11/97

TUBE

TUBE
TUBE
TUBE
TUBE
TUBE
TUBE
TUBE
TUBE
TUBE

TUBE

The

Invention

of

Television

David E. Fisher *and* Marshall Jon Fisher

COUNTERPOINT
WASHINGTON, D.C.

Library of Congress Cataloging-in-Publication Data
Fisher, David E., 1932–
    Tube : the invention of television / David E. Fisher and Marshall Jon
Fisher.
    Includes bibliographical references.
    1. Television—Receivers and reception—History.   I. Fisher,
Marshall.   II. Title.
  TK6637.F57   1996
  621.388'009—dc20   96-15480
ISBN 1-887178-17-1 (alk. paper)

FIRST PRINTING
Printed in the United States of America on acid-free paper that meets the American National Standards Institute Z39-48 Standard.

Designed by David Bullen
Typeset by Wilsted & Taylor

☥ A CORNELIA AND MICHAEL BESSIE BOOK

COUNTERPOINT
P.O. Box 65793
Washington, D.C. 20035-5793

Distributed by Publishers Group West

For Leila and Mileta

Preface to the Sloan Technology Series

Technology is the application of science, engineering, and industrial organization to create a human-built world. It has led, in developed nations, to a standard of living inconceivable a hundred years ago. The process, however, is not free of stress; by its very nature, technology brings change in society and undermines convention. It affects virtually every aspect of human endeavor: private and public institutions, economic systems, communications networks, political structures, international affiliations, the organization of societies, and the condition of human lives. The effects are not one-way; just as technology changes society, so too do societal structures, attitudes, and mores affect technology. But perhaps because technology is so rapidly and completely assimilated, the profound interplay of technology and other social endeavors in modern history has not been sufficiently recognized.

The Sloan Foundation has had a long-standing interest in deepening public understanding about modern technology, its origins, and its impact on our lives. The Sloan Technology Series, of which the present volume is a part, seeks to present to the general reader the story of the development of critical twentieth-century technologies. The aim of the series is to convey both the technical and human dimensions of the subject: the invention and effort entailed in devising the technologies and the comforts and stresses they have introduced into contemporary life. As the century draws to an end, it is hoped that the Series will disclose a past that might provide perspective on the present and inform the future.

The Foundation has been guided in its development of the Sloan Technology Series by a distinguished advisory committee. We express deep gratitude to John Armstrong, Simon Michael Bessie, Samuel Y. Gibbon, Thomas P. Hughes, Victor McElheny, Robert K. Merton, Elting E. Morison (deceased), and Richard Rhodes. The Foundation has been represented on the committee by Ralph E. Gomory, Arthur L. Singer, Jr., Hirsch G. Cohen, A. Frank Mayadas, and Doron Weber.

Alfred P. Sloan Foundation

THE SLOAN TECHNOLOGY SERIES

Dark Sun: The Making of the Hydrogen Bomb by Richard Rhodes

Dream Reaper: The Story of an Old-fashioned Inventor in the High-Tech, High-Stakes World of Modern Agriculture by Craig Canine

Turbulent Skies: The History of Commercial Aviation by Thomas A. Heppenheimer

Tube: The Invention of Television by David E. Fisher and Marshall Jon Fisher

The Invention That Changed the World: How a Small Group of Radar Pioneers Won the Second World War and Launched a Technological Revolution by Robert Buderi

Computer: A History of the Information Machine by Martin Campbell-Kelly and William Aspray

Naked to the Bone: Medical Imaging in the Twentieth Century by Bettyann Holtzmann Kevles

A Commotion in the Blood: A Century of Using the Immune System to Battle Cancer and Other Diseases by Stephen S. Hall

Beyond Engineering: A New Way of Thinking About Technology by Robert Pool

The One Best Way: Frederick Winslow Taylor and the Enigma of Efficiency by Robert Kanigel

Crystal Fire: The Birth of the Information Age by Michael Riordan and Lillian Hoddesen

Contents

Acknowledgments

In the course of our research, many people went out of their way to offer their time and expertise. Loren Jones was a particularly enthusiastic and valuable interviewee and also led us to his former colleague Ted Smith, one of RCA's early television patent holders and a treasury of information on RCA in the 1930s. Manfred von Ardenne was a gracious host and interviewee at his home in Dresden, and Fred Olessi generously made available his unpublished biographical writings on Vladimir Zworykin. Phyllis Smith at the David Sarnoff Research Center was invaluable, providing leads to many interviews as well as access to Zworykin's journals. Denis Robinson led us back through his memories of Zworykin and the early days of British television. John Anderson at GE's Hall of History, Ellen Fladger at the Union College Schaffer Library, and Nancy Young, Lorraine Crouse, and the rest of the staff at the University of Utah Archives were also a great help. Charles Jenkins's grandniece, Mrs. Virginia Roach, graciously shared memories, iced tea and cookies, and Jenkins's unpublished autobiography. The facilities and staff of the British Film Institute and the Westminster Reference Library in London and the Broadcast Pioneers Library in Washington, D.C., were of great help, as were Helen Albertson and Kay Hale of the University of Miami's RSMAS library.

Malcolm Baird generously allowed us to quote and use photographs from his father's autobiography, which is not available in the U.S. We would also like to thank Elma Farnsworth for permission to quote from her memoir, *Distant Vision: Romance and Discovery on an Invisible Frontier*. It is available from PemberlyKent Publishers, Salt Lake City.

We are particularly grateful to Michael Bessie, who brought the book to Counterpoint, and to Elizabeth Shreve, Erika Goldman, Nancy Palmer Jones, and Carole McCurdy for their dedicated editing. Our primary thanks, however, must go to Art Singer and the Alfred P. Sloan Foundation Technology Series committee, without whose support this book would never have been written.

So easy it seemed, once found;
Which yet unfound most would have
        thought impossible.

John Milton, *Paradise Lost*

Never before have I witnessed compressed into
a single device so much ingenuity, so much
brain power, so much development, and such
phenomenal results.   David Sarnoff

Preface

*Someday somebody will disclose the full story of the world
race for perfected television which began in the two years or
so before 1930 and lasted until 1936, but it is a lengthy
episode fraught with contradictions and unsubstantiated
claims and spiced here and there with commercial politics.*

John Swift, 1950

Every author of history owes an introductory word
of explanation to his public: if the story he tells is unknown, he should
explain why it is worthy of their attention; if the story is familiar, he
should explain why one more book on the subject is needed. Interest-
ingly, the story we have to tell needs neither of these explanations.

Television itself needs no excuse, no proclamatory words establishing its importance. Not a day goes by but nearly everyone in this country turns to it or is affected by it. As other nations struggle toward the
status of "developed countries," the first thing their people want, before
air conditioners or cars or computers, before they even emerge above
the poverty line, is a television set. The first condition for a history—
obvious importance—is clearly met.

What is amazing is that the second condition does not apply. Everyone knows that the Wright brothers invented the airplane, Alexander
Graham Bell the telephone, Edison the electric light. A new book on
these subjects would have to explain why it was needed. But who invented television? Nobody knows.

Television did not arise like Venus, springing newborn and whole from an oyster shell. It was not invented like the atomic bomb, which came with a flash of insight followed by massive experimentation and theoretical work by a dedicated group of scientists. There was no sudden moment of victory, as with the Wright brothers' first flight. Instead, television sidled up to us from a corner, then receded into the mists that obscure the future, never to return in quite the same form. It came back from a different corner, changed in shape and substance, and once again it faded like a Cheshire cat, leaving behind only the grin of its promise. Different men chased into different corners after it, and one by one they failed to find it. Finally it was dragged kicking and screaming out of the mists, out of the theoretical uncertainties and technical difficulties that had masked and disguised it, and was made to work.

The story of its invention is the story of a diverse body of men, working alone and in groups, guided by personalities that spanned the spectrum of human behavior, each seeking the lodestone by a different route, none of them certain of the path, each aware of the others struggling along different paths and afraid that his own path might not be the right one, might lead him nowhere, might end at any moment in failure.

In England, the traditional home of eccentricity, John Logie Baird dabbled in patent medicines and cheap soaps before trying to pull electric visions out of the air. In America, the self-styled home of lone inventors along the lines of Edison, Charles Francis Jenkins was robbed in Edison's name of one of his greatest inventions before turning to his greatest failure, television. In corporate America, the home of scientific conglomerates, the greatest corporate engineer of them all used the capital and assets of General Electric to track down the elusive demon—and failed. At the Bell Telephone Laboratories of AT&T, in Germany and Russia, in Japan and France, separate groups of bright-eyed visionaries followed their own paths toward the Holy Grail.

All these workers were gambling on the success of a simple mechanical device called the Nipkow disk. It was slow and it was awkward, and the pictures it produced were small and blurry and jerky. But it worked. It sent moving pictures through the air from the transmitting station to the receiver. Each of these researchers hoped to improve the picture quality to the point where it could bring commercial success.

And meanwhile two others, a Russian immigrant with a Ph.D. in physics and a Mormon farm boy with a high school education, were working separately on opposite sides of the American continent, marching to the beat of a different drum that no one else could hear. The drumbeat of a billion electrons . . .

PART ONE

Clever
Rogues

Prologue:
A Note from
the General

The past is prologue to the future.
Arnold Toynbee

During the first two decades of the twentieth century, the invention that promised the most revolutionary changes in everyone's life was radio. Instantaneous worldwide communication would bring sports and opera, wars and conferences, comedy and drama, understanding among peoples and universal brotherhood into every home. But it had one very serious problem right from the start: noise.

The foundation for radio had been laid as early as 1832 when Samuel Morse realized, first, that electric currents could be induced along wires of virtually infinite length and, second, that the presence of such electric currents could be easily detected. With that, he conceived his scheme of interrupting the current by breaking it into dots and dashes and letting each combination of dots and dashes represent a letter of the alphabet.

Liberation from the limitation of wires came some sixty years later when Heinrich Hertz showed that electromagnetic waves of varying wavelength, different from those of visible light, could be generated and propagated through the air just as visible light is. Almost immediately, Guglielmo Marconi found that the energy of these "radiating," or "radio," waves could, upon contact with an appropriate wire—called an "aerial"—generate an electric current in that wire. In effect, the radio waves carried the electric current from transmitter to receiver just as Morse's wires did, and so now we had "wireless" telegraphy, or "radio." When Alexander Graham Bell showed how to convert electric motion into mechanical motion—such as the motion of a vibrating diaphragm—and thence into sound, we had "telephony."

In order to convert the radio waves into recognizable sound, however, the waves had to be shaped, or modulated, somehow. The obvious, natural way was to modulate the amplitude, or intensity, of the wave. But the problem was that the atmosphere was already saturated with radio waves of various amplitudes, all of them naturally modulated.

And there are many natural sources of radio waves, since any motion of electrons produces them. Lightning is the most intense and obvious source, but there are many others, including all the man-made electric appliances; whenever you turn on the toaster or the vacuum cleaner you're opening a switch that forces electrons to cascade through the wires and thus to generate unintentional, randomly modulated radio waves. Even when the apparatus is off, the natural motion of the electrons in the metal generates low-amplitude waves. The air around us—and around every radio set—is filled with these natural electromagnetic waves, which upon hitting the aerial generate sound: noisy, incomprehensible sound, since the modulation is not intentionally set up to correspond to human voices or music. We call it static. It was an inescapable feature of radio until Edwin Howard Armstrong came along.

Armstrong—or the Major, as he liked to be called, since he had attained that rank during World War I—was one of the primary inventors of radio. It was he who discovered that if part of a received radio signal was fed back into an amplifier, it almost instantaneously cycled back and forth through the receiver and amplifier, being amplified each time so that its strength was magnified tremendously. This effect accounts for the familiar screech when microphones are turned on and improperly tuned; it also makes radio possible. Before this discovery, called regenerative feedback or the feedback circuit, the signal received from distant radio transmitters wasn't strong enough to be heard clearly over the background static.

By the late 1920s the Major had turned his attention to the problem of eliminating static altogether. A fiercely independent and iconoclastic worker, he had repeatedly refused employment with any radio or engineering firm. But his regenerative feedback discoveries, licensed to RCA, had made that corporation the dominant force in radio—and had made Armstrong the largest single RCA stockholder. David Sarnoff, who almost single-handedly had guided and driven RCA from its inception, repeatedly broached the subject to Armstrong. "Give me a little magic box," he said. "Get rid of the static."

The General—characteristically, Sarnoff's title was grander and less legitimate than Armstrong's—offered Armstrong all the technical help RCA had, but Armstrong just smiled and shook his head. He always worked alone.

Sarnoff and Armstrong made an interesting team: the lonely, introverted inventor and the grand, overpowering, immigrant executive. They understood each other, envied each other, competed with and compensated for each other. They fought against each other in the courts, fought for each other at the annual RCA stockholders' meetings, and competed with each other for Marion MacInnes, whom the General had hired and made his personal secretary and whom the Major stole away to be his wife.

In 1933 Armstrong invited Sarnoff to visit his laboratories at Columbia University to see the "little magic box." It turned out to be an apparatus more complex than that simple description, but it did just what Sarnoff had asked for. Armstrong turned on a normal radio set and tuned it to a transmitter in the next room. The sound of music filled the air. Next he turned on some electrical machinery, analogous to a toaster or a vacuum cleaner, and the familiar static overpowered the music.

Then he turned on his new black box, and again the sound of music filled the air—but now there was no static. He turned the interfering machinery on and off, and there was no difference in the music. Not only that, but the music was richer, deeper than had ever been heard on radio, reproducing both higher and lower frequency ranges than ever before.

What Armstrong had done was to invent a new kind of radio broadcasting. Instead of modulating the amplitude of the transmitted waves, he had devised a way of modulating the *frequency*: he had produced FM (frequency modulation) sound.

In ordinary AM (or amplitude modulation) radio, the sound of a voice speaking or singing is carried as an amplitude change in a standard carrier wave. In other words, when nothing is being broadcast, the transmitter puts out an unchanging carrier wave that looks like this:

When an intelligible sound is added, it changes (or *modulates*) the amplitude of the carrier wave to look something like this:

As we've discussed, the problem is that all other forms of added sound, such as those generated by a lightning storm or an electrical appliance or just by the vibration of the electrons in the wires, also look like that; they modify the amplitude of the carrier wave and show up in the radio as static. Armstrong devised a new way of carrying the intelligible signal, by modifying not the amplitude but the frequency of the carrier wave:

The radio set receiving this frequency-modulated signal was built so that it would pay no attention to any changes in amplitude; this meant that the natural static was filtered out and only the intended signal came through. It sounds simple, but at the time Armstrong began his research, the idea had already been discarded by everyone else working in the field. The consensus was that it was impossible to build a set that would work in this way, and Armstrong's success—which came only after years of lonely work—is a tribute to stubborn faith in the face of universal scorn. It was a truly magnificent achievement, and it ended up killing him.

At the moment, though, his new system needed thorough testing, and he was happy to accept Sarnoff's offer of help. He had given birth; now what was needed was a roomful of good nannies.

Sarnoff turned over the most ideal research space in the world: RCA's new experimental laboratories on the roof of the Empire State Building. From there Armstrong's FM transmitter could send its modulated waves out to New Jersey and Long Island, where receivers were set up to test each possible modification over commercially important distances. RCA's engineering staff, led personally by Armstrong, spent long days and nights there testing, experimenting, measuring, and modifying, month after month. "This is not an ordinary invention," Sarnoff decreed. "This is a revolution."

And then in April 1935, without warning or preamble, the Major received a curt note from the General. It was polite—Sarnoff was always polite—but it was clear, forceful, and final. It told Armstrong to vacate the laboratories on top of the Empire State Building immediately. RCA was no longer interested in FM.

Bewildered and enraged, Armstrong had no choice but to comply. But what had happened?

Another revolution had happened. A different magic box had appeared, one that offered more—much more—than static-free radio. At first, it was called *visual listening*, or *audiovision*, or *telectroscopy*, *telephonoscope*, or *hear-seeing*. It was also called *raduo* and *electric vision* and *radiovision*. Finally, it acquired a name that looked like it might stick. They called it *television*.

ONE

The Dream

Television? The word is half Greek and half Latin. No good will come of it.   C P Scott, editor, *Manchester Guardian*

1 . In 1935 the technology was new, but the dream was old. The ancient Greeks used seers to interpret the entrails of birds that had flown beyond the horizon, trying to see what the birds had seen; they endowed their gods with the ability to watch scenes of human struggle all over the world from the comfort of their Olympus perch. Shakespeare's *Henry IV, Part Two,* opens with a rumination on the powers of Rumor, upon whom the people relied for news due to their inability to see what was happening in the far corners of the kingdom. The dream of seeing beyond the horizon is as old as the human imagination.

The dream took its first step toward reality in 1872 when Joseph May, a worker at England's Telegraph Construction and Maintenance Company, noticed—and paid attention to—a most peculiar circumstance. The company was charged with maintaining the transatlantic undersea telegraph cable to America and was using rods made of selenium as electrical resistors to check the transmission of the cable. May, working in the company's tiny station at Valentia, on the coast of Ireland, noticed that his selenium rod was giving variable results in test runs: its resistance was not constant, as it should have been. His desk happened to be near a window, and eventually he realized that it was when a shaft of sunlight happened to fall on his selenium rod that its resistance changed; a battery-supplied constant current surged through the selenium when it was lying in the sunlight but merely crept through it when it was in the dark.

The company's chief electrician, Willoughby Smith, followed up with a detailed investigation of this phenomenon. At the next annual meeting of the Society of Telegraph Engineers, held in February 1873, the vice president of the society read a communication from Mr. Smith:

> Wharf Road
> 4th February, 1873
>
> My dear Latimer Clark,
> Being desirous of obtaining a more suitable high resistance for use at the shore station in connection with my system of testing and signaling during the submersion of long submarine cables, I was induced to experiment with bars of selenium. . . .
> The early experiments did not place selenium in a very favorable light. . . . There was a great discrepancy in the tests, and seldom did different operators obtain the same result. Whilst investigating the cause of such great differences in the resistances of bars, it was found that the resistance altered materially according to the intensity of light to which they were subjected. When the bars were fixed in a box with a sliding cover, so as to exclude all light, their resistance was at its highest, and remained very constant . . . but immediately the cover of the box was removed, the conductivity increased from 15 to 100 percent. . . .
> I am sorry I shall not be able to attend the meeting of the Society of Telegraph Engineers tomorrow evening. If, however, you think this communication of sufficient interest, perhaps you will bring it before the meeting. . . .
>
> I remain, yours faithfully,
> Willoughby Smith

The minutes of the meeting go on to say that the chairman "remarked that he thought this was a very interesting scientific discovery, and one on which it was probable they would hear a good deal in future." He was not, however, predicting the coming of television; what he meant by "interesting" was that he felt the phenomenon might "afford a most reliable means of measuring the intensity of light, and to constitute a perfect photometer."

Among the interesting features of this letter is that Mr. Smith never once mentions to the society the name of Joseph May. This will be a recurring theme throughout the story of television: angling for fame, appropriating the work of others, claiming to be "first," so that in the end there are at least four different and independent "Fathers of Television."

At any rate, Smith followed up with strong experiments. "Selenium's sensibility to light is extraordinary," he reported, "that of a mere lucifer match being sufficient to effect its conductive powers." He soon proposed a system of "visual telegraphy," in which light shining on a selenium cell would allow it to transmit a burst of electricity. By breaking a picture down into a mosaic of selenium blocks and by turning the electric currents back into light at the receiving end, one could transmit pictures. Joseph May himself went even further, building a machine to transmit pictures by wire. But the machine never worked, and very quickly the basis for both schemes was shot down when Lieutenant R. E. Sale of the Royal Engineers showed that only half of the effect is instantaneous: light impinging on selenium would result in a burst of electricity due to the sudden decrease in resistance, but when the light was removed the selenium only slowly returned to its former high-resistance state. The slowness of the overall response precluded any immediate invention (for it meant, in effect, that there was no way to create an "on-off" switch), as did also the very slight currents produced by the selenium cells.

Not that people didn't try. In the next few years there were many stories of "seeing by radio," and in 1880 an article in the prestigious scientific journal *Nature* mentioned casually that "complete means of seeing by telegraphy have been known for some time by scientific men."

But it was all nonsense. There was no technology that even came close to working. Selenium was too slow and its currents too weak. There was nothing but the dream.

2.   Looking back now on the many schemes to transmit pictures that followed the May/Smith discovery of selenium's photoconductive properties, one is struck by their simplicity and naïveté. Still, how could anyone have foreseen the remarkable complexities that would have to be mastered before television could be born?

From the *English Mechanic,* February 7, 1879:

AN ELECTRIC TELESCOPE

It may be of interest to your readers to know the details of some experiments on which I have been engaged during the last few months, with the object of transmitting a luminous image by electricity.

To transmit light alone all that is required is a battery circuit with a piece of selenium introduced at the transmitting end, the resistance of which falling as it is exposed to light increases the strength of the current, and renders a piece of platinum incandescent at the receiving end thus reproducing the light at the distant station.

By using a number of circuits, each containing selenium and platinum arranged at each end, just as the rods and cones are in the retina, the selenium end being exposed in a camera, I have succeeded in transmitting built-up images of very simple luminous objects.

An attempt to reproduce images with a single circuit failed through the selenium requiring some time to recover its resistance. The principle adopted was that of the copying telegraph, namely, giving both the platinum and selenium a rapid synchronous movement of a complicated nature, so that every portion of the image of the lines should act on the circuit ten times in a second, in which case the image would be formed just as a rapidly-whirled stick forms a circle of fire. Though unsuccessful in the latter experiment, I do not despair of yet accomplishing my object as I am at present on the track of a more suitable substance than selenium.

Denis D. Redmond
Belmont Lodge, Sandford, Dublin

With that last surge of optimism Mr. Redmond fades out of history. The search for a "more suitable substance than selenium" would take more years than he had left to live. But others followed in rapid succession. Indeed, just one week earlier the *English Mechanic* had relayed a story of a similar invention in France, where "M. Senleq, of Ardres, has recently submitted to the examination . . . a plan of an apparatus intended to reproduce telegraphically at a distance the images obtained in the camera obscura." Senleq's idea was to place a focused image of the object on a piece of unpolished glass. The object would be traced by a piece of selenium held by springs, and as it moved back and forth over the glass, the gradations of light coming through would be transmitted to the receiver, consisting of a pencil vibrating under the influence of an electromagnet. The pressure of the pencil would be controlled by the electromagnet, which would in turn be controlled by the intensity of electricity transmitted by the selenium, which would be controlled by the intensity of light from the focused image on the glass.

The theory was the same as in the game many of us played as children, in which we placed a piece of paper over a penny and rubbed a pencil back and forth, magically reproducing on the paper the image of Lincoln's head. Senleq worked on his scheme for several years but never achieved success.

The next year, 1880, Alexander Graham Bell announced that he had filed at the Franklin Institute a "sealed description of a method of seeing by telegraph," as *Scientific American* reported. Stung by this, two English professors, John Ayrton and William Perry, immediately retorted in *Nature*:

> While we are still quite in ignorance of the nature of this invention, it may be well to intimate that a complete means for seeing by telegraphy have been known for some time by scientific men. The following plan has often been discussed by us with our friends, and no doubt has suggested itself to others acquainted with the physical discoveries of the last four years. It has not been carried out because of its elaborate nature and on account of its expensive character. Nor should we recommend its being carried out.

And in fact, their plan never was carried out. The Bell announcement spurred a series of similar replies; *Scientific American* announced that a man named Carey in Boston had a system "ready to go into the stores," and a Dr. Hicks of Bethlehem, Pennsylvania, "announced his invention of an apparatus which he calls the diaphote." Other systems were reported in Portugal, France, Russia, England, and Italy.

But it was all illusions and imaginings. The Bell invention, the photophone, turned out to have nothing to do with television but was instead a system that used light waves to transmit sound. And one by one the other systems floundered and disappeared, until once again, nothing was left but the dream.

3 .   Photoconductivity was the basic concept that would eventually lead to television. All the earliest schemes worked along these lines: Suppose that this page was printed on selenium instead of paper. Suppose it was composed of a million tiny squares of selenium, each of which was connected by wire to another "page" a thousand miles away, composed of tiny electric lightbulbs. If you shone a light on the selenium page, all the pieces would send an electric charge to the lightbulb page *except* for those selenium squares that were covered with ink, where the words are, preventing the light from reaching them. The lightbulb page would then light up, except for those squares corresponding to where the writing is—and thus this page would be duplicated a thousand miles away.

The problem is that you'd need a lot of squares to define each letter properly; if you divided this page into, say, only a hundred or even a thousand squares, you couldn't do it. But if you had enough squares, you could duplicate a printed page or even a picture and send it instantaneously anywhere you wanted. All that is needed to transmit a more complex figure is a greater array of selenium cells: the more cells, the more detail.

You could even send a *moving* picture by sending a simple picture as just described, then moving the picture a space or two to the left and transmitting another picture. A succession of such pictures would give the impression of the object moving to the left.

But it wouldn't give a very good impression of motion. To achieve that you would have to send the pictures within intervals of less than a tenth of a second. This is because of a phenomenon known as *persis-*

tence of vision. The human retina retains an image for about that length of time, so if the next image is received within roughly that tenth of a second, it superimposes on the first. The two then merge into one, and an impression of motion is transmitted to the brain.

This tenth of a second is also approximately the time interval important in the normal perception of motion. If you transmitted a picture of a woman walking and didn't transmit the second picture for, say, another two seconds, the second picture would show her several steps away from where she was in the first. The impression would be that she had spontaneously jumped: the movement would be jerky. This was exactly what happened in the first motion pictures, which displayed the now familiar Charlie Chaplin mode of locomotion.

This was an insurmountable problem with selenium cells, as Lieutenant Sale had pointed out. Since the selenium didn't react instantaneously to a beam of light, a certain lapse of time was necessary. You could show a simple picture, but then when you moved it, you would have to wait several seconds for the previously lit cells to stop transmitting and for the newly lit cells to begin transmitting. This made any semblance of real motion simply impossible.

So people began looking for something like selenium, only better. And while they were looking, a French engineer, an English mechanic, and a German student came up with the next major step toward the development of television.

4.   In 1880 the French engineer Maurice LeBlanc published an article in *La Lumière Électrique* describing a scanning mechanism that capitalized on the retina's finite capacity to temporarily retain an image. Instead of multiple "photocells"—the generic name given to something like the selenium rod that would transmit electricity when light shone on it—LeBlanc envisaged a single photocell that would register only part of the picture to be transmitted at a time. It would start its transmission at the upper left corner of this page, for instance, proceed on across the page, and then, like a typewriter, return to repeat the process from a slightly lower point on the left-hand side. When it came to a bit of ink from a letter, it would shut off its transmitted charge, then turn it on again when it hit blank paper, and continue on in this way until the entire page was scanned, in a manner similar to that in which you are reading this page. A receiver would be synchronized with the transmitter, and it would produce a reconstruction of the original page at the receiving station, line by line.

To this day, this concept remains the basis of all television. But in 1880, the next question was, How to achieve the scanning? The entire picture would have to be scanned within a tenth of a second, and the receiving set would have to be perfectly synchronized in order to reproduce the picture. LeBlanc was not able to do this. He suggested a system based on a set of vibrating mirrors; as the mirrors vibrated they would "look" at different portions of the scene to be transmitted. It was an impossibly complex system, and nothing came of it. But even though the problem of practical achievement seemed unsolvable, the concept of scanning took root.

Two years later William Lucas published his ideas in the journal *English Mechanic*. While LeBlanc never specifically referred to reproducing a *moving* picture (though his device, if it worked at all, would have been capable of that), Lucas had this goal clearly in mind: "An image in light and shade will be formed upon the screen [which will be] an exact counterpart of that at the transmitting end; *and, more than that, every exact change in the image in the transmitter will be faithfully depicted upon the screen of the receiver.*" He envisaged a set of lenses that would direct a spot of light on the scene to be transmitted, and by rotating the lenses both vertically and horizontally he would scan across the scene. A synchronized and movable selenium cell on the receiving end would duplicate the scanning motion, projecting a spot of light on the viewing screen in exact duplication of the transmitter.

Alas, it never worked. Like LeBlanc's scheme, Lucas's was too complex for this primitive world. Both LeBlanc and Lucas had described the necessary solution to the problem, but neither of them was able to implement that solution. The apparatus for solving the problem had to be simpler.

The answer, in practical terms, came from a German engineer, Paul

Nipkow, who never produced a working television set himself but who did come up with the first simple and workable method of scanning, thus setting the stage for the first models.

Nipkow had graduated from technical schools in Berlin and Charlottenburg and was working as an engineer in Berlin when on Christmas Eve, 1883, the solution to the scanning problem came to him. Early the next year, at the age of twenty-three, he took out German patent number 30105, for an *elektrisches Telescop,* based on a simple rotating perforated disk for both the transmitter and receiver. The two disks would be connected by wires. "It was television over the telephone wires that appeared before me," he later wrote. "Hertz had not yet taught; Marconi had not yet telegraphed. How then could such far-flung ideas as pictures through the air have come to a modest student?"

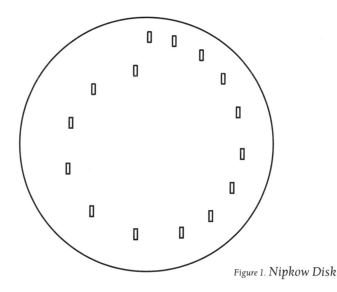

Figure 1. Nipkow Disk

Pictures through wires were far-flung enough—too far-flung, in fact, for his time. His patent pictured a disk perforated with a sequence of holes that spiraled inward (Figure 1). The disk would be placed so that it cut off the light from the viewed object to the photocell. When it was rotated, the first hole would sweep across the picture, essentially scanning over the first line of this page. The next hole would scan one line down, and so on; one complete revolution of the disk would give one complete scan.

The photocell would transmit to another system set up in reverse, so that as the receiving cell received a jolt of electricity, it would light a bulb; when it did not, the bulb would remain dark. In this manner a picture of the original object would be transmitted through the wires one bit at a time, and if the entire scan took less than a tenth of a second, the human eye would see the result as one complete picture. If the object were moving, the second revolution of the disk would show it again, but a moment later, as it had moved; and successive revolutions would produce successive pictures of, for example, a man walking across a room.

The Nipkow disk, as it came to be called, would become the basis for the first working television systems—but not for many years. Paul Nipkow faced difficulties in building such a system that were totally insurmountable at that time:

1. The disk had to be much larger than the transmitted picture if the scanning holes were to approximate a straight line as they moved across the image (see Figure 2). Since there were inherent difficulties involved in spinning a large disk at the necessary speeds, this meant that the transmitted picture—the viewing screen—had to be very small.

2. A time delay was necessarily involved with the use of any selenium photocells.

3. The electrical currents transmitted were very weak.

4. The small size of each hole, which allowed only a tiny fraction of the total illumination to pass through, called for lighting equipment of truly gargantuan intensity.

5. The limited number and size of the holes restricted the amount of detail that could be transmitted, so that only simple objects could be televised.

Possible solutions to some of these problems were mutually incompatible. For example, if you tried to improve the amount of detail trans-

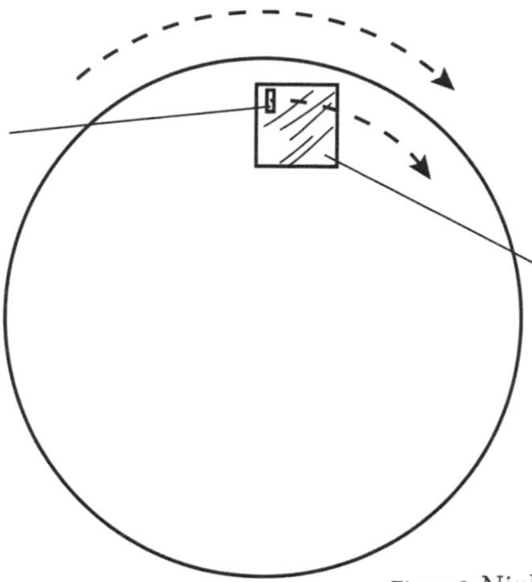

The scanning hole ————

The picture
to be transmitted

Figure 2. Nipkow Disk in Motion

mitted by making the holes smaller and more numerous, each hole would allow even less light to come through, necessitating even greater illumination. Taken altogether, these problems called for a significant number of improvements to be made before any real results could be achieved.

Nipkow himself abandoned his idea and went on to other pursuits. But in 1935, when Germany began what it loved to call the "first regular television programming in the world," he enjoyed a sort of public renaissance. The Nazi government, which had rushed the "public television service" into operation just in time to beat the British to the mark, loved the idea that the seed of television had been sown right there in the Fatherland. Accordingly, even though by that time the mechanical method of television, based on the Nipkow disk, had been proved inferior to the coming electronic systems, "a national technological myth was created and was eagerly popularized." The Berlin transmitting station that began the German broadcasting was renamed " 'Paul Nipkow' Television, Berlin," and the seventy-four-year-old inventor, suffering a bit from senility, was paraded out for thousands of propaganda photographs. Later, Hitler signed an edict proclaiming Nipkow the only person recognized by Der Führer as the inventor of television. In this way, his name became synonymous with German superiority, and Hitler could credit Germany with achieving the miracle of television.

Nipkow died in Berlin in 1940. He lived long enough to see television become a reality and to see the Nazis triumphant. One wonders what he thought of it all, but there is no record.

$\mathcal{P}$uir $\mathcal{J}$ohnnie

Never since the days when King Robert Bruce, inspired by the example of a spider, freed his country from an oppressor, has Scotland produced a more romantic hero than John Logie Baird, the man who made his wildest dreams come true, and, successfully combating ill-health and poverty, by dogged perseverance achieved what nearly every one regarded as the impossible.   Lord Angus Kennedy

1 .   Nipkow's spinning disk, which he had put forward in 1884, inspired a series of attempts in nearly every country at making a working television set. Forty years later, a lonely, eccentric Scotsman finally succeeded.

The anxiety and excitement of the First World War had come and gone; now the British people wanted only "tranquility and freedom from adventure," as the new prime minister, Bonar Law, claimed in his successful campaign of 1923. But it was not to be. While politics might be retreating to prewar conservatism, technology was not. The infernal internal combustion engine had made its appearance before the war and now was exhilaratingly promulgating itself throughout the byways of England. There were now more motorcars on the roads than horse-drawn vehicles, although in the smaller towns the ratio was still nearly fifty-fifty.

Inside people's homes, instead of the tinkle of the piano or the low hum of conversation, another sound was beginning to be heard: the static of radio sets. Marconi had demonstrated his wireless telegraphy as early as 1896; now, more than two decades later, it had begun to take its hold on the public. At first, when it was married to Alexander Graham Bell's new telephone to produce wireless telephony, optimism was great. People could talk to each other without regard to distance or to the expensive laying of telephone wires. But a crucial deficiency soon became apparent: anyone with a wireless receiver could listen in on anyone else's conversation. Privacy was impossible.

Enthusiasm fizzled until a few farsighted individuals proposed the concept of what was to be called "broadcasting." While the airwaves might not be appropriate for confidential business messages or words of love, they could be used for advertising. Mass communication, which had taken its first crawling movements in 1455 with the printing of the first book, now began to stride forward lustily.

The first broadcast in England took place in 1920, when the Marconi Company conducted two weeks of experimental transmissions of speech and music. In June of that year, Dame Nellie Melba sang to the listening public. Then the Post Office, which had been granted supervision of radio transmissions under the Wireless Telegraphy Act of 1904, prohibited "broadcasting" because it interfered with "wireless telephony."

But Post Office officials couldn't stop the radio tide, and by 1921 they had retreated in the face of mounting protests from enthusiastic radio amateurs. In that year, they allowed Marconi to broadcast for fifteen minutes every day.

By 1922 the tide was proving irresistible. In the United States, twenty-five thousand radio sets were being sold each month, and everyone, it seemed, was broadcasting. The transmissions were interfering with each other, and radio anarchy was flooding the land. In Britain, the Post Office decided it had to regulate the new industry, and so it established the British Broadcasting Company (BBC) and licensed eight radio stations.

Meanwhile, the dream of sending visual images over the airwaves was getting old and going nowhere, and the same might be said of a thirty-five-year-old Scotsman, John Logie Baird. If his friend Billy Barnes's invention of a cure for hemorrhoids had worked, John Logie might have been a successful marketing executive, but it hadn't and he wasn't. Nor had he succeeded in the imported marmalade or the cheap soap businesses, nor in a job as engineering assistant to the city of Glasgow, nor had he been able to create diamonds. The only success he had to look back on was his Undersock, and that had been only temporary.

He was born in 1888 in a small town near Glasgow where his father was the parish minister. A serious illness, never well defined, struck him at the age of two and left him sickly and almost pathologically imaginative for the rest of his life. As a youth he lived in a strange lonely world of his own making, and he failed disastrously to find his place in society as an adult. According to a member of his family who remembered him years later, "when his name was mentioned, relatives would smile and say, 'Puir Johnnie, puir Johnnie . . .' "

Still, by 1909 he had graduated from a sort of junior college, the Glasgow and West Scotland College of Technology, after taking an extra year to complete his studies due, as he later said, to bouts of "frequent ill-health, combined with simple lack of ability and stupidity." But he never went on to get the bachelor of science degree, and without it the only work he could find in the economically depressed Scotland of that time was just one step up from a laborer: assistant mains engineer in the Clyde Valley Company. "It was a horrible job," he recalled, but he had to make a decent living in order to support his lady love, a young Glasgow woman whose name Baird always concealed, for reasons that will become evident later. They were passionately in love but, like most young Glaswegians of those years, could not marry until the man had found a secure economic niche. Baird lay in bed alone at night, tortured by thoughts of the woman he could physically love only intermittently, for the privacy of a bedroom was unavailable without the discomfort and distaste of sneaking her into his own digs, out again before daylight, and back into her parents' home without being seen.

Talking one day with his mates about his need to find a better-paying job, Baird got into a discussion with Billy Barnes about piles.

Baird suffered from piles along with, it seemed, every other misery known to humanity, and Billy had a cure for it: a "mysterious white ointment." Baird realized how much money there was to be made in marketing such a "specific," as they called it. He would set up a small business to merchandise the cure and split the profits with Billy. But first, he'd try the stuff himself. He left the plant that night a happy man, dreaming of freedom from that most annoying of aggravations combined with a flood of money pouring in from his fellow sufferers.

His dreams later that night, after applying Billy's ointment, were not so good. They were interrupted, in fact, by an intense itching, rising to pain, from the afflicted region. Nor did morning bring any relief: "I wasn't able to sit down for a week," he said.

Nor was he able to continue at his job, once he blew up the city's power supply in a disastrous attempt to utilize the electrical mains to create diamonds in a pot of cement. Now how was he to earn a living? He was fit more for the creative than for the mundane sort of life, but he was not fit to be an actor or an artist; his training was in engineering. The way was obvious: he would be an inventor.

But of what? The diamond-producing scheme hadn't worked; perhaps he'd better try something simpler. And so he came up with the idea of the "Baird Undersock."

All his life he had suffered from cold feet. Summer or winter, rain or snow, his feet were cold. In Scotland in those days, there was no central heating for a working man like him, and he found that even socks taken straight from the drawer were cold and damp. As an engineer, he knew that if he could keep his feet dry, they would stay warm—and not only *his* feet but everyone's.

He had discovered that keeping your shoes dry with overshoes or galoshes was useless when the socks inside were wet. And the very overshoes that kept out the water of the gutters kept *in* the water of sweat; with no opportunity for sweat to evaporate, the feet necessarily became wetter and wetter, colder and colder.

He hit on the solution almost as soon as he verbalized the problem. He wrapped a layer of newspaper around his feet under his socks and found that the sweat evaporated or diffused into the paper and his feet stayed dry.

There was a bit more to be done. He realized he couldn't charge people for a supply of day-old newspapers, but he soon found that an extra layer of cotton worked just as well. Next came the problem of merchandising, and here he showed himself to be ahead of his time. He conceived the idea of hiring a platoon of women and hanging boards around their heads, and on the boards he printed in large letters "THE BAIRD UNDERSOCK for the Soldier's Foot."

His women took Glasgow by storm. There were photographs in the papers, giving him his first taste of free publicity—a taste he would indulge more and more as the years went by. To those papers that didn't find the scheme newsworthy, he offered a small financial inducement under the table, and within a year he had cleared sixteen hundred pounds, roughly ten times what his salary had been at the electrical plant.

When he got lumbered again with his yearly cold, he lay in bed and counted his profits and decided there was no point in going on like this: he would leave Scotland, get out of the dreadful climate, go somewhere nice and warm. He could always find something to invent or to sell when he got there.

He discussed this plan with his beloved. She was doubtful. He had made a lot of money with his undersock, but the future still looked daunting and unpredictable. She was afraid to go with him into the unknown.

Never mind, he told her. He'd go first by himself, get settled and secure, and send for her—as soon he invented something.

What would it be? she asked.

Well, that would depend on the local situation, he replied. There was certain to be something.

So he set off for Trinidad. But the only things he found there were heat, humidity, mosquitoes, dysentery, and fever. After a disastrous attempt to start a jam-making business using the local citrus fruits and guava, he returned to England more dead than alive and with more than three-quarters of his capital gone. He wrote to his lover, explaining what had happened and asking for her continued patience, and found that while he was in Trinidad she had married a Glasgow boy who had a regular job.

John Logie was living in London now, in an "appalling" boardinghouse. His rent of twenty-five shillings a week included meals: for breakfast, ham and bread and butter, with an occasional egg; for dinner, soup "of the dishwater type" followed by a watery stew and mash. The inventor's life had lost some of its charm.

He paid a hundred pounds for a small horticultural business but fell ill again and was lucky to sell it for what he had paid. He was laid up for six months this time and was down to his last hundred pounds. He invested it in soap.

"Baird's Speedy Cleaner," a double-wrapped pale yellow soap, seemed to be just the thing. It was, by his own admission, a very bad soap indeed. But it was cheap, and business took off, with sales to cheap hotels and boardinghouses. He was able to move into a slightly better hotel, paying thirty shillings for bed and breakfast, with Sunday meals included.

This slight economic recovery gave him a spiritual boost as well, and he took the train to Glasgow to reclaim his love, married though she might be. He reached her house while her husband was at work, and before that man returned, Baird had persuaded her first into bed and then into agreeing to fly away with him. They were packing her clothes wildly when the front door opened and her husband walked in.

He appears to have been a most agreeable man. He didn't take out a gun or even knock John Logie down. Instead, they all sat down with a cup of tea to discuss the situation. He saw John Logie's point; he had, as it were, stolen the woman while John was overseas. But he insisted that John see it from his point of view: the woman was now his wife, and he loved her passionately.

As it turned out, there was passion enough to spare for all of them. She agreed to sleep with both, and for the next several years, while she continued to live in Glasgow with her husband, John would journey up whenever he could and she would travel down to join him when he couldn't.

This arrangement agreed on, John Logie returned to London—only to be struck, almost immediately, by capitalism and the free market, in the form of a cake of soap called "Hutchinson's Rapid Washer." It proved to be just as good (or just as bad) as Baird's Speedy Cleaner, and it was being sold for a penny less. Baird got in touch with the proprietor, a Captain Oliver George Hutchinson, and they agreed to meet at the Café Royal. Hutchinson, "a hearty, jovial young Irishman," and Baird got along famously. They ended up drinking old brandy long into the night and deciding to merge their talents and corner all of England's cheap soap business. But next morning Baird fell sick again. Hutchinson came to pay a social call and was frightened by the sight of him. He called a doctor, who told Baird that his only hope was to get out of London and to a place with a healthier climate.

So in the early winter of 1923, Baird sold his soap business to Hutchinson, left London, and took up lodgings with an old friend in the seaside town of Hastings, where nothing of note had happened for more than 850 years.

John Logie Baird was soon to change that.

"Coughing, choking and spluttering," Baird was to write, "and so thin as to be almost transparent, I arrived at Hastings station, assets totalling two hundred pounds, prospects nothing. . . . What was to be done? I must invent something."

He designed a glass rustless razor, but it was not a success. "After cutting myself rather badly I decided to try pneumatic soles."

The pneumatic tire had just been invented for the automobiles that were beginning to fill the streets of Hastings with their noise and noxious fumes. Baird thought to apply the same principle to walking shoes. He put two partially inflated balloons inside a pair of extra-large boots and took off down the street for a trial run: "I walked a hundred yards in a succession of drunken and uncontrollable lurches followed by a few delighted urchins, then the demonstration was brought to a conclusion by one of my tyres bursting."

But he had to invent *something*, or starve. He got up the next morning and set off for a long walk, determined not to return home until he had settled on his future career. His digs were on a side street called Linton Crescent, a curving road lined with three-story brick homes, only a few blocks from the railroad station, the center of town, and the English Channel. He headed east, and within a mile he was out beyond the cluttered houses and boarding hotels, out into the Kentish moors. These heather-strewn fields rise and fall in long, undulating, uneven rows, stretching out toward the gray waters of the Channel to the south and to the cliffs of Dover to the east. He went for a long walk eastward over these moors, finally reaching the stark beauty of Fairlight Glen, which is unchanged to this day—a desolate, moody, inspiring spot. And there, staring out across the fields and the Channel, standing where William the Conqueror had changed the fate of England, John Logie Baird envisioned a feat that would bring just as great a change to the entire world.

He had to invent something, he thought. Well, why not television?

2. Back around the turn of the century, when he was thirteen or fourteen years old, Baird had experimented with electricity, which was then at the cutting edge of technology. He had bought a secondhand oil engine, a stack of lead plates, and several gallons of sulfuric acid. He poured the sulfuric acid into a bunch of jars he scrounged from around the house, dropped the lead plates into them, and hooked the whole thing up with wires to the engine. When running, the engine charged up the plates, which then provided electrical power to light his father's house, and the vicarage at Helensburgh became the first house in town to have electric lights.

He went on from there to hook up his own private telephone exchange, from plans provided in the *Boys Book of Stories and Pastimes*.

He ran wires from his bedroom to those of four schoolboy friends several streets away. The whole setup worked beautifully—until one "dark and stormy night."

Old MacIntyre the cabby was driving the streets late that night, sitting up high on the box of his cab, urging his horses home, when he ran into the wires. Unseen in the dark and dangling low from the wind, they caught him under the chin, yanked him off the cab, and threw him into the street. "Shaking with anger," Baird says, old MacIntyre drove furiously to the home of the manager of the local telephone exchange, banged on his door until he woke, and then cursed him for letting his damned wires hang so low.

The manager put on his mackintosh and went out with MacIntyre to investigate. It was an easy matter to trace the wires back to the vicarage. "Fortunately, MacIntyre was a good friend of my father and the affair was settled quietly, but it was the end of the telephone exchange. . . . It was about this time that the idea of trying to produce television first occurred to me," Baird wrote later.

The word itself had just come into use: a Frenchman, Constantin Perskyi, had coined it at the International Electricity Congress (part of the 1900 Paris Exhibition), but it had not yet taken precedence over "electrical telescope" or "radiovision" or half a dozen other alternatives. The main research efforts at the time were occurring in Germany. Baird got hold of Ernst Ruhmer's *Das Selen und seine Bedeutung in Elektronischer Technik* (*Selenium and Its Importance in Electronics*) and worked his way through it. He was clever enough to construct a selenium cell and smart enough to see that it wouldn't work because the currents produced were so weak.

But by 1923 this problem had been at least partially solved. Radio researchers had constructed vacuum tubes that could amplify weak radio signals, and these could be applied to television. The amplification wasn't quite enough; television would struggle for another decade with insufficiently amplified currents, but the solution was at least within sight.

The slowness of the response still remained a problem, but somehow Baird's vision flitted over that and settled on the final reality. He came back from his walk over the cliffs of Hastings "filled with an influx of new life. Over the raisin pudding I broke the news to Mephy."

Mephy was his schoolboy friend Guy Robertson, a tall, thin young man who had acquired his nickname for a marked resemblance to Mephistopheles. Baird had moved to Hastings because of Mephy, who had met him at the train station when he came down from London and had insisted that Baird share his lodgings. They were the closest of friends until the Second World War, when Mephy took his own life in a fit of despair.

"Well, sir," Baird now told him, "you will be pleased to hear that I have invented a means of seeing by wireless."

Mephy had been involved in all of Baird's schoolboy science projects. He had been a charter member of the photography society that Baird had formed and had been one of the Telephone Four. But he was less than impressed with this new idea. "Oh," he said, "I hope that doesn't mean you are going to become one of those wireless nitwits. Far better keep to soap."

Those "nitwits" had proliferated in the first two decades of the century. Seven years earlier Georges Rignoux in France had developed a system to send images of letters through electric wires. But he had not yet attempted to send moving pictures, nor had he tried to transmit through the air. Charles Francis Jenkins in America would apply for his first television patent in 1923, and at the end of that year Edouard Belin would give a demonstration of his system in Paris, but Baird knew nothing of these two as yet.

Nor did Mephy's lack of enthusiasm hamper him. He went down to the Hastings public library and found "a musty and torn copy of a book in German called *Handbuch der Phototelegraphie* published in 1911 by A. Korn and B. Glatzel," and by the time he had merged what was then known about television—which wasn't much—with his own vision, it all seemed clear to him. "The only ominous cloud on the horizon," he later wrote, "was that, in spite of the apparent simplicity of the task, no one had produced television."

Never mind. As a historian put it in the magazine *Electronics and*

Power many years later, "he had little money, no laboratory facilities for the construction and repair of equipment, no access to specialist expertise, and no experience of research and development work in electrical engineering." Luckily, John Logie didn't happen to see things that way. All he really saw was his vision.

It is a popular idea that people of genius see farther and clearer than other people, but perhaps the truth is actually the opposite. Ordinary people who might be tempted to build something like a working television system would sit down and study the problem and see all the obstacles, and then decide that it couldn't be done. A man like Baird did not see more clearly than others; he saw things much *less* clearly. His vision wasn't sharp enough to pick out all the obstacles that lay in his way; instead, it all looked perfectly simple to him. What frightened him was not the difficulty but the "apparent simplicity of the task." And so without further ado he got to work.

He began to build what would become the world's first working television set by purchasing an old hatbox and a pair of scissors, some darning needles, a few bicycle lamp lenses, a used tea chest, and a great deal of sealing wax and glue. The contraption that he assembled from these variegated pieces of equipment soon "grew and filled my bedroom. Electric batteries were added to it, wireless valves and transformers and neon lamps appeared, and at last to my great joy I was able to show the shadow of a little cross transmitted over a few feet."

What he had done was to cut a circle of cardboard out of the hatbox, and from this he fashioned a Nipkow disk by cutting a spiraling series of small holes with the scissors, adding one large hole in the center. Through the central hole he pushed the darning needle, which served as a spindle around which the disk could be revolved. The electric lamp shone through the lens onto a cardboard cross and cast a shadow on the disk. As the disk rotated, the light passed through its holes and fell on the selenium cell, generating a current that lit a neon lamp, which thus glowed at the same instant. A second Nipkow disk, revolving synchronously with the first, caught the light of the neon lamp and reproduced the original image on a screen behind the second disk. At least, that was how it worked, after many months of struggle, on the great day when the two disks revolved and the lamp shone and suddenly the shadow of the cross was seen on the far side of the contraption, two feet away from the cross itself.

It wasn't all that simple, of course, nor is Baird's own account the only one we have. According to Norman Loxdale, who was a schoolboy at the time, Baird "was no good with his hands. He could describe what he wanted, but he couldn't make it himself." Loxdale was one of several unpaid volunteers who helped Baird put things together. Some of these young assistants simply showed up at Baird's workshop, curious about the goings-on that had been rumored throughout the town. If Baird was in a good humor when the youngsters showed up, he would invite them in. If their questions were bright enough, he would answer them, and after a few minutes they might find themselves cutting out disks or soldering wires together.

Others were sought out by Baird himself. Victor Mills was known in town as a wireless buff, and though they had never met, Baird, according to Mills, rang his doorbell one night because he was having a problem with "a terrific noise" in his apparatus and wasn't able to find the source. Mills accompanied him back to his workshop—"he had a collection of junk, that's what it boils down to; no, quite truly, I wouldn't have given two pounds to sell the lot"—and found the problem, which had to do with the selenium cells being too large.

Despite his first appraisal of the equipment as "junk," Mills became one of Baird's unpaid workers, bringing along with him, he later claimed, much of his own equipment because he "couldn't trust anything that Baird had got." And finally, one night while the equipment was being tested, Mills put his hand in front of the transmitter to check on the illumination level and heard Baird shout from the other room, "It's here! It's here!"

"And that was the first picture he'd ever seen, it was a true picture of my hand."

No matter whether the first picture was of a cross or a hand, by the spring of 1923 Baird was seeing something being transmitted by wireless. "I was much elated," he wrote. "A start had been made. I was on the right track."

Baird's hope now was somehow to attract private funding from people who could see the commercial advantages to come. But of course he had no Ph.D. with which to impress, and his one previous success as an inventor had been an undersock. He gave a demonstration for the press, "hoping to attract capital," but as he later realized, his whole setup was much "too embryonic." With the vision of a genius or a madman, one could see where it all might lead; with the vision of an ordinary reporter, what was there to see? The shadow of a cross two feet away from the cross itself? Big bloody deal. The only result was a small story in the local *Daily News;* the only person impressed by it was John Logie's father, who sent him fifty pounds, which enabled him to take the second step. He rented a tiny room on the second floor above a flower shop in the Hastings Queen's Arcade, paying five shillings per week.

The Queen's Arcade is now, as it was then, a high, narrow, glass-roofed alley lined with shops that leads from the Queen's Road to the main promenade. In a lovely bit of historic coincidence, the small room in which John Logie invented television is now occupied by a television store. In the window is a small snapshot of the man himself, standing next to his first working contraption.

The apparatus in the bedroom that Baird and Mephy shared had grown so large that the two of them had to do an intricate dance around it and each other in order to find their places in bed each night. Now, with Baird's move to a room of his own, the machine could grow and grow, sprouting tangles of wires like the head of Medusa, until "it became a nightmare cobweb of wires and batteries and little lamp bulbs and whirling disks." Soon Baird was able to transmit the "shadows of letters and simple outlines" of things.

But the going was difficult. Every day brought a different problem. Baird would leave his little shop in frustration and wander down the promenade to be refreshed by the view of the Channel. "It was mostly his back we saw," remembers a Hastings resident. "He had his hands stuck in his coat pockets, staring at the sea. Then he would suddenly say, 'Ah!,' as if he had seen something, and turn and go quickly into the room . . . that he used as a laboratory. I did not know then who he was, but the barber who used to cut my hair told me that he was 'one of those inventor chaps.'"

Once again the money ran out. By now Baird knew that what he was able to demonstrate would not impress the ordinary mind, but he thought there must be some people out there who could appreciate what he was doing. So he dug into his shallow pockets and ran an advertisement in the London *Times,* on June 27, 1923:

> Seeing by wireless. Inventor of apparatus wishes to hear from someone who will assist, not financially, in making working model. Write Box S 686. *The Times.* E.C.4.

He was careful not to mention funding. He wanted to find someone simpatico; *then* he would ask for money. He may have been a madman, but he was not stupid.

3.   He had two replies. One was from Mr. J. W. B. Odhams, a London publisher, who sent one of his editors, E. H. Robinson of *Broadcasting* magazine, to take a look. Robinson took with him Captain A. G. D. West, chief research engineer of the BBC. "Both were favorably impressed, but both agreed that I had a long way to go."

Odhams invited Baird to London for tea; emboldened, Baird offered him a 20 percent share of his invention—including all future profits—for one hundred pounds. Odhams declined the offer. Baird asked him what he could do to convince him of the feasibility of television. Odhams replied that if he could transmit a living face from one room to another, he could have "all the money you want. But we can see no future," he concluded, "for a device which can only send shadows."

The second reply was from Will Day, a well-to-do merchant in both the wireless and cinema businesses. Day proposed to buy a one-third interest in Baird's invention for two hundred pounds, and Baird jumped at the offer. Day's solicitor—"an ancient and crafty gentleman in a dirty collar"—insisted on an agreement that was totally unfair:

Baird would have to pay all future expenses; Day was to contribute nothing more than the initial payment of two hundred pounds, and he would not even share in the costs of obtaining patents worldwide once the invention was solidly established. But that didn't matter: "I would have signed away my immortal soul for two hundred pounds," Baird roared, and he signed the contract without a quibble. (In the end, the document was found to be so riddled with legal errors that it was unenforceable.)

Baird and Mephy ate a lavish dinner to celebrate and next morning ran out to the stores to buy hundreds of flash lamp batteries in the hope of improving the electrical supply to two thousand volts. Within a few days they were all set up in Baird's little workroom, and he began the task of wiring them together. As he was finishing the connections he touched something he shouldn't have, and the full two thousand volts jumped out of the line and through his body. There was a flash of light, a quick moment of agony, and then his body convulsed and was thrown across the room, breaking the connection and saving his life.

Unfortunately, the noise and light brought a crowd to his door, and the next day he got his publicity, although not the kind he had wanted: "Serious Explosion in Hastings Laboratory." This was followed almost immediately by a note from his landlord, saying that any such experiments must be terminated at once.

Baird ignored this, of course. But Mr. Twigg, the landlord, was insistent. He showed up at the office (as he viewed it), or at the laboratory (as Baird viewed it), and began to shout that he would not have experiments going on in his room.

Baird replied that he would do as he pleased so long as he was paying the rent on time. But Mr. Twigg would have none of it, and the exchange between the two rose to such a pitch that a crowd gathered to see what was happening. Baird, embarrassed by the scene, thrust his hands in his pockets "in a dignified fashion" and turned his back on Mr. Twigg and the crowd, intending to march off haughtily.

But he was "rather astonished by a roar of laughter from the crowd, and a few minutes later I discovered that it was caused by the fact that, in thrusting my hands violently into my trouser pockets, I had strained this dilapidated garment and torn a large rent in the seat of my trousers."

A few days later Baird received a formal eviction notice. But Will Day had already found him another space, a small fifth-floor attic walk-up at 22 Frith Street, in the Soho district of London. And so it was back to the dank miasma Baird had fled the year before.

Shortly after Baird set up his apparatus in London, E. H. Robinson, the editor who had come down to Hastings, published in the *Kinematograph Weekly* a more positive report of what he had seen: "I myself saw a cross, the letter H, and the fingers of my own hand reproduced by this apparatus across the width of the laboratory. The images were quite sharp and clear although perhaps a little unsteady. This, however, was mostly due to mechanical defects in the apparatus and not to any fault in the system."

In those last few words, however, Mr. Robinson was unfortunately wrong. The Nipkow disk was simply not fast enough and the holes in it could not possibly be made small enough or spaced closely enough ever to produce a system that would be good enough to make television an integral part of people's lives.

The fault *was* in the system; it was doomed from the start.

THREE

The Three Lessons of Invention

Without courage, initiative, and sacrifice, a new art cannot be created or a new industry born.   David Sarnoff

Thousands of amateurs fascinatingly watch the pantomime picture in their receiver sets as dainty little Jans Marie performs tricks with her bouncing ball, Miss Constance hangs up her doll wash in a drying wind, and diminutive Jacqueline does athletic dances with her clever partner Master Fremont.   Charles Francis Jenkins

1. The final, insurmountable problems with any form of mechanical scanning would always be the limited number of scans that could be produced per second (the speed at which a disk could revolve) and the large size of each spot of light it used. There is simply too much inertia in any mechanical moving part to enable it to move fast enough to avoid visible flicker, and one cannot cut or bore holes small enough or close enough together to give good resolution. These problems are obvious, of course, only with the aid of hindsight. At the time, people were still optimistic. A Frenchman named Armengaud, for example, was quoted in the British journal *Nature* in 1908 that his system was nearly perfected and that "within one year we shall be watching one another across distances hundreds of miles apart." He was wrong; his apparatus never worked at all.

One possible solution, which would in fact become the television of the future, was suggested in 1908 by A. A. Campbell Swinton, a gentleman who made his living as a consulting engineer in the fields of electric lighting and steam power but who was also respected enough as a scientist to have been elected a Fellow of the Royal Society and the president of the Röntgen Society. He was born in 1863 in Edinburgh, and by the age of six had designed a gallows for hanging Fenians. His interest in scientific invention was frustrated by the schooling of the time, and at the age of seventeen he left formal education, apprenticing himself to a shipbuilder near Newcastle upon Tyne. He continued his studies on his own, and at twenty-one he published a textbook on the new field of electric lighting. He then left Newcastle and set up in London as an electrical contractor and consulting engineer, earning his living primarily by installing the new electric lights in town and manor houses and earning his reputation through a series of experiments and scientific publications.

In 1908, responding to an article in *Nature* about the possibility of television, he wrote that the systems proposed in that journal were not even remotely possible but that the "problem can probably be solved by the employment of two beams of kathode rays (one at the transmitting and one at the receiving station) synchronously deflected by the varying fields of two electromagnets placed at right angles to one another and energised by two alternating electric currents of widely different frequencies, so that the moving extremities of the two beams are caused to sweep synchronously over the whole of the required surfaces within the one-tenth of a second necessary to take advantage of visual persistence."

A dozen years later, in 1920, he spoke to the Radio Society of Great Britain on "The Possibilities of Television." During the discussion that followed the lecture, he regretfully concluded that the real problem with television "is that it is probably scarcely worth anybody's while to pursue it. I think you would have to spend some years in hard work, and then would the result be worth anything financially?"

There were, however, a few dissenters. Five thousand miles away, David Sarnoff (then commercial manager of the newly formed Radio Corporation of America) was lecturing at the University of Missouri at precisely the same moment, telling his audience that soon the entire world would be able to watch the best orators in the comfort of their own living rooms and that they would not only hear the words but they would see "every play of emotion on the preacher's face as he exhorts the congregation to the path of religion." Television, he assured his audience, was coming.

2.   It was coming, perhaps, but slowly. Its glory was still in the barely foreseeable future. In the 1920s it wasn't yet possible to project a picture by Campbell Swinton's "kathode rays"; there was still too much groundwork to be done. Instead, work continued on mechanical systems, by John Logie Baird and his American competitor, Father Number Two of television: Charles Francis Jenkins.

Francis, as he was known to his friends, was born of Quaker parents in the farm country north of Dayton, Ohio, in 1867 and grew into a red-haired, freckle-faced boy. Like Baird, he was a precocious mechanical whiz, fixing machinery, hooking up a rudimentary telephone line from the house to the barn, inventing little things to make life a bit easier. He attended country schools before entering Earlham College in Richmond, Indiana. After just one year there, he left in 1885 to spend some time "exploring the wheat fields and timber regions of the Northwest, and the cattle ranges and mining camps of the Southwest." He worked his way across the country by picking up odd jobs fixing equipment that had broken down in places where there were no repair services. His first steady job was at a sawmill in the state of Washington; then he worked as an accountant for silver mines in New Mexico and Colorado. Next, work on the railroad took him to Mexico. In Washington he had taken a course in stenography; now, back home on vacation, he took a civil service exam, and in 1890 he began a clerkship in Washington,

D.C., serving as secretary to Sumner Kimball, who had founded the United States Life Saving Service (which later became the Coast Guard).

But the routine of a government job wasn't for him. It provided him with a living but not with a life. His mind was too restless to be satisfied with clerking for Mr. Kimball, and it turned to the only dream he had ever had: inventing things. What things? Everything, anything—it didn't matter. The game was in the playing.

As a child on the farm he had invented a jack to raise wagon wheels for greasing. His intention was to save himself some heavy work, but when he found how useful the jack was, he decided to build some extras and sell them. He made five and painted three of them a bright red before he got tired and figured the color wasn't important anyway. He took them to market one Saturday and sold the three red ones—but not the two that were unpainted. He always said that he learned the first valuable lesson for an inventor that day: an invention that isn't marketed properly isn't going to sell.

First, however, he needed to invent something. But what?

Just a year or two earlier, in 1889, Thomas Edison had bought two dollars and fifty cents' worth of George Eastman's new cellulose nitrate film and found that this new material was just what he needed to turn his previously unsuccessful tries at motion-picture photography into an accomplished, if primitive, fact. His Kinetoscope was a peep-show type of machine, which ran a loop of Eastman's film between a magnifying lens and a bulb and projected a jerky sort of moving-picture sequence.

Here, Jenkins thought, was the ideal opportunity for an inventor: a system that showed promise but that didn't quite work yet. The first thing he did was to build a kinetoscope himself; next he modified it to make it work better. He tried various methods, and by the fall of 1895 he had a working model of the world's first practical motion-picture projector, the "Projecting Phantoscope." The Edison Kinetoscope simply ran a loop of film, with successive images of a moving scene, through the camera shutter, and the resulting "moving" picture was a jumbled blur of motion. Jenkins's new machine was the first projector to allow each frame of the film to be illuminated for a long time compared to the shifting period during which the next frame was advanced. In essence, the eye saw a single, static picture that was then immediately replaced by another and then another, all in sequence and each lasting less than a tenth of a second. The eye of the viewer would then inform the brain of each individual scene, and the brain would run them together in a true moving picture. It is from this concept that the entire motion-picture industry has grown.

A few months later the only working model was stolen from Jenkins's home by his financial backer and sold to the Gammon theater chain, which then marketed it all over the world as the "Edison Vitascope." After a lengthy court battle, Jenkins accepted $2,500 as payment in full, and despite the Franklin Institute's award of a gold medal to Jenkins for the invention of the world's first movie projector, to the public it has always been Edison who invented the movies.

"It's the old story over again," Jenkins wrote. "The inventor gets the experience and the capitalist gets the invention. I'll know better the next time."

He had learned the second lesson.

But at least he now had a couple of thousand dollars in his pocket, and by the time it had run out he was making a good living as a consulting engineer in the photography and motion-picture field and was branching out into new areas. He built the first "horseless carriage" ever to cruise the streets of Washington, D.C., a steam-driven contraption that could go "eight miles an hour, perhaps, when everything worked fine," as he put it. Usually everything did not work fine, and the machine didn't go quite fast enough "to prevent small boys from running rings around it, with derisive thumbs at their noses." He built a twenty-passenger bus, intending to set up a commercial mass transit system in Washington, but the plan went bust and he went broke, having spent his savings on research and development. He finally sold the machine to New York City as a sight-seeing bus, but he didn't recoup his losses. Once again he was in financial trouble.

Never mind. He had learned the third lesson: the life of an inventor is never as secure as that of a government clerk, and if you have the right sort of outlook, that's half the fun. He never thought of giving up and getting another job with a guaranteed income; he simply picked himself up, dusted himself off, and set to work again—inventing things.

Milk bottles, for example. They were always breaking, and he wondered if he couldn't invent something better than glass. He fiddled a while with the thought of making a more permanent bottle, and then suddenly had an inspiration: how about making a bottle *less* permanent? A disposable bottle. And so he came up with the idea of a container made by winding a strip of paraffin-lined paper in a spiral; this formed the basis for today's whole disposable container industry.

In time he became a wealthy and respected inventor, one of the most prolific in history, with more than four hundred patents in his name. Sometimes it seemed as if he couldn't turn his brain off, couldn't get any rest from all the creative thoughts that piled up and threatened to crush him with their weight.

In 1910 he broke down from sheer exhaustion. His doctor told him that if he didn't rest, he would die. So he bought a new car and took it and his new wife, Grace Love, to Atlantic City. He drove the car onto the beach and backed it up until its rear wheels were in the waters of the Atlantic. Then he drove it due west until its front wheels were resting in the Pacific.

In 1910 a cross-country automobile trip was not exactly what the doctors had meant by resting. On the way, in fact, Jenkins invented the self-starter. He had to: the damned machine was always stalling, and it nearly broke his arm when he had to spin the starter to get it running again.

One of Jenkins's first projects, even before he turned to inventing full time, had been what he always called "radiovision." In 1894 he had proposed a method for "transmitting images to a distance by electricity," but his proposal was only theoretical; he wasn't able to build anything that worked, and he quickly dropped the idea.

Twenty years later he came back to "radiovision," claiming that he knew how to transmit pictures in motion, but again he failed to construct a workable system. His first real work on television came as a result of a motion-picture invention he made in 1920. In an effort to eliminate the erratic images produced by the early film projectors, he replaced the projector's shutter with a prismatic ring: a thick glass disk with an outer rim consisting of a continually curving prism, shaped so as to be capable of bending light. As Jenkins's disk revolved, the light would be bent at a continually changing angle. With this he could send a beam of light straight ahead (zero bending) or bend it at an angle great enough to deflect it away from the screen.

The advantage that the prismatic disk had over the shutter in a film projector lay in this continual rather than open-shut motion; in fact, the prismatic disk made the high-speed (slow-motion) camera possible. The best that the shutter-type projectors could do was to run slow motion at about 10 percent of real speed; with the Jenkins prismatic rings, projectors were soon able to slow up motion by more than a thousand times.

It was immediately obvious to Jenkins that he had something else here, as well: a scanning device for television, one that might be superior to the Nipkow disk.

Imagine a ring operating as just described. As the disk rotates, the entering beam of light is moved successively downward. If now another disk, positioned so that its prismatic edge overlaps the first, rotates at right angles to the first, it will intercept the same beam of light but will move it horizontally instead of vertically. Using the two in conjunction produces a beam of light that can be continually moved in such a manner as to scan a picture: right to left and top to bottom. Such an apparatus would eliminate two of the inherent deficiencies of the Nipkow disk: it would have no holes to limit resolution or the amount of light coming through.

Just one year later, in 1921, Jenkins incorporated the Jenkins Laboratories in Washington, D.C., for the sole purpose of "developing radio movies to be broadcast for entertainment in the home," and by 1922 he had put together a prismatic-ring system capable of sending still pictures by radio. On May 19 he did this to his own satisfaction, and on

October 3 he held a public demonstration, sending a series of photographs by telephone wire from his Washington, D.C., office to the Anacostia Naval Air Station; from there the pictures were broadcast by wireless back to the Post Office in Washington.

The very next month *Scientific American* published an article heralding the new discovery and taking it a bit further than had been demonstrated. Titled "Motion Pictures by Radio," the piece began by lauding the invention: "In spite of the startling character of the idea conveyed in the title," it said, moving pictures broadcast throughout the country would soon be here. The invention "opens up the possibility of broadcasting the image of a man. For instance, the picture of a criminal suspect might appear simultaneously in a thousand police headquarters for identification." In the brave new world of the twentieth century, crime would be driven out of existence by science.

Furthermore, they went on, "there is no reason why we should not, with the new service, broadcast an entire theatrical or operatic performance. . . . It is merely a matter of sending [the pictures] rapidly enough. With light and electricity both moving at velocities of 186,000 miles per second, the capacities of neither projection nor receiving apparatus would be even touched by the broadcasting of sixteen pictures per second [ordinary movie projection speed]."

Jenkins himself was modestly pleased with his achievement. "Invention is to me a very satisfying occupation, a pleasant recreation that equally benefits one's fellowman. . . . Of course I must make some money out of it; that is, I must make inventing pay or I could not go on. Beyond that I care little. The accumulation of great wealth does not seem to me an ambition which promises very great happiness."

3.　A few months later Jenkins successfully sent a picture of President Harding from the navy's radio station in Anacostia to a newspaper in Philadelphia. The navy bought his invention and began sending weather maps to ships at sea. This was promising, but what he had in mind was true television: the broadcasting of moving pictures of real people. As an intermediary step, he concentrated on learning how to send moving pictures taken from film rather than from real life, and in another two years he had succeeded. In June of 1925 he demonstrated a moving picture of a windmill to an assembled group including the heads of the Bureau of Standards, the navy, and the Commerce Department. In the Anacostia radio station a ten-minute film of a windmill was projected through the air by radio and received in Jenkins's Washington laboratory. The assembled group watched a ten-by-twelve-inch screen, and while an accompanying radio broadcast told them that the "windmill will now turn forwards. . . it will now stop . . . now it will turn backwards," they saw the vanes of the windmill move. Afterward, Jenkins himself would refer to this as "the first public demonstration of radiovision," although he must have known that he had come in second: Baird had publicly demonstrated a working television set at Selfridge's department store in London just two months earlier (see Chapter Four), and the event had been well covered in the newspapers.

At any rate, this was the first demonstration in America, and despite the rather mundane nature of the program, the assembled group was not bored. "Congratulations were in order," Jenkins wrote, describing the event, "but they seemed to be given in a rather awed manner as the unfathomable possibilities of this new extension of human vision came to be more and more realized." Hugo Gernsback, one of the pioneer radio writers in the early years of this century, who was also the leading exponent of science fiction in America, wrote in *Radio News*, "I have just left the laboratory of Mr. C. Francis Jenkins of Washington, D.C., and am still under the influence of what I consider to be the most marvelous invention of the age." The newspapers abounded with predictions of the wonders this new technology would bring into the home, and not the least of these predictions consisted of direct quotes from Jenkins himself: "Folks in California and Maine, and all the way between, will be able to see the inauguration ceremonies of their President in Washington, the Army and Navy football game in Philadelphia. . . . The new machine will come to the fireside . . . with photoplays, the opera, and a direct vision of world activities."

The press reported that "in a more or less perfect form it will be a common thing within a year," but Jenkins's system, which he now called a "teloramaphone," was far from perfect. It produced pictures of only forty-eight lines. (Each line consists of one scan across the image. Jenkins's televised picture was composed of forty-eight such scans, from top to bottom, which is not enough to delineate any detail. Hundreds of lines would be necessary to produce a reasonable picture; today's sets use 525 lines in the United States or 625 lines in England, and new "high-definition" systems will have more than a thousand lines.) Thus, Jenkins's system could show only silhouettes, with no shadings of light intensity. When he transmitted a picture of President Harding, an enthusiastic observer (who began his resulting magazine article with the startling pronouncement: "The transmission of photographs through space by means of radio apparatus is an accomplished fact!") admitted later in the article that "the likeness of President Harding [is] not clear from a photographic viewpoint."

Several years were to pass in Jenkins's laboratory without noticeable improvement. And meanwhile, back in dank London, "puir Johnnie" was enjoying some success.

FOUR

They All Laughed...

I think it will be admitted by all, that to have exploited so good a scientific invention for the purpose and pursuit of entertainment alone would have been a prostitution of its powers and an insult to the character and intelligence of the people. John Reith, first president of the BBC

Memo from BBC producer to House superintendent, 1932, during first months of BBC television programming: "For your information, I shall be giving an audition to a performing ape, with the Director of Programmes' sanction, on Monday, September 12. I understand that he must be admitted by the goods entrance."

1 . John Logie Baird's success hadn't come easily, though. When he first moved back to London in 1925 and began to set up his little laboratory in the fifth-floor attic in Soho, he was still operating on a shoestring. In an attempt to obtain some financial backing, he took himself one morning to a Mr. Gray, the general manager of the Marconi Company, who had at one time been a neighbor of his father's in Helensburgh. When he told the receptionist he was "Mr. Baird from Helensburgh," Mr. Gray welcomed him into his office. Baird later related the exchange of views:

"Good morning," I said.
"Good morning," said Mr. Gray.
"Are you interested in television," said I.
"Not in the very slightest degree. No interest whatsoever," said Mr. Gray.
"I am sorry to have wasted your time. Good morning," I said and immediately walked out in high dudgeon.

Nor was Mr. Gray the only one to have no interest in television. One day Baird, still seeking funds, tried to garner some publicity by visiting the editor of the *Daily Express*. He asked if the paper might be interested in doing a story about his television invention.

"Television? What's that?"

"Seeing by wireless," Baird explained. "An apparatus that will let you see the people who are being broadcast by the BBC, or speaking on the telephone."

"Astounding," said the gentleman. He then excused himself, saying he would send in one of his colleagues to take down the story. A "large, brawny" man soon came in, and Baird gave him all the details. The man listened attentively and enthusiastically and told him they would write it all up for the next day's front page.

Ecstatic, Baird went home and rose early next morning to pick up the *Express*. But there was not a word in it about television. It was years later, when he happened to meet the "large, brawny" reporter again, that he found out what had happened. The editor had come bursting into the newsroom and picked the largest man there. "Jackson," he said, "go down to the reception room and get rid of a lunatic who is down there. He says he's got a machine for seeing by wireless. Watch him carefully, he may have a razor hidden."

But despite these setbacks the work went on, and somehow the word got out. One day early in 1925 Gordon Selfridge Jr., the owner of the

London department store, came to call. Selfridge's would be celebrating its birthday in April of that year, and he wanted a snappy exhibition to gather public interest. Baird demonstrated his apparatus, and Selfridge offered him twenty pounds a week to do a three-week exhibit at the store.

SELFRIDGE'S
PRESENT THE FIRST PUBLIC
DEMONSTRATION OF TELEVISION
In the Electrical Section (First Floor)

Television is to light what telephony is to sound—it means the INSTANTANEOUS transmission of a picture, so that the observer at the "receiving" end can see, to all intents and purposes, what is a cinematographic view of what is happening at the "sending" end.

For many years experiments have been conducted with this end in view; the apparatus that is here being demonstrated, is the first to be successful.

In actuality, the hundreds of viewers who came to see "television" looked through a narrow tube and "were able to see outlines of shapes transmitted only a few yards by a crude wireless transmitter"—hardly a "cinematographic view of what is happening at the 'sending' end." But by and large the audiences were suitably impressed, though none was impressed enough to come forward and offer to buy an interest in the invention.

Baird tried everything he could think of to bring in money. He sent a flyer out to every doctor in England—three thousand of them—offering to sell shares in his company. He received six replies and a total of seventy-five pounds.

Although it wasn't much, it was a start. A representative from an electrical business called Hart's Accumulators called, trying to sell him some batteries. Baird described what he needed, and the man said the price would be about two hundred pounds. Baird said that he had just ten pounds to spare. The man smiled and went away, but a few days later a letter arrived, announcing that Hart's was going to donate the batteries in the interest of "encouraging pioneer work." England's General Electric Company soon joined Hart's, providing Baird with two hundred pounds' worth of valves. And so the work continued.

2. It wasn't simply a question of making the system work but of whether or not the system would *ever* work. Baird was assailed by skepticism on all sides. The lay public, typified by the *Daily Express* editor, could be excused their ignorance, but the general manager of the Marconi Company should have known better. These people simply didn't think any form of "seeing by wireless" would ever be possible. They were frustrating because among them were people who could have provided the funds so desperately needed, but they were not discouraging because their ignorance was so apparent that their attitude warranted no consideration. They were the same people who had thought the Wright brothers and Marconi himself were crazy, the people about whom George Gershwin had written, "They all laughed at Christopher Columbus when he said the world was round . . ."

Far worse was the attitude of some in the scientific community who said he was on the wrong track. News of the work in America came over only in muted echoes, but in England there were others trying to crack the secret of seeing by wireless. Foremost among these in 1925 was Dr. E. E. Fournier D'Albe, who published an article in *Nature* proving that Baird's system could never work.

Dr. D'Albe attacked the one concept that Baird had right: sending pictures by scanning, by breaking them down into small parts that would be sent separately and reassembled on the receiving end. In this procedure, the sending and receiving apparatus must be synchronized, so the question arose as to just how perfect the synchronization needed to be. D'Albe showed that any synchronization less than absolutely perfect would result in a scrambled picture, and since perfection is unattainable, it followed that the concept of scanning was fatally flawed.

It did not follow that television was impossible, only that scanning had to be avoided. D'Albe was working on a system in which the total picture was to be broken down into small parts with each part transmitted simultaneously instead of in a scanned sequence. To achieve simultaneous transmission, D'Albe suggested that each picture particle be transmitted on an individual frequency.

If this system had succeeded, it would have meant that the entire spectrum of wavelengths would have been taken up to transmit just one program; it would have been impossible for different stations to transmit on different channels (that is, at different frequencies).

D'Albe's was a hopelessly complicated idea, from which no workable system was ever developed. Still, D'Albe's article in *Nature* seemed quite convincing, even though by the time it appeared, Baird had shown that slight errors in synchronization did not scramble the picture at all but only added a small vibration to it.

Why didn't Baird answer D'Albe's article? He probably felt that he could not compete in scientific terms with *real* scientists; after all, he didn't even have a bachelor's degree. He was a tinkerer, really, not a proper scientist. So he tried to ignore the scientific arguments raging in the journals, although the weight of scientific opinion settled heavily on his shoulders.

By this time Baird was aware not only of D'Albe's work but of that of several others around the world. Three years before, in 1922, the London *Times* had reported that Edouard Belin in Paris had "proved the practicality of television beyond question." As Belin himself put it,

> I cannot make you see the Statue of Liberty at New York, but I can transmit the image of a point of light by wireless, and thus show you the principle on which, when the proper apparatus is developed, you will be able to see the Statue of Liberty while sitting in a room in London or Paris. . . . If a single point can be transmitted by wireless, so can a million. . . . There is no serious difficulty in its construction.

Although Belin faded in and out of the newspaper headlines for another couple of years, his system never worked. The next year, however, the magazine *Radio News* reported on Jenkins's work: "Although the machine is not as yet entirely perfected . . . I was able to see my hand projected by radio vision." And in Germany a Hungarian, Dénes von Mihály, filed a patent application for what he called a "Phototelegraphic Apparatus." His book, *Das elektrische Fernsehen und das Tele-hor,* was the first book exclusively about television. There was talk of the giant corporation American Telephone and Telegraph (AT&T) joining the race in America; Kenjiro Takayanagi began to publish in Japan; Max Dieckmann and Rudolf Hell were competing with Mihály in Germany . . .

The race was on, and nearly everyone else in the running had university credentials. Some of them thought Baird was on the wrong track, and those who didn't were on the same track themselves but had better laboratories and sounder funding. As Baird himself confessed, he was nothing but "a wretched nonentity working with soap boxes in a garret."

Never mind. He shut all his problems and all his competitors out of his thoughts. He *knew* where he was going. He knew what had to be done.

3 . The selenium cell had two major disadvantages: it produced a very weak electric current, and it did not turn this current on and off instantaneously. The first problem, however, had recently been solved when J. Ambrose Fleming invented a two-electrode variation on the vacuum tube that he called the *diode,* a by-product of an interesting puzzle called the Edison effect.

Edison's first successful incandescent lamp used a carbon filament in an evacuated bulb. The idea was that the flow of electricity, carried to the bulb by copper wires, would bump into the carbon filament and encounter a much increased resistance. As the electricity forced its way through the carbon, friction would heat the filament until it glowed. In order to keep the hot carbon from oxidizing and falling apart, Edison pumped the air out of the bulb.

It worked, but there was one unexpected problem: as the bulb burned, it got dimmer because a thin layer of black carbon began to build up on the inside of the glass. What was happening, he realized, was that the heat of the filament was causing carbon particles to evaporate and be deposited on the first cold surface they came to: the glass walls.

He assigned a couple of his workers to try to find a solution but they were unsuccessful, and Edison soon turned his attention to finding a nonevaporative substitute for carbon as the filament material.

This was in 1883, some sixteen years before the discovery of the electron, so there was no way to imagine that in addition to carbon, electrons were being ejected from the filament because of its heat. But in 1903, Fleming (Edison's former assistant who was now working for Marconi) remembered the experiment and put it to use as a detector of radio waves, solving in an ingenious way the problem of the weakness of the received signal.

When a radio wave hits a receiving antenna, it causes the electrons in the antenna to vibrate. This vibration creates an alternating current in the wire running from the antenna to whatever detecting device is in use. But because a radio wave spreads out in all directions, by the time it reaches the antenna some distance away it is naturally much weaker than when it was generated, making it hard to detect. In 1903, dots and dashes could be distinguished at great distances, but only with difficulty; the subtle variations of speech were lost.

Imagine a simple detector in which a needle will swing when an electric signal hits it, as shown in Figure 3(a). Since the signal is weak, the needle will barely move, and as soon as it moves to the right, the alternating current will reverse itself and cause the needle to move to the left. The result will be that as soon as the needle starts to move, it reverses itself so that the total motion is hardly more than a quiver, and the transmitted dots and dashes are difficult to read.

What Fleming did was to line up the electrons so they flowed in one direction only. It had been found that in the Edison effect the evaporated electrons flowed only when a positive plate was inserted into the bulb to pull them away from the filament. Fleming now realized that when an alternating current (such as is generated by the arrival of a radio signal at an antenna) is applied to the plate, the plate will alternate between positive and negative, and the electrons will flow to it only

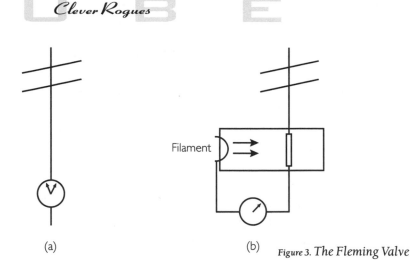

(a)   (b)   Figure 3. The Fleming Valve

when it is positive. So if the plate is connected to an antenna, as shown in Figure 3(b), it will attract a flow of electrons from the filament only when it is positive; when it is negative, the electron flow is simply cut off. The result is that a pulsing flow of electrons from the filament, moving in one direction only, will be generated by the received alternating-current radio wave. In this manner the alternating current set up in the antenna by the reception of a radio wave is converted into a secondary current, which moves the needle in only one direction, and the signal is more easily seen.

The Fleming valve, or *diode,* was the first vacuum tube to be used for the reception of radio waves. (It was pumped down to a vacuum to keep the filaments from oxidizing and burning up under the impact of the electrons.) It had been further improved when Lee De Forest, a Yale Ph.D. who was struggling to break into the newly burgeoning radio business, added a third stage in 1906, making the valve a *triode,* which he named the Audion.

De Forest, described by radio historian Susan Douglas as "a wonderful character, a churl, a rogue, a cad, a thief, a romantic, and yet probably the man most responsible for bringing radio broadcasting to the American public," accomplished this by inserting a zigzag wire, called a grid, between the positive and negative plates of Fleming's vacuum tube. A separate current applied to the grid could charge it positively or negatively with respect to the others, impeding or accelerating the electron flow. In fact, this "grid current" acted much like a venetian blind; just as a small adjustment in the angle of the blinds makes a great difference in the amount of light allowed through, so a small change in grid current made possible a large amplification in the radio signal.

Baird therefore thought he no longer had to worry about the weakness of the transmitted signal, radio and television signals being electromagnetically identical in this respect. But the problem of the time lag remained.

He tried to solve this by using the new photoelectric cells that had recently been developed, based not on selenium but on sodium or potassium. Following the discovery of the photoelectric effect in the late nineteenth century (in which ultraviolet light knocked electrons out of metals), several workers had found that the alkali earth elements sodium and potassium were photoconductive: their electrons were mobile enough that the energy of ordinary light was enough to make them flow from one atom to another, providing an electric current. Unfortunately, these elements are also extremely reactive: in air they soon react with oxygen to form an oxide coating that shields them from the light and thus inhibits their release of electrons; when this happens, the photoconductive effect quickly disappears.

Researchers in Germany had begun to overcome this problem by amalgamating the sodium and potassium with mercury. The mercury protected them from ambient oxygen without affecting the mobility of their outer electrons. The mercury effect was not permanent, however; it merely slowed down the metals' reaction with oxygen, so eventually the photoconductive effect was still lost. The next step was to enclose the metal in a glass cylinder and to replace the air with an inert gas such as nitrogen or argon. With no water vapor or oxygen to react with, the metals remained pure. This marked the beginnings of modern photocells. Later work, through the 1920s, extended the effect by finding that sodium and potassium hydrides (compounds with hydrogen) deposited in thin layers were hundreds of times more efficient.

Baird conducted a long series of experiments with such photocells, and they formed part of the heart of his system, which he guarded jealously. "The exact nature of my light-sensitive device is being kept secret" is all he would tell reporters. But we may surmise from his results at the time that he had hit on the idea of pumping the air out of the glass cylinder and maintaining a vacuum instead of replacing it with another gas. This type of photocell, as is now well known, has the advantage of responding quickly to the presence of light: light shines and current flows; light is removed and the current stops.

These photocells provided an instantaneous burst of electricity, but they had a corresponding disadvantage: they needed a large amount of light to induce the effect. Baird's apparatus, remember, consisted of a Nipkow disk fashioned from the top of a ladies' hatbox, and the small amount of light coming through the perforations wasn't bright enough to trigger a response from the photocell.

So he tried building bigger Nipkow disks, finally creating an eight-foot one out of plywood, with lenses eight inches in diameter to focus the light onto the photocells. The disk "nearly filled the little lab" and was spun around at two and a half revolutions per second, 150 per minute. "On more than one occasion lenses broke loose," Baird recalled, "striking the walls or roof like bomb shells. The apparatus would then get out of balance and jump from one side of the lab to the other until it was stopped or the disk tore itself to pieces. I had some exciting moments."

Unable to make the photocells work, he decided to try something else. He had read that "the light sensitivity of the human eye . . . resides in a purple fluid found in the retina of the eye, and called visual purple. I decided to make an experimental cell using the substance." With the chutzpah of the truly mad, he called in at Charing Cross Ophthalmic Hospital, asked for the chief surgeon, and matter-of-factly told him he needed an eye for "some research work I was doing on visual purple."

The surgeon evidently took him for a doctor and told him he had come at just the right time; he was just about to take out a patient's eye. So Baird sat down and waited, and as soon as the operation was over the surgeon came in to see him, carrying the eye wrapped carelessly in cotton wool. Baird took it back to the Frith Street attic and tried to dissect it with a razor, but made a mess of it and ended up throwing the eye into a nearby canal.

Pounding the walls in frustration, venting an honest Scottish rage at a recalcitrant universe that refused to cooperate, he went back to the selenium cells. But the time lag problem had not cured itself in the interim. He tried chopping the light into packets by passing it through a serrated disk, hoping that if the selenium saw a succession of sudden bursts of light instead of a steady source, it would respond with equal suddenness.

But nothing worked. "One could not help feeling sorry for his restless nature," one of his assistants later wrote, "watching him as he paced up and down the laboratory."

Still, he was transmitting *something,* and occasionally he got a bit of encouragement. The editor of a popular science magazine, *Discovery,* visited his laboratory and reported:

> I attended a demonstration of Mr. Baird's apparatus and was very favourably impressed with the results. His machinery is, however, astonishingly crude and the apparatus in general is built out of derelict odds and ends. The optical system is composed of lenses out of bicycle lamps. The framework is an unimpressive erection of old sugar boxes and the electrical wiring a nightmare cobweb of improvisations. The outstanding miracle is that he has been able to produce any result at all with the indifferent material at his disposal.

But there *were* results:

> The hand appeared only as a blurred outline, the human face only as a white oval with dark patches for the eyes and mouth. The mouth, however, can be clearly discerned opening and closing and it is possible to detect a wink.

This was not enough to satisfy the inventor, who was trying to transmit clear and recognizable scenes. He had progressed by now past the stage of trying to transmit simple figures like crosses or letters and was using a ventriloquist's dummy, focusing on and trying to reproduce the head. All he got, though, time after time was "a streaky blob."

He was down to his last thirty pounds when at last, on the first Friday in October 1925, with a final flurry of twisting knobs and crossed fingers, it quite suddenly worked. "The dummy's head formed itself on the screen with what appeared to me almost unbelievable clarity," Baird wrote. "I had got it! I could scarcely believe my eyes, and felt myself shaking with excitement."

He had to see a human face on television—that would be the real test. He ran down the four flights of stairs and grabbed hold of the office boy working there. He pulled him upstairs, trying to explain but too excited to be coherent, and sat him down in front of the transmitter. Then he ran into the other room where the receiver was, and looked into it—and saw nothing.

His spirits sank. He ran back to the first room, and there he saw that the boy—William Taynton by name—had backed out of the lights; they were too bright, they hurt his eyes. Baird gave him two shillings and sixpence and sat him back down again, making him promise not to move. And "this time he came through. On the screen I saw the flickering, but clearly recognisable, image of William's face—the first face seen by television."

4. After this first successful television run, Baird went from triumph to triumph. He showed that distance was no factor when he transmitted through telephone lines to the BBC studio and that even wires weren't necessary: the BBC transmitted their received signal (from the telephone lines) over the air and Baird received it back in his laboratory—the first wireless transmission of a television image, though this was done informally and soon stopped by "someone up above" at the BBC.

The excitement now built steadily. True television had been obtained, but how should they announce it to the world? "I was extremely nervous in case while I waited, someone else achieved television and gave a show before I did," related Baird. His financial partners, on the other hand, opposed any public announcement; they were "terrified that someone would copy my work, and particularly frightened [with very good cause] that the big wireless concerns would be given an impetus to take up television research, and use my work as a guide."

Baird's concerns won out over those of his backers, and he invited the Royal Institution to a demonstration. To maintain the dignity of the occasion, the *Times* was the only newspaper invited. On Tuesday, January 26, 1926, the small attic room on Frith Street was jammed full of distinguished visitors in full evening dress. "This gorgeous gathering found that they were expected to climb three flights [actually four] of narrow stone stairs, and then to stand in a narrow draughty passage, while batches of six at a time were brought into the two tiny attic rooms which formed my laboratory."

Baird was afraid that the enormous Nipkow disk, spinning at a rapid rate, might shake loose one of its lenses—as it not infrequently did— sending dangerous glass shards flying around the room like shrapnel. He had visions of next morning's *Times*: "Royal Institution Massacre in Soho!"

But the worst that happened was that one of the members who volunteered to be televised sat too close to the disk and his long white beard got caught in it. Fortunately his hair was yanked out before his face got pulled into the whirling disk. Aside from that, all went swimmingly, and the audience responded with great enthusiasm. "Baird has got it!" one of them said. "The rest is merely a matter of pounds, shillings, and pence."

Well, not quite. But he was certainly off and running. The *Times* published a laudatory, if cautionary, piece, stating that they had examined the "apparatus designed by Mr. J. L. Baird, who claims to have solved the problem of television. . . . It has yet to be seen to what extent further developments will carry Mr. Baird's system towards practical use." Other papers picked up the story, however, without the cautionary aspects. The *New York Times* reported that "the international race for the perfection of television has been won by Great Britain. . . . Within a few months, it was declared, a central television station may be erected. . . . Movements of [the subject's] face were clearly seen in another room," and the *Radio News* headlined, "Television an Accomplished Fact."

The following days saw hordes of reporters from the lesser papers climbing the rickety stairs of 22 Frith Street. Baird gave demonstrations "to every newspaper from the *Times* to *Tit-bits,* and to everyone who was willing to come, from the office boy to the Prime Minister." Gone was any lingering attempt to preserve "dignity"; he was consumed with the idea that he must get his achievement before the public, both to raise private funds and to establish his own priority of invention.

It wasn't easy to overcome the skepticism of the public. Many people suspected trickery—for example, that he was hiding someone behind the receiver or was using mirrors to fool them. "I remember being called away in the middle of a demonstration to a distinguished scientist," Baird wrote. "I came back suddenly and was surprised to find this venerable old gentleman crawling about under the apparatus. He was a little embarrassed, but pointed out that as he had to make a report it was his duty to satisfy himself that there was no trickery."

As a stunt, Baird set up a transmitter that used infrared instead of visible light. This allowed him to televise a scene in utter darkness. It wasn't clear what use this could be—and indeed it still isn't—but it was the sort of thing that titillated the public. As he was coming down to breakfast in his hotel, a young lady stopped him on the stair and asked if it was really true that he had a device that could see in the dark. He replied that it was, and she said, with a coy smile, "That explains the queer tickling sensation I had last night in bed." *You naughty man,* she probably added under her breath.

In a circus atmosphere such as this, it is no wonder that scientists witnessing Baird's exhibitions thought there might be chicanery involved. But little by little they were convinced. A. A. Campbell Swinton, the theoretical pioneer who had first discussed the concept of cathode-ray television, was heard to remark at his club: "I have been converted! I have been converted!" When questioned, he answered that it was not religion he was talking about but television. He wrote to the *Times* that television had arrived, and he himself had witnessed it and could vouch for it.

5. With Baird's new success appeared an old friend. Captain Oliver George Hutchinson, with whom he had spent one sociable evening back in London drinking brandy and planning to merge their cheap soap businesses, read in the papers about this new marvel of the age and showed up one morning at the Frith Street laboratory. Hutchinson had prospered, and he was now ready to invest in something else. He clapped Baird on the back, they shook hands, Hutchinson bought out Will Day, and he and Baird formed a partnership. Baird would work with his beloved wires and disks, and Hutchinson would be business manager.

"Hutchey's" first recommendation was that they should take advantage of the publicity by forming a public company and selling stock. They found a firm of stockbrokers willing to undertake the proposition, and with the solemn assurance from Baird that he had a complete monopoly on television—that no one else in the world could do what he was doing—the venture was solidified. On a cold day in February 1927, the final papers were signed, setting up a board of directors with Sir Edward Manville, the chairman of Daimler Motors, as chair; Baird, Hutchinson, and a vice president of Guaranty Trust of New York completed the board. Baird and Hutchey served as joint managing directors, with the munificent salary of fifteen hundred pounds per year.

For a brief interlude Baird was able to enjoy the fruits of financial success. He lunched every day with Hutchey at the Café Ivy across the street from their new laboratory. Instead of his usual midday meal of tea with one scone and two pats of butter, he was now starting off lunch with cocktails and hors d'oeuvres, then "a nice bowl of rich pea soup, fritto misto, curried chicken and Bombe Gladys Cooper, washed down with copious draughts of Chateau Y'quem, followed by coffee and petits-fours washed down with Bisque d'Bouche Brandy. . . . Those were the days!"

Baird would later regret his naïveté of these years, when he did not take advantage of his celebrity "to get into the right circles. I turned down all sorts of invitations and continued to shuffle around in the lab in a state of dirt and dishevelment, absorbed in my bits and pieces. I paid for my carelessness later on, when big business got hold of television and of myself. Oh! Why did I not cash in while the going was good?"

Of course, becoming a corporation wasn't all petits fours and brandy. There were drawbacks as well. The first chairman, Sir Edward Manville, was a nuisance at board meetings, where he would pontificate and bore Baird, but this was easily handled by Baird's simply nodding off. Quite another matter was the nuisance of Sir Edward's being an engineer by training and having the notion that this entitled and even obligated him to take an interest in the technical aspects of television and to offer Baird his continual advice. "Ever and again I was interrupted by the intrusion of his portly figure. He boomed at me through a cloud of cigar smoke, asked innumerable pointless questions, and, what was worse, he made impossible suggestions. When I tried to explain that they were impossible his booming became angry and ominous, and he glared indignantly and overbearingly at me over his impressive facade of double chins."

Baird couldn't compete with him on his own terms, but he was cleverer than Sir Edward. When the company moved into new space in Long Acre, London, Baird had the door to the laboratory "made just wide enough to let myself through and far too narrow to admit Sir Edward. The first time he appeared there was a most heart-rending and embarrassing scene—he was an obstinate and determined man—and he got through! But he lost several buttons from his waistcoat and dropped his cigar and tramped on it in the process. He never visited my laboratory again."

Baird' spirits dampened when the winter weather arrived; he caught his "usual chill," but this time he couldn't seem to recover. His doctor diagnosed a liver ailment and associated disorders. A diet of boiled fish, soda water, and toast replaced the Ivy feasts, and slowly his health came back. But not completely: he consulted one specialist after another and received diagnoses of polyps in the nose, tonsillitis, inflammation of the antrum, inflamed gums, sinusitis, and streptococcus discharge. He took one treatment after another but remained sickly the rest of his life.

Nor was his health the only cloud on the horizon, for "by an astounding coincidence," as he later recalled, "the very next morning [the day after the final papers had been signed, in February of 1927] the London newspapers were filled with headlines: 'American Telephone and Telegraph Company Gives Television Demonstration.'"

The Baird monopoly was over. American Big Business was here; Goliath was about to tackle David.

FIVE

Slumbering Giants

*Human genius has now destroyed the impediment
of distance.* Herbert Hoover, 1927

1 . Actually, it was not until April 7, 1927, that American Telephone and Telegraph broke out of the laboratory and surprised the world with their television accomplishments. The newspaper headlines screamed:

FAR-OFF SPEAKERS SEEN
AS WELL AS HEARD HERE
IN A TEST OF TELEVISION

A PHOTO COME TO LIFE

HOOVER'S FACE PLAINLY
IMAGED AS HE SPEAKS
IN WASHINGTON

THE FIRST TIME IN HISTORY

The *New York Times* was properly enthusiastic—as well as chauvinistic, ignoring Baird's work in England. This was to become characteristic of the television race: each group's accomplishment was hailed as "the first in history," especially by the group itself. In AT&T's case, however, even if their demonstration wasn't the first, it was still pretty impressive. As befit a major corporation, AT&T put on a damn good show, all the more surprising because until then they had kept a discreet silence regarding the television research being conducted by Dr. Herbert E. Ives and his research team. Ives had been working since 1924 on a television/telephone system, with the object of establishing both visual and aural two-way communications across the country.

On April 7, AT&T gathered together a distinguished audience of college professors and scientists, reporters and politicians, engineers and administrators at the building of their New York subsidiary, the Bell Telephone Laboratories. First the audience was taken on a tour of the equipment: two Nipkow disks, each fifteen inches in diameter with fifty holes; one disk was for transmission and the other for reception. Ives's team had devised a technique to avoid the terribly bright lights needed for illumination; the scene was lit by a bright light that shone only in a thin pencil beam through the holes of the transmitting disk, so that instead of being bathed in light, the subject was lit by a searchlight-like beam that scanned over him as the disk revolved.

Two screens were shown. One, two feet by two and a half feet, was intended as "an adjunct to a public address system"; the other, two by two and a half inches, "was suitable for viewing by a single person [seated at] the telephone."

After the tour, the demonstration began. Herbert Hoover, then secretary of commerce, spoke first. (Television was not yet powerful enough to command a presidential appearance.) Through a telephone he told the watchers and listeners that he was proud "to have a part in this historic occasion . . . the transmission of sight, for the first time in the world's history. Human genius has now destroyed the impediment of distance in a new respect, and in a manner hitherto unknown. What its uses may finally be, no one can tell. . . . We may all take pride in the fact that its actual accomplishment is brought about by American genius and its first demonstration is staged in our own country."

It's easy to imagine Baird's rage when he read that. The *New York Times* went on to report that "at times the face of the Secretary could not be clearly distinguished . . . [but] near the close of his talk he turned his head to one side, and in profile his features became clear and full of detail. On the smaller screen the face and action were reproduced with perfect fidelity."

Hoover was followed by an AT&T vice president and several others. "The speaker on the New York end looked the Washington man in the eye, as he talked to him. On the small screen before him appeared the living face of the man to whom he was talking. Time as well as space was eliminated."

The first part of the demonstration was transmitted over telephone lines; the people in Washington had been physically linked to the people in New York by AT&T's cables. But in the second part—which featured a couple of vaudeville comedians—there was no connection at all; the pictures were sent through the air by radio waves, originating from a studio in New Jersey. Everyone present suddenly realized that it would soon be possible to see and talk to people anywhere on the face of the earth.

AT&T was not interested in going into broadcasting but only in advancing one-on-one radiotelephonic-television connections. And they soon decided that television did not offer enough promise in this field to justify their spending the money on research that would be needed to compete effectively with everyone else. So Baird, as it turned out, had nothing to fear from them. Instead, it would be two other corporate giants, General Electric and Westinghouse—brought under the aegis of the Radio Corporation of America—that would finally defeat him.

2. On January 11, 1927, the *New York Times* had carried another story that somehow Baird hadn't noticed. It reported that Dr. E. F. W. Alexanderson of the General Electric Company, in a demonstration to the Institute of Wireless Engineers in New York, had sent photographs via radio. Not merely still photographs but a film strip. "It was crude reproduction," the paper reported, "but it moved." The next day the London *Times* announced that "the broadcasting by wireless of moving pictures is an accomplished fact."

Unknown to Baird and his backers, active television research had been going on at GE for several years. On March 10, 1923 (the same year that Baird began his quest), Ernst Alexanderson, consulting engineer at GE in Schenectady, had written a memo to Mr. Ira Adams of the GE patent department:

> Our work in developing methods for transmitting pictures by our system of radio telegraphy has led me to figure on the possibilities of transmitting moving pictures by radio.

Now, in 1927, with the first public demonstration of his work, Alexanderson would become one of the select group who dominated the press coverage of the race to bring television to the people. But television was not the object of obsession or the focal point of his life's work, as it was for Baird. Nor was it the culmination of a lifelong interest in tinkering and invention, as it was for Jenkins. Instead, it was yet another noteworthy episode in a career focused on scientific investigation. He alone of the three was a trained scientist, and early in his career he had developed the philosophy that scientific progress should occur as a natural evolution; inventions should come about as logical "stepping-stones" rather than as bursts of genius separated from the collective work of the scientific community. He came to television with the bemused and tempered excitement of an already famous and accomplished scientist settling confidently into middle age.

Ernst Fredrik Werner Alexanderson had been born in Uppsala, Sweden, in 1878, the same year that Edison formed his Electric Light Company (GE's forerunner) in New Jersey. The son of a professor of classical languages and a mother who came from military nobility, Ernst grew up in an atmosphere of erudition and academic accomplishment. His parents encouraged him in every creative endeavor, and he particularly enjoyed playing in his father's home workshop, where he built a toy steamboat at a young age and developed an interest in becoming an engineer. This eventually led him to the Royal Institute of Technology in Stockholm.

At the time of his graduation from the institute in 1900, electrical power was all the rage, and the best young scientific minds were flocking to the field of electrical engineering. Many of them were also flocking to America, which was considered the capital of big-time, cutting-edge electrical work. And the electrical capital of America was Schenectady, New York, home of General Electric's research laboratory. By 1902, about twenty-five of Alexanderson's Royal Institute of Technology classmates were employed there. And early in that year, Alexanderson himself managed to join them. By now twenty-three years old, he was five-foot nine, with brown eyes and blond hair, and he already sported his trademark handlebar mustache, carefully groomed in the style to be made famous by Kaiser Wilhelm.

Within a few years of his arrival at GE, he had invented a new type of alternator that resulted in the transmission of radio signals across the ocean. His original annual salary of $750, which had risen to $2,900 by 1907, jumped to $4,000 in 1910. He became an American citizen in January 1908 and married Edith Lewin, a GE secretary. Ten years out of the Royal Institute of Technology, he had made a permanent home in America and a place for himself in the scientific world.

In 1917, with America on the brink of entering the World War, Alexanderson asked one of his assistants, Charles Hoxie, to begin experiments on the photographic reception of radio signals. His idea was to transmit pictures as a method of communication with airplanes, undisturbed by cockpit noise. The idea didn't work, but six years later, in 1923, this interest in the transmission of visual images would come back and stick.

By then he was at the top of his profession, a charter member of GE's new Consulting Engineering Department, which had been set up to "enable a few elite engineers to select challenging problems and be provided with the resources needed to solve them." The autonomy that this provided allowed him to follow his interests into the field of television. He was forty-five years old, happily married to his second wife (his first had died in 1912, two weeks after giving birth to their second child), and was already becoming a legend at GE for his mental abstraction as well as his genius. "You'd be talking to him," recalled colleague Harold Beverage, "and all of a sudden he'd start talking in Swedish.

You'd have to say, 'Hold on, back to English.'" His daughter Edith remembered, "I once met him at the corner of Erie and State, and he bowed to me. I finally said, 'Daddy, hello!' He didn't know who I was."

This abstraction didn't prevent his career from blossoming. During the war he had overseen the establishment of a transoceanic radio system based on his own new high-powered alternator. When the Radio Corporation of America (RCA) was formed in 1919, he was appointed its first chief engineer, while continuing to work for GE at an opulent combined salary of $20,000. He received the Institute of Radio Engineers' Gold Medal for his alternator, "a major advance in the science or art of radio communication," and went on to serve as the IRE's vice president in 1920 and president in 1921.

On January 5, 1923, he wrote to Adams of the patent department:

At the luncheon and dinner given this week for General Harbord the possibilities were touched upon by Mr. [Owen] Young and others of sending pictures by radio. It seems like a coincidence that just a week before I specially asked Mr. Ranger to look into the possibility of sending pictures over our existing oceanic circuit as a way of increasing the earnings of the station. I outlined to him a method by which this can be done using only apparatus that already exists at present.

Then came the March memo to Adams regarding the possibility of transmitting moving pictures. In it, he envisioned a mechanical scanner sweeping a beam of light across the image, connected to an apparatus of one hundred separate radio transmitters operating in parallel, "acting simultaneously upon 100 photo-electric cells which thereby modulate one hundred circuits," in order to tackle the seemingly insurmountable problem that "600,000 unit impressions must be transmitted in one second."

"This feat is conceivable," he wrote, and with that statement he joined the ranks of the television "nitwits."

Alexanderson's renewed interest in television coincided with and was heightened by his entry into the field of shortwave propagation. Early in the 1920s, amateur radio transmitters discovered that shortwaves could be used to transmit over great distances, and soon the entire radio industry was experimenting with them. On July 24, 1924, Alexanderson wrote to F. C. Pratt, a GE vice president:

> Personally, I believe that short waves hold possibilities of opening up whole new systems of communication of a scope that we can at present only vaguely foresee. . . . Short waves are particularly adapted for radio transmission of pictures; even moving pictures by radio such as broadcasting of a boxing match is conceivable by the use of short waves.

The evolution of his television ideas was well under way. By August 1924 he had trimmed down his concept of one hundred separate radio channels to "sixteen independent photo channels, each covering one-sixteenth of the picture." Alexanderson was convinced at this point that Baird's notion of scanning—of sending a series of separate pictures and requiring "the eye . . . to retain the image for a sixteenth of a second"—was misguided. "I believe," he wrote, "that such a process would cause a great eye strain. . . . I therefore believe it essential in realizing television that the field of vision should be illuminated continuously, or nearly continuously."

But by December 1924 he had changed his mind. He described to the patent department the latest design of his and Hoxie's, which used a Nipkow disk to scan the scene, much as Baird was doing. "I have seen this device in operation," Alexanderson wrote, "and am satisfied that the impression on the eye is the same as if the whole picture were constantly illuminated." Using the disk at the transmitting end, Hoxie pointed a camera at the window on December 12, and Alexanderson "listened on a telephone connected directly to the photoelectric cell and could distinctly hear the high-pitched sound appear and disappear when a writing pad was held at the spot in the window opening which was focused on the photoelectric cell." They hadn't even begun to try to turn the signal back into a picture at the receiving end, but already Alexanderson concluded that his disk system was "more practical than the system of rotating lenses developed by Mr. Jenkins in Washington."

By the next week he was already speaking of projecting a television picture onto "a moving picture screen three feet square."

At the same time, David Sarnoff, who was by now general manager of RCA, asked Alexanderson to evaluate Jenkins's work in detail and advise RCA about whether they should consider buying his patent rights. (RCA had been formed in 1919 as a subsidiary of GE and now constituted a virtual monopoly of the American radio communication business.) On December 19 Alexanderson reported to the GE patent department:

> I have no reason to change my opinion regarding the value of the Jenkins patent situation. . . . Mr. Jenkins makes certain claims for television which he has not substantiated. The demonstration which I saw in Washington two years ago was very crude and so far as I have been able to learn he has not made much progress in that time.

Of course, Alexanderson himself to date had not done as much as either Jenkins or Baird, but he was confident: "[We have] . . . designed a very promising form of television projector. . . . I believe . . . that we will control this situation provided that we are the first to give a practical demonstration."

On January 17, 1925, Alexanderson conducted his first demonstration in which a picture was reproduced at the receiving end. The image was a horizontal bar of light, which was passed through a prism and projected onto a photoelectric cell. The resulting current was transmitted by radio to his laboratory, where it was amplified and used to control the mirror of a standard oscillograph. A system of lenses and an arc light produced a light beam that was passed through another crystal and focused on a screen. Crude as it was, said Alexanderson, "the test demonstrated the operativeness of all the principles which we consider necessary for development of practical television."

Over the next two years his team worked on a succession of television-related topics, related mainly to working with the long-wave telegraphy lines that GE already had operating. By the end of 1926, he was envisioning the possibility of transmitting a picture "in one-tenth of a second, and we will thus have the machinery for transmitting moving pictures of real objects [rather than merely film strips]."

He still wasn't able to demonstrate a working television set, but this didn't dim his confidence. He claimed to the patent department: "Our work on picture transmission and television has progressed to the point where we are now laying out a definite program for the commercial application." The most profitable commercial application of television in the short term, he felt, would be the instant transmission of movie films for projection in theaters. What he was envisioning was a revolution in the distribution of films, with no impact whatever on the medium itself.

On December 15, 1926, Alexanderson was the featured speaker at the annual meeting of the American Institute of Electrical Engineers in Saint Louis. His talk, "Radio Photography and Television," was the first public announcement that GE was engaged in television research and was tempered by a conservatism and hesitancy not present in his claims to his patent department.

He began his talk by describing a scene from George Bernard Shaw's recent play, *Back to Methuselah,* in which the British prime minister holds conferences with ministers hundreds of miles away: "He has at his desk a switchboard and in the background of the room is a silver screen. When he selects the proper key at the switchboard, a life-size image of the person with whom he is speaking is flashed on the screen at the same time that he hears the voice." He then announced that GE had at last achieved a "radio picture service across the Atlantic Ocean." Achieving television, however, would mean reducing the transmission time from twenty minutes to one-sixteenth of a second.

"When we embark on such an ambitious program as television," he continued, "it behooves us to reason out, as far as possible, whether the results we expect to get will be worthwhile even if our most sanguine hopes are fulfilled."

We have before us a struggle with imperfections of our technique, with problems which are difficult but which may be solved. In every branch of engineering there are, however, limitations which are not within our control. There is the question whether the medium with which we are dealing is capable of functioning in accordance with our expectations and desires. . . . The use of the radio wave itself imposes certain speed limitations on account of the limited scale of available wavelengths. The question therefore remains, what quality of reproduction may we ultimately expect in a television system if we succeed in taking full advantage of the ultimate working speed of the radio wave?

Another problem, he pointed out, was projecting a large enough picture at the receiving end. To scan enough lines at that size, fast enough to produce a seamless moving image, "seems at first inconceivable."

At the root of this situation is the fact that we have to depend upon moving mechanical parts.

If we knew of any way of sweeping a ray of light back and forth without the use of mechanical motion, the solution of the problem would be simplified. Perhaps some such way will be discovered, but we are not willing to wait for a discovery that may never come. A cathode ray can be deflected by purely electromagnetic means, and the use of the cathode ray oscillograph for television has been suggested. If, however, we confine our attention to the problem as first stated, of projecting a picture on a fair-size screen, we know of no way except by the use of mechanical motion.

Unwilling to dream of electronic television, Alexanderson pinned all his hopes on a mechanical apparatus: "How long it will take to make television possible we do not know, but our work has already proved . . . that it may be accomplished with means that are in our possession at the present day."

Paradoxically, it is in the scientist, Alexanderson, not in the amateur inventors, Baird and Jenkins, that we can truly detect the limitations of the mind-set of the times. How is it that the foremost electronic engineer of the foremost electronic corporation in the world could not see the possibilities of purely electronic television?

Perhaps it was Alexanderson's previous successes that doomed him.

He had won his wings, so to speak, in 1910 with a spinning-disk alternator that had made transoceanic radio a practical possibility. By 1926, when he spoke publicly on the possibilities of television, he was recognized as an electrical authority and quoted in newspapers all over the country, in stories that proclaimed him the father of long-distance radio. The *Brooklyn Eagle,* for example, described him as the man who "Made Radio Encircle the Globe" and who had the world's "foremost mind in the electrical field." All this adulation was based on his spinning-disk approach to radio. Perhaps this early success subconsciously influenced him, keeping him fixated on the Nipkow disk as the answer to television.

Whatever the reason, as 1926 drew to a close, Alexanderson plunged ahead with his mechanical experiments, determined to give GE the first commercial television system, while Baird raced against him in England and Jenkins worked doggedly in Washington.

And meanwhile, unknown to them, the seeds of something quite different were sprouting. Eventually it would grow to a towering organism that would cut off all mechanical light.

SIX

The Path to Glory

*Great as has been the success of the talking movies, they
may easily be outdone by radio-television if the technical
difficulties are overcome.*   New York Times

1. But not quite yet. Electronic television was
still a mewling baby, and no one could tell what it would grow into. Of
its two main inventors, one was a Russian immigrant who was spending these years trying desperately to find a job—any job—in the American engineering industry, and the other was a Utah farm boy with a
high school education who was trying to convince someone—anyone—to invest a little money in order to give him a chance to prove that
his ideas would work.

There was the occasional short article in the newspapers. Early in
1928 the *New York Times* carried a story picked up from the *San Francisco Examiner*: "The *Examiner* says today that Philo T. Farnsworth,
young San Francisco inventor, has perfected a new system of radio television which does away with the revolving disk feature, reproduces objects in great detail, and can be manufactured to retail at $100 or less."
The handwriting that would spell the end of Baird's work was on the
wall, but in the thrill of daily accomplishment at the Long Acre laboratories, nobody was yet paying attention.

Nor was anyone else. Most of the headline news about television
told of the spectacular successes of the Nipkow disk and the mechanical systems based on it, particularly those of Baird and Jenkins. Both of

these men worried about the progress of the other and about being overtaken by AT&T or GE or by researchers in France or Germany, but they thought not at all of those peculiar people fooling around with cathode-ray tubes.

The picture that Baird was transmitting at the time of his first success in 1925 was composed of thirty vertical strips lined up side by side to make a picture with a vertical-to-horizontal ratio of seven to three, and it was transmitted at the rate of twelve and a half complete scans per second. This combination of number of strips and rate was chosen as a compromise between what he called flicker and detail. The more detail you transmitted, the more flicker the picture had. The less flicker, the less detail. He began with fifteen strips and a low frequency of scanning, and one by one he increased first one and then the other until the picture transmitted became clearer and clearer as the detail increased, and he continued this process until the picture began to get less clear because of the increasing flicker. In this stepwise process he arrived at the maximum clarity his equipment could transmit.

His experiments went further: he tried color television, for example, by assembling a Nipkow disk with three spiral series of holes, each covered by separate colored filters: red, blue, and green. As the disk spun, the transmitted scene was sent out first in red, then blue, then green light. At the reception station these were recombined on a similar disk. The results were not yet of commercial quality, but they were reasonable enough to evoke much interest when demonstrated at the 1928 annual meeting of the British Association. It wasn't until a year later, on June 27, 1929, that the Bell Laboratories gave the first demonstration of color TV in America. (The *New York Times* typically omitted those somewhat crucial words "in America" in their announcement of this development.)

Baird also experimented with stereoscopic television, by using disks with two concentric spirals, one for the view as seen by the right eye and the other for the left. He claimed that "quite effective stereoscopic relief" was obtained, but clearly something was lacking since, except for a few demonstrations, he never followed up on it.

In 1928 Baird "decided to have a shot at transmitting across the Atlantic." He later wrote, "There was absolutely no technical reason that I could see against it." There were, however, technical details to be overcome. Hutchinson went to New York to set up the receiving system, and night after night Baird tried to get an intelligible signal across the waters, "listening to the whirr of the transmitter and hoping for the best." At first the tuning fork used to synchronize the waves interfered; this was cured by putting it in another house blocks away and connecting it by telephone. Then it turned out that the signal was too faint, and the power of the transmitter had to be increased. Finally the dummy's head was seen faintly, and from then on it was merely a matter of tuning up the apparatus.

Baird arranged for a famous actress of the London stage, Elissa Landi, to be the first person to be "sent" across the Atlantic. But on the arranged night, the signal simply wouldn't cross the waters; nothing was received in New York. The next night Baird tried again, this time with a journalist's wife as subject, and this time it did work. The press in New York was wildly enthusiastic as the lady's face appeared on the screen in front of them. It was an achievement that "ranks with Marconi's sending of the letter *S* across the Atlantic," the *New York Times* trumpeted.

Success was coming thick and fast in those exciting days. As Baird later recalled, "the shares in the company rushed upwards. Fortunes were made by active speculators and I sat like my own dummy and neither bought nor sold, and did not make one penny. . . . I was not interested in shares or money. . . . I felt I was doing something worth doing. It was interesting enough to make me work willingly night after night until three or four in the morning. These were happy days; I lived in the laboratory surrounded by my bits and pieces, trying this and trying that. Ominous clouds were gathering on the horizon and threatening rumbles were becoming audible, but they were still far off."

In 1928 the recently formed Television Society introduced a new magazine, *Television*, which featured such articles as "All About Television, the Invisible Ray," and "How to Make a Selenium Cell." The first issue sold 150,000 copies and showed on its front cover the stage of a concert hall in the misty distance, while up front a lady and gentleman, properly dressed in evening gown and white tie respectively, reclined in the comfort of their living room and watched the spectacle on television. It was hardly an accurate premonition of either the programming or audience of the future, but it sold copies.

At about this time Baird Television was transmitting daily. They were also making receivers, but they sold few to the public; the high price (twenty-five guineas) and the paucity of programming meant that television was as yet only a fad for the well-off or for those who were putting together their own receivers. Baird felt strongly that the future rested with broadcasts from the BBC, and he tried to interest them, but they were recalcitrant. He called for an interview with the BBC's chief at the time, Sir John Reith, with whom he had gone to school. They had never been friendly: Reith was the sort whose manner and bearing had made him popular at school, despite a lack of much actual accomplishment either in sports or scholastics. Baird, on the other hand, had been a sickly, skinny boy who had led his fellow introverts in rather arcane pursuits; at school he had formed a science club, a wireless club, a telephone club, and so on.

Now Baird entered Sir John's vast office at Portland Place, sat beneath the stained-glass window, and had a very cordial conversation. Sir John "was at that time, I think," Baird reported, "really wishful to be friendly; he offered to support a government grant to my company for the furtherance of our research. We parted in a very friendly fashion, but it was not to continue. Our relations with the BBC formed such a tangle of intrigue and conspiracy and cross purposes, that what and which threads of the cobweb were involved at any one time is, I now find, extremely difficult to remember."

What brought it all to a head was the fact that the Baird broadcast station was close to Admiralty House, and the Royal Navy began to complain of interference with their radio reception. Since this was integral to communication with the fleet at sea and since nothing in Britain could be allowed to irritate the navy, something had to change. Baird felt strongly that all broadcasting should be done by the BBC and that he should be involved only in the design and sale of receiving sets, but the BBC refused to broadcast television. In September of 1928 Baird

Television Ltd. appealed to the Post Office, which to this day oversees radio (and television); they are, in effect, the parent organization of the BBC. Baird gave a demonstration to the Post Office's chief engineer, who reported back favorably and said that the BBC should provide television broadcast facilities.

The BBC asked that a similar demonstration be given to them so they could evaluate the system for themselves. Although it went just as well as the first one had, the BBC once again refused to broadcast. This refusal was part of what Baird meant when he referred to "a tangle of intrigue and conspiracy," but really the argument involved a difference in technological philosophy. A memo written by the BBC's chief engineer after the demonstration stated baldly that "the Baird apparatus not only does not deserve a public trial, but also has reached the limit of its development owing to the basic technical limitations of the method employed."

It was clear to the BBC that despite Baird's achievement, mechanical scanning could never possibly deliver enough scanning lines with enough resolution to produce a clear picture. In mid July of 1928 Campbell Swinton, the man who had first proposed electronic television and who had earlier been "converted" by Baird, now regretted that conversion. With the fervor of a reformed apostate, he wrote to the *Times* to express his anger at the "very absurd prognostications that have appeared in the daily press. . . . At present, with the mechanically operated devices employed by all demonstrators, both in this country and in America, all that has been found possible is to transmit very simple pictures [which] can with a certain amount of imagination be recognized. Now however, the public are being led to expect, in the near future, that, sitting at home in their armchairs, they will be able, with comparatively inexpensive apparatus, to witness moving images approximating in quality to those of the cinematograph. . . . Such achievements are obviously beyond the possible capacity of any mechanism with material moving parts . . . and the only way it can ever be accomplished is by . . . using the vastly superior agency of electrons."

He later wrote to a friend at the BBC complaining that the *Times* had not published his letter in full. He had gone on to say that "Baird and

Hutchinson are rogues, clever rogues and quite unscrupulous, who are fleecing the ignorant public." The *Times* evidently thought such vituperation unsuitable for a "gentleman's newspaper."

The BBC agreed with Campbell Swinton. They wrote privately to the Post Office that the demonstration had been "an insult to the intelligence of those invited" to witness it, that Baird's system was "either an intentional fraud or a hopeless mechanical failure," and that it "would be merely ludicrous if its financial implications didn't make it sinister." Though the exact wording of this BBC report was never transmitted to Baird, he got the gist of it, and when he argued that the Post Office's own staff had obviously felt differently after their demonstration, a special committee of Parliament was set up to take a look. They decided that Baird should set up a television transmitter at the BBC headquarters and transmit a demonstration program to the General Post Office (GPO) facility at Saint Martins Le Grand, where it would be viewed on four receivers "of the type sold to the general public."

You couldn't ask for a better shot than that, but it put Baird into a terrible state. "It was a nerve wracking ordeal, as we were to stand or fall by the result of one crucial demonstration. A wire slipping or a valve burning out at the critical moment, and the demonstration would be a failure and we would have been faced with a devastating fiasco."

Baird spent a "dreadful nightmare night" setting up the transmitter, but by the morning of March 5, 1929, it all seemed to be working properly. He motored out to the GPO and watched with "infinite relief" as the program—"consisting of head and shoulders views of singers and comedians"—came through loud and clear. Three weeks later the committee reported that Baird's television was a "notable scientific achievement" and that in their opinion the BBC should be directed to begin regular television broadcasts. "This demonstration was a turning point and gave a crushing answer to innuendos, hints and significant shrugging of shoulders, implying that the whole thing was a fraud or a trick," Baird wrote. The BBC gave in with good grace and offered to broadcast television programs for fifteen minutes once a week, beginning at midnight.

"What?" Baird asked incredulously.

"That is, of course, if you agree to pay all expenses" came the laconic answer. "And one transmitter only." Which meant that he could broadcast sight or sound but not both simultaneously. Baird was "rightly indignant." A series of antagonistic conferences followed, with Baird each time threatening to go back to Parliament and the BBC each time giving up another hard-fought inch. Finally, "rather than be held up indefinitely," Baird agreed to three half-hours per week . . .

Beginning at midnight.

2. Between the BBC's somewhat backhanded concession and the commencement of broadcasts, Baird took his campaign abroad. In May 1929 he traveled to Germany at the invitation of Dr. Hans Bredow, former secretary of state and now broadcast commissioner of the Reichspost. Bredow and his staff had been in London the previous December and had been impressed with a Baird demonstration. They consequently invited him to come and use their famous radio transmitter, in the Witzleben section of Berlin, for experimental broadcasts.

Up to this point, Germany had taken no backseat to America or England in the development of the new "art." It was a German who had invented the Nipkow disk, after all, and another German, Karl Ferdinand Braun, had put together the first cathode-ray tube; the Germans had published the first book exclusively about television, and their government had been the first publicly to sponsor its development.

Dénes von Mihály was the young Hungarian physicist and former Hussar cavalry captain who had published that first book about television six years previously. The year before Baird's visit, on May 11, 1928, Mihály, now working together with the German Reichspost, presented his newest system to a Berlin audience of fifty invited guests. Misleadingly called "the first true demonstration of electrical television," Mihály's system used the Nipkow disk and transmitted thirty-line pictures onto a screen four centimeters by four centimeters. The thirty lines provided only a crude picture of silhouettes, but the demonstration sparked great German interest in television. As one spectator wrote, "there can no longer be any doubt that the question of television has found its solution."

A few months later, at the Berlin Radio Exhibition held from August 31 until September 9, Mihály pitted his newest "Telehor" machine against the television apparatus of August Karolus. Karolus, a forty-five-year-old former schoolteacher who had turned to physics in his thirties, had begun working on television in 1923 as a special assistant in applied electricity at the University of Leipzig. In 1925 he had developed a light valve that Ernst Alexanderson had incorporated into his mechanical television system. Now Karolus, with the support of the Telefunken company, showed up in Berlin with two systems: one, using Nipkow disks, produced a picture of eight by ten centimeters, big enough to be viewed by several spectators at once; and another, using ninety-six mirrors and his special light valve, projected onto a large screen of seventy-five centimeters square.

To the engineering experts in attendance, Karolus's systems were the obvious winners, but for the general audience, Mihály stole the show. The Hungarian immigrant proved to possess a gift for publicity that rivaled even Baird's. Walter Bruch, who would later work for Mihály and become an important television engineer himself, said, "Mihály spoke to the interests of the little man, suggesting to him that in the foreseeable future television devices would be available for 100 marks." No matter that the "little man" might suffer less eyestrain before Karolus's larger screens; the enduring famous photograph of the 1928 exhibition is of a line of spectators waiting for their turn to peek into the tiny aperture of Mihály's Telehor.

Then a new publicity hound showed up in Berlin. From May 15 to June 13, 1929, Baird made his broadcasts and collected support. "Other broadcasting authorities are more interested in my television transmission than you are," he had warned the BBC, and he was right. On June 11, he entered into a formal partnership with three successful German companies—Loewe, Bosch, and Zeiss-Ikon—to form a new company dedicated to the development of television. Fernseh A. G. ("Television,

Inc.") was born and would do battle against the more established Tele-funken throughout the coming years of television development. The plan was that Loewe would bring to the conglomerate its expertise with signal amplifiers; Bosch would provide knowledge of mechanics and measurement technology; and Zeiss-Ikon would add its mastery of lenses and photographic matters. For the guts of the machine, though—the means of turning pictures to electricity and back to pictures—Fernseh would put its money on the spinning disks and contagious confidence of John Logie Baird.

3. Ernst Alexanderson's 1926 lecture in Saint Louis served a purpose he almost certainly had not had in mind: to place him in the American public's mind as the leading television pioneer. On January 2, 1927, the *Tulsa World* proclaimed him "the inventor of television, which would soon become as common a household item as the telephone." It was the first of many articles, but Alexanderson resisted such declarations. In an interview in the *New York Herald* in May, he insisted that he was but one of many who had contributed to the development of television. He restated his philosophy of scientific progress: the important thing was not to come up with one great invention that changes your life but rather to be a part of the constantly running machine of science, to "go straight ahead and one thing leads to the next." "The march of progress is necessarily slow," he told an audience in April; "it is an evolution and not a revolution."

In January 1927, Alexanderson gave a lecture at a meeting of the Institute of Radio Engineers in New York City; while he spoke, a receiver on the podium picked up radio pictures transmitted over WGY from Schenectady. The next day an article in the *New York Tribune* agreed with Alexanderson's prediction that within ten years every home would have a television.

Everyone, it seemed, agreed with that prediction. What people couldn't agree on was what were to be the basic components of a workable television system. The leading contender for the basic ingredient, the scanning system, was the Nipkow disk; but as we have seen, Jen-

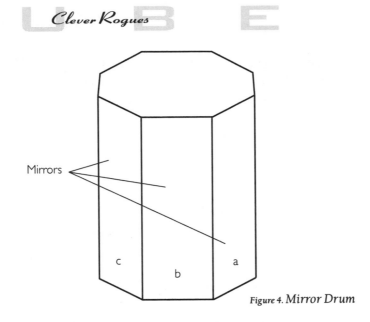

Mirrors

c   b   a

Figure 4. Mirror Drum

kins had switched over to his prismatic rings, and others were trying to get the cathode-ray tube to work. There were still other schemes as well. As an earlier historian of television put it, "almost every conceivable type of scanner was suggested in the period 1877–1936. There were vibrating mirrors, rocking mirrors, rotating mirrors, mirror polyhedra, mirror drums, mirror screws, mirror discs and scintillating studs; there were lens discs, lens drums, circles of lenses, lenticular slices, reciprocating lenses, lens cascades, and eccentrically rotating lenses; there were rocking prisms, sliding prisms, reciprocating prisms, prism discs, prism rings, electric prisms, lens prisms and rotating prism pairs; there were apertured discs, apertured bands, apertured drums, vibrating apertures, intersecting slots, multispiral apertures, and ancillary slotted discs; there were cell banks, lamp banks, rotary cell discs, neon discs, corona discs, convolute neon tubes, tubes with bubbles in them; there were cathode-ray tubes, Lenard tubes, X-ray tubes, tubes with fluorescent screens, glass screens, photoelectric matrices, secondary-emitting surfaces, electroscope screens, Schlieren screens and no screens at all."

In 1927 Alexanderson's team at GE joined the non-Nipkow (but still mechanical) battalions. In May Alexanderson made an important move in bringing Ray Kell over from the testing department. Kell had already devised a way to synchronize picture signals by means of a hand control; before long he was in charge of Alexanderson's television lab. Immediately, he and Paul Kober set to work on a system using a twenty-four-mirror drum instead of a Nipkow disk as a scanning device.

The mirror drum was based on an idea proposed in 1889 by a French worker, Lazare Weiller. Weiller had called his television set the "phoro-scope," and though it had never been successful, the idea had been used by several people since then. The outside cylindrical surface of a drum was covered with twenty-four flat mirrors, as shown in Figure 4 (for simplicity, we show an eight-mirror drum).

Mirror *a* would pick up a beam of light from one point of the scene to be televised and reflect it onto the photocell (light from other points would reflect in other directions). As the drum rotated, mirror *a* would reflect additional points from one line of the scene onto the photocell (Figure 5).

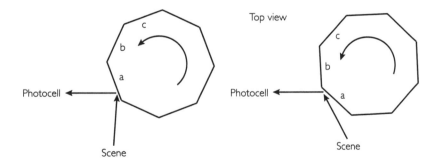

Figure 5. *Angle of Reflected Light Shifts as Drum Rotates*

In this manner mirror *a* would scan across one line of the televised scene. The next mirror on the drum, mirror *b*, was fixed at a different angle, so it would scan the same way but one line lower. Mirror *c* would follow, tilted just a bit more, and in this way as the drum rotated, the twenty-four mirrors would scan the entire scene, left to right and top to bottom, thus having the same effect as a Nipkow disk with twenty-four holes.

GE's version of Weiller's idea used two light beams, which produced a picture of forty-eight lines from the twenty-four mirrors. "The two beams work alternately," Alexanderson reported, "so that one beam traces every other second line in the picture and the other beam the intermediate lines." A couple of weeks later, he wrote:

> I witnessed today a test of our television system. . . . An image was projected on a small screen and . . . we could clearly distinguish the image of a hand, the opening and closing of the fingers.

By October, he was able to write: "A test was made today at my home of a television receiver developed for home use. We were able to clearly recognize the features of persons who posed before the transmitter in the laboratory." Though he admitted that the basic principle was "old and well-known," he felt that his group had added several new features that could be patented:

> One of the important simplifications is the system of synchronization. . . . To operate this television receiver it is only necessary to throw the switch which connects the receiver with the house lighting circuit and observe the changing patterns until a clear image of the object appears. With the help of a telegraph key this image can then be held in the field of vision indefinitely. . . . I believe that the simplicity of [this] system of synchronism will prove an important factor in widely popularizing television.

He was referring to the problem every television system of that time had: it took a trained engineer to find and focus the picture on the receiver, and one with the patience of a saint to keep it from flickering away. Even if someone were able to produce a working set, who would buy it if they couldn't operate it?

Because of the simplicity of this new GE system, Alexanderson called this test the first to show the feasibility of home television, and he declared his next step: to begin transmitting home television entertainment to the Schenectady area.

On January 13, 1928, Alexanderson took that next step, gathering twenty to thirty reporters, company officials, and engineers at the GE laboratories to announce the beginning of television broadcasting and to demonstrate their system. He explained his research to date and declared the demonstration to be "the starting point of practical and popular television." Then David Sarnoff spoke, calling the demo "an epoch-making development" akin to Marconi's demonstration of sending radio signals a mile or two through the air.

> The greatest significance of the present demonstration is in the fact that the radio art has bridged the gap between the laboratory and the home. Television has been demonstrated both in this country and abroad prior to this event, but it did not seem possible within so short a time to so simplify the elaborate and costly apparatus of television reception, that the first step might be taken towards the development of television receivers for the home.

While he warned that television was not yet ready for mass consumption, he predicted that within five years television would be "an art and an industry."

And then the demonstration began. The visitors were led into a small dark room and clustered about two receiver cabinets, each about four feet high with a screen of three inches square. Then over the radio loudspeakers came the voice of Leslie Wilkins, a member of the testing department, who was poised in the broadcasting alcove in another building: "I understand there is an audience in the receiving room now, so we will start."

> In the small openings of each of the cabinets appeared the image of his face.
>   "Now I will take off my spectacles and put them on again," he said. The picture suited his words.

"Here is a cigarette. You can see the smoke," he continued.

The audience saw him breathe out a smoke ring and watched it drift upward across his face.

Wilkins was succeeded on screen by regular WGY announcer Louis Dean, who played "Ain't She Sweet?" on his ukulele. The picture would occasionally waver to the left or right but was kept fairly well in place by the new synchronizing knob.

The demonstration was transmitted simultaneously to receiver sets in the homes of Alexanderson and two members of the board. The picture, composed of forty-eight lines at sixteen frames per second, was transmitted by station 2XAF at a wavelength of 37.8 meters, and the sound came on WGY at 379.5 meters. Ignoring the fact that the basic principles of television had been known for years and that others had already demonstrated their use, GE issued a press release: "Home television was developed by Dr. E. F. W. Alexanderson, consulting engineer of the Radio Corporation of America and the General Electric Company, and his assistants."

The reporters at the demonstration swallowed this story whole. The *New York Times* announced:

> A diminutive moving picture of a smiling, gesticulating gentleman wavered slowly within a small cabinet in a darkened room of the General Electric Company's radio laboratories this afternoon and heralded another human conquest of space.
>
> Sent through the air like the voice which accompanied the picture, it marked, the demonstrators declared, the first demonstration of television broadcasting and gave the first absolute proof of the possibility of connecting homes throughout the world by sight as they have already been connected by voice.

Forget Jenkins and Baird. The publicity department of General Electric was playing by one of the standard rules of invention: bravado is just as important as achievement.

The race for recognition was in full swing.

4.   And Francis Jenkins was in it for keeps, though by now he had abandoned his prismatic lens system. It had rekindled his interest in television, but it didn't work. He never was able to get the rings to rotate fast enough or to be synchronized perfectly enough to give a good picture, and he soon admitted defeat. He didn't, however, give up on mechanical television. Instead he went back to the Nipkow disk, using a fifteen-inch disk with forty-eight holes, which provided a forty-eight-line picture of reasonable clarity. But the Nipkow disk was unacceptably bulky, and by 1925 Jenkins still had not been able to reduce its size. As he himself admitted, "a 36-inch diameter disk is required for a 2-inch-square picture. A 4-inch picture would require a 6-foot diameter disk—a rather impractical proposition in apparatus for home entertainment."

However, he was now hooked on television, and if one system didn't work, perhaps another would. He abandoned the prism and the Nipkow disk and went to a drum scanner. Using a drum seven inches in diameter and projecting the picture through a magnifying glass gave an acceptable six-inch-square picture. "The whole family," he joyfully pronounced, "can very conveniently enjoy the story told in the moving picture." By 1927, just in time to take advantage of the flood of publicity accompanying the AT&T demonstration, Jenkins was ready to market his "Radiovisor."

That same year the Federal Radio Commission granted its first television station license; it went to station W3XK of the Jenkins Laboratories, and in May of 1928 he was ready to begin regularly scheduled television broadcasts. He announced his intention by sending out invitations to viewers, proclaiming the "birth of a new industry—Radio Movies—i.e., Pantomime Pictures by Radio for Home Entertainment."

The nature of his broadcasts was to be just that: pantomime stories, showing silhouettes only, in black and white, without sound. The entertainment value lay solely in the miracle of seeing these flickering images in your own home, transmitted as if by magic through the air. There was a "Little Girl Bouncing a Ball," and "Red Mike," who could be seen sawing through the bars of a jail and climbing out the window, and the always popular Sambo. There were musicians playing—although without sound it isn't clear just how entertaining that might be. Silent movies were broadcast; a description sent in by a viewer described one movie as consisting of "much love at the breakfast table, many embraces, kissing and a goodbye and then the husband going back to the job swinging the pickaxe and stopping to limber up his muscles and finally streaking for home and more embraces."

For those who couldn't afford his Radiovisor, Jenkins went on to give clear and detailed instructions for constructing a television set from easily obtained materials: "Needed will be a ³/₄ inch board 8 × 15 inches, a block ³/₄ × 1.5 × 2 inches, with a ¹/₄-inch hole bored through it endwise. . . . You will also want four round-head wood screws No. 10, 1.5 inches long, together with a half pound of ten-penny nails." Also needed was a store-bought or home-built radio set, to which the television apparatus would be attached.

The Jenkins broadcasts began on July 2, 1928, and, typically, there is an air of exaggeration in his memories:

> That evening the first scheduled broadcast of picture story entertainment was made, to be followed every evening thereafter (except Sundays and holidays).

The claim to be "the first scheduled broadcast" depends on the definition of what constitutes "picture story entertainment"; remember that GE had commenced its regular programming the previous month. And as it turned out, Jenkins's programs aired not every day but on Monday, Wednesday, and Friday evenings at 8:00 P.M. Despite the limitations of his programming, Jenkins was enthusiastic: his "magic mirror," he said, "reflects a pantomime picture story so realistic one's initial astonishment is lost in the fascination of the weirdly told tale."

A growing legion of viewers was responding just as enthusiastically, writing to him and to magazines such as *Radio News:* "For the past week I have been able to receive all of the Jenkins 46.7 meter broadcasts on a rather simple outfit built up at home in one evening. . . . When reception on the [radio] broadcast band was almost impossible, we received the entire silhouette broadcast, and had no difficulty in following the movements of the girl bouncing the ball and seeing the ball itself bounce up and down."

It may not sound like much to us now, but at the time it was a thrilling harbinger of wonders to come. This was the Jazz Age, and science was the new messiah. Lee De Forest, creator of the Audion, voiced the expectations of the nation:

> What thrilling lectures on solar physics will such pictures permit! . . . What could be a more fitting theme for a weekly half-hour of television than a quiet parade through some famous art gallery, pausing a moment before each masterpiece while the gifted commentator dwells briefly upon its characteristics, explains its meaning, recounts the story of its creation, its creator? What could be more richly entertaining, more uplifting, than such experience? . . . Can we imagine a more potent means for teaching the public the art of careful driving safety upon our highways than a weekly talk by some earnest police traffic officer, illustrated with diagrams and photographs?

Wall Street responded. In December 1928, the establishment of the Jenkins Television Corporation was announced, with a capitalization of ten million dollars in common stock. It was founded in order to manufacture, distribute, and sell the television receivers that came out of the Jenkins Laboratories, which would be bought by the public to "receive movies by radio." The president of the De Forest Radio Company, James Garside, became its first president; the next year the De Forest Company became the majority stockholder of the rapidly growing corporation.

Jenkins was not the only one to take up the baton from Alexanderson. Once these two had shown that television was a real possibility, others began building transmitters and receivers, and during the first few months of 1928, radio stations in New York, Boston, and Chicago began televising, with thousands of people across the country buying or building receivers.

By the end of that year there were eighteen stations throughout the United States broadcasting their own TV programs. Several companies started selling kits, for those who didn't want to make their own sets from scratch ("Synchronism is obtained by moving the motor board to or from the center of the scanning disc, by the screw S shown in Fig. 6 . . ."), and soon there were ready-to-view complete sets being sold in the stores. Tuning was difficult even in these and was usually done by twirling two dials simultaneously in an attempt to steer the picture into view: "Now, the picture may be upside down or it may be wrong right and left. . . . However, except in reading titles this is not often important." Indeed, this was a major part of the sport.

The First Great Television Boom was on, spurred forward by the media. Kits, supplies, and store-bought sets were snapped up, as everyone wanted to be the first on the block to own this marvelous gadget. *Radio News* had announced in 1925 that "in a more or less perfect form [TV] will be a common thing within a year. The main difficulties in the problem have been successfully worked out." Finally, this prediction seemed to be coming true.

In Brooklyn, Theodore Nakken designed a transmitter, and the Pilot Electrical Company built his receivers (or "televisors," as Nakken called them). In August, Hugo Gernsback, the publisher of *Radio News* and the owner of New York's radio station WRNY, began sending Nakken's television pictures out over his radio wave band, broadcasting sight and sound alternately rather than simultaneously: first you would see the face of a performer, and a few seconds later you would hear the voice. The performances took place for five minutes every hour and were designed to lure the radio audience into buying "televisor" sets from Pilot.

In Chicago, station WCFL began broadcasting in June, using equipment designed by Ulysis Sanabria, who would remain competitive for several years, and in Boston the *Post* sponsored telecasts in April and May, hoping that reports on them would make interesting reading for its subscribers. The Raytheon Company, which manufactured the neon tubes used in receivers, was thinking of entering the race; they became associated with Massachusetts radio station W1XAY, which began television broadcasts by the end of 1928.

None of these early broadcasts showed much promise of things to come. GE's transmissions were of men "talking, laughing, or smoking." In Boston and Chicago, movie films "of the kind used in theaters" were broadcast and were sometimes almost recognizable. In New York, viewers were treated to still pictures, diagrams, and occasionally a human head that moved.

Most of the transmissions used the Nipkow disk, transmitting forty-eight-line pictures, and the quality of reception was terrible. But it was in the anticipation of something better that people began to buy television sets. In 1928 they remembered the silent motion pictures, for sound had been introduced only a few years before. There was every reason to expect television to progress in the same manner, and when Jenkins issued a clarion call for amateur viewers to help with its development by putting together their own receivers and writing to tell him what kind of reception they were getting, they responded by the thousands.

He was on the path to glory, he thought.

5. Nineteen twenty-eight seemed to Alexanderson, too, to be the beginning of something big. After the January demonstration, his team concentrated on improving their existing system and made great strides. Still ignoring cathode-ray television, they were intent on bringing their mechanical system to commercial fruition.

On March 13 they demonstrated a picture projected onto a silver screen eighteen inches square. This dramatic enlargement from January's three-inch screen was accomplished by using a new, patentable light-control system. "This test appears convincing that this patent will control the art of projecting large television pictures," wrote Alexanderson. (As things would turn out, it did not.)

Two months later, on May 11, 1928, GE fulfilled the promise announced at their January 13 demonstration by inaugurating the country's first regular television broadcasting schedule. This was a full two months before Jenkins's "first scheduled broadcast of picture story entertainment." Jenkins's claim was based on program content, for GE's broadcasts were less ambitious in this regard. A press release announced that television programs would be broadcast on Tuesday, Thursday, and Friday afternoons from 1:30 to 2:00,

> primarily to enable Dr. Alexanderson and his assistants to pursue their investigations. . . . At the same time, the television broadcast offers the amateur, provided with such receivers as he may design or acquire, an opportunity to pick up the signals and carry on independent investigations.

Over the summer, the Alexanderson team used these experimental broadcasts to work on televising outdoor scenes. On July 26 they made some tests using a "portable" camera with only a twenty-four-hole disk and transmitted pictures of men boxing. Soon afterward, they were using a forty-eight-hole disk and showing clear pictures of the skyline and of smoke rising from chimneys. By late August they were ready to make history.

On August 22, New York Governor Alfred E. Smith stood before the usual cluster of radio microphones and newsreel cameras to make his speech accepting the Democratic nomination for president of the United States. For the first time ever, the media apparatus included a television camera: WGY's newest Alexanderson model.

Governor Smith was quite amenable, agreeing to rehearse beforehand for the television crews and also putting up with the camera, which consisted of one box housing a thousand-watt bulb and twenty-four-hole spinning disk, and two tripod-mounted photoelectric cells to convert the image into electrical signals, all within three feet of his face. Although it was an outdoor broadcast, the necessary illumination came from the camera's light source. The camera transmitted its signals to WGY eighteen miles away, where the signal was amplified and retransmitted to the surrounding area. The picture was also broadcast on shortwave by stations 2XAF and 2XAD. Those listening with ordinary radios heard "a peculiar high-pitched tone, broken at varying intervals. This was the face of the Democratic candidate for president. The peculiar tones heard on the loudspeaker were convertible into the moving image of Governor Smith by those who were equipped with proper receiving equipment."

At any rate, so said the subsequent GE press release, which called the broadcast "another great advance in the fascinating art of television . . . the first practical application of the equipment." The reality was less impressive; although the rehearsals went well, the huge arc lights of the newsreel cameras ruined the actual event, overpowering the television camera's thousand-watt bulb and rendering the picture a whiteout.

At times Alexanderson spoke of television with such reserve that we have to assume he was either determined to temper the optimism fomented by the GE public relations corps or else was disingenuously trying to lull his competition. In a statement issued in New York on September 4, 1928, he announced that GE would have a television exhibit at the upcoming Radio World's Fair in New York. The exhibit would consist of a television projector showing a life-sized picture of a person's head, but he "made clear at the outset that the television [would be] transmitted over a short wire line and that [they were] not prepared to transmit television of the same quality over any considerable distance."

The reason, he said, was the greatest obstacle facing commercial television: the difficulties in transmitting moving pictures via radio waves. He explained how the speed of light, though enormous, was not fast enough to make up for the varying paths the radio waves took from transmitter to receiver. Light, he said, travels fifty miles in the time required to produce one-fourth of one line in a television image. "Thus," he said, "if two rays have traveled from the transmitting to the receiving station through different paths and the length of these path differs by only 50 miles they will register separate images differing as much as ¼th of the picture." Some rays would fly directly from transmitter to receiver, but he saw no way to prevent other rays from arriving along circuitous routes—bouncing off buildings or mountains or even bouncing back and forth between different atmospheric layers. The effect of many rays arriving via different routes would be a blurred image.

He did concede that perhaps, after more research, "some wave length may be selected which will not produce these mirage effects," and in fact he would experiment in the coming years with shorter and shorter wavelengths for this purpose. "The history of radio in the past," he said, "has shown that obstacles that appeared insurmountable have been overcome." Still, he cautioned, "our conclusions regarding television are that it is a subject which should be of intense interest to the skilled experimenter at the present time, whereas it will be some time yet before it will be available as an entertainment for the general public."

Alexanderson could afford such modesty as others could not; no matter how much he demurred, the newspapers would follow his every move. The public was hungry for television, and GE was the most obvious place to look for progress.

This impression was reinforced a week later, on September 12, when the *New York Times* carried a front-page story about the latest television stride taken in Schenectady. "PLAY IS BROADCAST BY VOICE AND ACTING IN RADIO-TELEVISION," shouted the headline. Using the same apparatus as in the Smith speech broadcast, WGY had become the first station to televise a drama. The play was *The Queen's Messenger,* a one-act spy melodrama written thirty years before by J. Hartley Manners and a staple of community and school productions around the country. With only two characters and no necessary movement, it lent itself to the limited capabilities of the cameras. Three cameras were used, each consisting of three tripod-mounted boxes; two contained photoelectric cells, and one had an arc lamp and spinning Nipkow disk. One camera was trained on the head of each actor, and the third camera showed the hands of "doubles" handling small props, such as wine and glasses, keys, a ring, and a revolver. WGY radio director Mortimer Stewart stood between the two "head" cameras and controlled the transmitted picture with a small box with two knobs. One knob allowed him to choose which camera was "live," and the other let him fade pictures in and out; a receiver set in front of him let him monitor the broadcast.

The picture signal was carried by wire to the WGY transmitter four miles away and broadcast on the regular 379.5-meter wavelength as well as on a shortwave of 21.4 meters; the sound came in on 31.96 meters. However, it is unlikely that anyone outside of the GE laboratory was able to pick up the broadcast; if they did, they failed to notify GE. An invited audience of journalists and dignitaries watched the performance next door to the studio on a GE receiver with a three-inch-square screen.

"The pictures . . . were sometimes blurred and confused, were not always in the center of the receiving screen, and were sometimes hard on the eyes because of the way in which they flickered," said the *Times*. "It was recalled that ordinary moving pictures suffered from worse mechanical defects in their early days. . . . Great as has been the success of the talking movies, they may easily be outdone by radio-television if the technical difficulties are overcome." Alexanderson spoke to the audience and repeated his belief that it would be some time before television was perfected for public consumption.

6.   Francis Jenkins disagreed. On July 22, 1929, he opened a new broadcast station in Jersey City and broadcast every night except Sunday, from 8:00 to 9:00 P.M. The programs were received as far away as Indiana; a viewer there wrote that "the picture of the little Dutch girl comes in good. I notice she sets a bucket under the pump, which is a pitcher pump, and pumps it full of water."

Jenkins was inordinately proud of this programming. "We write our own scenarios, we built and operate our own movie studio, the only one of its kind in the world, we designed, built, and operate our own film developing and printing equipment, and do our own editing and cutting."

All that took money, and where was it to come from? The station license approved by the Federal Radio Commission was for experimental work only, which meant that Jenkins couldn't sell advertising time.

He didn't want to commercialize like that, anyway; it would have di-
minished his dream of what television was for—to bring news and cul-
ture to people all over the country. In his vision, the project would
make money by the sale of Jenkins television receivers, so that people
could watch the wonderful programs he was providing. The problem
was that other people were also making television sets, and every dollar
spent on them was lost to him. So he began a series of "public service"
announcements:

> We offer the radio amateur kit parts for the construction of an excel-
> lent receiver for our broadcast movie stories. The kit includes every
> essential in the construction of a really excellent receiver.

In 1930 the FRC came down on him, deciding that these were commercial messages—that is, advertisements. Jenkins's argument was
that he wasn't trying to make money but only to establish a network of
viewers who would write to him with details of their reception, thus
enabling him to improve his system. These people were part of the experiment, he claimed.

It's ironic that the FRC didn't buy this argument, because in fact Jenkins wasn't making any money this way. His kits "cost the amateur but
$7.50 packed and postage paid," which was less than his actual cost.
Like the old joke goes, he hoped to make it up in volume.

Still, although he was forbidden to advertise these sets on his broadcasts, word spread from one person to the next. By 1931 the Jenkins
Universal Television Receiver was selling for $82.95, complete and
ready to operate, while the kit was up to $42.50 plus $5.00 for the magnifying glass. The programming had also improved; broadcasts were
now running three hours every day (Sundays were still excluded), and
the viewer could tune in simultaneously to a radio broadcast that provided sound. They now had readings of poetry and plays, singing, and
vaudeville-style skits. The program would usually open with a woman
singing "The Television Song" ("Conjured up in sound and sight / By
the magic rays of light / That bring television to you . . ."). A second
camera would then pick up her partner who would sing a verse, and

then the two would blend together and finally fade out to give way to a singing and jesting skit. The program would close with a brief lecture on the mechanics of television.

Business flourished. In April 1931 W2XCR (Jenkins's second station, owned by his Television Corporation) moved from its original site in Jersey City to a luxurious new residence at 655 Fifth Avenue in New York. It had five thousand watts of power and could transmit sixty-line pictures instead of the old standard forty-eight. It announced a schedule of four hours each day, *including* Sunday. (Jenkins didn't feel right about intruding on the Lord's day, but business is business. He was a television pioneer in more ways than one.)

The new station opened with appropriate hoopla on April 27, with a cast of Broadway stars, including Gertrude Lawrence, and a public viewing at the Aeolian Hall, just down Fifth Avenue from the station. The public responded, and the money came flowing in. Others followed Jenkins's lead. In July the Columbia Broadcasting System (CBS), formed just three years previously, began broadcasting six hours daily from station W2XAB, using Jenkins equipment. In October Ulysis A. Sanabria, who had been designing his own television system in Chicago, brought it to New York for a theater demonstration. The act "that caught the fancy of the audience was a conversation carried on between an African parrot, John Tio, and its owner."

RCA had begun two-hour daily broadcasts in 1929 from station W2XBS in Van Cortlandt Park. By 1931 the station had been transferred to NBC, transmitting from Forty-second Street, west of Broadway, and it too was broadcasting six hours a day, although on an experimental basis only. That is, instead of entertainment they were transmitting signs, statues that revolved, and photographs—subjects that enabled their engineers to determine the quality of the picture at various reception points.

There were other television systems and stations popping up all over the country—in Boston and Milwaukee, Chicago and Los Angeles. But how often can you sit in your living room and watch a little girl bouncing a ball? And even with the new improvements—a sixty-line picture and synchronized radio sound—the image was often hard to see clearly, so much so that sometimes an announcer would describe the scene, telling the audience what they should be seeing. It was found that this "aided the eye in completing the picture."

It wasn't enough. The flush of excitement began to wear off, sales dropped, and the cutbacks began. By January 1932, Jenkins stopped broadcasting films; he no longer had enough money to produce them or even enough to rent them.

The boom had been riding on a crest of enthusiasm fed by dreams of profit. The first broadcasting stations were sponsored by or connected with companies manufacturing and selling television sets and kits. No one was yet aware of the immense amounts of money to be made by paid advertising, but they did see the prospect of selling millions instead of thousands of receivers. And so their advertisements, and the stores that accompanied them, continually spread the word that television was here and that future improvements in picture quality could easily be handled by minor changes in the equipment now being sold.

But while these advertisements convinced some of the public, convincing the government was another matter. The Federal Radio Commission and, later, its successor the Federal Communications Commission were not impressed by Jenkins's claim that "forty-eight lines per picture frame is as logical in this new industry as four wheels were in automobiles." They refused to endorse the present systems, refused to allow them full commercialization. Television, they decided, was in its infancy, and while further experimentation should be encouraged, it would be wrong to tell the public that a working system had already arrived. It was quite likely, they decided, that future advances would render the current sets useless. Television broadcasting was to be undertaken only on an experimental basis, and the public was so advised.

This accelerated the decline in sales, as did the arrival of the depression. By February of 1932 the boom had gone bust, and the Jenkins Television Corporation was liquidated, its assets sold to the De Forest Company. Later in the year, that company folded too, selling its assets, including all television patents, to RCA for five hundred thousand dollars.

The saddest note is that RCA didn't even care about the patents. They were simply buying out De Forest to eliminate one possible source of distraction for the public concerning television. They filed the patents away and forgot them. They didn't need Jenkins. They had Zworykin.

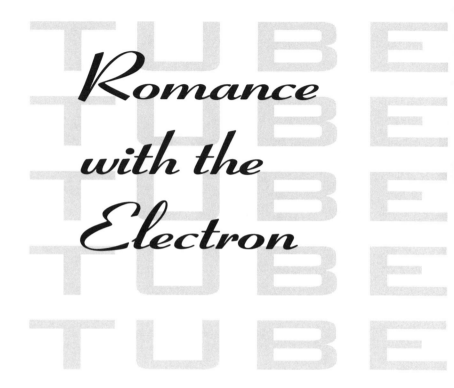

PART TWO

Romance with the Electron

Prologue:

The Wireless

Operator

And what rough beast, its hour come round at last,
slouches towards Bethlehem to be born?
W. B. Yeats, "The Second Coming"

The Radio Corporation of America (RCA) has long since evolved into a typical American conglomerate. But its conception was unique: it was formed to rectify an unfortunate circumstance.

The four great inventions of the early years of this century were the telegraph, the telephone, the airplane, and radio. The telegraph was invented by Samuel Morse of Boston, and the airplane by the Wright brothers of Dayton, Ohio. The telephone was invented by Alexander Graham Bell, a native of Scotland who had emigrated to America and who was acknowledged to be as good an American citizen as any.

But it was an Italian named Marconi who invented radio. In the early 1920s, Guglielmo Marconi intended to market his invention in America. He had already taken over the market in England with his British Marconi, Ltd. The American Marconi Company, set up in 1919, was clearly not an American company set up by Marconi but was rather his

British company's setup to take over radio sales in America. A subtle distinction but one of overwhelming importance.

From an American standpoint, this could not be allowed to happen. The recent world war had demonstrated the crucial role of radio in national defense; the United States could not leave the research and production capabilities of such an invention in the hands of foreigners.

Emerging from the First World War, the United States was resolved to stand alone as a military and commercial power. When General Electric announced that British Marconi wanted to buy twenty-four GE Alexanderson two-hundred-kilowatt alternators for five million dollars (including worldwide exclusive rights to their use), word came from President Wilson—who was in Paris negotiating the peace settlement—that the sale must be blocked. A letter on April 4, 1919, from Acting Secretary of the Navy Franklin D. Roosevelt to Owen Young, GE general counsel, asked Owen to confer with the U.S. Navy (which had controlled American wireless operations during the war) before signing the deal. Four days later, Young, Rear Admiral W. H. G. Bullard, and Commander Hooper of the Naval Radio Bureau presented "the outline of a proposal that would alter the structure of American communications."

As compensation for GE turning down the British Marconi deal, the navy would join its myriad wartime radio patents with those of GE and American Marconi in a royalty-free patent pool, run by a new subsidiary of GE. To keep it all in American hands, the new company would be created by a buyout of American Marconi stock. Since American Marconi's competitors had long since fallen by the wayside, the new company would constitute a private monopoly. It would also be not only a new source of profit for GE but also a completely American worldwide powerhouse, thus appealing to the growing postwar nationalism. Accordingly, the name GE chose for the new company was the Radio Corporation of America.

On October 17, 1919, RCA was incorporated from the remains of American Marconi, with staff and shareholders transferring smoothly from the old company to the new. GE's Owen Young was appointed chairman of the board, and a twenty-eight-year-old Russian Jew named David Sarnoff was named commercial manager.

David Sarnoff is the epitome of "what made America great": the oppressed and impoverished but bright, energetic, hardworking immigrant who found gold in the streets of New York.

He was born in 1891 in Uzlian, a shtetl in the province of Minsk, deep within the Russian pale where Jews had been forced to live for a hundred years. His father was a housepainter and paperhanger, his mother a descendant of a long line of rabbis, and young David was quickly put to work studying the Talmud while his consumptive father struggled to put food on the table.

When David was four, his father left for America, joining the great wave of Jews from Russia and Eastern Europe fleeing poverty and persecution, hoping for the better life about which they'd heard. He would send for his family when he could.

David was "hermetically sealed off from childhood," as he said years later. In the absence of his father, his maternal grandfather began grooming him for the rabbinate, putting the small boy through a strict regimen of study and prayer. After a year of living in his grandparents' house with his mother and brothers as well as eight aunts and uncles and their families, David was sent to live with his granduncle a hundred miles away, where he spent four years in complete isolation from his family, studying the Talmud and the prophets "from sunup to sundown."

By 1900, when David was nine, his father had finally saved enough money to send for his family. After an arduous monthlong journey by horse-drawn cart, freighter, and steamship to Montreal and then train and steamboat to New York City, he and his mother and brothers were finally reunited with his father.

But the apartment to which Abraham Sarnoff took his family in the Jewish ghetto on the Lower East Side provided an immediate lesson in the reality of the American dream; it was a tiny three-room railroad flat in a decrepit building with "a single befouled toilet" serving the entire floor. His father was not in much better shape than the building; weakened by consumption and the effort to finance his family's passage, he was clearly unable to support a large household. Only days after his arrival, David was competing with the other Jewish boys in the selling of Yiddish-language newspapers. After school began in September, he would rise at four, deliver the papers, and devote the rest of the day to the study of English.

His capacity for hard work, forged in the shtetl, made him a young lion in the Darwinian jungle of the ghetto; he learned English faster than the other immigrants and excelled at the newspaper game, soon running his own newsstand. When he was fifteen, he graduated from the eighth grade and easily qualified for a college prep school, but his father was sicker than ever, and it fell to David to support the family.

After selling newspapers for six years, it was only natural for him to aspire to a career in journalism. So he put on his only suit and tie and walked up Broadway to Herald Square, into what he thought was the lobby of the *New York Herald*. He went to the first window he saw and informed the man behind it that he was looking for any job that the *Herald* had available.

Unfortunately, he was in the wrong place. He had blundered into the Commercial Cable Company, not the *Herald*. Fortunately, however, they were looking for a messenger boy. The pay was five dollars a week, with ten cents per hour for overtime. Without a second's pause, Sarnoff accepted.

When not busy delivering cablegrams by bicycle around the city, the new messenger boy hung around the office, fascinated by the telegraph machines in operation. He bought his own telegraph key and mastered the Morse code, practicing at night in bed or in the morning before work. Soon the telegraph operators were letting him fill in for them on occasion. When he was fired for refusing to work on the Jewish High Holidays (not for religious reasons but because he made more money singing soprano in temple), he took his telegraph key and went to the small branch office of American Marconi down on William Street in the financial district. They didn't need any junior operators, they told him, but they could use an office boy. He immediately accepted, for $5.50 a week.

The Italian inventor whom Sarnoff now considered his "boss" became his idol as well. Marconi too had emigrated to a new country, and with genius and hard work had raised himself into one of the most successful and famous men in the world. Sarnoff made it his business to learn everything about his new employer, as well as everything about the wireless business. He became not only a messenger boy but also assistant repairman, library custodian, and office factotum.

When Marconi visited the New York office, Sarnoff was determined to meet him. With an outstretched hand, David introduced himself, ingratiated himself with the older man, and volunteered to be his personal messenger during his visit. Marconi accepted, and a mentor relationship was quickly established. Sarnoff served as Marconi's personal assistant on future visits as well, and before his first year as a Marconi employee was out, shortly after his sixteenth birthday, Sarnoff, with the help of the inventor's personal recommendation, got a position as junior wireless telegraph operator, with a raise to $7.50 a week. His father had succumbed to tuberculosis, so he needed this salary to support his family, whom he now moved out of the slum and into the Brownsville section of Brooklyn.

In 1908, at seventeen, Sarnoff volunteered for duty as telegraph operator at the remote Marconi station on Nantucket. Because of the isolated location, the position paid extra—seventy dollars a month—and he felt that the excellent technical library at the station could provide him with a substitute education. He did so well in his eighteen months there that he was recalled to New York to become manager and chief operator of the Sea Gate station. For the first time in his life he was giving orders, and to men many years his senior.

Just before his twentieth birthday, Sarnoff resigned his Sea Gate position to volunteer as operator of a Marconi wireless unit aboard a wintertime seal-hunting expedition to the Arctic. For six weeks he manned the wireless, keeping contact with the other ships in the fleet as they traded hunting information. When he returned, he negotiated his first commercial contract, for the permanent installation and servicing of wireless equipment on that fleet.

He now parlayed his success on the Arctic expedition into a new position, as manager of the new Marconi station installed in the John Wanamaker department store—ostensibly a tool for information exchange between the New York and Philadelphia stores but in reality more of a promotional gimmick. This set the stage for one of the most consequential events—or nonevents—in David Sarnoff's life.

In 1912, just as Sarnoff was taking the Wanamaker job, the British White Star Line finished building a ship called the *Titanic*—advertised as the most luxurious and most unsinkable ship ever built—and they sent it off across the Atlantic, and it hit an iceberg and sank. It had been only a few years since Marconi first sent radio messages from ships at sea to stations on shore, and the *Titanic* was one of the few that had a radio transmitter on board. As the ship listed and went down, the radio operator stayed at his post and tapped out his message calling for help. Nearby ships that did not have wireless equipment passed by in the night without knowing of the tragedy; others farther away heard the distress call and hurried to help, thus saving some of the passengers. . . .

Fade out and segue to Wanamaker's department store in New York City, where a young Russian immigrant is sitting bored in front of an odd-looking box, earphones on his head, listening to dots and dashes no one else can hear. Suddenly he stiffens: the dots and dashes have taken on a new meaning. Quickly he turns them into letters, into a tale of horror: "S S *Titanic* ran into iceberg. Sinking fast."

The operator calls the police, the Coast Guard, the newspapers. Day after day, night after night, he stays at his post, listening to the airwaves, passing out information on who is saved and who is lost to crowds of reporters and relatives who have converged on his small office in the department store. Without sleep, without food, our hero remains the one point of contact between the waiting world and the tragedy unfolding in the dark sea. . . .

A great story, and Sarnoff made the most of it to build up a public persona. He talked about it often; he wrote a story about it for the *Saturday Evening Post:* "Seventy-two hours I crouched tense in the station. I felt my responsibility keenly, and weary though I was, could not have slept. . . ." But it never happened. The *Titanic* sank on a Sunday, and Wanamaker's was closed that day. *Time, Newsweek,* and the *New York Times* all gave lengthy coverage to the disaster, but none of them mentioned the Wanamaker station or David Sarnoff at all. The first list of survivors came not from Wanamaker's but from the Marconi station at Cape Race in Newfoundland, and the next day another list came in from a station in Boston.

Sarnoff was one of the operators who picked up some of the early—though not the first—accounts of the sinking; soon after that, the Marconi Company closed down all its stations except four, in an effort to concentrate its response. And Sarnoff's station in the Wanamaker building was not one of those that remained open.

But as far as the story's effect on Sarnoff's public image went, its authenticity was beside the point. Erik Barnouw, who in a 1975 book passed on the Sarnoff fable as true, wrote in 1990, "Accounts of how he stuck to his telegraph key . . . acquired over the years a legendary quality that seemed to suit his life story." As Tom Lewis pointed out, "of all the wireless operators from Newfoundland to Cape Sable, Siasconset to New York [who were involved in the disaster] . . . Sarnoff alone had the prescience to embellish his role as the sole wireless link between the *Titanic* and the mainland."

As Sarnoff liked to say in later years, "the *Titanic* disaster brought radio to the front, and incidentally me." Not quite incidentally and certainly not inconsequentially. Though the episode didn't make him a public hero, as he later "remembered," his handling of the situation at Wanamaker's did reflect well on him among Marconi management. Ensuing U.S. legislation required all large ships to carry wireless equipment (quickly doubling the value of Marconi stock), and Sarnoff was appointed chief inspector of all ships carrying Marconi equipment. His salary was tripled since his first days as an operator, and he was able to move his family once again, this time to a clean new five-room apartment in the Bronx with electric lights, hot water, steam heat, and indoor plumbing. He also began accumulating more expensive suits and smoking what would become his trademark cigars.

To his list of duties was soon added the title of contract manager, which put him in charge of negotiating all sales and service contracts for onboard equipment. He began sending a deluge of memos to his superiors in New York as well as to Marconi himself in England, and he soon had a reputation as the premier fount of technical knowledge and marketing savvy in the company. World War I brought an increased need for wireless communication, and both American Marconi and its young prodigy thrived. In 1917 Sarnoff was put in charge of a brand-new department devoted exclusively to contract and business operations; he now had a salary of $11,000 a year and 725 employees working under him. And on July 4 of that year he married Lizette Hermant, a pretty blonde French Jewish immigrant who lived with her family near the Sarnoffs in the Bronx. A year later she gave birth to the first of their three sons. At the age of twenty-seven, Sarnoff was a wealthy American family man.

He was also an important player in the exploding world of wireless communications. During the war he had spent much of his time in Washington negotiating navy contracts and cultivating relationships with senators, members of Congress, and other powerful people. By 1919, his immigrant background lay buried deep beneath his expensive suits, Havana cigars, and "deeply resonant" American speech, and so with his position as commercial manager of the new Radio Corporation of America, David Sarnoff stood poised to lead the American communications industry to new heights of technology and profit.

He soon gained the confidence and respect of his new boss, Owen Young, and was given the important job of negotiating with AT&T and Westinghouse to bring their radiotelephony resources into RCA in exchange for a percentage of ownership. He accomplished this in 1921, priming RCA to be the leader in the new radio home entertainment market.

All he had to do next was to create that market, and by dint of his technical knowledge—which led him to support the right engineers, such as Howard Armstrong—and his marketing capability, he did just that. And when, in 1935, he had Major Armstrong evicted from the experimental transmission station on top of the Empire State Building, it was only because he was now ready to create an entirely new market.

SEVEN

Two Russian Immigrants and One Farm Boy

The spirit of man
Is a bird in a cage . . .
    Hugh MacDiarmid

1. The sequence of events that led to Major Armstrong's eviction from the Empire State Building began one day in early January of 1929, when two Russian immigrants met at the New York offices of the Radio Corporation of America. David Sarnoff, thirty-seven years old, sat behind an immense desk smoking an immense cigar, as befit the vice president and general manager of RCA. Facing him was Vladimir Kosmo Zworykin, a thirty-nine-year-old engineer for the Westinghouse Electric and Manufacturing Company of East Pittsburgh, who had fled the Bolsheviks in poverty and danger and come to America to pursue his dream of developing electronic television. With the feverish relish of a madman whose delusions are finally being taken seriously, Zworykin began to speak, controlling his exuberance in calm, confident waves of heavily accented English. The key, he explained, lay in the electron . . .

Michael Faraday, the first person to harness electricity (in 1824), never really understood what it was. (When he demonstrated his first dynamo, which generated only infinitesimal amounts of electricity, Sir Robert Peel, the British prime minister, asked, "Of what use is this?" And Faraday answered, "I don't know, but I'll wager that someday you'll tax it.") He tried transmitting electricity through a variety of different materials and found that some materials conduct it well and others do not. When in 1854 Heinrich Geissler created the first man-made vacuum by blowing a glass tube and pumping it out with his new vacuum pump, it was only natural for scientists to see if the vacuum would conduct electricity.

The first experiments with the "Geissler tube" showed that it did not. The concept is simple enough; Figure 6 helps to illustrate it. In the

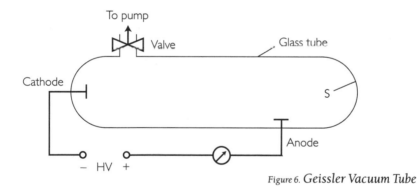

Figure 6. Geissler Vacuum Tube

original setup, before a vacuum was created, two metal poles, or electrodes, labeled cathode and anode, were connected to an electrical source such as a battery or an induction coil, labeled HV (high voltage) in the figure. No electrical current flowed since the two electrodes were connected on one side (the wire attached to the HV) but not on the other. It was already well known at the time that if a wire did not form a closed loop, no current could flow through it; the circuit was "not complete," in the expression of the day. When the setup was enclosed in a glass tube, of course nothing changed, as expected. The saving grace of science, however, is that sometimes—not often, but once in a while—the unexpected happens. In this case, when the air in the tube was gradually pumped out, a current began to flow, even though there was still no connection inside the tube; it grew in intensity as the air pressure decreased. But no one understood why.

The scientists approached the answer when they noticed that if they pumped enough air out of the tube, and if they turned the voltage sufficiently high, a spot on the glass tube directly behind the anode (labeled S) began to fluoresce—that is, to glow with an eerie green light.

This phenomenon of fluorescence had been recognized but not understood since the year 1602, when a Bolognese shoe cobbler and part-time alchemist, Vincenzo Cascariolo, was climbing Mount Pesara and noticed a heavy mineral reflecting the sun's rays with a particularly brilliant light. He brought it home and gave it to his wife, who placed it in their bedroom. That night he was awakened by his wife's screams: she had got up to use the chamber pot and opened her eyes to see the devil's mineral shining at her in the dark.

Some materials, it had been found since then, have the ability to absorb light and to give it out again later. Different materials retain the light for different lengths of time: hours, days, minutes, or seconds. The glass in the evacuated tube was evidently doing something very similar, absorbing the electrical current and then giving off light. It had a very short retention time: when the high voltage was turned on, the glass instantly began to glow; when it was turned off, the glow faded away within a second or two.

In 1876, after experiments by a number of investigators, a German physicist, Eugen Goldstein, recognized that the current through the tube was carried by mysterious "kathode rays," which could only penetrate from cathode to anode when the interfering air molecules were sufficiently pumped away. If the voltage was turned up higher, these rays would flow through the tube with more energy. If the vacuum in the tube was good enough—that is, if there were few air molecules to interfere—and if the voltage was turned up high enough, some of these high-energy rays would zoom right by the anode and hit the glass wall, inducing the fluorescence phenomenon (normal sunlight didn't have enough energy to make the glass fluoresce). This was proved, and the nature of the rays understood, by means of experiments using vertical and horizontal deflector plates. By magnetizing these or by attaching a voltage to them, the cathode rays could be bent up or down or to one side or the other. One could follow the rays' changing pathways by watching the movement of the fluorescing spot on the glass wall. William Crookes in England was the first to characterize these cathode rays as streams of electrically charged particles (which we now call electrons).

In 1906 a German engineer, Max Dieckmann, was the first person to attempt to create a sort of a picture with the Geissler tube. He based his experiments on the two phenomena just described: the fluorescence of the glass when struck with the cathode rays and the ability to "steer" the cathode rays with the deflector plates. His ideas can be visualized as shown in Figure 7.

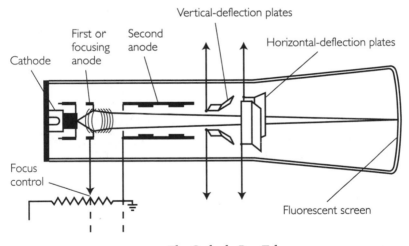

Figure 7. The Cathode-Ray Tube

The electrons streaming out from the cathode are magnetically or electrically focused so they emerge from the barrel in a thin beam. If nothing else were to happen to them, they would continue in a straight line and strike the fluorescent screen at the end of the tube, causing a bright point of light there. But on the way, they pass through two electrostatic deflectors, each consisting of a pair of metal plates that produce a field when a voltage is applied.

The first trap deflects the beam vertically. When a signal, in the form of a voltage, is applied to the pair of plates, the electron beam passing between them will be attracted to the more positive plate; the amount it is deflected is proportional to the voltage, so the greater the strength of the incoming signal, the greater the deflection. The second pair of plates works exactly the same way and deflects the beam in a horizontal direction. The image to be reproduced is electronically translated into a continuing series of pulses that deflect the beam vertically and at the same time horizontally; the result of these two simultaneous effects is to draw the beam out from its central position in a manner similar to the children's toy in which one manipulates two knobs to steer a black line across a screen and draw a picture. The electrons are so small they can react instantaneously to the incoming signal, while the fluorescent screen can be made of chemical phosphors that continue to glow for several seconds after the electrons strike them; this means that the indicating line will remain visible after the brief incoming signal has vanished.

On September 12, 1906, Dieckmann (together with the first of a series of colleagues) filed a patent application for the "transmission of written material and line drawing by means of cathode-ray tubes." His cathode beam was steered by magnetic coils (rather than by the electrical plates shown in Figure 7), and they reproduced the movement of a pen that was connected to two sets of sliding resistors (which produced a variable current on both an X and Y axis). If you signed your name or drew a picture, the pen's movement against the two sets of resistors was reproduced by two sets of current flowing through a wire and connected to the magnetic coils of the cathode-ray tube, moving the cathode rays in a duplicate manner so that an image of your signature would appear on the fluorescing glass wall of the tube.

This idea resembles a fax machine rather than true television, and in any case, Dieckmann never got it to work. But for the next twenty years he kept trying different schemes. During the First World War, he became director of a research laboratory near Munich, and he spent the war years trying without success to perfect an apparatus enabling "aeroplanes" to send pictures of what they saw directly to forces on the ground. By 1925 he had devised a true cathode-ray television system, which he attempted to demonstrate at the German Transport and Traffic Exhibition in his hometown of Munich. Anecdotal descriptions claim that the system could transmit moving pictures but in stark black-and-white silhouette form only, and there remains no firm evidence that the system actually worked at all. He applied for a patent but it was never granted, and although his camera was similar in principle to those that were to come later, there is no indication that the people who ended up giving us cathode-ray television ever heard of Dieckmann—or, at least, there is no evidence that their work was influenced by his. And with this brief note, Max Dieckmann passes out of the television picture.

In 1907 Boris Rosing, a lecturer at the Saint Petersburg Technological Institute, put together equipment consisting of a mechanical scanner and a cathode-ray receiver. At the time—and this applies to both Dieckmann and Rosing—the electron beam in a cathode tube was not very well focused, and the picture quality could not have been great. There is in fact no record of any successful demonstration of actual television by either Rosing or Dieckmann, but Rosing's name lives on because he had one thing Dieckmann did not: a fascinated and brilliant student.

The student's name was Vladimir Kosmo Zworykin.

2.　Zworykin was born in 1889 in the thriving provincial town of Mourom, into a prominent mercantile family—his father had a wholesale grain business as well as a steamship line on the Oka River. Vladimir enjoyed an idyllic childhood as a member of Russia's prerevolutionary upper-class bourgeoisie. He lived in a huge stone mansion and grew up happily diverted by horseback riding, hunting, and croquet. As a student in Saint Petersburg, he dallied in revolutionary activities, as was the fashion for the intelligentsia of the time, and slaked his thirst for opera and art.

Above all, though, he had a passion for science. "When I was a student," he said six decades later, "we suddenly underwent a sort of revolution in physics, which produced the new possibility of using technology and science for human welfare." This was the age of relativity and quantum mechanics, when new insights and approaches were inspiring a young generation of physicists. It was at this time of scientific infatuation that he met Professor Rosing.

In early 1910, Rosing noticed the young Zworykin helping other students in the physics laboratory and invited him to assist in the experiments he was conducting across the street at the Bureau of Standards. The following Saturday Zworykin showed up at Rosing's lab and was introduced to the new art of television.

In 1907 Rosing had applied for his first television patent, for a system using a mechanical scanner at the pickup end and a cold cathode tube as a receiver. This was probably the most important television patent since Nipkow's 1884 spinning disk; here was an actual design for a working electronic television receiver. When Zworykin entered Rosing's lab three years later, Rosing was still trying to get that system to operate. For the next two years, Zworykin spent most of his free time in Rosing's laboratory, assisting in experiments and learning physics.

Rosing's ideas were more advanced than the technology of the day: the photocells that were available were far too insensitive, vacuum pumps were manually operated and required tremendous work to create a vacuum tube, the tubes leaked continually, and proper glass bulbs were not available. As a result, Rosing and his new assistant had to become expert glassblowers and put in hours lifting heavy bottles of mercury up and down to create a vacuum in their tubes. They also built their own photoelectric cells—glass bulbs containing rarified hydrogen or helium and sodium, potassium, cesium, or rubidium amalgam, with a platinum electrode for an anode. Their camera consisted of a box containing a mechanical scanner and all the gearing, connected with wires to a separate photoelectric cell.

The mentor and his protégé were able to conjure up an apparatus that produced crude results. On May 9, 1911, Rosing wrote in his notebook, "A distinct image was seen for the first time, consisting of four luminous bands."

That was about as close as they got to actual television. Still, by the time Zworykin's affiliation with Rosing ended, with his graduation in 1912, Rosing's system had shown enough promise to win the gold medal from the Russian Technical Society. More importantly, although work on mechanical television would continue around the world for two more decades, Rosing had managed to pass on to Zworykin the conviction that the future lay in the potential of the cathode-ray tube.

Zworykin might have stayed in Saint Petersburg after graduation in 1912 and continued to work with Rosing, but his father decreed that he should return home to work in the family business—unless, that is, he wished to study abroad. The choice was easy; with Rosing's recommendation, Zworykin went to Paris and joined the prestigious laboratory of physicist Paul Langevin. Under the tutelage of the future Nobel laureate, Zworykin conducted experiments concerning the diffraction of X-rays by crystals. After a year in Paris, he left Langevin and went to Berlin where he spent a year at the university attending lectures in physics. His time in Berlin, however, was cut short in the summer of 1914 by the declaration of war; he woke up on August 3 to find he was suddenly an enemy alien, and though he didn't realize it, his life as a privileged member of the Russian upper classes was over.

He left Berlin and returned via Denmark and Finland to Russia, where he was immediately mobilized into the Russian Army. Because of his background, he was made a radio communications specialist and stationed near Grodno, on Germany's eastern front. After a year he was posted back to Saint Petersburg, renamed Petrograd, where he was commissioned as an officer and where he met and married his first wife, Tatiana Vasilieff.

While in Petrograd, Zworykin was assigned to work at the Russian Marconi factory. One day he got into conversation with the director and told him about his work with Rosing. The two of them agreed that after the war Zworykin would join the company and form a team to develop electronic television. In the meantime, Zworykin concentrated on military radio applications.

In February 1917, when the Russian Revolution broke out, privates suddenly wielded the power, and officers were often abused, beaten, arrested, or summarily shot. Zworykin fled one such attack and ended up with his wife in Kiev behind German lines, out of uniform. Marital problems that had been building for some time came to a head there, and they went their separate ways, she to Berlin and he back to Russia. At home he found that his father had died the month before, and the family mansion had been requisitioned by the Soviets for a museum; his mother and oldest sister had been granted only a couple of rooms.

Zworykin resumed his job at Russian Marconi but found that work at the factory had slowed to a crawl. The entire country was tumbling into chaos, with the Bolsheviks fighting the Mensheviks and both of them struggling with the remaining Czarists. By October, when the Bolsheviks claimed victory, all work had come grinding to a halt. Sick of the war and the revolutionary turmoil that precluded any serious scientific effort, Zworykin decided to get himself to America.

This was not easily done, however, especially for a former bourgeois officer who might appear to be betraying the revolution, or at least fleeing it. Zworykin had friends in a cooperative organization who gave him an official assignment to the Siberian city of Omsk. After weeks spent getting his papers in order, he left abruptly when a friend tipped him off that the police had learned that he was a former officer and were looking for him at his apartment. After an arduous journey by steamer and train, imperiled by constant military patrols suspicious of his business, he finally reached Omsk, where he was able to join the Arctic expedition of a Russian geologist. He also received an official assignment from the Siberian government to procure radio equipment. He sailed with the scientists in July 1918 to Archangel, which was occupied by British, French, and American troops. From there he was able to secure a visa to England, and from there to the United States. He arrived at last in New York on the SS *Carmania* on New Year's Eve, 1919.

But life in New York, then as now, was difficult without a job, and it was difficult to get a job without a good command of English. A few months later the Omsk government, which still considered him a Soviet citizen, ordered him back to Siberia as a radio specialist. Discouraged by his inability to find work, he obeyed, traveling back to Russia by way of California and the Pacific.

He quickly found, however, that life in Russia had not improved in his absence, and almost immediately he resolved to return to America. By the end of 1919 he was back in New York, determined to make it there as a scientist one way or another.

Badly in need of a job, Zworykin accepted a position at the Russian Purchasing Commission in New York as a mechanical adding-machine operator. He found a room at a boardinghouse in Brooklyn and began to study English furiously. He had been out of touch with his wife for months, but he finally procured her address in Berlin. They agreed to give the marriage another try, and he borrowed money to finance her trip to New York. Soon afterward he received an offer of an engineering job at the Westinghouse Research Laboratory in Pittsburgh. It paid him only half his current salary, but he was determined to make his living as an engineer, not a purchasing agent, and he accepted. Tatiana was pregnant by this time, and as soon as the baby was born, Zworykin moved with his family to Pittsburgh to begin, finally, his true career at the age of thirty.

After six years of war and revolution, he wasn't terribly upset by the fact that his new superiors were cold to his ideas of television research. He took quickly to his assignments, working to develop new radio amplifying tubes. But when he was forced, with all the engineers, to take a 10 percent pay cut because of hard financial times for the company, he resigned on the spot and took a position with C&C, an oil development company in Kansas City. His job there was to prove that a patent design the company held for the use of electrical currents in oil refining would actually work. Unfortunately, when Zworykin carried out the tests, he found that the design would *not* work, so the company had no further use for him and he was laid off. He stayed in Kansas City building custom-made radio receivers and acting as consultant to a small radio manufacturing company. He designed a car radio, but the local police thought it was a dangerous device that could distract the driver from the complex business of driving, and they put him out of business. In 1923, Westinghouse contacted him with a new offer of higher salary and job security, together with the promise of allowing him to work at least part time on his television concept. Happily, he packed up the family again and returned to Pittsburgh.

Westinghouse was as good as its word, and he set to work putting his ideas into practical form. Although the rudimentary television receivers that Zworykin and Rosing had made back in Russia hadn't worked very well, the principle—if not the picture—was clear. What was not clear was whether it would be possible to transmit as well as receive pictures electronically. This, it seemed to Zworykin in 1923, was the key, for without a completely electronic system, the advantages over mechanical systems would be largely lost. Just as a chain is only as strong as its weakest link, the rapidity and resolution of a scanning electron beam would be wasted if the transmission was limited by mechanical components.

In February of 1923 he began work on a camera tube similar to that envisioned by Campbell Swinton in 1911, with one major exception: Swinton had proposed a mosaic of individual cubes of rubidium to gather the light and turn it into electric current, each cube providing one element of the final picture. The number of such cubes that could fit together into a camera of reasonable size was obviously limited, and this would limit the clarity of the televised picture. Zworykin designed instead a plate composed of a photoelectric surface deposited on an insulating layer of aluminum oxide. The light from the televised scene would be focused on this surface and would knock off electrons according to the brightness, leaving behind a series of positively charged atoms.

Unfortunately, the positive charge on the plate's surface quickly dissipated. Zworykin had to go back to Swinton's ideas of separate little packets of photoelectric material instead of a continuous surface. But he couldn't make enough little cubes of rubidium to provide the necessary detail. Finally, after two years of intensive research, he hit on a workable substitute. He formed a mosaic of hundreds of thousands of tiny, individual droplets of potassium hydride evaporated onto a plate of aluminum foil, the surface of which was oxidized.

The potassium hydride droplets, like Swinton's cubes of rubidium, were photoelectric. Because the aluminum oxide was an insulator, each droplet was maintained electrically separate from its neighbors so that charges could not dissipate. Now the brightly lit parts of the scene remained positively charged.

At this point, Zworykin had transformed a visual scene into an electrical one. What he needed next was a means of gathering and transmitting the electrical information.

For this purpose, he designed a scanning electron beam, similar to that diagrammed in Figure 7. In this case, used as a camera, the beam would scan over the back side of the aluminum sheet, pass right through it, and impinge on the potassium hydride mosaic. The beam would bounce off dark portions of the mosaic. But when a lit portion, from which electrons had been ejected by the light (leaving it positively charged), was hit by the beam, the negatively charged electrons from the beam would be absorbed, replacing those previously lost. This would result in a quick surge of electricity, which could be accurately measured and which would constitute a message that a bright portion of the scene had been encountered.

As the beam scanned across and down the scene, the succession of messages would be defined by the distribution of brightnesses in the original scene. This mass of information could then be passed on to a similar cathode-ray tube in which a scanning electron beam impinged on a fluorescent screen, as in Figure 7, with high intensities corresponding to the bright points and low intensities corresponding to the dark points. In this manner, a reproduction of the original scene would be built up.

The images this system produced were coarse and flickering, they faded in and out like teasing ghosts, and the screen would go blank and stay blank for no reason. Still, no matter how crude the system was, something important was happening during those years in Pittsburgh: a purely electronic television system was taking shape.

3.   A few years before, on a crisp clear morning in the spring of 1921, far from the sophisticated electronics laboratories of East Coast corporate America, a fourteen-year-old boy named Philo Farnsworth was mowing the hay on his father's 140-acre farm in Bybee, Idaho. Up since four, he had already studied for an hour, milked the cows, and fed all the animals. By sunrise, he had two horses tethered to the single-disk mower and was ready for the monotonous but peaceful routine of clearing the fields. He welcomed this task, for it gave him time to think. But while most fourteen-year-olds would be dreaming of football or baseball as they worked their way across the fields, Philo was on another plane altogether: he was inventing television.

When the Farnsworths had moved to their previous house in nearby Rigby, Philo had found piles of back issues of *Science and Invention* and other popular technical magazines that had been left behind, and he pored over them just as kids twenty years later would read *Superman*. One enterprise chronicled in their pages stuck with him and would shape the rest of his life: the effort to transmit pictures by radio. He read of the early television systems being worked on, all of which used a Nipkow disk. Instinctively, he knew that this method would never be fast enough to produce a clear picture of live action. He had also read about work with cathode-ray tubes and how electron beams could be manipulated with magnetic fields. He was convinced that these concepts were the key to high-quality television.

Now, nearing the ripe age of fifteen, Philo Farnsworth turned his team of horses around at the edge of the field and surveyed his work. Before him lay his mowed hay field, clearly delineated rows cut in alternating directions. Suddenly the future hit him with a vision so startling he could hardly sit still: a vision of television images formed by an electron beam scanning a picture in horizontal lines. He could create an image line by line just like the hay field in front of him, and the electrons would scan so fast that the human eye would see it as one instantaneous picture. "He humbly acknowledged an influence beyond himself," as his wife wrote later.

This story about the idea of electronic scanning coming to Farnsworth in a flash of insight must, however, be taken with a grain or two of salt. Swinton had published his ideas thirteen years previously, and the concept of scanning was inherent in all work done with the Nipkow disk, with which Philo was familiar. Nevertheless, whether divinely inspired or simply hardworking and brilliant, Philo Taylor Farnsworth, the Mormon schoolboy working alone and untutored on an Idaho farm, became the next Father of Television.

Philo was named for his paternal grandfather, one of Brigham Young's lieutenants who had helped build the original Mormon Temple in Nauvoo, Illinois. When the local Illinoisans, unappreciative of polygamy and other "heretical" practices, burned down the church in 1848, Farnsworth followed Young on the arduous journey west to the promised land in Utah. His grandson, Philo, was born in Beaver City, Utah, in 1906 and grew up in a house without a radio. At the age of six, encountering for the first time the Bell telephone and the Edison gramophone, he declared to his parents that he, too, would become an inventor.

When Philo's father moved his family to his brother's Bungalow Ranch in the Snake River Valley near Rigby, Idaho, in 1919, Philo soon taught himself how the ranch's Delco power system for lighting and electricity worked, making the twelve-year-old the only one in the family who knew how to run and fix it. The family took to calling him "the engineer," and rumor had it that he would occasionally render the unit inoperative just so that he could take it apart and put it together again. He also rigged it so that it would run the manual washing machine, thereby eliminating one of his household chores.

On entering Rigby High School, Farnsworth's precociousness and enthusiasm drove him to ask the school superintendent, Justin Tolman, whether he could compress the entire four-year high school curriculum into one year. Advised to register as a normal freshman, Philo was back in Tolman's office a few days later to ask if he could enter Tolman's senior chemistry class. Turned down again, Philo took the normal freshman load but supplemented his work with outside reading in electronics, physics, and chemistry. Halfway through the semester, he begged Tolman at least to be allowed to sit in on the chemistry class. Tolman agreed, and before long Farnsworth was his prize pupil. He was even put in charge of study hall from time to time, and one day Tolman entered the room to find Philo giving his senior classmates a lecture on Einstein's theory of relativity with "clarity and dramatic force . . . [like] a good salesman."

By the time Philo was fifteen, his idea for television had become the focus of his life, dominating his free time. Finally he had to tell someone about it, so in the early spring of 1922 he went to the only person he knew who he felt would be responsive. Instead of his usual after-school chemistry session with Tolman, he began to use the time to explain to his teacher his television design. Though Tolman had never so much as heard of television—even radio was in its infancy—he listened day after day as Philo explained his system in detail.

The basic concept of Farnsworth's proposal was similar to Zworykin's. These two men, born on opposite sides of the world, separately zeroed in on the same concept: focusing an image through a lens at one end of a cylindrical, flat-ended tube onto a plate at the other end coated with a mosaic of many photoelectric cells, then scanning the electrical image formed by the cells.

The difference in Farnsworth's design was that instead of using an electron beam to scan the image, he would use an "anode finger": a metal cylinder the size of a pencil with a small aperture. The electrical image formed on the cathode end would be emitted and sent across the tube toward the anode (Figure 8). As magnetic coils moved the entire electrical image over the anode finger's aperture, from left to right, line by line, the electrons would flow into the finger and become electric current. An electrical "picture" would form, corresponding exactly to the original light image. This design had been part of an earlier patent application by Dieckmann that had never been granted, but Farnsworth could not have known this.

As in Zworykin's scheme, the output current from the camera tube

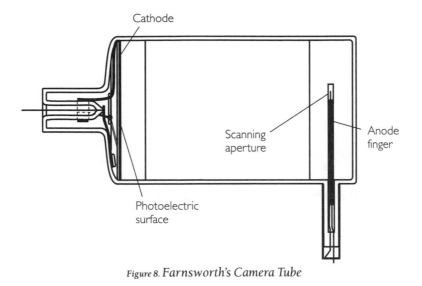

Cathode

Scanning
aperture

Anode
finger

Photoelectric
surface

Figure 8. Farnsworth's Camera Tube

would create a corresponding current in another cathode-ray tube. This in turn would create an electron beam that would cause a fluorescent surface on the end of the tube to glow. The intensity of light at each spot, Philo told his teacher, was determined by the strength of the current, which in turn was determined by the intensity of the corresponding spot in the original image. This electron beam would be moved by magnetic coils horizontally and vertically just as in the camera, thus painting a picture of the subject. Because of "persistence of vision," the human eye would see the image, repeating itself many times per second, as a solid picture.

Someday, Philo told his teacher, everyone in America would own one of these receiving tubes.

After his freshman year at Rigby High, Farnsworth's family had to move to a part of the ranch holdings in Bybee, outside the Rigby school district. Even in "metropolitan" Rigby, Philo had needed to take senior chemistry and supplement it with outside reading and advanced personal tutoring in order to satisfy his scientific curiosity; in his new far-flung locale, the public school wasn't an acceptable option for someone who'd already designed an electronic television system. Instead, he moved to Glen's Ferry, Idaho, where his half-brother worked for the railroad, and got a job with the Oregon Short Line. The next year, 1923, joining his family at their new home in Provo, Utah, Philo reentered high school and simultaneously entered Brigham Young University as a special student. With the death of his father in January of 1924, however, Farnsworth had to abandon his education for a real job.

After a brief stint in the navy, Phil (as he now chose to be called) returned to Provo, where he worked part time and enrolled again at BYU. There he confided his ideas for television to some of his professors. Impressed, they encouraged him to take relevant physics and mathematics courses and gave him unlimited access to the laboratory facilities. Although he made no demonstrable progress in constructing his invention, he began to build the thorough background in scientific knowledge that would be necessary to navigate the complex route to a working television system.

He also made a significant discovery of another kind: Elma (Pem) Gardner, a high school student and close friend of his sister. She was instantly captivated by this young man with "the deepest blue eyes [she] had ever seen" who "radiated a sense of strength and vitality," and he was similarly inclined.

In that fall of 1924, as he was learning the principles he would need to build the television he had already envisioned, radio itself was still a novelty. Although he had a job at the Bates Furniture Store delivering and installing radio sets, many of his friends at BYU had never even heard one. Phil decided to borrow a top-of-the-line set from the store and have a "radio party." His guests were amazed to hear stations in Los Angeles and Cincinnati (the only ones powerful enough to reach Utah) dedicating songs "to Phil Farnsworth and party in Provo, Utah." (Phil had written the stations in advance with the date and time of the party.)

By the end of 1925, his part-time jobs were insufficient to support his mother and siblings as well as his own studies, so Farnsworth left the university and moved to Salt Lake City where he found work as a radio repairman. Pem's brother Cliff joined him, and together they lived in rented rooms on minimal wages and sent the bulk of their paychecks home. They still managed to come back on occasional weekends for dances, however, and on February 25, 1926, Pem's eighteenth birthday, she and Phil became engaged.

That spring, George Everson and Leslie Gorrell arrived in Salt Lake City for a campaign to raise money for a local community chest. Everson was a San Francisco bachelor, a "congenial fellow with the average substantial build of a man in his early forties who enjoyed good food and spent his weekends playing golf to keep fit," as Pem would report later. After graduate studies at Columbia and then several years doing social work, he had decided not only to strike out on his own but to create a new profession for himself: director of fund-raising campaigns. He hooked up in San Francisco with Gorrell, a "young, tall, smartly dressed man-about-town, with blond hair and a stylishly thin mustache" and a "friendly sense of humor."

As usual when arriving in a new town to begin a campaign, they hired a group of local young people to help out; two of those were Phil Farnsworth and Cliff Gardner. Everson remembered years later that Farnsworth "looked much older than his nineteen years. He was of moderate height and slight build and gave the impression of being undernourished. There was a nervous tension about him . . . he had the appearance of a clerk too closely confined to his work." (To his fiancée, Pem, he appeared quite different: he had "broad shoulders, a lean body, and deep blue eyes. . . . His sandy-colored hair had a tendency to curl, making it a bit unruly, and his broad, infectious smile revealed strong white teeth.")

Before long Farnsworth had impressed Everson with his "characteristic purposefulness," not to mention his success in fixing Everson's lemon of an automobile after two mechanics had failed. Soon Phil had convinced Everson to hire Pem as a secretary, and the two men were becoming friends. When asked if he was returning to school, Phil told Everson he couldn't afford it. He was more interested in trying to find a way to finance an invention of his, but he hadn't had any luck. He was so discouraged, he said, that he was considering just writing up his ideas for *Popular Science*. He thought he might get a hundred dollars.

Although Everson and Gorrell "regarded his story at the moment as little more than the interesting daydream of an ambitious youngster," Farnsworth convinced them to listen to his ideas in more detail a few days later. Given the chance to expound on his obsession, Farnsworth made the transformation that would characterize him throughout his life when discussing his work. "Farnsworth's personality seemed to change," Everson later wrote. "His eyes, always pleasant, began burning with eagerness and conviction; his speech, which usually was halting, became fluent to the point of eloquence. . . . He became a supersalesman."

Farnsworth explained that everyone else working on television at the time was on the futile path of mechanical spinning disks. Only his all-electronic system could ever hope to be fast enough to produce a seemingly continuous image, he argued. To Everson's objection that the powerhouse laboratories of the electric and telephone companies must have thought of this too, Farnsworth replied by telling him about Baird and Jenkins, both of them stuck on mechanical disks. (Zworykin had already patented his first electronic receiving tube but was still working with mechanical transmitters; at any rate, no mention of his work had yet appeared in public, and Farnsworth had never heard of him.)

Everson was particularly struck with Farnsworth's familiarity with the technical details of his proposed system; the boy had an ease about him when talking of the mathematical foundations "that was phenomenal considering his lack of formal training." He didn't waffle on in vague generalities but pinned his listener down with solid facts, quoting authorities and textbooks, sketching diagrams, listing the parameters that were known and those variables still to be determined.

Farnsworth had no money to take out a patent on his ideas, and he had the same obsessing fear that stalked Baird: his conception of television seemed so simple, so obvious, that surely someone else would think of it tomorrow. "Every time I pick up an amateur journal," he told Everson, "I'm afraid I'll see that someone has turned up with the same ideas I have."

Over the ensuing weeks, during breaks in their fund-raising work, the three men discussed Farnsworth's ideas, and the older two became nearly as enraptured with the concept as Phil was. Finally, one day Everson asked Farnsworth how much money he thought he'd need to produce a working system. "It's pretty hard to say," said Farnsworth, "but I should think five thousand dollars would be enough."

With no background in science, Everson knew he was hardly competent to evaluate the worthiness of Farnsworth's design, and Gorrell's degree in mining engineering included little of the kind of electronics involved here. But Everson had a special bank account in San Francisco with six thousand dollars in it; he had been saving his money with the idea that one day he'd take a long-shot gamble on something, hoping to make a killing. Call it the intelligent hunch of an experienced financial man or a reckless bet on what even he called "as wild a gamble as I can imagine," but Everson pledged Farnsworth his money in order to create a working patentable television system.

They drew up an agreement forming a partnership, alphabetically named Everson, Farnsworth, and Gorrell. Farnsworth owned one half of the partnership and was to devote himself full time to the project. Everson and Gorrell split the other half, with Gorrell (who didn't have the cash) promising to pay back Everson his share if the money were lost. Both men agreed that Farnsworth would owe them nothing if the project failed.

Since the fund-raisers' next job would be in southern California and because the California Institute of Technology offered resources greater than could be found in Utah, the new triumvirate decided that their laboratory should be set up in Los Angeles. Nineteen-year-old Farnsworth, with characteristic forcefulness, determined not to leave his fiancée behind. Everson, after first arguing that Philo should forget about marriage until he had made some practical progress, quickly gave in to the boy's stubbornness and even insisted on lending his Chandler Roadster as well as some cash so that the couple could be married in Provo before catching the train in Salt Lake City.

Three days later, on May 27, 1926, after quieting everyone's fears that he was too young to support a family and after getting his mother to cosign the marriage license (he was under the age of consent), Philo T. Farnsworth married Elma Gardner in the duplex their families shared. After the reception they drove Everson's Roadster back to Salt Lake City, where they spent the night in an inexpensive motel near the train station. In the morning, they boarded the Southern Pacific Railroad's *City of Los Angeles* to begin a marriage and fulfill a prophecy: to turn glimmering rows of hay into electronic television.

EIGHT

The Damned
Thing Works!

Every act of progress the world has ever known first began with a dreamer. After him came the scientist or the statesman, the expert or the technician. But first came the dreamer.   Rabbi Maurice Davis

1 .   On December 29, 1923, Vladimir Zworykin applied for a patent on an all-electronic television system. U.S. Patent Number 2,141,059 would be the focus of mountains of legal paperwork over the next fifteen years, including eleven patent interferences filed by Farnsworth, before what was left of the application would be granted in 1938. In the meantime Zworykin was settling into his new life as an American. In 1924 he received his naturalization papers, and he applied to a special program at Pittsburgh University in which Westinghouse scientists could get credit for advanced degrees for original laboratory work. A second daughter was born, and the Zworykins built a comfortable social life in Pittsburgh.

By October 1925, Zworykin had made improvements in his 1923 design. The main change was the use of the mosaic of fine potassium hydride droplets as a photoelectric surface, instead of a single continuous layer of potassium hydride. He also introduced a fine mesh screen instead of the aluminum foil, allowing the scanning beam to penetrate more easily. By late 1925 he had reached what he thought was a turning point. And indeed it was, but not of the sort he envisaged.

By this time he had a system that actually worked, but compared to his dream it was a primitive setup. He was able to transmit simple geometric figures in a recognizable form, but he needed additional funding and space if he was going to make any further significant progress. He decided to demonstrate his system to his immediate superior, S. M. Kintner, and to the general manager of Westinghouse, Harry Davis. He was sure they would be impressed and would order a full-scale development effort.

"I will never forget that day," he remembered. The evening before the test he spent hours with the equipment, tuning it to perfection. Just before leaving for the night, he gave the dial one more infinitesimal twist—and he blew a couple of condensers. The whole setup crashed, the image disappeared into darkness, and so did his future.

He spent the rest of the night soldering and splicing, cursing and pleading, and by morning, just in time for the demonstration, the equipment worked again. His visitors stood around and talked while he turned it on and tuned it. The image of a cross was projected onto the camera tube, and lo and behold "a similar cross appeared . . . on the screen of the [receiving] cathode-ray tube." Zworykin beamed proudly. His administrative bosses, however, saw nothing on that dimly lit screen that excited their corporate imaginations. In Zworykin's own later words, the image had "low contrast and rather poor definition." They asked him what came next, and Zworykin, in his own words, "scotched [his] case." They wanted to hear that a commercially viable system would be available in the near future. But Zworykin wanted to impress them with his needs so they would authorize more money and space for him. And so he dwelled not on the future possibilities—which to him were so obvious that they hardly required articulation—but on his immediate problems. He impressed them so much with the problems, with all the work which had to be done before they could lay their hands on a practical system, that they decided it wasn't worth the effort. "Mr. Davis asked me a few questions," Zworykin recalled, "mostly as to how much time I spent building the installation, and left after saying something to Mr. Kintner which I did not hear. Later, I found out that he had told him to put 'this guy' to work on something more useful."

Zworykin was ordered to forget about television and to work on projects of more immediate use to Westinghouse. He obeyed, turning to research in photographic sound recording and in photocells for use in motion pictures. He continued to work on television on his own time, but the closest he came to official television research over the next two or three years was some work on facsimile transmission.

On June 25, 1926, Zworykin closed this chapter in his television work by dutifully penning an in-house research report entitled "Problems of Television." In it he briefly described the system he had demonstrated the previous winter and concluded, "This development has been temporarily discontinued in order to work with the mechanical method of picture transmission, which is still in progress."

He was referring to Westinghouse's work on mechanical television under Dr. Frank Conrad, an early radio pioneer. Conrad's work continued for a few years, and in the summer of 1928 Westinghouse gave a public demonstration of his "radio-movies" system, which used a thirty-five-millimeter film projector and a sixty-hole Nipkow disk. The signal was sent two miles by wire to a broadcast station and then returned to the receiving units by radio waves. The demonstration was a success, considering the state of the art at the time, but eventually Westinghouse's mechanical work faded out of history, its place usurped by electronic television. For now, however, Zworykin had no choice but to bide his time until the right moment arrived to bring his cathode-ray dreams back to the forefront.

2 .   In June of 1926 Phil and Pem Farnsworth rented an efficiency apartment for fifty dollars a month at 1339 North New Hampshire Street in Hollywood and began turning it into a television laboratory. The arrangement with Everson and Gorrell had given them $150 a month for living expenses as well as some immediate start-up money for the lab. By the time Everson and Gorrell arrived two weeks later,

Farnsworth had a motor generator in the garage, a shop work space in the rear carport, and a closet and dining room full of electrical equipment.

His biggest initial worry was finding a glassblower who would be able to create the tube he had imagined. He needed a vacuum tube with one end thin and one end wide, the wide end with a flat surface coated with a photoelectric material, and an electric lead coming out of the thin end. It sounds like a simple design, but scientific glassblowing was then, as it is now, more a black art than an engineering discipline, and there were problems.

First, there was the size. The wide end had to be large enough to carry a visible picture, and it was difficult to forge a glass tube both big enough for a good picture and strong enough to withstand the atmospheric pressure on the outside pushing against a vacuum on the inside. We tend to ignore atmospheric pressure because it's all around us, but it's tremendously potent.

The problem of size was compounded by the requirement for a flat surface on which to "paint" the picture. The strongest structure, with respect to implosion, is a sphere; flattening one end would seriously weaken it. This difficult problem wasn't fully solved for many years. (When the first commercial television sets were being sold in the late thirties and forties, implosion of the tubes was a well-known danger.)

Finally Farnsworth found a scientific glassblower in town who said he could approximate his design; three days later, Farnsworth carried home the primitive progenitor of his original design of a camera tube. It wasn't as large as he wanted, and the "flat" surface was somewhat curved, but it was a beginning.

Now the three partners combed the city picking up the various materials Phil would need. They bought nichrome wire at the Roebling sales branch; they picked up radio tubes, resistors, and transformers where they could find them; and in a lapidary shop they found a crystal needed for an experiment requiring polarized light. For the magnetic coils to focus and deflect the electron beam, they found copper wires of varying thicknesses as well as a manually operated coil-winding machine with a counter to keep track of the number of windings. They brought these, along with shellac and heavy paper strips to separate the windings, back to New Hampshire Street and set up a coil-winding shop in the backyard.

Pem Farnsworth remembered her husband conducting experiments on light refraction on the dining room table with an arc lamp and "a glittering array of crystals, prisms, and lenses," while in the backyard Everson was busy winding the first deflecting coils. The young financier's famous sartorial fastidiousness fell victim to his enthusiasm for the project on which he had unloaded his special savings, and his expensive hand-tailored suits were soon blotted with the orange malodorous gooey shellac used to insulate the copper wires and hold them in place.

As the small team became engrossed in their work and began to make progress, the home lab took on a suspicious appearance, especially during Prohibition. "Strange packages were being brought in," said Pem, "and the curtains were drawn for demonstrating the light relay." It wasn't long before the police came by and searched the house. Everson, horrified at the thought of being discovered in such a slovenly condition, tried to escape out the back but was caught and returned with his hands up. "It's okay, Joe," the first officer told Everson's captor; "there ain't no still here. They're doing something kookie they call electric vision or something, but they ain't got no still."

As the summer of 1926 wore on, the Farnsworth team prepared for their first major experiment. Working with the glassblower, Phil had been perfecting his camera tube, and after months of trial and error they produced what they hoped would be the first working tube. Phil named it the Image Dissector because of its basic function: to break down a visual image into a stream of electrons. With great care, Farnsworth and Everson carried it home and installed it in a stable chassis. Gorrell came over to witness the demonstration. After checking the entire circuit to see that it was connected properly, Farnsworth started the generator, and all watched in anticipation of seeing a beam of electrons deflected accurately by magnetic coils. Instead, "there was a Bang! Pop! Sizzle! and smoke and terrible acrid smells began to rise from the assorted devices. Phil quickly cut the power, but it was too late." He had not foreseen the power surge that would occur as the generator started, and every tube in the circuit had instantly burned out, including the precious Image Dissector itself. Gesturing to the ruined apparatus, Farnsworth said, "That's all I have to show you for your investment, George."

To Farnsworth's surprise and relief, the investors were not deterred. Still, it was now apparent, even apart from the power-surge oversight, that Everson's six thousand dollars would not be nearly enough to produce a working system. And Everson and Gorrell were committed to be in El Paso, Texas, on the first of September for a new fund-raising campaign. The team therefore decided to draw up as complete a plan as possible of their television system, obtain as much patent coverage as possible, and then find more substantial financial backing.

Farnsworth set to work writing a detailed description of the system he was developing. They hired a stenographer to type it up, and Gorrell, with Pem's help, turned Phil's rough sketches into finished drawings.

Lawyer friends of Gorrell's recommended the patent-law firm of Lyon and Lyon. When Everson called Leonard Lyon, a former lecturer on patent law at Stanford, Lyon told him, "If you have what you think you've got, you have the world by the tail; but if you haven't got it, the sooner you find it out the better." Several days later, Everson, Gorrell, and Farnsworth went to a meeting at the firm's offices with Lyon, his brother and technical partner Richard, and a second technical expert, Dr. Mott Smith of Cal Tech.

Farnsworth got up to explain his work and was quiet and hesitant at first. But his passion for the subject quickly transformed him as usual, and he proceeded to take his audience through a whirlwind but coherent tour of his television system. As Everson recalled,

> It became apparent that Farnsworth knew more about the subject in hand than either of the technical men. He completely overwhelmed them with the brilliance and originality of his conception. During

the conference Richard Lyon often got up from his chair and walked the floor, pounding his hands together behind his back and exclaiming, "This is a monstrous idea—a monstrous idea!"

When Farnsworth was finished, Everson stood up and said he wanted to ask three questions to determine whether they should begin seeking financial backing. To his first question, whether the system was scientifically sound, Dr. Smith simply said, "Yes." To his second, whether it was original, Smith replied that he knew of no other similar research, although a patent search would confirm that. And to his third question, whether it would be feasible to construct a working unit, Richard Lyon spoke up, "You will have great difficulty in doing it, but we see no insuperable obstacles at this time."

When Dr. Smith announced his fee for consultation, he said, "I'm afraid I will have to add to that the amount of a fine for parking overtime, because I left my car on the street and came up here feeling sure I could throw this scheme into the discard in a half hour."

Philo Farnsworth was collecting believers in his "kookie electric vision."

Believers were nice to have, but what an inventor really needs is some substantial financial investment. Everson asked Farnsworth how much money and time he now felt he would need to build a working television system that would secure recognition for his invention. Farnsworth, realizing he may have been a bit too optimistic with his earlier estimate, said that he would need a thousand dollars a month for twelve months. He was confident he would have a picture within six months, and then he would have another six months to work out any bugs. Everson, however, remembered that his six thousand dollars had disappeared in just three months that summer. He decided to ask investors for twenty-five thousand dollars to ensure there would be enough to produce the system.

Everson set out on the trail of the big-money investors with whom he had dealt in his various fund-raising campaigns in southern California. One, who had made a fortune in yeast, said, "I'm sorely tempted, but my judgment says that I'd better stick to bacteria." Another, the head of a group of scientific investors, declared the entire scheme futile since, he said, Western Electric (a subsidiary of AT&T) already owned controlling patents over the entire television field. But after restudying the Bell Laboratory journals, Farnsworth was again convinced that nothing threatened the uniqueness of his invention. Bell Labs, the research division of AT&T, reported work only on mechanical disks. Nowhere was there mention of an all-electronic system like Farnsworth's. (Although Zworykin at Westinghouse and Max Dieckmann in Germany were already hot on the trail, nothing of their research was discovered by the Farnsworth group at this time.)

Everson and some friends discussed the idea of forming a syndicate among themselves to put together twenty-five thousand dollars, but Everson had a hunch that even that amount wasn't going to be enough. He journeyed up to San Francisco to talk to his friend and former associate, Jesse McCargar, vice president of the Crocker First National Bank. When he got there he found that McCargar was on vacation for several weeks, and Everson was due in El Paso before he would return. His despondency, however, caught the eye of James Fagan, the bank's executive vice president.

Fagan was one of the few remaining bankers from the old days; he had experienced the California bonanza era of the 1890s and then helped rebuild San Francisco after the disastrous earthquake and fire of 1906. He was considered "the soundest and most conservative banker on the Pacific Coast." His financial judgment was legendary at the bank; they said he had a sixth sense that immediately distinguished between promising long shots and doomed failures. He was famous for sniffing out future financial crises and getting the relevant accounts out of the bank before a disaster occurred. In short, his word was considered gold.

Fagan insisted that Everson tell him all about the venture for which he was seeking capital. After listening to the entire story of Farnsworth's work and ideas, he calmly proclaimed, "Well, that is a damn fool idea, but somebody ought to put money into it. Someone who can afford to lose it," he added.

Fagan had a technical expert inspect the plan and in the meantime aroused the interest of W. W. Crocker, the bank's owner. Everson wired for Farnsworth to drive up in the Roadster. When he arrived, Everson took one good look at him and realized that he would need more than his inventive ideas to make the right impression: "His clothes were shabby and ill-fitting, and generally speaking he had the appearance of a poor inventor." Everson immediately took him to the Knox Shop, one of San Francisco's finest clothiers, where he bought him a new hat and suit, insisting that the alterations be ready by the next morning. (As Jenkins had already found out, you have to paint your invention—and inventor—bright red if you want someone to buy it.)

The next day Everson and Farnsworth met with Roy Bishop, an engineer and capitalist whom Fagan had asked to evaluate the project, and another engineer. Bishop seemed convinced of the soundness of Farnsworth's ideas, but after they left lunch and had spent the rest of the afternoon in Bishop's offices, he expressed his doubts that the system could actually be made to work.

On hearing this, Farnsworth, without so much as an exchange of glances with Everson, "rose from his seat, picked up his briefcase, and with a courteous gesture thanked Mr. Bishop for his kindness in spending so much time discussing the matter and expressed regret that he could not see the possibilities that [they] saw in the invention." Following his lead, Everson joined him at the door. As they were closing it behind them, Bishop asked them to wait one second. After a whispered conversation with his colleague, Bishop asked them to see one more engineer, Harlan Honn from the Crocker Research Laboratories. "Honn is a hard-boiled, competent engineer," said Bishop. "If you can convince him that your proposition is sound and can be worked out, I think we will find ways of backing you."

By the end of the day, Farnsworth had won over Honn, who made his favorable report to the McCargar-Fagan-Crocker group. Everson stayed in town to wait for McCargar's return, after which the banking group asked Farnsworth and Everson to meet them at the bank. Once again, Farnsworth went through all the details of his invention, calmly and confidently answering any objections that were raised. The bankers agreed to provide the twenty-five thousand dollars, as well as laboratory space they owned in San Francisco at 202 Green Street. In return, they would control 60 percent of the new syndicate, the remaining 40 percent to be divided among Farnsworth, Everson, and Gorrell.

"Well, Mr. Everson," said Bishop after the agreement was reached, "this is the first time anyone has ever come into this room and got anything out of us without laying something on the table for it. We are backing nothing here except the ideas in this boy's head. Believe me, we are going to treat him like a racehorse."

"Colt" would have been more appropriate. When it came time to sign the papers, a technicality had to be taken care of, namely the appointment of Everson as Farnsworth's legal guardian. The inventor on whom San Francisco's oldest and most respected banker was betting was still under age.

A few weeks later, on September 22, 1926, Cliff Gardner sat himself down on the curb at the corner of California and Powell streets in downtown San Francisco, where he had sat for several hours each of the last three days. Across the intersection was Nob Hill's Fairmont Hotel, its majestic outline by now etched into his brain. In his hands was a telegram, soft and discolored from constant folding and reopening:

HAVE BACKING FROM SAN FRANCISCO BANKERS STOP JOB FOR YOU STOP
MEET US CORNER CALIFORNIA AND POWELL STREETS NOON EACH DAY
STARTING SEPT 19 UNTIL WE GET THERE STOP PHIL

As soon as he had signed his new contract, Farnsworth had wired his brother-in-law in Baker, Oregon, where he was working. Gardner had immediately quit his job, packed his few belongings, and said good-bye to his girlfriend and to his sister, with whom he had been living. He and Phil had been through a slew of temporary jobs together, all the while dreaming of making Phil's invention a reality; he wouldn't have missed this next step for anything.

The view from California and Powell, however, was becoming a bit too familiar. He was running out of money fast, and he couldn't afford to stay in his hotel much longer. To pass the time and keep from worrying, he imagined what their new lab would be like and how he might contribute.

Suddenly his ears picked up the familiar leaky muffler on Everson's Chandler Roadster. He jumped up to greet his sister and brother-in-law, and they immediately set out to find 202 Green Street, the address of their new lab. From the downtown area they rolled gently up and down Sansome Street heading north, each street on the right offering a view of the bay and the Oakland hills beyond. When they reached Green Street, they turned left and parked. The two-story gray stucco building occupied the entire north side of a dead-end alley ending in a sheer cliff that formed the eastern side of Telegraph Hill. As they got out of the car, they could smell the fresh litchis from nearby Chinatown. On the ground floor were a garage and a carpenter's shop; a sign on the second floor announced the Crocker Research Laboratory. Inside, Farnsworth walked around the empty loft allotted for his television work: twenty by thirty feet, with a high-beamed roof and plenty of sunlight. "Behold," he said softly, "the future home of electronic television."

By the first of October, the lab was set up enough to begin constructing the first Image Dissector tubes. Farnsworth and Gardner had built a four-foot-by-ten-foot stable glassblowing table complete with a vacuum pump and nearby plumbing. Since the only tubes made at the time had curved ends and Farnsworth needed flat ends on which to project an image, one of the first orders of business was to learn the art of glassblowing. Gardner, unschooled in the advanced electronics Farnsworth would be dealing with, jumped at the chance to contribute in this way.

Their first attempts at building tubes, however, were futile. When they tried to insert a cathode into a tube softened by flame, the glass inevitably cracked on cooling. Frustrated, they visited the University of California campus at Berkeley and found a Mr. Bill Cummings, head of the glassblowing lab. Cummings was intrigued by their project and agreed to help in his spare time. If they would bring him their cathode, he would try to install it in a tube and bring it over to their lab, along with the ingredients for a good vacuum setup.

Farnsworth and Gardner set out buying additional elements Cummings suggested, including liquid air, which is cold enough to condense mercury vapor (from the pump) and keep it from entering the vacuum tube. Two days later Cummings showed up with the cathode tube and various vacuum paraphernalia: roughing pumps, a high-vacuum mercury-diffusion pump, and various glassware. He spent most of the afternoon sealing the Dissector tube connections to the pump; finally, late that night, the three men left the vacuum pump to do its work.

The next day, after deeming the vacuum pure enough, they began the process of coating one end with potassium, which would serve as their photosensitive material. Farnsworth had learned how to do this from Dr. Herbert Metcalf, a radio engineer and physicist (and friend of Everson) who had worked extensively with cathode-ray tubes. Potassium pellets had already been put into one of several fingerlike appendages built into one end of the tube. Now Farnsworth heated that finger until the potassium vaporized. By slowly moving the flame along, he was able to force the potassium into the main chamber and over to the cathode side. Now he had Pem hold cotton soaked in ice water to the wires leading to the cathode as he heated the tube walls, and the potassium condensed and coated the cathode end of the tube. Within a few months, they would be adding a step: while the potassium was against the cathode but still in vapor form, they would introduce hydrogen gas. The resulting product that cooled and coated the cathode was potassium hydride, a more efficient photoelectric surface.

Next Farnsworth sealed the tube off from the pump as Cummings had shown him, melting the connecting tubulation with an oxyhydrogen torch and carefully pulling it away. With asbestos gloves he laid the first Image Dissector tube on the bench. When it cooled, he tested it by connecting a meter to the cathode and shining light on the potassium hydride surface. Disappointingly, the meter barely registered. Farnsworth was undeterred, however. He had hardly expected that the very first tube would function properly. Clearly he would have to go through many models and much fine tuning before he had a working tube. He quickly determined that he would need a thicker coating of potassium hydride and realized he could get it by inserting the solid pellets at a point closer to the cathode. The second model of the Image Dissector was on the drawing boards.

In the ensuing weeks and months Farnsworth went through a variegated landscape of tubes, each one slightly modified from the one before. Cummings was an unexpected boon during this period, taking Phil's suggestions and returning with an improved tube time after time, squeezing the work in between university jobs. By December 1926, Farnsworth was becoming ever more impatient to get patent protection for his work. He finally got the backing group to agree, and on December 7 he left for Los Angeles to make a patent application with Lyon and Lyon.

On December 21 Farnsworth signed U.S. Patent application number 159,540, his first, before a San Francisco notary; it was officially filed with the U.S. Patent Office on January 7, 1927. The application detailed Farnsworth's television system as it had progressed so far. In it, he mentioned that the photoelectric surface could be made of potassium, sodium, or rubidium. He also claimed that his system would scan images with five hundred horizontal lines at a rate of ten cycles per second. Unknown to Farnsworth, this rate—in fact his entire camera design—was nearly identical to the camera tube in a patent application filed a year and a half earlier (but still not issued) by Max Dieckmann and Rudolf Hell in Germany.

Dieckmann had been working on television systems since 1906 but was never able to construct a successfully operating system. His 1925 design was finally on the right track, but there is no firm evidence that it ever worked. Because of this, the patent was never issued. So as far as Farnsworth knew, his new camera tube was the first of its kind in the world.

It was at about this time that Cummings began teaching Gardner the art of glassblowing. It turned out to be the perfect use of Gardner's abilities, for although he was not an engineering expert, he was a dexterous, meticulous worker with his hands. His sister Pem remembered how "Cliff's skills increased, along with his knowledge of and feel for the various materials used in experimental tube work. Within a year he was making tubes other glassblowers had called impossible."

Gardner was also put in charge of purifying the potassium for the photoelectric surface. This involved removing the highly reactive chemical from the oil in which it came packed, sealing it in a vacuum (it was explosive when exposed to water or air), and distilling it. Obviously this could be a dangerous job, and in fact one day the vacuum tube in which he was working exploded, spraying molten potassium in every direction, including into Gardner's eyes.

He was able to wash his eyes out without damage, but such accidents were not uncommon in the lab. After all, the team was working in an experimental field with techniques that were new to them, without the benefit of safety codes.

In early 1927 Farnsworth's optimistic vision was running far ahead of his lab's actual accomplishments. On February 13 he wrote Everson:

> I had everything set up to show a line picture and would have had that all over by now but [the backers] decided it would be better to take a little longer and transmitt [sic] a real photograph. We can do that right away, Geo. . . . Television will then be the next step. We have about a week or ten days more work. . . . It is really about the same size job either way—line picture or photograph—I just hadn't prepared for the latter.

In reality, he was more than six months away from even a line transmission, but his impatience in no way hampered his hard work and steady progress. Throughout 1927 he continued to improve his tubes while at the same time tackling the two main problems: magnetic focusing and signal amplification. He used two sets of magnetic coils: one to move the electron image horizontally across the collecting anode and another to move it vertically by a small increment after each horizontal line scan. He was able to get this to work well enough for the moment, although he realized that to get a really sharp picture, improvements would have to be made.

The biggest challenge at this point, however, was amplification. The signal produced by the Image Dissector was far too weak to result in a visible image on the receiving tube, particularly in the presence of stray interference from nearby radio and telegraph lines. Amplification in those days was performed by Lee De Forest's Audion vacuum tubes. To get the necessary signal, Farnsworth had to use several of these in a series, each amplifying the signal from the previous one, which created other problems as the "noise" or weakness of each tube was itself magnified by the succeeding one until it built up into an uncontrollable oscillating, or "motorboating," of the whole amplifier system.

No matter what the Farnsworth team tried over that summer of 1927, they were unable to produce enough amplification without creating concomitant problems. Farnsworth decided that an entirely new type of amplifier tube was needed. He designed what he called a shielded grid tube, or "tetrode"; an extra grid would isolate the input and output electrodes to give better gain and frequency response. As Pem Farnsworth wrote:

> Because there were no shield-grid tubes on the market at the time, incredibly, Phil and Cliff started making their own. I do not mean they went out and bought existing tubes and modified them; they started from basic materials and made their own. It was a little like making one's own automobile tires.

By the end of the summer, the workforce at 202 Green Street had increased to six: Pem was working with them full time as stenographer, office assistant, and an extra lab hand when necessary (at a monthly salary of ten dollars), and Farnsworth had hired his cousin Arthur Crawford, a physicist who had helped him tremendously when both were at BYU. He had also hired two engineers: Carl Christensen was "a tall, angular man a few years Phil's senior, with a quiet dignity," who was doing postgraduate work in radio and electronic engineering; and Robert Humphries was a young radio engineer who had "red curly hair and a happy disposition." Together, the small lab worked twelve hours a day, six days a week, in an effort to get a working picture by the fall. They would have worked seven days a week except that Farnsworth, despite his workaholic tendencies and obsession with his goal, remembered his orthodox Mormon background and would allow no work on the Sabbath.

Everson and Gorrell showed up often to check on progress and lend support. Their standard greeting was "Hi, Phil! Got the damned thing working yet?"

Then, on August 30, Farnsworth took a new Dissector tube off the assembly pump, hooked it up to the new amplifier chassis, and prepared to attempt transmission. With magnetic deflection only on the horizontal axis, he limited his attempt to the transmission of a straight line. From his journal entry for that day:

> The Image Dissector tube was excited by the ten-cycle current only and was coupled to the receiving oscillograph in an attempt to obtain a line picture. Although lines appeared across the tube and the image would go bright and dark with changes in the illumination of the object, still I did not believe it to be a transmission, but only due to other currents on the input of the amplifier. This was experiment number 11.

Farnsworth's cool, controlled reporting in his notebook belied his excitement; in fact, experiment eleven convinced him that he was on the verge of an early success. The next week he and his team attacked the present apparatus at every possible weakness, making slight improvements wherever they could. Gardner concentrated on the high-voltage source, a rotary static machine charging a large condenser; Humphries and Christensen turned their attention to the magnetic focusing and deflection coils and the sine-wave generators that drove them. Farnsworth fussed over the whole project like a master chef, offering advice here and approving of tinkering there.

On Monday, September 5, Farnsworth took the new and improved Dissector tube they had produced and performed the potassium hydride operation. He sealed it off from the vacuum pump, mounted it on the horizontal deflection "yoke," and spent the rest of the day making minor adjustments. The next day he connected all the generators and tubes and made sure everything was set just right. On Tuesday night they locked up the lab, leaving the assembly in a ready position until the morning.

"The morning of September 7th, 1927, dawned with the high fog typical of San Francisco in autumn, but it had already begun to clear as we drove to the lab," remembered Pem. Phil asked her to continue her work on drawings of the apparatus while the others made the final preparations. Several hours later he finally appeared at her door and asked her to come into the next room, where everyone was gathered around the receiver tube. Farnsworth began to call out instructions to Gardner, who was in the next room with the Dissector transmitting setup.

> "Put in the slide, Cliff," called Phil.
> "Okay, it's in. Can you see it?" Gardner's voice came back.
> An unmistakable line appeared across the small bluish square of light on the end of the [receiving] tube. It was pretty fuzzy, but Phil adjusted the focusing coil, and the line became well defined.

Farnsworth called out for Gardner to turn the slide, and in a few seconds the line on the screen rotated ninety degrees.

> "That's it, folks! We've done it! There you have electronic television," Phil announced, with a trace of a tremor in his voice.

Even the engineers who had been working on the machine with such devotion could hardly believe what they had achieved. When Gardner switched places with his brother-in-law so he could see the result, he exclaimed, "Well, I'll be damned!" Christensen's response was equally incredulous: "If I wasn't seeing it with my own two eyes, I wouldn't believe it."

Farnsworth's journal entry for that day has the same calm professional tone as those of previous days:

The Received line picture was evident this time. Lines of various widths could be transmitted and any movement at right angles to the line was easily recognized.

This was experiment #12.

But in the lab the spirit was appropriately festive. While they were all still congratulating each other, Everson arrived and was given a demonstration. Realizing the significance of this first transmission, he "became very jubilant, pumping Phil's hand and slapping him on the back at the same time." Together, they went out and sent a wire to Gorrell in Los Angeles:

THE DAMNED THING WORKS!

NINE

Two Years and One Hundred Thousand Dollars

Had I known as much about it then as I do now I doubt whether I could have gone into the scheme as wholeheartedly as I did.
George Everson

1. The damned thing may indeed have worked, but the newspaper headlines of 1927 and 1928 ignored Farnsworth, featuring instead the advances of Baird, Jenkins, and Alexanderson. Almost every day seemed to bring forth another triumph, another story in the papers, another climb in the stock offerings being issued by the builders of mechanical television receivers. The boom was on, and the small, unknown group in San Francisco was definitely on the outside looking in.

Farnsworth's financial backers were worried by what they saw. As the first months of 1928 unfolded and Farnsworth made strong but subtle progress in the laboratory, the Crocker group began to show signs of impatience, wondering when they would "see some dollars" in Farnsworth's invention. They worried that General Electric was taking over television. Farnsworth assured them that GE was on the wrong track, that despite all the current publicity, electronic television would win in the end. In a February 18 letter to Everson, who was also becoming edgy, Farnsworth wrote:

> There has been a lot in the papers lately alright about Television, but that just means we're going to make a million out of this. . . . We have them all scooped a mile as I believe they themselves would agree. . . . We've been making rapid strides lately. Have been working on telephoto transmission and it is going to be easy. . . . I have spent the last week in studying and playing with the telephoto set up my gosh Geo. it certainly looks encouraging. . . . I certainly wish that we could organize to transmitt [sic] a picture from the Lab here and have the picture received by several small receiving sets in the Locality. That is not a big step now—I don't see why we can't do it, do you?

But as always, Farnsworth's work in the lab, as recorded in his daily private notebook, showed slower progress than his confident predictions indicated. Only three weeks earlier he had written in his journal, "Line pictures can be transmitted with the amplifier system as it is, but I always get practically negative results when I attempt to show variations in two dimensions . . . although I cannot discover anything wrong."

As time progressed, Farnsworth came to realize that his thousand-dollar monthly laboratory expense allowance, which had seemed such a luxurious sum at first, really covered only the basics in chemicals, radio parts, and salaries. There was nothing left over for the high-priced equipment that the larger corporate laboratories at GE had available for testing all their ideas. "The result," said Everson, "was that from the very first Phil never seemed to have all of the facilities the task required. He often spoke of this as an advantage, since it made for resourcefulness and invention and often led to a simplicity and directness of approach to a problem that might otherwise have become too deep."

And hunger is good for the artist's soul . . . but what Van Gogh wouldn't have given for a good steak dinner! And what Farnsworth wouldn't have given for a stockroom full of electronic equipment . . .

Still, he determined to make do with what he had. He realized from the very beginning that one of his main challenges was to create a signal strong enough to produce a clear picture—in other words, to amplify the weak signal from his camera without distorting it. This problem would plague him to the end and remain one of the drawbacks of the Farnsworth system. He had first attacked the problem by trying to design a new type of amplifier; the results were initially encouraging, but then no further progress was made.

So he turned to a different angle of attack. Instead of amplifying the signal, he began to search for a better photoelectric surface, something that would produce a stronger signal at the beginning of the process. After much experimentation, he settled on cesium oxide. It was very difficult at first to produce this coating in such a way as to emit consistent levels of electrons, but the reward was a stronger electron flow than they had achieved with the potassium.

Still, there was no breakthrough; each element of the system needed improvement. The receiver tubes were functioning, but not well enough. Farnsworth sent the Corning Glass Company in New York state a design for a Pyrex glass envelope, and the company produced a limited supply. Gardner took these and blew them into the necessary pear shape, with one end a narrow stem and the other a nearly flat surface on which to project the image.

Farnsworth then had to coat the flat side with a fluorescent substance that would glow when hit with an electron beam but almost instantly turn off again. Once more, much experimentation followed before he settled on willemite, a zinc silicate. A special apparatus was constructed to grind the granules down to a fine powder, which could then be applied to the surface much as the photoelectric surface was put onto the Dissector camera tube. After much trial and error, the team was able to produce a willemite coating that produced satisfactory results. They named this tube the Oscillite, because it produced an image when it was bombarded with an oscillating beam of electrons. Other work at this time concentrated on producing an electron gun for the stem of the Oscillite that could sufficiently focus an electron beam to produce a sharp picture. The team was also working to synchronize the scanning coils at the receiving end with those at the transmitter. To do this they sent a series of synchronizing pulses over a wire separate from the one used for picture transmission.

But this caused another problem. The synchronizing currents interfered with the picture, distorting and twisting it, and vice versa: transmission of light and dark areas in the picture caused power surges in the synchronizing generators, which in turn created interference in the signal between camera and receiver.

After countless futile strategies, Farnsworth solved the problem, and by the spring of 1928 a workable system had begun to take shape. Everson recalled the setup:

> In one room the dissector tube with its coils and amplifiers was placed on a small stand before a windowlike aperture in the room. The room itself was copper-lined [to keep out radio interference]. The dissector tube was hooked up to some panels containing the scanning generators. Leads were fed into a black box containing the amplifier. A copper tube led out of the amplifier into the receiving room, where another box contained the receiving tube and the necessary receiving set apparatus. It was all very handmade and crude-looking.

And the results were often equally crude. They desperately needed more money for sophisticated equipment. So in an attempt to attract corporate funding, Farnsworth went into the lion's den. On March 1, he gave a demonstration to two GE engineers. The results were disappointing, and GE showed no interest in his work. (Alexanderson's low opinion of electronic television was partly based on reports such as the one the GE engineers sent back to corporate headquarters.) "We showed them the ability of our tube to analyze an image," Farnsworth wrote in his journal. "Fine lines could be transmitted and recognized as they moved on the receiving tube. The demonstration was not satisfactory, however. The Disector [sic] coil system heats up very badly. In fact one tube was spoiled by the potassium becoming hot and distilling off the cathode. It was decided to get our equipment in shape to give a [better] Television demonstration."

In May, Farnsworth decided he was ready to try to transmit a two-dimensional picture. When Everson arrived on the appointed day, he found Farnsworth in his office. "I think we will have a picture as soon as the boys get the new circuits wired up," Farnsworth told him, and then added quietly, "I don't know how good it will be. The signal is very low, and we may not be able to get it out over the noise." When everything was ready, everyone gathered as they had the previous September around the receiver, which now consisted of the cathode-ray tube with its auxiliary apparatus mounted on an oblong box of imitation mahogany. Gardner was again in the other room with the transmitter, ready with a slide of a black triangle and a carbon arc for a light source. Everson remembered Farnsworth turning on the set:

> A square luminescent field of bluish cast appeared on the end of the receiving tube. A series of fairly sharp bright lines was unsteadily limned on the screen, which was about four inches square.
>
> "Put the slide in," Phil told Cliff.
>
> Cliff did so. The luminescent field was disturbed and settled down with a messy blur in the center. By no stretch of the imagination could it be recognized as the black triangle that we were supposed to see. Phil and I looked at the blur with a sickening sense of disappointment.
>
> Phil suggested some adjustments on the amplifier and the scanning generator circuits. There was a lot of feverish puttering around with no improvement in the results. I felt that I was making the fellows nervous, so I went back to Phil's office to wait. Phil was so certain he was going to get results that I didn't have the heart to leave the lab.
>
> Finally, after a couple of hours of struggle, Phil came to the door and announced, "I think we've got it now."
>
> We again went into the receiving room. Things were turned on again. The bluish field lighted up. Cliff put the slide in again. A fuzzy, blurry, but wholly recognizable image of the black triangle instantly filled the center of the picture field. We gazed spellbound for a while.

The men shook hands all around, and Pem gave her husband "a very big, unbusinesslike hug." There were some blurred spots on the picture due to irregularities in the willemite, but it was clearly a success.

"There it is, folks," announced Farnsworth, "a two-dimensional picture!"

But suddenly, with everyone still staring at the screen, the triangle disappeared and was replaced with what appeared to be billows of smoke. Alarmed, Farnsworth rushed to the transmitting room, only to reappear in a minute with a relieved smile. Cliff came in behind him, explaining, "I was just trying something. First I put my face in sideways, between the arc light and the camera, but I got no response, and it was too hot anyway. Then I blew a cloud of smoke from my cigarette so it would rise up past the viewing area."

Once again, everyone was "shaking hands and slapping backs." But according to Everson, "this interlude of satisfaction endured but for an instant. Then Phil burst forth with a shower of ideas, telling the boys in hurried, feverish words of changes to be made."

Next came a demonstration for R. J. Hanna, vice president of Standard Oil of California, W. H. Crocker and his son W. W. Crocker, Fagan, and Bishop. It had been nearly two years and forty thousand dollars since this group had convened and granted Farnsworth one year and twenty-five thousand dollars to create television. Everson met with them regularly to report on progress from Green Street, but more and more he was greeted with the same refrain from Fagan: when were they going to "see some dollars in that thing?"

Finally Everson had an answer. The distinguished group gathered around the receiving apparatus in a jovial mood, delighted at the chance finally to see some results. As the set warmed up, Farnsworth explained cautiously that all they would see at this point were simple geometric figures. Then, just as the bankers were beginning to fidget in doubt, the television screen seized their attention. In the middle of the small bluish screen had appeared the unmistakable vision of a "$" sign.

After the initial laughter and congratulations, Bishop spoke for the backers. Despite Farnsworth's original miscalculation of time and money, they felt that the venture was a success. Uncertain expenses and difficulties were to be expected in a pioneering field like television, and Farnsworth had indeed done what he'd promised—he'd scanned a picture electronically and reproduced it at the other end of a transmission. They, too, had held up their end of the agreement, funding his lab with no questions asked. Now, though, it seemed a new stage was to begin, and it seemed clear that a prodigious amount of capital would be necessary to fulfill the dream of commercial television. Consequently, they felt that the venture should now be sold to one of the large corporations already in the broadcasting field, which would have the resources necessary to complete the invention.

Farnsworth listened to this in grim surprise. But though he was determined to avoid at all costs being bought out by a large company, he kept his silence and his temper, saying only that he agreed, suggesting that perhaps they should wait a bit longer before selling out, until he could realize his immediate goals of televising directly from motion-picture film and from still photos. "Either one of these," he told them, "could bring us to the point of realizing a much greater profit than we would realize if we sell out now." As he told Pem that night, "if I can persuade the backers not to sell out now, then once television does become commercial, we'll have all the money we could ever dream of." He told them he could achieve these goals in one more month.

The backers left, having agreed to give him that month before making a decision. Once again alone in their lab, the Farnsworth team looked at each other with both satisfaction and trepidation. They had learned over the past two years just how short a month is.

Farnsworth knew now that he needed to be clever in the boardroom as well as in the laboratory; he was learning the same lessons that had been so painful for Baird. Farnsworth had been naive; now he would be sly. He had made them agree to give him a month, and he meant to slide them along, month by month, until he had accomplished all he had in mind.

But he was about to learn the meaning of such words as *naive* and *sly*. His backers had given him a month, but just a few days after that promise was given, on May 22, Roy Bishop wrote the General Electric patent department expressing a desire to sell the Farnsworth patents. After the unimpressive demonstration for GE of March 1, however, Alexanderson was not interested. Farnsworth had done little to challenge Alexanderson's views about electronic television. Albert Davis of GE did offer to hire Farnsworth; they would buy whatever patents he held up to that time, and then "whatever he invents while in our employ comes to us under the regular television engineering contract." Of course, Farnsworth never even considered this offer.

In June, Carl Christensen received his graduate degree and went home to Utah, leaving the lab shorthanded. To replace him, Farnsworth hired Robert "Tobe" Rutherford, an expert in circuitry, despite the fact that he would have to be paid much more than Christensen. When the backers heard of this, they insisted that no new workers be added, even to replace old ones. Farnsworth was forced to let Rutherford go, with the promise that he would be rehired as soon as possible.

Near the end of June the backers called another meeting: the monthlong extension was up. Farnsworth was not able to make good his promise of televising directly from motion-picture film and from still photos, and their attempts to sell out to General Electric had brought them nothing. But during the month's hectic attempts in these directions, young W. W. (Willie) Crocker (W. H. Crocker's son) had become a regular fixture in the lab, observing from a stool-top perch, asking questions, and showing great interest. He became a great asset to Farnsworth at the meeting when it came time to evaluate the situation. With his support, as well as with the increasing public interest in television, the backing syndicate agreed on a compromise: they would go on funding the project while Farnsworth continued his work, and at the same time they would seek a large corporate buyer. It was also agreed that the three original partners, Farnsworth, Everson, and Gorrell, would contribute capital commensurate with the size of their individual holdings. This meant that Farnsworth, the largest single shareholder, would have to sell off some of his shares in order to meet his commitment. He was willing to do this in order to keep his lab going until he had a system that would enable him to break free of outside backing.

Throughout the summer of 1928 the Farnsworth group worked feverishly to improve their system. As always, amplification of the signal remained a constant struggle. The black box in which Farnsworth tried out many different sorts of apparatus for this purpose became known as the "Jonah," since it was a large black thing swallowing up all their money. Everson recalled walking into the lab one day to see the men taking apart the Jonah and salvaging whatever parts might be used again, cutting their losses on one particular effort that had cost them five thousand dollars and several wasted months.

A related problem was that a television picture contains much more information than a radio signal. This means that more information has to be transmitted, which in turn means it needs a wider highway—or, in electronic terms, a wider wave band—on which to travel. The greater the clarity required for the picture, the more information must be sent, and this means ever wider wave bands. This would lead to trouble in the future when television stations began fighting the already established radio industry for the limited space available in the electromagnetic wave-band spectrum. In 1928, however, it meant that Farnsworth was trying to amplify signals over wider wave bands than had ever been used for radio.

The solution that Farnsworth finally hit on was what would eventually become known as an electron-multiplier, or multipactor, tube. It was based on the fact, long known to experimental physicists, that metals have free electrons located near their surfaces that are released when bombarded with other electrons.

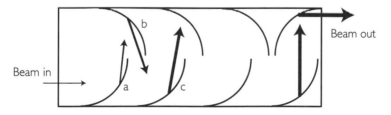

Figure 9. Operation of the Multipactor Tube

Farnsworth conceived of a tube in which a series of curved plates of a particular metal faced one another as in Figure 9. When the first plate, *a,* is bombarded by the electron beam from the cathode photoelectric surface, it emits a number of electrons for every one it receives and knocks them against the next plate, *b*. From that plate, too, more electrons are emitted for every one impacting, and so forth. Electrons rebound back and forth between the plates, multiplying at nearly the speed of light and enormously amplifying the picture signal in a fraction of a second, finally sending a much stronger beam out to the receiving tube.

The multipactor tube, in modified form, is used in a variety of electronic machinery today, but it would be some time before the right metal and design were found. Eventually it would provide the key for outdoor television without artificial lighting.

At this point Farnsworth decided it was time to attempt transmitting from motion-picture films. This was a logical intermediate step to live-action transmission, which was problematic due to the insensitivity of the camera tube and the resulting amplification problems. A powerful projector lamp shining directly through film would provide enough light to overcome this.

The transmission of movies, however, presented its own difficulties. For one thing, it was not feasible to use a regular shutter-type projector. Movies are normally shown by an apparatus that presents twenty-four separate picture frames a second; the human eye sees these separate frames as continuous motion. To prevent blurring of the picture while each frame is moved into place, a shutter blocks out the light while the film is moving and then pulls away to give the viewer an instantaneous view of each frame. (This was Francis Jenkins's invention; it made motion pictures possible.) Through "persistence of vision," the image of each frame remains on the eye's retina during the subsequent blackout, until a new image replaces it. Hence the viewer perceives a continuous, unblurred picture.

The television scanner, however, continued to scan the picture when the shutter was in place, resulting in a disturbing flicker on the screen. Farnsworth decided to try to run the projector continuously without a shutter and to synchronize the scanner with the motion of the film.

He purchased an old secondhand movie projector and began customizing it, removing the shutter and using a bright carbon arc light instead of the regular, lower-intensity projector light. He also installed a special wide-angle lens on the television camera to focus the movie image onto the photoelectric surface. Each modification required countless adjustments and trials, but finally Farnsworth called Everson to tell him he was ready for the first motion-picture transmission.

The film was of a hockey game, and though the transmitted figures were blurry, Everson recalled being able definitely to make out the players as they skated about the rink. At this first transmission the puck was invisible, but it too would come into focus as further adjustments were made.

Farnsworth pored over movie reels culled from a local film exchange to pick out scenes that were "telegenic," particularly those that had sharp contrasts of black and white. Two favorites were a bootleg film of the famous long-count episode in the Dempsey-Tunney fight in Philadelphia and an excerpt from *The Taming of the Shrew,* starring Mary Pickford and Douglas Fairbanks. One particular scene of Pickford at her dressing table was played hundreds of times; at first, only Pickford's hair came through well defined, but continuous adjustments resulted in a gradual lightening of background items, such as the details of her clothing and the frame of the casement window. As Everson put it, "Mary Pickford combed her hair at least a million times for the benefit of science and the development of television."

Cliff Gardner had by this time become an expert at blowing glass tubes, using a hand-held torch and an air tube held in his mouth. During this summer Farnsworth urged him on to do what most glassblowers called impossible: create a cathode-ray tube with a perfectly flat end. Years later, Gardner recalled the process:

All the other glassblowers thought the tube would implode. I didn't know any better, so I went ahead. At first I had the devil of a time, because in those days we didn't have such things as glass lathes or multiple stationary fires that you could move your work around in.

Finally, I got a turntable used to grind lenses and mounted a small furnace I had made on it. Then I clamped the tube inside in a vertical position and closed the furnace, bringing the temperature up to where I could work on it. Tobe [Rutherford, recently rehired] had ground a piece of optically clear glass, used in furnace doors, to the required thickness and size, then polished it. This I laid on top of the tube. Once it was in place, it was fairly simple to heat it up and make the seal. I got so that by turning the work slowly, I could seal it in only one time around. I would let it cool down, then open the furnace and go on to finish the tube.

Tubes did occasionally implode, but Gardner was able by and large to produce tubes that provided a better picture, one that the backers suddenly decided was good enough to impress any prospective buyer. Without warning they closed the lab down. Clearly they were anxious to sell the company before expenses climbed out of their price range. Quickly, however, Farnsworth and Everson were able to convince them that a continuous working lab was necessary to provide the demonstrations that would sell the project, and the lab was reopened.

On August 24, 1928, Farnsworth gave a demonstration to the Pacific Telephone Company. The viewers described seeing a blurry picture of low intensity on a screen one and a quarter by one and a half inches, but with motion easy to follow. The Dissector tube impressed them, as well as the fact that the system was all electronic, but apparently they were not interested professionally in the future of the Farnsworth system.

Nine days later, on Sunday, September 2, in San Francisco, Farnsworth gave his first demonstration to the press. Back in May, Farnsworth had recorded in his journal that "a picture having 2,500 elements can be transmitted quite well." Now, a few months later, he demonstrated in public a picture with 8,000 elements, at a rate of twenty pictures a second. Reporters described the picture, on a screen only one and a quarter inches square, as "a queer-looking little image in bluish light, one that frequently smudges and blurs," but sounded confident that "perfection is now a matter of engineering." The Dissector tube was "about the size of an ordinary quart jar that a housewife uses for preserving fruit, and the receiving tube containing the screen is even smaller." Taking a visionary leap of faith, Farnsworth told reporters that the receiving apparatus could be attached to an ordinary radio set and that it could be sold at retail for under one hundred dollars.

Monday morning the *San Francisco Chronicle* carried the headline:

S.F. Man's Invention to Revolutionize Television

NEW PLAN BANS ROTATING DISC IN BLACK LIGHT

W. W. Crocker, R. N. Bishop Head Local Capitalists Backing Genius

An accompanying photo showed a dapper, well-dressed, mustachioed Farnsworth holding a Dissector transmitting tube in one hand and a cathode-ray receiving tube in the other. The farm boy had become a big-city celebrity.

Fame, however, didn't necessarily mean that corporations were beating down the door to buy the Farnsworth enterprise. In fact, most companies were still betting that the mechanical spinning-disk systems that had been dominating television research would be the way of the future. In late 1928 the Crocker group, still without a buyer, decided that to pour any more money into the Farnsworth project would only dilute their equity. They voted to withdraw their support and informed Farnsworth that no more funds would be forthcoming while they continued to search for a buyer.

Farnsworth told his team he would do everything he could to raise enough money to keep the lab going, but in the meantime he would be unable to pay them their regular salaries. Unanimously they agreed to take a minimal living wage and also to chip in at whatever odd jobs would bring in cash. A local representative of the Federal Radio Commission dropped by around that time and mentioned that local radio stations were having problems straying off frequency. Farnsworth took the lead, and before long his lab was producing and selling thermal units to keep the stations on line.

After a month or so, Everson was once again able to persuade the backers that they couldn't sell their interests without an operating lab, and reluctantly they agreed to provide more money. But with such erratic support, Farnsworth now felt more pressure than ever to bring his work to a commercially viable stage.

Shaky financial support was not to be the only setback, however. On October 28, the weekly Sunday morning tennis game between Phil and Pem and Cliff and his new wife Lola was interrupted by a police officer.

"Are you Farnsworth?" he asked. "You might want to get down to your laboratory right away. The place is on fire."

Led by the police cruiser with his siren screaming, they arrived at Green Street minutes later, to see firefighters confounded by the odd nature of the blaze. Their water hoses, rather than quenching the flames, seemed to be catalyzing new explosions. Farnsworth shouted out the explanation: the lab was full of potassium and sodium, which react violently with water. By the time the fire department, with Farnsworth's advice, was able to subdue the fire, it had effectively destroyed the entire lab. "The place was a shambles," remembered Pem. "The wax container holding hydrofluoric acid had melted, and the acid had eaten a hole in the wooden floor and was dripping down into the machine shop below."

Though everyone spent a restless night unsure whether the lab was well enough covered by insurance, the morning brought the good news that it was. Within a month, by the first of December, they were back in business. Farnsworth took advantage of the time off to work with his patent attorney, Don Lippincott, on patent applications for the work so far accomplished.

The workforce at 202 Green Street was now back up to five with two recent hires: Harry Lubcke, a young electrical engineer from the University of California, and Harry Lyman, a radio expert who specialized in the transmission of the television signal by radio waves. Rutherford was trying to perfect the motion-picture film apparatus, and Gardner was busy with his tubes, continually making small improvements, some of which led to patents of his own. Farnsworth, meanwhile, was throwing himself at the problem of narrowing the wave-band requirements for television, a quest that seemed critical if television was ever to compete with radio and have commercial possibilities.

By March 1929, work in the lab was progressing well. Jesse Mc-

Cargar decided to commit himself completely to the commercial future of television and be the backing syndicate's liaison with the Farnsworth project. On March 27, Television Laboratories was incorporated under the laws of California, with McCargar as president, Farnsworth vice president in charge of research, and Everson secretary-treasurer. Twenty thousand shares of stock were created, half issued to the company for patents and half divided between the syndicate and the original partnership of Farnsworth, Everson, and Gorrell. As before, each shareholder would contribute according to his stake: one dollar for each share. Farnsworth again was the largest single shareholder and therefore the prime financial backer of his own research. Soon after the incorporation, Everson sold one-fortieth of his share for $2,500, indicating that at this time Farnsworth, still only twenty-two years old, had a potential personal wealth of over $100,000 (making him a millionaire by today's standards). In this sense his invention was already a great success.

2. Zworykin, meanwhile, had been removed from television work by Westinghouse, which was banking on Frank Conrad's mechanical system. On his own time, however, with materials appropriated without official permission, Zworykin continued to work on improving his television tubes. Much of his work lay along the same lines as Farnsworth's, although neither of the men was aware of the other. The low sensitivity of potassium as a photoelectric material, for example, posed a challenge for both men. They each turned to cesium instead, but cesium had its own problems; in particular, it was too volatile, which made it unsuitable for making and maintaining a stable photoelectric surface. The trick, as it turned out, was to alloy it with another element. Farnsworth devised a substitute made of cesium oxide, as we have said, while in March 1928, Zworykin applied for a patent for a new photoelectric tube consisting of a base layer of magnesium covered with a thin film of cesium trinitride. But he was still unable to improve on the crude pictures he had demonstrated three years before.

Then, in November of 1928, Westinghouse sent Zworykin to Europe to inspect various electrical laboratories that had contractual connections to the company. Among the laboratories he visited was the Paris workshop of Edouard Belin, where he stumbled onto two great discoveries.

The first was Gregory Ogloblinsky, Belin's chief engineer. A fellow Russian by birth, Ogloblinsky was tall, blond, good-looking, with a "Russian charm" and an easy smile that made him instantly likable. Trained as a physicist but with an engineer's practical turn of mind, he was just the man Zworykin needed. It also didn't hurt that he was intimately familiar with all the work carried out in the Belin laboratory. Zworykin hired him away from Belin, and beginning with his arrival the following summer, he became one of Zworykin's chief assistants in the next few, crucial years. Zworykin already had Harley Iams, a physicist who would also be integral to the television project. So, even without a company mandate, Zworykin was assembling the team that he planned to lead to victory in electronic television.

The second Paris discovery was a new kind of picture tube that Belin showed him, which used a totally different method of controlling the electron beam. Theoretically, the electrons that go whizzing through cathode-ray tubes can be steered and focused with either magnetic or electric fields. In practice, everyone was using magnetic fields. The method was cumbersome and lacked finesse, since secondary effects were always present. Magnetic fields deflected the beam and accelerated the electrons in ways that were difficult to control; the result was that the scanned image lost sharpness and brightness. In addition, the high voltage that had to be applied to energize the electrons so that a bright image would result interfered with the magnetic steering fields and made the whole operation difficult to control. Still, magnetic focusing was the method of choice, because electrostatic focusing had not yet been made to work.

Now, in November of 1928, Zworykin found that two scientists at Edouard Belin's laboratory, Fernand Holweck and Pierre Émile Louis Chevallier, had discovered that if a cathode tube was pumped out to a very high vacuum, electrostatic focusing would work. They had actually put together such a picture tube, and although the results were no better than those of comparable magnetically focused tubes, Zworykin saw where their discovery could be improved. He had already gone as far as he could with magnetic focusing; now, with the Belin tube, suddenly he saw a light at the end of the tunnel.

As Holweck and Chevallier explained how their tube worked and what its limitations were, Zworykin saw that he could relocate the electric steering field, placing it closer to the electron source than they had it. This would allow him to steer the beam before it was accelerated with high voltages to gain brightness, and this would give him much better control. He would accelerate it after it had already been steered in the proper direction; then the acceleration would not disturb the steering, so he would not have to worry about losing focus—all this would enable him to get a brighter picture. In addition, he saw how he could avoid a major disadvantage of the Belin tube, which was that it had to be maintained at an ultra-high vacuum. The French accomplished this by using a metallic tube that was continuously pumped out—unthinkable in a commercial television set. Zworykin knew that his people back in America, unlike the French, were capable of turning out glass tubes that could maintain the requisite vacuum without continuous pumping.

The final problem was that the electron beam striking the glass surface would build up a negative charge there, which would begin to repel further electrons; in effect, the tube would shut itself off after a short time. Zworykin would avoid this problem by coating the inside of the glass with a metallic layer. This would provide a pathway for the electrons to return to the electron gun, avoiding the charge buildup on the screen.

Putting it all together in his mind, Zworykin saw the future.

He came back to Westinghouse fired with enthusiasm. But those in charge of the company were still convinced that electronic television could never work, and almost everyone in the game agreed with them. A private note written in 1929 by the chief of television development at the Bell Telephone Laboratory sums up the prevailing view that Zworykin was "chiefly talk. . . . His method of reception . . . offers very little promise. The images are quite small and faint and all the talk about this development promising the display of television to large audiences is quite wild."

Finally, Sam Kintner, vice president and one of Zworykin's few supporters at Westinghouse, suggested he take his ideas to New York and David Sarnoff, RCA's executive vice president. Sarnoff was famous for gambling on new, progressive ideas. If Zworykin could convince him of the future profitability of his television system, he'd never have to worry again about scraping around for research funds.

"I had learned by this time," Zworykin recalled later, "that it is impossible to work on an idea in commercial research without camouflaging it, unless you can convince commercial people of its immediate profitableness." And by now, he had the skills to do this convincing. According to Loren Jones, at the time an RCA engineer and close friend of Zworykin's, "he didn't like to admit it, but he was a marketeer . . . very good at selling his ideas. . . . He was very generous, very sociable, and greatly liked and admired by most people; but he was disliked by some people because of his hard drive to get things done."

Certain of his work's promise and of the necessity of getting RCA money behind it, Zworykin took Kintner's advice and called Sarnoff's secretary to make an appointment. It would be the most important marketing assignment of his career.

3 . If you had to sell a bold idea to a corporate executive, you couldn't have asked for a better customer than David Sarnoff. Sarnoff had pulled himself up the ladder by hard work and intelligence as well as by chicanery and intrigue—but above all by keeping an eye out for groundshaking innovations.

Early in his career, as a twenty-four-year-old inspector of Marconi ships, he had sent the president of the company what would years later become famous as the "Radio Music Box" memo. Up to that point, radio had been used solely as a means of transmitting information, first in the form of Morse dots and dashes and then by the human voice. But Sarnoff had a new idea:

I have in mind a plan of development which would make radio a "household utility" in the same sense as the piano or phonograph. The idea is to bring music into the house by wireless. . . .

For example, a radiotelephone transmitter having a range of, say, 25 to 50 miles can be installed at a fixed point where instrumental or vocal music or both are produced. . . . All the receivers attuned to the transmitting wavelength should be capable of receiving such music. The receiver can be designed in the form of a simple "Radio Music Box" and arranged for several different wavelengths, which should be changeable with the throwing of a single switch or pressing of a single button.

He also predicted the use of the box to receive news broadcasts, baseball scores, and other entertainment possibilities, but he wasn't just a starry-eyed visionary; he combined his concept with hardheaded business strategy. He suggested that the company could build receivers and sell them for about seventy-five dollars; if only 7 percent of American families, or one million households, bought one, "it would, at the figure mentioned, mean a gross business of about $75 million, which should yield considerable revenue. Aside from the profit to be derived from this proposition, the possibilities for advertising for the company are tremendous."

Sarnoff's proposal seemed a bit fanciful at the time. The year was 1915, America was drifting toward war, and American Marconi was being deluged by orders from the navy. The memo was pigeonholed and forgotten by all but Sarnoff, who would wait five years before making another push.

The delay, however, would cost him the chance to spearhead the premier radio home entertainment in America; Westinghouse beat him to it in 1920, led by Frank Conrad (the man who would later be in charge of Westinghouse's mechanical television program). Conrad, like Sarnoff, was a grade school dropout. He had started his career on a production line at Westinghouse and worked his way up to become one of their top patent-producing engineers. As a hobby, he had built a "ham" radio transmitter in his house. One Sunday afternoon, on a whim, he began broadcasting recorded music from it. The response from other amateur radio operators in Pittsburgh was enormous and was followed by an agreement with the Joseph Horne department store; the store advertised the broadcasts and then sold the receivers with which to enjoy them. Horne's sold out of sets within days.

When Westinghouse executive Harry Davis caught wind of this, he experienced an epiphany similar to Sarnoff's five years before—a vision of "limitless opportunity," as he put it. He financed the building of a bigger transmitter for Conrad and applied for a station license from the Department of Commerce. On October 27, 1920, KDKA became the official Westinghouse broadcast station.

Not only had Sarnoff been beaten to the punch by Conrad and Davis but he was encountering problems of his own at RCA. His brash, confident style had fomented a growing resentment among many of his fellow executives; he was much younger than his colleagues, and being the only Jewish executive probably didn't help. Invitations to company social functions began to bypass his desk, and annoying, time-wasting visitors were politely directed to his office.

The best way to deal with this "hazing," he decided, was to cement relations with the top man, Owen Young. Sarnoff rented a private dining room at Delmonico's restaurant and spent a leisurely four-hour dinner telling the chairman of the board of his poor beginnings, his long road through the ranks, and his plans for RCA's future. Almost immediately the hazing ceased, as word got around that Sarnoff was Young's right-hand man. And in April 1921, two months after his thirtieth birthday, Sarnoff was made general manager and corporate officer of RCA.

This put him in a stronger position to challenge Westinghouse's early home-radio domination, and he quickly moved to do so, targeting for his first event "the sporting match of the century"—the Jack Dempsey–Georges Carpentier heavyweight title bout. On July 2, after courting the fight promoter, rerouting equipment that was headed for the Navy Department in Washington, and "pluck[ing] what [he] needed from whatever departments had a little cash in the till," Sarnoff succeeded in producing the first live broadcast of a major sporting event. It was a huge success: RCA received worldwide praise and recognition, and Sarnoff received permission to start an RCA broadcast station in New York. The radio boom had begun, and Sarnoff had managed, barely, to get his company in on the ground floor.

The ensuing years were an era of giddy ascension—for the economy, for radio, for RCA, and for David Sarnoff. Sarnoff engineered a no-holds-barred campaign to solidify RCA's position as the leader in home-radio receivers, attacking patent infringers in court and refusing to sell to distributors if they also sold other brand sets. As a result, RCA took in over eleven million dollars in gross income from radio sets in 1922, and Sarnoff's salary swelled to a luxurious fifteen thousand dollars a year.

By 1926, when RCA launched its new subsidiary, the National Broadcasting Company (NBC), with an extravaganza broadcast from the Waldorf Astoria Hotel in New York City, Sarnoff was a wealthy man. His yearly salary was now sixty thousand dollars, and he was truly the king of radio.

Yet even as his concept of home-radio entertainment was exploding into a new megaindustry, another dream was germinating in his mind. Always pursuing the frontiers of technology, Sarnoff was well aware of the efforts of Jenkins and Baird. In an April 25, 1923, memo to the RCA board of directors, he had written:

> I believe that television, which is the technical name for seeing instead of hearing by radio, will come to pass in due course. . . . Thus, it may well be expected that radio development will provide a situation whereby we shall be able actually to see as well as hear in New York, within an hour or so, the event taking place in London, Buenos Aires, or Tokyo.

Sarnoff did not jump right into full-scale funding of television research, watching instead from the sidelines for a few years while he monitored its development by the various scientists and enthusiasts. RCA did have some research going on and, in December 1924, transmitted photographs from London to New York under the direction of Richard Ranger. The company also built a transmitting station at Van Cortlandt Park in New York City and was granted the first permit ever issued in the United States for a television station, using Alex-anderson's forty-eight-line mechanical system.

In public, Sarnoff was already beginning his push for the new medium. In a speech before the Chicago Association of Commerce on June 8, 1927, referring to AT&T's demonstration televising Hoover's speech, he declared television "an accomplished fact." He continued: "It is the glory of man that he has never quailed before the apparently insurmountable obstacles of space and time. In the circumstances, it is inconceivable that he will not make the fullest possible use of a medium of communications which bridges the distance between himself and the objects of his interest." It should have been equally inconceivable to anyone following Sarnoff's career that he would not find a way to put himself and his company in the forefront of the new medium's development and in a position to reap the lion's share of its gargantuan potential profits.

So at the end of 1928, when he received a request for a meeting from Zworykin on the subject of television, he perked up. He knew something of Zworykin's attempts to build an all-electronic system, and he was beginning to wonder if the mechanical systems under development would ever be fast enough to produce a large, seamless picture. If RCA could develop electronic television, they could lead the way to commercial TV and dominate the new market.

All he needed was the right scientist. He told his secretary to make an appointment with Zworykin for after New Year's. He would hear what the Westinghouse engineer had to say.

On that January day in 1929, David Sarnoff was thirty-seven years old and far removed from the Jewish ghetto. He sat behind an immense desk smoking an immense cigar, as befit the vice president and general manager of RCA. He listened carefully as Zworykin, two years his elder, described for him in heavily accented English his work on a television system that would no longer depend on the Nipkow disk or any other moving parts. He could produce a television set, he claimed, that would be cheap and small enough to sit in an average family's living room, that would be maintenance free and could be operated as simply as a radio.

Sarnoff stared intently across his desk at "the slight, sandy-haired inventor whose blue eyes sparkled behind thick-lensed glasses." The man's origins mattered little to him; Sarnoff considered himself as American as Herbert Hoover, and in any case, Zworykin's privileged Russian family would have seemed as foreign as Texans to the poor Jewish boy in the shtetl. No, all Sarnoff saw now was a brilliant inventor with vision and enthusiasm to match his own. "Zworykin had the spark in his eye, the determination to do something," remembered his colleague Loren Jones. "Sarnoff immediately saw in him the man he wanted."

The feeling was mutual, as Zworykin later remembered:

My first impression of Sarnoff was as a man of tremendous energy, drive, and vision. He listened without interrupting my story, asked a few questions to clear some points that I didn't make sufficiently clear, and then asked how long it would take . . . and how much it would cost . . . to build [the electronic] system.

Two years and one hundred thousand dollars, said Zworykin.

The estimate was only slightly more accurate than Farnsworth's of six months and five thousand dollars. It didn't matter. It's unlikely that Sarnoff took the inventor's estimate literally; he also probably didn't realize that RCA would spend almost fifty million dollars on television before recording a profit. Whatever his own private projections were, however, he pledged RCA's immediate support.

According to David Sarnoff's biographer Kenneth Bilby, this encounter "proved to be one of the most decisive in industrial annals. It brought together television's leading inventor and the executive who would guide its development. Their spirit of kinship . . . would lead to a fundamental alteration in the direction of technology and its management."

One month later Sarnoff set out for Europe to participate in the German Reparations Conference. He left behind a rejuvenated Zworykin. He had Sarnoff's blessing and, even more important, his line of credit; Westinghouse would bill RCA for all of Zworykin's expenses. The process of filling out his staff of television engineers was put in motion, and on February 1, 1929, the first shipment of new glass bulbs from the Corning Glass Company to the Westinghouse labs in Pittsburgh signaled the beginning of the RCA push for electronic television.

Dr. Zworykin began his new experiments.

TEN

Tube Wars

*Whether the general public will be enough interested or get
enough satisfaction out of television to make it possible to
commercialize home sets for television is still to be seen.*
Ernst Alexanderson

1 .   While electronic television was inching its
way slowly toward the objective of transmitting a recognizable moving
picture of a complex object, mechanical television had already accomplished this and was progressing rapidly, taking no heed of
its embryonic competitor. John Logie Baird worried about Jenkins
and Alexanderson and similar workers in France and Germany, but
thought not at all of those peculiar men fooling around with cathode-
ray tubes.

He also worried about the recalcitrance and blind obstinacy of the
BBC. Reluctantly they had agreed, under pressure from their Post Office superiors, to broadcast his television transmissions, but the only
time slot they gave him was at midnight. Still, he took what he could
get, and once he started, the situation quickly improved. He met with
Captain Eckersley, the BBC's chief engineer, and the two of them—
each prepared to meet his mortal enemy—found instead that they got
along like old friends, sitting up till one in the morning drinking old
brandy and talking technology. Eckersley evidently had been convinced that Baird was a charlatan and that the whole television business
was nothing but a scam from which he, Eckersley, had to save the Brit-

ish public. Now he recognized a kindred engineering spirit in Baird and told him, "If we had only met sooner, all this trouble over television would never have arisen."

By March of 1930 Baird had a second transmitter, so he could broadcast sound along with the televised images. (Since the past September, his broadcasts had consisted of a few minutes of silent visual images followed by several minutes of sound without sight, and so on, sight and sound alternating rather than being broadcast simultaneously.) Soon the BBC was broadcasting his programs three times a week at 11:30 P.M. instead of midnight. Thank heaven for small blessings.

The BBC then introduced an additional two evenings of half-hour broadcasts, which began once again at midnight. Baird Television still had to pay all expenses, including a fee for the BBC's overhead studio expenses, even though Baird was providing all the equipment.

But in a sense, John Logie had won, for the BBC was broadcasting Baird television, and the future appeared bright and clear.

In 1929 His Master's Voice (HMV) Gramophone Company, Ltd., the English arm of the Victor Talking Machine Company, had bought the Marconiphone Company from its parent organization, Marconi Company, Ltd. Since Victor was a subdivision of RCA, Gramophone was routinely notified of the RCA work on television. Intrigued, it began its own modest experimental work. At the same time, the Marconi Wireless Telegraph Company was the RCA affiliate in England, so they too were aware of what RCA was doing in the television field.

The new company's work was directed by Isaac (later Sir Isaac) Schoenberg, whose family had fled the czarist pogroms in 1913. He had been in the employ of the Russian Marconi company and quickly got a job with its English counterpart. By the time of the merger with HMV, he was director of research. He was able to hire a brilliant group of scientists and engineers who were willing to do anything at the height of the Great Depression, even work in so speculative a venture as television. J. D. McGee, for example, remembers being told, "You had better take this offer, since jobs are scarce. I don't think this television business will ever come to much, but it will keep you going until we can get you a proper job." Another member of the team, Dr. L. F. Broadway, gave up his Cambridge scholarship to accept HMV's offer because it paid him fifty pounds a year more.

Schoenberg badgered his group and protected them, treating them like a family, fighting for research funds from above and for results from below. And in 1931 they dropped their big bomb. On January 6, Gramophone announced that "new strides in television" had been accomplished in their laboratories; they had "attained such perfection in transmission that even such small details as . . . the number of a tramcar are plainly visible." Their system, they pointed out, was not associated in any way with the Baird system.

At the Physical and Optical Society's Twenty-first Annual Exhibition that year in South Kensington, London, where HMV demonstrated their working television apparatus, they explained that they were not interested in developing a commercial television system but were only working experimentally. Nevertheless, Baird Television filed an immediate lawsuit to prohibit any further work or exhibition by HMV.

The basis of their claim was that they had invented television, and anyone else experimenting in the field would be infringing on their patents. But the Gramophone Company's system was distinctly different from Baird's, relying more on RCA patents, for which they were the licensed organization in England. Baird's argument was thrown out.

Four months later HMV Gramophone merged with Columbia Gramophone to form a new company, Electric and Musical Industries Ltd., to be known as EMI. Since, in America, RCA had bought out the Victor Talking Machine Company to form RCA Victor and since the original Victor had been the progenitor of Gramophone, RCA Victor ended up owning more than a quarter of EMI's stock. EMI looked over the experimental work on television that had been carried out by the Gramophone staff and found it interesting. They also asked for, and received, information on the RCA work, particularly the cathode-tube experiments being carried out by Zworykin.

The future of English television began to look rather complex.

But despite these inner and outer aggravations, Baird Television still prospered. The transatlantic transmission had resulted in a great deal of publicity in America, and they decided to form an American company. Baird International Ltd. was created as the parent company, with Hutchinson and Baird as joint managing directors.

This American venture quickly faded out, however, taking with it "Hutchey," who believed in it so strongly he resigned when the board disagreed with him. He was granted an eighteen-month option on American rights, but nothing ever came of these.

Still, new avenues continued to open. Baird had worked out a new sort of receiving apparatus: a six-foot-by-three-foot screen composed of 2,100 flash lamp bulbs, "which gave a remarkably bright and spectacular television picture." In July of 1929 this was installed at the Coliseum Theatre in London, and the three daily shows were generally sold out. This was the beginning of "pay TV" and was to provide an outlet for Baird Television Ltd. when other options began to dry up. Soon they had set up similar systems in Paris, Stockholm, and Berlin.

By 1932 Baird had devised a nine-foot-by-six-foot screen, using a different technology, to refine the rough picture provided by the earlier system. Now he had three transmitters wired together, sending out three pictures simultaneously side by side, and these were reproduced on the giant Metropole Cinema screen as one cohesive picture. This apparatus was set up to show the Derby from Epsom, attracting a vast audience. The system worked perfectly, the crowd roared with approval and cheered the winner, and Baird was brought onstage to say a few words, "but was too overcome to say more than thank you."

John Logie didn't realize it, but his personal roller coaster was nearing the peak of its ascent just then; soon it would go over the top and begin to drop. The science and engineering aspects of Baird Television were moving along quite nicely, but the financial outlook was darkening. Though the BBC was transmitting television programs almost daily, it was still not paying Baird anything; as we've said, Baird had to pay the BBC for the privilege. The only source of income was from the sale of television receivers, and this wasn't enough to cover all the costs of research and development. At the first flush of success, the company had reorganized and expanded, and the public had bought up all available shares. But by 1928 this money was gone, and with no certain financial pigeon in view, the shares began to plummet. By the early 1930s, despite some technical successes, internal bickering and dissension erupted, and Baird International Television Ltd. went into receivership. Finally, it was sold off to Gaumont British, a gigantic theater combine.

Out of all this Baird himself got only three thousand pounds. "If an inventor reads this," he wrote, "let him by this be admonished to do what Graham Bell (the inventor of the telephone) did, and sell at once for cash. Inventors are no match for financiers where stocks and shares are concerned, and will, if they hold on, find out that the financiers have the cash and they have the paper."

And so Baird Television was no longer John Logie Baird's company. Mr. Baird was just an employee. And his job description was . . . figurehead.

The engineering was now being done by a large staff, with Baird puttering around in his laboratory among his beloved wires and valves; more and more, he was accomplishing less and less. In 1931 he was sent to the United States to see if he could salvage anything out of the aborted American connection. He stayed in America three months for a whirling round of business lunches and dinners and cocktail parties, accomplishing nothing—except to get married.

He was then in his early forties, and the pressures of his background had begun to take hold: it was time, and past time, to start a family. His sex life up till then had been virtually (though not totally) monogamous, consisting mostly of the long-standing triangle with his Scottish mistress and her husband. Before he sailed to America, he decided to marry "a beautiful young woman with raven black hair"—Margaret Albu, a South African–born pianist who was nearly twenty years younger than he.

He left her behind when he sailed for New York, but his loneliness and desire grew until he called her by transatlantic phone and asked her to join him. She took the next steamer over, and they were married a few days later at their hotel by a judge. John Logie, ill with his usual flu, wore carpet slippers and was so nervous he couldn't stand still during the ceremony. He kept wandering away while the judge droned on, and as Mrs. Baird recalled, "at one point I think poor Knight [the witness] was standing closer to me than Logie and thought he was being married in error."

Since they were already on a longer trip than most couples take for a honeymoon, they made no changes in their itinerary. Indeed, the groom spent his wedding day, according to his wife, writing to his mistress: "The situation had become hopeless but he was kind and loyal and did not want to hurt her. However, he just could not find the words and the room was strewn with discarded bits of paper. Eventually, I wrote it for him. This proved futile, as she read about the wedding in a newspaper the same day while in a London restaurant, and fainted on the spot."

John Logie was not a man to dwell on such things: the description of his marriage takes just one paragraph in his autobiography, and there is not a single word about his wife—not even her name is mentioned anywhere in the book.

In the end, the American venture came to nothing. "The only way to get anything done in America," Baird said, "is to sell out for what you can get to an American company, and let Americans fight Americans."

He had good reason to be so jaded. He had reached an arrangement with a New York station, WMCA, to broadcast using Baird equipment. Together Baird and the station's representatives traveled to Washington to testify before the Wireless Committee, which approved the arrangement and issued the necessary permit. David Sarnoff and the Radio Corporation of America appealed the decision and asked for a ruling specifying that no foreign-controlled company should be allowed to broadcast in the United States. The Federal Commission granted the appeal, and with that decision Baird Television Ltd. withdrew from America, taking nothing back with them from a very expensive three months except one new bride.

2.   Even as Zworykin was unwrapping his new glass bulbs in Pittsburgh, RCA was continuing their work on mechanical systems in New

York. At Van Cortlandt Park the new television transmitter was completed by mid March of 1929, and tests based on Frank Conrad's mechanical system at Westinghouse began under Alfred Goldsmith and Ted Smith.

Smith soon had a patent application out for interlaced scanning to reduce flicker: two consecutive fields, one consisting of only the odd-numbered lines and the other of the even-numbered lines, blended to form one complete picture frame. So, for example, one could create a picture of forty-eight lines while still scanning only twenty-four lines per field. Their picture was so improved that by April, Goldsmith was reporting to the *New York Times* that television receivers would be on the market before long. Sarnoff was in Europe at the time, but this news reached RCA president General James Harbord, a greatly respected former military man whom Owen Young had hired away from GE in 1922. Within days a memo reached Goldsmith ordering that all further publicity releases must first be cleared with Harbord. This edict must certainly have reflected the wishes of Harbord's vice president, Sarnoff, whom he trusted on all technical matters. Although Sarnoff wanted television for RCA, at this time he felt that nothing must take attention away from radio and the still nascent NBC.

Meanwhile, in Pittsburgh in the summer of 1929, the Zworykin team was taking shape. Harley Iams, who had been working with Zworykin since the previous November, was designing receivers; John Batchelor had arrived in April and was concentrating on picture tubes; Arthur Vance came in May and turned to deflection circuits and high-voltage supplies; and in July, Gregory Ogloblinsky arrived and began work on a cathode-ray camera tube.

The first camera model, completed before the end of the year, consisted of a tube based on the one that Zworykin had seen in Belin's laboratory in Paris, using a cesium photoelectric mosaic. It transmitted only twelve-line pictures, but according to a Westinghouse research report, "the result proved to be quite promising. A rough picture was actually transmitted across the room using cathode ray tubes for both transmitter and receiver."

More importantly, and inadvertently, a new principle had been discovered. In the building of this tube, each element of the mosaic was

electrically isolated—that is, each element was an electrically conducting island surrounded by an aluminum oxide insulator. It turned out
that this had a far-reaching consequence. When the visual scene was
focused on the mosaic, electrons were continually ejected from each element as long as light from the scene reached it, with each electron lost
resulting in a net positive charge left on the element. Since each of the
elements was isolated, each could not release this buildup of positive
charge until the scanning beam hit that particular point. Thus, while
the beam was scanning the picture, a positive charge was being built up
at all points; at any given moment in time the beam was striking one
point only, and all other points were increasing their charge and storing
it until they too were hit. Then, after the beam had passed, each element would start all over again, storing its steadily accumulating
charge until the beam came around again. This "storage" ability increased the electric signal—because it increased the amount of current
released by the scanning beam when it hit each element—thus increasing the brightness of the televised picture. Achieving sufficient brightness, remember, was one of the major problems every one of the
researchers faced, so this was a major turning point in the development
of television.

And then in October the stock market crashed. Great business executives saw their fortunes evaporate, and workers all over America began to lose their jobs. RCA's chairman Owen Young quickly fell into
deep personal debt, and RCA saw its stock plummet from 110 to less
than 20. But Sarnoff had escaped the worst. The previous June, on a
hunch, he had sold off his stock. He also would not allow his television
project to suffer. Protected by Sarnoff, Zworykin and his men continued their work undisturbed.

Though work on the camera tube was slow, great progress was made
on the receiver. On November 16, 1929, Zworykin applied for what
would become a momentous patent. The result of the work begun the
previous year, based on Belin's tube in Paris, it solved the dilemma between screen intensity and fine focusing by focusing the ray via electrostatic deflection before accelerating it.

Two days later, Zworykin traveled to Rochester to describe his new

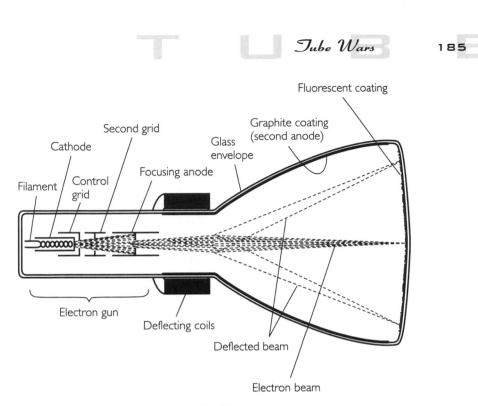

Figure 10. The Kinescope

invention to the Institute of Radio Engineers. The Kinescope (Figure 10), as he now called it, was presented as the first practical receiver without moving parts that could be operated by any layperson and that was bright enough to be viewed in normal household conditions. In fact, Westinghouse had already built seven receiver sets, one of which sat in Zworykin's living room. (At the last moment, Zworykin was only allowed to hint at his historic invention. Westinghouse and RCA had been secretive about his work up to then and would become more so now; the Kinescope would not be given a public demonstration for three more years.)

Zworykin still didn't have an electronic camera tube—the system he described in Rochester used a mechanical transmitter. Nonetheless, the announcement marked a great triumph. There were skeptical reactions, of course, from those consumed with mechanical research. The British periodical *Television* referred to Zworykin's "utopian idea," and

Herbert Ives of AT&T, in a memo the next month, called the new tube "chiefly talk" and "of very little promise." But the fact is that although Zworykin didn't demonstrate his Kinescope, he did have it built and running. In fact, he had been receiving pictures at his home and laboratory from the Westinghouse transmitting station KDKA late at night since August of 1929. According to television historian Albert Abramson, "Zworykin's tube was the most important single technical advancement ever made in the history of television."

But it was still only a receiver tube; Zworykin needed a camera tube of equally high quality before he could claim to have developed true electronic television. This would have to wait until after the new year—that is, until after a restructuring of the entire RCA research organization, engineered by Sarnoff, had taken place. A new corporation, the RCA Victor Company, was formed with joint ownership by RCA (50 percent), General Electric (30 percent), and Westinghouse (20 percent); Sarnoff, of course, became the new director of all research activities.

Under the new plan, Alexanderson continued his mechanical work in Schenectady, and Alfred Goldsmith still ran the RCA transmitter from Van Cortlandt Park, but most of the television personnel and equipment from the three companies moved to new facilities at Camden, New Jersey. Television was not the only order of business at Camden. There were two major research divisions set up, advanced development and general research, and under the former there were three main labs: radio receivers; acoustics; and television, under the direction of Vladimir Zworykin.

Then, on January 3, 1930, the governing structure of RCA was totally reorganized. Owen Young, chairman of the board since its inception, was reeling from the stock market crash and his subsequent three million dollars of debt, as well as from his wife's incapacitating illness. He resigned his chairmanship to assume the less stressful role of chairman of RCA's executive committee. To replace himself, he chose current president Harbord, now elderly and more of a figurehead than anything else, who welcomed the chance to move from the stress of daily decisions to the more restful atmosphere of the board. And as RCA's new president, Young selected David Sarnoff. Not yet thirty-nine, supported by two amiable gentlemen who wanted nothing better than to sit back and watch him take over, the penniless immigrant had become the leader of one of the country's mightiest corporations.

3. After several months spent setting up the new laboratories, the television projects of Westinghouse, GE, and the Van Cortlandt lab were officially transferred to Camden on April 1. The next week Zworykin set out for the West Coast to visit the laboratory of a relatively obscure rival.

David Sarnoff and the RCA patent attorneys were well aware of Farnsworth's activities. He had begun to get a bit of publicity lately, particularly in the San Francisco papers, and clippings had been sent east; what was to be a long series of patent litigation suits between the two groups had already begun; and his backers had already contacted Westinghouse asking if the corporation would like to invest in their protégé, or perhaps even buy them out. The RCA patent attorneys thought the impossibly young inventor probably didn't have anything they could use, but who knew?

David Sarnoff wanted to know. He asked Vladimir Zworykin to go out to Farnsworth's laboratory and have a look around.

In that small California laboratory, a series of minor technical breakthroughs had been carrying the Farnsworth team forward for the past couple of years. They managed, for example, to "incorporate the electron multiplier into the Oscillight tube, now enlarged to a seven-inch picture." As a result, on August 1, 1929, Farnsworth was able to transmit for the first time a recognizable picture using light from a simple room lamp, rather than the hot, overwhelmingly bright light sources previously needed. "This marks an important step," he wrote.

Farnsworth and Lubcke were now also able to attack the problem of sine-wave scanning. The pictures at this time were plagued by two problems: a double image blurred the scene, and a dark smudge ran down the center. Farnsworth figured out that both problems were related to the same source: the scanning of the scene was accomplished with a five-hundred-cycle generator that produced a scanning current in the natural electrical wave form called a "sine wave" (shown in Figure 11).

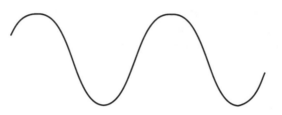

Figure 11. *Sine-Wave Scanning Current*

The double image was caused by the symmetry: the upslope, or left side of the "hump," corresponds to the left-to-right scanning of the image, and the downslope, or right side, to the "carriage return" back to the left. When the scanning electron beam finished scanning a line and returned to the left side to begin the next line (like a typewriter when the carriage return is hit), it continued to scan as it returned, producing a shadow image.

The dark central smudge was caused by the sine wave's changing slope: at the peaks and valleys, the curve was horizontal, which meant it had a zero slope. In between, the curve was moving up or down, with a continually changing positive or negative slope. These changes of slope, as it turned out, corresponded to changes in the rate of scanning. During the portions that were closest to being vertical, between peaks and valleys, the picture was being scanned fastest, so fewer electrons were emitted and a weaker signal was produced. As a scanning line began, the wave was at the valley; as the scanning progressed across the line, the slope increased to a maximum halfway up, then began to decrease again to zero at the top of the peak. This corresponded to one scan across the line, so at the beginning and at the end of the line, where there was almost no slope, the rate of scanning was slower than in the middle. The center part of the screen corresponded to the middle part of the rising sine wave, where scanning was faster; thus, it received a weaker signal, and this produced a dark smudge.

During the spring and summer of 1929, Farnsworth and Lubcke were able to remedy both problems by eliminating their common source, the five-hundred-cycle generator. Farnsworth had written in his journal back in December 1926 that "it is necessary to supply the plates of the disector [sic] cell and also the image builders with straight-line currents." Now he had figured out how to accomplish this: he proposed "charging a very large capacity condenser and allowing it to discharge itself through the dissector coils." With this, he and Lubcke were able to build a vacuum-tube pulse generator for the scanning, which produced a "sawtooth" wave instead of the sine wave (Figure 12).

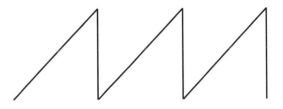

Figure 12. *Sawtooth-Wave Scanning Current*

Now the slope of the rising curve was constant, which translated into a constant scanning speed so that the electrons were emitted at a constant rate, eliminating the dark smudge at the center of the screen. The "carriage-return" motion of the scanning beam took place at the vertical portion of the curve, and the steep slope at that point meant that the return scan was so swift it was as if the pulse turned off while the scanner returned to the left side, eliminating the double image.

In reality, a perfectly vertical line—and therefore an infinite slope— was impossible to attain. But the more nearly vertical it was, the better the result would be. Farnsworth figured that the ratio of the long up-slope to the quick drop had to reach ten to one before the smudge would disappear. Over the months, as the team improved the generator, the ratio grew and the smudge gradually thinned out and disappeared.

An indication of the originality involved in this solution to the problems is the patent litigation that followed. It lasted through eleven years of interference suits and ended in total victory for Farnsworth.

The vacuum-tube generator also gave Farnsworth a truly all-electronic system for the first time, since now even the motor generator was gone. He now had the only complete television system in the world with no moving parts whatsoever.

Public interest in the mysterious work of the young "genius" continued to grow. The lab at 202 Green Street became the scene of regular demonstrations to visitors, who ranged from corporate emissaries interested in buying into the operation to high-profile tourists. In early 1930 Robert Fairbanks, business manager for the United Artists Film Company, called to ask if he could bring Douglas Fairbanks and his wife and costar Mary Pickford to see the new television system.

The day before they were to arrive, Farnsworth was making some last-minute improvements when suddenly the picture went bad. The whole lab worked late into the night but couldn't locate the problem, and when the visitors arrived, Farnsworth had to show them a picture of far less quality than the lab had been producing recently. The movie stars seemed pleased, however; either any picture at all was impressive to newcomers, or they were reassured that television after all would never make the movies obsolete. Or perhaps they were simply being polite.

That night, while Mary Pickford was writing Farnsworth a gracious thank-you note from her train cabin, Tobe Rutherford found the source of their troubles: a minuscule well-hidden wire had become disconnected during the last-minute changes. When it was reconnected, with Pickford and Fairbanks speeding away on the *Los Angeles Express,* the Farnsworth group viewed "their best picture yet."

———

In April, Farnsworth received a visitor more important to him than any movie star. Though the average American would have looked straight through him on a city street, Vladimir Zworykin was considered by Farnsworth to be his greatest colleague. Having studied his work through articles, patents, and the already numerous patent interferences between them, Farnsworth had the greatest respect and admiration for his rival, and he felt that Zworykin's visit to his laboratory was a true honor.

Farnsworth knew as well as anyone, however, that the two of them were involved not in pure scientific research but in laying the groundwork for what would be a multimillion-dollar industry. So while McCargar was hoping the visit would lead to a sale of the operation to Westinghouse or RCA, and while Sarnoff was waiting to see what he had to fear, Farnsworth was thinking more along the lines of a patent license deal. Oblivious to the hidden agendas of the RCA management and his own backers, Farnsworth looked forward to a mutual exchange of information and ideas that would stimulate both his and Zworykin's work.

"Dr. Zworykin spent three days in the laboratory," he later wrote laconically in his journal. "Demonstrations were given on moving-picture transmission, admittance-neutralized receiver, slope wave, mutual conductance, etc. The demonstrations were all successful." Zworykin was gracious and complimentary throughout his stay and particularly enthusiastic about Farnsworth's Dissector transmitting tube. He marveled at the flat, optically clear Pyrex glass end Gardner had been able to seal onto the tube; all the experts back east had told him it was impossible. "They told us that too," Farnsworth told him, "but we needed it, so we just went ahead and made it."

At Zworykin's request, Gardner built a Dissector tube while he watched. Afterward, he sat at Farnsworth's desk, holding the finished Dissector in his hand. "This is a beautiful instrument," he mused. "I wish that I might have invented it."

Indeed, Farnsworth's Dissector, given the sufficient light from slides or movies, produced a sharp, comprehensive picture signal, better than Zworykin's best efforts so far. Zworykin did recognize, however, in his subsequent report, the problem that Farnsworth had been struggling with: the insensitivity of the Dissector. It had no storage capability and therefore relied on the bright light of a projector. Although Farnsworth had televised scenes with only ambient light, the resulting pictures were relatively dim. And Farnsworth's Oscillite picture tube, Zworykin knew, could not compete with his new Kinescope; its pictures were, in comparison, dim and small, the size limited by the magnetic coils used to focus the electron beam.

Leaving Farnsworth's lab in a shared spirit of goodwill, Zworykin stopped in Los Angeles on his way home and wired Dr. E. Wilson of Westinghouse in Pittsburgh with instructions for building some Farnsworth Dissectors for the purpose of study and further experimentation. He stopped in Pittsburgh long enough to pick up the tubes and continued on to New Jersey to begin work at the new Camden laboratory.

While Farnsworth may have considered Zworykin a comrade-in-arms, the possible consequences of the visit did not escape the backing syndicate. Within days, Farnsworth received a letter demanding a full report including "all time spent with Zworykin, both at the laboratory and elsewhere, mentioning subjects discussed generally and the tests and observations made at the laboratory. We want your signature witnessed by a notary. If any data or photographs were furnished him, attach copies to your report; if any apparatus was given him, include description of such apparatus."

This was no ivory tower or open scientific forum: this was capitalism. This was war.

4. Zworykin's report on his Farnsworth visit is no longer available, but it was certainly taken seriously at the time. Although Alexanderson dismissed Farnsworth's work as "clever" but unimportant to the future of television, Zworykin was not so sure. Farnsworth's cathode-ray picture tube couldn't produce as bright a picture as his own Kinescope, but the younger man's Image Dissector camera tube was far superior to the first crude electronic camera tubes he was building in Camden. And Farnsworth was, at this time, the only one to have perfected a working, fully electronic television system.

Sarnoff, unconvinced by either man, sent Albert Murray, director of the advanced development division, and a patent attorney to the Green Street lab, and he made a note to visit Farnsworth himself.

As for Zworykin, his glimpse at the Image Dissector clearly spurred him on to develop his own camera tube. On May 1, just after returning home, he filed his first camera patent application in five years. This tube, like the Kinescope, used a gas-free vacuum, with two separate accelerating anodes for focus and acceleration. It was a "two-sided" tube—that is, the image was focused onto one side of a plate containing a mosaic of pins or rivets coated with a cesium-oxide photoelectric layer, while the electron beam scanned the other side of the plate.

Unfortunately, the tube proved very difficult to construct. Zworykin's men were able to get it to work, but not nearly as well as the duplicates of the Farnsworth tube that Wilson had built. On June 20, Zworykin wrote to Harley Iams, "Ogloblinsky got very nice results with the transmitting tube, which is a modified Farnsworth type."

One way in which he planned to improve Farnsworth's tube, however, was the method of focusing. "M. Farnsworth developed a transmitting tube using a magnetic focussing [sic]," he wrote in his notebook on May 15. "The disadvantage of this kind of focussing is the interaction between the focussing magnetic field and the deflecting fields, which rotate the image and distort it. It occured [sic] to me that the electrostatic focussing similar to that used in our Kinescope with two anodes can be used for the purpose. Our experiment was arranged by M. Ogloblinsky which proved that such a focussing is entirely possible."

They were well on their way, but now a new obstacle appeared. Alexanderson—who was, after all, the premier scientist at General Electric and one of the world's most respected electrical engineers—made a strong push to have the corporation go ahead with commercial television based on his mechanical system. On April 2, 1930, he wrote a memo to Sarnoff:

> I believe that a public showing of the apparatus as now set up should first be made in Schenectady and then the apparatus should be transferred to New York where the entertainment can be properly staged. . . . In my opinion the time has come when we should take the public into our confidence by giving a short television act regularly in a New York theater.

In the nineteen months since the broadcast of *The Queen's Messenger,* the GE lab had concentrated on the projection of a television image onto a large screen for use in theaters, as well as on facsimile transmission. By 1930, office memos, drawings, and calculations were being sent from California to Schenectady at the rate of eight square inches a minute. Facsimile should, according to Alexanderson, replace airmail, and he urged GE and RCA to push for a commercial service. (In practical terms, however, since a normal sheet of paper, eight and a half by eleven inches, is ninety-three and a half square inches, it would have taken almost twelve minutes to transmit it. Long-distance telephone service was an expensive luxury in those days, so this slow fax system was not of interest to most people. Facsimile service had to wait another fifty years before improvements made it commercially attractive.)

Alexanderson had also by now considered the possibilities of electronic television, admitting at the end of 1928 that a working cathode-ray television tube would "be a step toward the television receiver of the future." But the future was distant and nebulous, and who knew when electronic television would be ready? For the present, he argued, mechanical systems deserved the lion's share of the RCA commitment. And for himself, he decided that the most worthwhile work was to perfect mechanical television as a commercial enterprise.

But commercial television was not Alexanderson's only concern at the time. On April 30, 1930, Major Mitchell and Lieutenant Hegenberger of the United States Army visited Schenectady "to discuss the development of television for war purposes." Alexanderson demonstrated his setup at the Proctor Theater, with a projector that threw the image onto a screen six feet square. He televised a street scene from outside and also discussed with Mitchell and Hegenberger his plans for airborne television; in his scheme, a scouting plane could either send direct pictures of the terrain it was traversing to the operating base or send its images to a machine that would print "a continuous map of the ground over which the plane flies." Alexanderson also envisioned fighter planes made "many times more deadly" by the addition of television to their onboard equipment, naval battles guided by scout planes with television, and future wars transformed by television into "a battle of brains between experts." These military advances, he said, were reason enough to pursue television, regardless of the entertainment possibilities.

Entertainment, though, was the spirit of the day three weeks later on May 22, when Alexanderson gave a demonstration to the public and press. Audiences in the afternoon and evening watched live performances by a full orchestra in the Proctor Theater's pit. The director, John Gamble, was present only as a life-size television image on the six-foot-square screen. He stood in front of a television camera miles away at the GE laboratory; from there his image was broadcast to the theater at a wavelength of 140 meters and his voice at 92 meters. Merrill Trainer, one of Alexanderson's assistants, also appeared on screen, explaining the apparatus to the audience. Other performers included a soprano, a harmonica player, and a vaudeville performer who first performed onstage at the theater and then rushed to the lab to give the same act via television.

The key to the television projection system was a high-intensity arc lamp designed by August Karolus. Alexanderson had met the German television researcher five years earlier on a European trip and had been using his powerful light systems ever since. The Karolus arc lamp, placed seventeen feet from the screen, flashed light corresponding to the signal received (about forty thousand signals a second) through a forty-eight-hole Nipkow disk, then through a series of lenses that magnified the image. Though the forty-eight-line, sixteen-frames-per-second picture swayed a bit and was far from perfect, the life-size images made an enormous impression on the audiences.

That night Alexanderson spoke at a "television dinner" for the press at the Mohawk Club in Schenectady and mused on the exciting and unknown future of television. "Television," he said, "is today in the same state as radio telephony was in 1915." Yet he was "not sure that the analogy [was] justifiable and that television [would] repeat the history of radio telephony. . . . Whether the general public will be enough interested or get enough satisfaction out of television to make it possible to commercialize home sets for television is still to be seen," he continued, but then he went on to explore the myriad possibilities for the new technology: news airplanes bringing scenes to theater audiences, unmanned flying projectiles that "can see the target and be steered by radio up to the moment when it hits," commercial aircraft guided through the fog by television.

Alexanderson would never get the chance to develop these ideas, however. The Proctor Theater demonstration would be his last great moment in the television spotlight.

At the beginning of June, Alexanderson received a copy of Zworykin's report from his visit to Farnsworth's Green Street lab in San Francisco. Basking in the glory of his recent Proctor's Theater demonstration, he responded with a note to the patent department:

> I have read Mr. Zworykin's report on Farnsworth's television system. Farnsworth has evidently done some very clever work but I do not think that television is going to develop along these lines. However, this is a question that can be settled only by competitive experimentation and I think that Farnsworth can do greater service as a competitor to the Radio Corporation group by settling this provided that he has financial backing. If he should be right, the Radio Corporation can afford to pay much more for his patent than we can justify now, whereas, if we buy his patents now it involves a moral obligation to bring this situation to a conclusion by experimentation at a high rate of expenditure.

No sooner had he passed judgment on Farnsworth's electronic system, however, than he was asked to submit his own system to the judgment of others. There was much dissension within the RCA group regarding the relative merits of mechanical and electronic television. The former Westinghouse people, under Zworykin's direction, were convinced that cathode-ray tubes were the only way to go, while Alexanderson and GE stood firmly by the merits of the spinning disk. To settle the matter, Sarnoff decided to stage something of a competition to decide which was the worthier system.

The week of July 15, 1930, at a test house in Collingswood, New Jersey, the two teams gave demonstrations. The Zworykin group presented their cathode-ray receiving tube, although they still used a Nipkow disk to transmit and a mechanical impulse generator for synchronization. Alexanderson demonstrated the same apparatus he'd used at Proctor's Theater.

The people at the Proctor Theater had been understandably impressed by the demonstration of working television, but the expert evaluators at RCA were a tougher audience. They were looking to the future for the prototype system that would lead to high-quality television in every home, not just for a good working demo to thrill the 1930s public. And like Farnsworth and Zworykin, they saw that electronic television would be the only way to capture effectively every nuance of high-speed motion and intricate shading. So although the Zworykin apparatus at that point could only televise from motion-picture films and slides, it won the competition hands down. It was only the insistence of GE management that their system was still worthwhile, as well as Alexanderson's preeminence, that garnered them 10 percent of RCA's television research budget; 90 percent would henceforth go to Zworykin and his cathode-ray work. Soon afterward, Ray Kell and other key television assistants left GE to work in Zworykin's lab at RCA.

Despite this setback, Alexanderson continued to work on his mechanical system with zeal. While Karolus was visiting Schenectady in the early fall, they conducted tests together, transmitting live images via shortwave to Leipzig, Germany. Engineers from Telefunken who were receiving the signal in Leipzig reported that Karolus was clearly visible; they could see him put his eyeglasses on and take them off and spell out words by holding up letters. The BBC also picked up the signals for observational purposes: everyone in this business had one eye over their shoulder.

On October 3, Alexanderson wrote to Sarnoff proposing "to construct a system of television for the theater which can be produced simultaneously in New York and Berlin." He claimed that the system would be "new in several essential respects," including the addition of color to the same large-size screen. He went on to ask for a budget of sixty thousand dollars over one year in order to complete the project. "P.S.," he wrote hopefully. "You may be interested to know that in yesterday's test Karolus was recognized in Germany by television with spectacles visible."

Less than three years before, Sarnoff had publicly declared Alexanderson the Marconi of television. Now he took more than a month to respond to the request. On November 11, Sarnoff's reply came: "I regret I cannot authorize the expenditure to which you refer." Zworykin had replaced Alexanderson in Sarnoff's eyes as the man who would make RCA the leader in television technology. Alexanderson's response, two days later, attempts to rationalize the rejection in financial terms, but it also reveals a growing sense of being swept aside by the tide of cathode-tube research:

> Dear Mr. Sarnoff:
> Your letter to me of November 11th was bad news, but I realize that I am not the only one who must face financial embarrassment in the present crisis.
> I just came back from a technical committee meeting where I had hoped to find you present. These meetings in the past have made me feel that I have many friends in the R.C.A. with whom I wish to continue my contact even if it must be only "for the love of the art."

Indeed, "the love of the art" would be all that would keep Alexanderson in television research for the next few years. His attachment to the mechanical system had held him back at the critical juncture when electronic television was beginning to emerge as the wave of the future. In early 1931, his Consulting Engineering Department report for the previous year announced that RCA had terminated several television and facsimile projects and that he would be concentrating in the coming year on more fundamental electrical research.

Still, Alexanderson was not yet ready to abandon television completely. He continued to feel that radio transmission was a fundamental obstacle to high-quality television, since rays arriving via paths of varying distance would cause a blurred picture. His research on ultrashort wave propagation led him to "explore still shorter waves, until [he] finally arrive[d] at light waves, which we know travel in straight lines and which can be accurately controlled by such optical means as mirrors and lenses." In late 1931, he announced that he had succeeded in transmitting a television picture "on a beam of light, utilizing a wave length of only billionths of a meter." He envisioned this as the basis for a local broadcasting system:

> The work thus far is highly experimental, yet some day we may see television broadcast from a powerful arc light, mounted atop a tower high above the city. These modulated light waves will be picked up in the homes by individual photoelectric tubes, or electric eyes, instead of the present-type wire antennae.

Once again he was on the wrong track; the system he envisaged never became practical. On May 2, 1933, Ernst Alexanderson filed his final television patent application of the pioneering era: an adaptation of Zworykin's cathode-ray receiver for color, using either red and green filters or different kinds of fluorescence. He would continue to take an interest in television development over the next twenty years, but it would be subordinated to his other work and to the outside demands placed on a great scientist nearing retirement.

ELEVEN

Coast to Coast

When television has fulfilled its ultimate destiny, man's sense of physical limitation will be swept away. . . . With this may come a new horizon, a new philosophy, a new sense of freedom, and greatest of all, perhaps, a finer and broader understanding between all the peoples of the world.

David Sarnoff, April 1931

1 . David Sarnoff had decided that the future of television lay in electronic systems, and the race to him seemed clearly to be between Farnsworth and Zworykin. But in Germany, birthplace of both the Nipkow disk and the cathode-ray tube, headlines appeared in the summer of 1931 that appeared to steal Zworykin's and Farnsworth's thunder. After all the claims of the previous decade that "the race for television has been won by England" or "by the United States," a new claimant suddenly took the stage. The star attraction of the Berlin Radio Exhibition that year was "the world's first all-electronic television system," designed and built by a twenty-four-year-old auto-didact and wunderkind, Baron Manfred von Ardenne.

Born in 1907 in Hamburg, von Ardenne was building his own radio sets in his bedroom by the time he was fourteen, picking up the sounds of opera while his parents slept. He also managed to meet Dr. Sieg-mund Loewe, who had broken away from Telefunken to start his own vacuum-tube laboratory. Impressed by the boy's knowledge and technical questions, Loewe invited him to visit his lab. Beginning the very next day, von Ardenne became a permanent guest.

Loewe, thirty-seven at the time, had been endeavoring for a while to produce a radio receiver so cheap as to become the "people's set." In 1925 von Ardenne convinced him that the key lay in developing a wideband amplifier, and together they patented a new method of building cheap receivers that had the power of the much bigger, more expensive sets. Retailing in 1926 at only thirty-nine reichsmarks, the new Loewe receivers dominated the market, selling millions of units, making Loewe the leading German radio manufacturer and von Ardenne a wealthy young man. At the age of twenty-one, von Ardenne was able to rent and then buy a beautiful two-story mansion in the Lichterfeld section of Berlin; this would be his home and laboratory until the end of the Second World War.

A few years later, working out of this private lab, von Ardenne decided on a new venture. "Using cathode-ray tubes for television was obvious to me," he said, "since I already had been working with the components and had everything right there in the lab." Indeed, the previous year he had formed a company to sell new cathode-ray oscillographs that he had designed. Now he told his assistant, glassblower Emil Lorenz, his plan, and together they sprang into action.

> Feverishly we took from our stock two cathode-ray tubes, put together two apparatus for the production of deflection voltage from the components of the low-frequency lab, prepared one of the wideband amplifiers, and borrowed from the optical lab a powerful lens and a low-inertia photocell.

Just two months later, on the night of December 14, 1930, they had their first success:

> I held a scissors in front of the screen of my "Light-spot Scanner" and actually saw its contours appear on the other end of the room on the screen of the receiving tube. We repeated the attempt with a slide and achieved a still more impressive success.

Ten days later, he repeated the demonstration for a small audience of engineers, and after New Year's he applied for a patent on the system, which was hailed as "the first all-electronic television picture in the world." But von Ardenne knew at the time that he was not the first to employ cathode-ray tubes for television. In the periodical *Fernsehen* (Television) in April 1931, he wrote that "of all the patented schemes, only the one due to Zworykin, using special tubes, seems to have met with any successful development—at any rate on the transmitting side."

In August 1931 at the Berlin Radio Exhibition, the Reichspost demonstrated Dénes von Mihály's latest mechanical television, and Fernseh displayed the Baird mechanical system. But the star of the show was Manfred von Ardenne's all-electronic system; transmitting pictures from an endless loop of film running through a motion-picture projector, it drew by far the biggest crowds. On August 16 the *New York Times* ran a photograph of the apparatus on their front page, hailing the twenty-four-year-old inventor. At the fair, and forever after in German history, this was celebrated as the "world premier of electronic television."

But this was true only if one considers "world premier" to mean "first public demonstration." For while von Ardenne was indeed the first to demonstrate cathode-ray television to the *public,* he was certainly not the first to develop it, or even to demonstrate it. He was aware that Zworykin had produced an electronic camera in the laboratory, and whether he was aware of it or not, Philo Farnsworth had demonstrated his all-electronic system to the San Francisco press a full three years earlier.

Farnsworth never seemed to get his due. But looking back a half-century later, von Ardenne would at least point out Zworykin's stature, as well as the tenuous nature of his own demonstration's claim to be the "world premier." He admitted that he hadn't really had a true "camera"; his scanner had no storage capability and could only transmit from a film projector or slide. He was the first to give a public demonstration mainly because he had the desire to do so. But while he was putting together his exhibit, he explained, Zworykin was busy in the laboratory perfecting the Iconoscope—a true electronic television camera.

2.   Zworykin had won the competition with Alexanderson by using a Nipkow disk at the transmitting end, but he knew that his team would only be triumphant when they had produced a camera tube that outperformed all mechanical devices.

RCA began construction of a 2.5-kilowatt transmitter at Camden and a receiving station at Collingswood in order for Zworykin to test transmissions. These stations were completed in February 1931, and a similar installation was finished at the Empire State Building in July 1931. Meanwhile, Zworykin's group was hard at work dissecting the Farnsworth Image Dissector and putting it back together again, better than it was before. Leslie Flory's first assignment on the team was to examine the Wilson version of Farnsworth's tube and see how it could be improved. By early 1931, the Camden group was able to use the Image Dissector to get good pictures outdoors by direct sunlight—a full two years before Farnsworth would be able to do it.

But Zworykin was more concerned with perfecting his own camera, a far more difficult task. The two-sided tubes he had been working with were very difficult to build and produced only the crudest of images. In May 1931 he hit on the idea of building a single-sided tube, one in which the projected image and the scanning electron beam both fell on the same side of the photoelectric plate. This had never been tried before because of what seemed an obvious and insurmountable obstacle: the photoelectric surface on which the visual scene was focused was by its very nature sensitive to electrons. Everyone thought that scanning this surface directly with a beam of energetic electrons would surely destroy it.

But when Zworykin actually tried the experiment, this turned out not to be so. It was another example of a lesson scientists have learned over and over again: intuition is no substitute for experiment. Flory,

Sanford Essig (who had recently been hired to work on chemical problems), and Iams were assigned to work on the new design under the leadership of Ogloblinsky. A month later, several prototype models were giving promising results, and they became the shape of things to come.

The main conceptual advantage Zworykin had over Farnsworth was in the idea of a storage tube, in which those portions of the scene not being scanned stored their accumulating electric charge until the scanning beam swept over them. This provided more charge per light intensity. The Camden team's toughest problem was with the mosaic, which they were forming on a mica layer by depositing silver over a fine mesh, or by etching through an unbroken silver layer, or by several other methods, none of which proved satisfactory. Then one day Essig "was baking one of the silver-covered mica targets in an oven and accidentally left it in too long. When it came out he found that the silver had broken into a beautiful uniform mosaic of insulated silver globules."

The team quickly jumped on this revelation, and before long they had perfected an elaborate ritual. After baking the silver mosaic, they introduced oxygen into the tube to form a silver oxide mosaic and then covered it with a layer of cesium. Finally, they pumped the tube out and baked it again. Essig eventually was issued a patent for the procedure.

According to Zworykin, this accidental discovery was the "final link" needed for the construction of his all-electronic television system. He was building and operating the world's first electronic camera tubes that used the storage principle. Through the late summer and early fall, Ogloblinsky's group went through a succession of models, producing better and better tubes, with the mosaic growing to as large as four by four inches.

To be sure, though, they were still far from a commercially viable camera. Their best still had low efficiency and produced a large amount of visual static. Ted Smith, the leader of the Van Cortlandt lab, who had just made the switch from research to marketing and management, remembered,

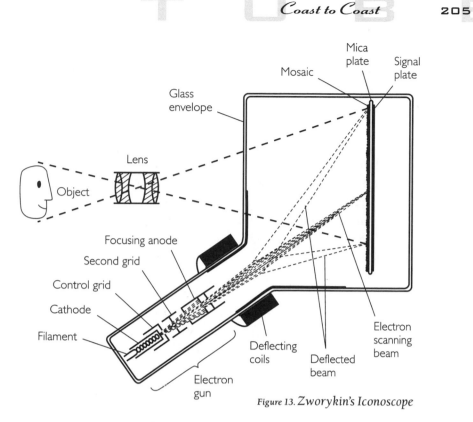

Figure 13. Zworykin's Iconoscope

Zworykin's tube was a great improvement over anything else that had been used, and that includes the Farnsworth tube, because it stored light. . . . However, it had some basic defects. The electrons that hit the plate were apt to bounce off and come back again. So you've got black and white areas all over the picture. So it was necessary to "shade" the area in order to get a good picture. This took twenty-two knobs that had to be adjusted. But [the tube] started things off at least.

The process of refinement continued, and a final design began to take shape (Figure 13). On October 23, in Zworykin's lab notebook, he named his new camera tube the Iconoscope, from the Greek words *eikon,* meaning image, and *skopion,* to look at. On November 9, "tube number 16" was tested; it was the first Iconoscope to produce a "reasonably good picture" and be considered a true success, worthy of patenting. Four days later, Zworykin filed his patent application for a "Method of and Apparatus for Producing Images of Objects."

(In Hungary, an engineer named Kolomon Tihany had been working on a similar design, and in fact several individual elements from Zworykin's patent had to be taken out later and given to Tihany, prompting claims that Tihany had actually invented the Iconoscope. But the design was for the most part Zworykin's, and he was certainly the only one to build an operable tube of this kind at the time.)

So Vladimir Zworykin finally had his camera tube; his all-electronic television system was complete. But the time for a public announcement was still not at hand. He needed to improve his tube so that he could properly impress the public with the superiority of his system. And his champion, Sarnoff, was in the middle of an all-consuming antitrust suit with the Justice Department. When the dust settled, in a year and a half, Zworykin would be ready to demonstrate what he and his team had done.

3.   David Sarnoff's tenure as RCA's president did not start off calmly. On May 30, 1930, while entering a stag dinner in honor of his new position, he was served with a summons from the Department of Justice charging that the original patent pool on which RCA had been founded constituted an illegal restraint of trade and violated the nation's antitrust laws. RCA had been set up in 1919 on the advice of and at the instigation of the United States Navy, for the purpose of securing control of American airwaves by Americans. But times change, and Justice Departments and political philosophies change, and by 1930 Americans were more afraid of American trusts than of foreign companies.

In typical fashion, Sarnoff looked at the suit not as a potential disaster that could render RCA little more than a small wireless operation with no radio-controlling patents, but rather as an opportunity to sever ties with GE and Westinghouse and keep patent power with RCA.

Throughout the next two and a half years of exhausting legal chess games, however, Sarnoff never lost sight of Zworykin's progress. He began making regular visits "from the empyrean tower of Rockefeller Center to Zworykin's small, cluttered Camden laboratory, and he made the trip often to observe, inquire, and exhort. In New York, he was an immaculately garbed corporate paladin; in Camden, he went to shirt sleeves in the bright lights and intense heat of the television labs, sweating, cigar or pipe clenched within his jaws. 'It was a question of confidence,' he would later say. 'The technical people had to know management was behind them, and I was management. I let them know I believed in them more than they believed in themselves.'"

Charles Jolliffe, one of the engineers, said, "We always knew someone up there understood us. We knew we were important to him. We knew the value of our work was recognized. I've never been more stimulated than through those long years of television's development. We felt we were doing the most important job in the world. That's how Sarnoff made us feel."

The promise of two years and one hundred thousand dollars was nearing an end, and Zworykin was nowhere near a commercially viable system, but Sarnoff was far too shrewd to be angry. He had known from the start that Zworykin was merely an optimistic visionary like himself. "Zworykin is the greatest salesman in history," he liked to say later. "He put a price tag of $100,000 on television, and I bought it." But Sarnoff knew from the start, perhaps better than Zworykin, that when the Iconoscope came through, the revenue would be so astronomical as to dwarf any initial outlay.

Unless someone else beat him to it, that is. So along with representing the RCA/GE/Westinghouse combine in Washington, taking care of business in New York, and following Zworykin's work in Camden, Sarnoff also kept a personal watch over what others were accomplishing in television research. After sending first Zworykin and then Murray and a patent lawyer to visit Farnsworth's lab, Sarnoff decided that the young man's iconoclastic work might be a danger to future RCA patent domination. So in April of 1931, right in the middle of the antitrust hearings, he paid a "casual" visit himself to 202 Green Street in San Francisco.

4.   Since Zworykin's visit in April 1930, work had continued at Green Street, spurred on by the issuance of the first Farnsworth patents: "Electric Oscillator System" on May 13, 1930, and "Television System" (the first of all his applications) and "Television Receiving System" on August 26. These applications had encountered much interference from the Zworykin group, and their survival boded well for the financial future of the Farnsworth enterprise.

The Farnsworth team now felt ready to attempt transmissions over some distance, and they set up a receiving apparatus at the Hobart Building, about a mile away from the lab. They then established a telephone connection, passing through two exchanges, and sent the signal over ordinary telephone lines. Farnsworth had felt that this was one possibility for future commercial transmission, but the pictures transmitted were poor, with "a great deal of distraction and noise," and he quickly turned his attention to the challenge of transmitting over the airwaves.

Lubcke installed a low-power four-meter transmitter at the Green Street lab, and a receiving apparatus was set up at the Merchants Exchange Building, also about a mile away. Although the picture was poor, they did succeed in transmitting the first all-electronic picture ever through the air. Funds were low at this point, though—McCargar was forever putting pressure on Farnsworth to keep his staff at a minimum—and Farnsworth was unable to pursue further experimentation on these air transmissions.

In December 1930 the Federal Radio Commission was holding informal hearings in Washington regarding the new art of television and possible wave-band assignments. At that time the federal airmail service was offering to carry a limited number of passengers to help defray their rising costs. Facing the monotony and wasted time of a four-day train trip and also excited at the prospect of air travel, Farnsworth jumped at the chance to fly to Washington, and he talked his patent attorney, Don Lippincott, into joining him. Their wives, who had protested in vain from the start, didn't hear a word from them for three days after their plane took off. Bad weather forced them down in Kansas

City, where they had to spend the night. They sent a telegram that never arrived, then were grounded again in Saint Louis, where they took the night train to Indianapolis. There they boarded another plane to Washington, arriving only a day ahead of the transcontinental train from California.

On December 3 Farnsworth appeared before the commission, delivering a paper describing his present system. As always when speaking about his invention, his shyness quickly melted away and he became a captivating, impassioned speaker, assuring the commission that his new all-electronic system made commercial television an immediate possibility. Unfortunately, on this occasion his enthusiasm led him to make some claims that had yet to be substantiated in the lab. Some of these claims, such as his insistence that subjects were now able to be televised outdoors without artificial lighting, would be achieved soon enough to verify his testimony, at least retroactively. But Farnsworth made the mistake of discussing at length his new theory for reducing the necessary wavelength band for television transmission, and his reputation would suffer for it.

As early as June of 1928, Farnsworth had written in his journal of the need to narrow the wave band across which television could be transmitted. The concept was an important one. One of the political battles yet to be fought—and a bloody one it would be—was over the allocation of space on the electromagnetic spectrum. There are only a limited number of frequencies (or wavelengths) suitable for radio or television transmission, and in its infancy, television was at a distinct disadvantage compared to radio. On the one hand, radio was already established and had its audience, while television was arguing for frequency allocation on the basis of experimental work only. On the other hand, television needed more frequencies (a wider wavelength band) for one station than radio did for many. If Farnsworth could narrow the waveband needed, it would be a big step forward.

For months Farnsworth had been working out a mathematical basis for doing this, and finally he had come up with a theory he believed in. He relied on a sophisticated mathematical technique (which he had mastered on his own) called Fourier analysis to create an "image compressor" that would suppress part of the frequency band, so that a frequency of only five or ten kilocycles was actually transmitted, while the suppressed portion was replaced at the receiving end. He had sent his calculations to mathematicians and engineers at the Naval Research Laboratories and other institutions, and no one had reported a flaw in his reasoning. He had not learned that most scientists, given a problem to look over that they are not particularly interested in, will give it only a shallow perusal; their lack of disapproval ought not to have been construed as an endorsement. But emboldened by what he took to be their assent, he had set out for Washington sure of his method's eventual success, even though he had not yet made it work in the laboratory—and in fact he never would.

His usual confidence, however, led him to claim that he had already successfully transmitted using this method in the lab. On October 25 he had written to McCargar, "We have succeeded in narrowing the wave band for sure this time. . . . I have not been able to grasp the full import of this idea yet; it has us all gasping for breath, since, as you will realize it permits television to be transmitted over all existing broadcasting networks." On November 22, he wrote to McCargar, "I am quite anxious to make an announcement of this development," and the next week, before the FRC, he did.

In a Bell Labs memo written two weeks later, Herbert Ives called the public revelation "perplexing," coming from "an ingenious and sincere experimenter. . . . If Mr. Farnsworth is doing what he says he is doing, we simply do not know how he does it." Other colleagues would not be so kind; according to Everson, "it later became a source of considerable embarrassment." Some historians contend that this premature proclamation was a major factor in Farnsworth's later relative obscurity in the annals of television.

For the moment, however, he was still riding a wave of confidence from his triumphant testimony, and when he stopped in New York City before returning west, the press was there to meet him. He told them of his receiving apparatus, which could be attached to existing radio sets and was "housed in a box slightly larger than a foot in dimension. If the delicate tube burns out the owner releases a catch, unscrews the tube

like changing a light bulb, and inserts the new one. The entire device and tube should cost less than $100." He also bragged of his band-reducing apparatus: "In my laboratory at the present time I have a system in operation which requires a wave band of only six kilocycles. I believe that television will be combined eventually with sound programs over one ten-kilocycle channel by placing the music or voice on one side of the carrier wave and the image on the other side."

Farnsworth's rash statements seem to be due to the understandable impatience of a precocious twenty-four-year-old. After all, Baird, Jenkins, Alexanderson, and Zworykin were receiving most of the publicity, and the young man from the West must have felt that others were running away with his dream. His system was better than theirs, he was convinced, or at least it soon would be. What was wrong with a little healthy optimism to push the program past the skeptics?

In the spring of 1931 Farnsworth made another East Coast trip. The Crocker group, more and more impatient to sell Television Laboratories, had placed ads all over the country looking for a buyer. At the same time the Philadelphia Storage Battery Company (soon to become Philco) decided to enter the emerging field of television.

David Sarnoff and RCA showed signs of taking over the fledgling industry, and the only all-electronic system with the potential to challenge Zworykin's belonged to Farnsworth. So in early 1931 Philadelphia Storage Battery had sent its vice president in charge of engineering, Walter Holland, to San Francisco to visit the Farnsworth lab, and he was so impressed that he stayed an extra few days to draw up a preliminary agreement. Farnsworth and McCargar were subsequently invited to Philadelphia to discuss a sale.

Before Philadelphia, however, Farnsworth and McCargar stopped in New York to discuss another deal. "A fast-talking promoter by the name of Cox" was trying to put together a conglomerate of radio, television, and movie leaders and had talked Farnsworth into discussing his ideas. Once in New York, however, they found that it was all a bit shaky. Cox turned out to be a somewhat shady character, and some of the other principals had already backed out of the deal. When Farnsworth did the same, Cox turned around and sued them all. While the suit eventually ended in a cash settlement, the legal proceedings, including a court restraining order, trapped Farnsworth and McCargar in New York City for almost five weeks. Halfway through the detainment, Pem took the train east to join her husband for their anniversary, and they managed to turn the situation into a good time. But it did delay the meeting with Philco.

It was during Farnsworth's frustrating waiting period in New York that David Sarnoff showed up in his Green Street lab in San Francisco. In Farnsworth's absence, Everson proudly showed the RCA president around the lab, later relating that

> Sarnoff seemed impressed with what he saw but told me that he felt Dr. Zworykin's work on the receiver made it possible for RCA to avoid the Farnsworth patents, and that at the transmitter they were using a mechanical mirror device that he thought would equal the results which we could obtain by our dissector-tube camera.

But Sarnoff's confidence was clearly a facade: before leaving, he made an offer of one hundred thousand dollars for the entire enterprise, including Farnsworth's services. Although this was a considerable sum during the depression, Farnsworth, contacted via wire, flatly refused. He insisted on a deal that would leave him in control of his invention, not simply a paid scientist in a larger lab. Sarnoff headed back to New York proclaiming disinterest: "There's nothing here we'll need."

But even in the spring of 1931, his words must have sounded more hopeful than certain.

5.   By the beginning of June 1931, Phil and Pem Farnsworth were out of their legal entanglements in New York and headed to Philadelphia; within days a formal contract was signed by Philco Corporation and Television Laboratories, Inc. Philco was to finance Farnsworth's move to Philadelphia, along with most of his lab equipment and staff, and set up a lab in the penthouse of their plant at Ontario and C Streets.

They would also provide funds to keep the Green Street lab in San Francisco running with a skeleton staff of two, to provide backup development work. In return, the Farnsworth company granted Philco nonexclusive licensing for the production of television receiver sets. Farnsworth would also help Philco construct an experimental broadcasting station, to be set up within a year.

The Farnsworths traveled back to San Francisco and began to pack up the lab. The process of carefully putting all the delicate equipment into boxes and loading it onto vans underscored their achievements. Five years in California had seen them go from nothing more than an idea in a nineteen-year-old's head to a television system worthy of an opulent offer from the king of broadcasting and a historic contract with the country's largest radio manufacturer. This time they would travel in style; instead of two excited newlyweds in the *City of Los Angeles* coach, Farnsworth chartered a Pullman car for his staff and their families. This now included the Farnsworths' sons Philo Jr. (twenty-two months) and Kenny (six months).

As the train crossed Utah, Phil Farnsworth's small congregation had a faith as strong as that with which his grandparents had followed Brigham Young in the opposite direction nearly a hundred years before. The faith in 1931 was that this young man who had already turned an intuition into an earthshaking invention could lead them to perfect the invention and transform it into fields of gold.

TWELVE

Mavericks
from the West

There was something in that simple picture that made me realise that television was going to be a power to contend with. I could see something happening miles away at that very moment, something unrehearsed, spontaneous.

A viewer, after watching the 1931 British Derby telecast

1. You could charter a Pullman car in 1931, but you couldn't air-condition it, and as the Farnsworth party rolled eastward across the Great Plains, they suffered a foreshadowing of the infamous Philadelphia summers. The children broke out in heat rashes, and their parents sat as still as they could, sweating out the journey.

Philadelphia was worse. The July heat was particularly bad in the new unventilated Farnsworth lab, and Philco ignored Farnsworth's request for a comprehensive system of exhaust fans. Work began under truly oppressive conditions.

Philadelphia at this time retained a more formal Victorian style than was practiced in California; even temperatures hovering near a hundred failed to relieve men of their coats, vests, long-sleeved shirts, ties, and hats. The Farnsworth group were more slaves to comfort: they put on ties to go out for lunch but left their sleeves rolled up and forsook vests and coats altogether. One day, William Grimditch, the new director of Philco's research department, told them they were undermining

Philco's high ethical standards and demanded that they put on the rest of their clothes. Farnsworth calmly informed Grimditch that until the heat subsided or something was done about it, this would continue to be their mode of dress.

Later that afternoon the issue came to a head, as Grimditch entered the television lab to find Gardner and his assistant topless, sweltering under the added heat of their blowtorches as they attempted to blow tubes. Calling them animals, Grimditch bellowed his order to put their shirts back on. Gardner replied with a desperate ultimatum: "Mr. Grimditch! Not only will we not put on our shirts, if we don't get exhaust fans within the hour, I quit!" At long last, their fans arrived. But from then on, the rest of the Philco staff would refer to the vestless television researchers as "those mavericks from the West."

By general agreement, Farnsworth's work at Philco was kept top secret, supposedly to keep Sarnoff and Zworykin from knowing what their main competition was up to—or even that they had competition at all from across the Delaware. Farnsworth may have had another reason for guardedness: he was still trying to figure out how to produce the results he had announced the previous year. "I have been working on [narrowing the wave band] for some time," he wrote in his journal in late 1931, continuing to propose possible methods a year after his proclamation of success.

But his determination to narrow the wave band didn't bring other lab work to a standstill. In fact, this objective wasn't even mentioned in the four major goals he outlined on April 10, 1932:

I. To simplify, overcome limitations, and generally improve present scanning chassis

II. Improvement and development of ultra short wave superheterodyne

III. Improve, develop, and simplify present Television Amplifier and generally improve picture

IV. Overcome difficulties in way of successful heat screen Oscillite.

By this time Farnsworth had made some significant improvements. On July 14, 1932, he applied for a patent on a new type of television receiver, with a uniquely different method of applying high voltage to the anode. The engineering details are highly complex, but it resulted in a great improvement and, in fact, is the method that is still in use today. On that same July day he applied for another patent, this one for a method of projecting the televised scene onto a screen two square feet in size.

With these developments, Philco was ready to begin television broadcasts. Farnsworth traveled to Washington to apply for an experimental broadcast license, and despite the protests of RCA, Bell Labs, Jenkins Television, and the Radio Amateurs Association, the Federal Radio Commission granted Philco a license with the call letters W3XE.

Now Farnsworth could make his own broadcasts—a necessary condition for the experimentation that would improve his system—but there was a flip side to the coin. For some time he had been picking up Zworykin's transmissions from RCA's labs just over the river in Camden, New Jersey, and he was thus able to gauge where the competition stood and evaluate his own progress against theirs. But now Zworykin was able to monitor his work just as easily, and RCA was not pleased that Philco, which had achieved stunning success in selling radio receivers partly due to their use of RCA patents, was working secretly to beat RCA to the television punch. Sarnoff had developed a particular resentment of Farnsworth, who had refused his generous offer and thus ruined his plans for complete television patent control. In the spring of 1933, RCA delivered an ultimatum to Philco: either drop Farnsworth altogether, or forget about renewal of RCA licensing agreements.

Relations between Farnsworth and Philco had been strained from the beginning. In March of 1932, the Farnsworths had suffered the tragic loss of their one-year-old son Kenny from a streptococcal infection. They were determined to bury their child back in Utah, but Philco informed Farnsworth that they could not afford to let him off for the time that trip would take; as a result, Pem had to take the train out west by herself with "[her] baby cold and alone in a coffin in the baggage car ahead."

On a less personal level, it had become clear that there was an incompatibility of grand designs: Philco wanted simply to be the leading producer of television sets, while Farnsworth was determined to construct an all-encompassing patent infrastructure through advanced laboratory research. He also suspected, unaware of the RCA ultimatum, that McCargar was planning to sell the Farnsworth company to Philco. Add to all this the fact that Philco relied on the RCA patents for their lucrative radio business, and it was clear that the two-year contract between Farnsworth and Philco would not be renewed. In the summer of 1933, Farnsworth and Philco parted ways.

The two-year liaison had been far from unproductive, though. In April 1933, twenty months into the partnership, Farnsworth applied for one of his most important and powerful patents. Titled simply "Image Dissector," it was actually much more than that: a design for a storage-type camera tube (Farnsworth's first) using a low-velocity electron scanning beam from a hot cathode. It was the first patent for a tube that decelerated the electron beam so that when the electrons reached the photoelectric plate they were hardly moving at all, and so was a progenitor for the low-velocity storage camera tubes of the future.

McCargar now wanted to bring the operation back to San Francisco, but Farnsworth was convinced that he needed to stay on the East Coast, where the new television frontier lay. He convinced McCargar and Everson of this necessity, and Television Laboratories, Inc., started up their new lab in the quiet neighborhood of Chestnut Hill, where the Farnsworths now lived. To keep operating costs down, Farnsworth agreed to cut the staff back down to just Gardner and Rutherford, a significant sacrifice for which he resented McCargar. Some stock was sold to raise funds, and in the summer of 1933 Farnsworth found himself once again with his own small lab, a maverick inventor with a staff of two.

2.   May 22, 1932, the *New York Times:*

TELEVISION IMAGES ARE LEAPING
FROM A SKYSCRAPER PINNACLE

Despite the still-primitive nature of the Iconoscope camera tube, Sarnoff had decided it was time to demonstrate Zworykin's Kinescope receiving tube. And so he stood in front of a Nipkow-disk mechanical camera at the Empire State Building and addressed a group of a hundred radio executives and engineers from fifty companies, who watched on a Kinescope at 153 East Twenty-fourth Street. He told his audience that the RCA receiving set was virtually ready for the market but that due to the depression they would wait to introduce it commercially until "the business sun is smiling . . . sometime in 1933."

Mysteriously, though, at least to the expectant public, a veil of secrecy then fell over RCA's television operations. Nothing more was heard for several months. In September, in response to a request from the Television Society in London for a paper on his research, Zworykin wrote, "Our Company still does not consider it advisable to release for publication the results of laboratory research before this development has reached the commercial stage." For this was science not only in the service of mankind but equally in the service of the dollar bill. Sarnoff most probably *did* feel that television would bring "a finer and broader understanding between all the peoples of the world"; but he'd be damned if it wasn't also going to bring a finer and broader profit margin to RCA.

The Zworykin system clearly wasn't ready for commercial television. The audience strained to see an image of four by five inches, and although the 120-line, twenty-four-frames-per-second picture was described as "fairly clear," it suffered in comparison with the home movies of the day. As if to concede the tenuousness of his predictions, Sarnoff had closed the May 22 demonstration to the press and public. And there were no more demonstrations scheduled; after this debut for the Kinescope, Sarnoff sent television back to the laboratory in Camden until a more impressive Iconoscope would allow him to present television in its final, all-electronic form. There would be no more RCA television demonstrations for four years.

In the meantime, both Zworykin and Sarnoff had their hands full. There was much pressure on Zworykin to improve the Iconoscope into a model that would allow his boss to claim the first commercial all-electronic system. And Sarnoff was deep in the final stages of negotiations with the Justice Department regarding the antitrust suit.

Indeed, Sarnoff was the central figure in what was perhaps the most complex antitrust proceeding up to that time. He coordinated the legal defenses of GE, Westinghouse, and RCA; he was the main contact between all of them and the antitrust department; and he was Owen Young's confidant and primary adviser. As the trial date of November 15 approached, Sarnoff became convinced that it would be disastrous for RCA. In a brilliant countermove, he decided that he would support the government's bid to break up the conglomeration, but under terms that would let RCA remain the leader in radio. Young, reeling under personal debt and his wife's illness, gave his approval.

A series of marathon negotiating sessions as the trial approached gave Sarnoff exactly what he wanted. GE and Westinghouse agreed to sever all ties with RCA, vowing not to compete in radio for two and a half years and resigning all personnel from the RCA board of directors. GE canceled half of RCA's eighteen-million-dollar debt, accepting in payment for the other half an issuance of debentures and RCA's new building at Lexington Avenue and Fifty-first Street. On November 11, 1932, four days before the trial and three days after Roosevelt's landslide victory in the presidential election, Sarnoff delivered the plan to the Justice Department, whom he had kept well apprised of every development. They postponed the trial a week in order to study the agreement, then accepted it and signed a decree on November 21. The trial was canceled.

While the press lauded the government's great victory against big-business monopolies, Sarnoff in private knew he was the victor. As historian Erik Barnouw later wrote:

> Miraculously, RCA emerged as a strong and self-sufficient entity. No longer owned by others, it had its own destiny in hand. It owned two networks, broadcasting stations, manufacturing facilities, international and ship-to-shore communications facilities.

Sarnoff himself became the sole leader of this new independent giant. Under the terms of the agreement, Young had to resign either from RCA or from GE, and his financial situation forced him to stick with the older, safer company. With Harbord, the chairman of the board, holding little more than an honorary title, RCA's president became its undisputed master. "I don't know how he did it," recalled RCA's Ted Smith. "It was a masterful job of diplomacy." David Sarnoff would never again share power at RCA.

And that meant he would never have to justify television research to a higher power. "Finally," he told an associate years later, "I had the authority to move television at my own pace. No executive layers above, no electric committees to question expenditures." He began taking board members on tours of the Camden laboratory and Empire State Building transmitter, and he consistently got their approval for further expenditures, which had already passed five million dollars since Zworykin's estimate of one hundred thousand dollars. He made no false promises to stockholders; he admitted that commercial television was years away but "told them bluntly that without courage, initiative, and sacrifice 'a new art cannot be created or a new industry born.'"

As Ted Smith remembered,

> Sarnoff was a genius. He wasn't given credit for much of what he did. He convinced the public who owned RCA stock to put up the money to develop this project alone against the rest of the world. And this was during the heart of the depression. We used to go to the stockholders' meetings and he would give a lecture about television and how it would be supreme. A great number of stockholders were Jewish people from Russia who had emigrated to this country, and they saw their man Sarnoff and were convinced he was honest, which he was, and so they went along and allowed him to spend as much money as he wanted. Very unusual corporate situation. People would get up and say, "I'll back him. Davey, he's our man."

With the hard-won support of the stockholders and the board of directors, Sarnoff set about the task of "creating" television. Developing the right tubes was just one part of it; as biographer Kenneth Bilby wrote, Sarnoff intended to make RCA the dominant force in every aspect of commercial television.

> It would not be enough just to have the best TV camera or the best home receiver. The leader must lead in all areas of the new art—in

the construction of transmitters and mobile equipment, in compo-
nentry and equipment servicing, in studio construction and net-
working, in the creation of the entertainment and informational
programs that would course through the apparatus of transmission
and reception. It was a total system approach to a new industry—
"the whole ball of wax," Sarnoff called it—and at the time it was
unique on the industrial landscape. . . . The followers would seek
competitive niches in one or more aspects of the system, but only
one would be involved in them all, and that would be RCA.

"In the whole world," said Ted Smith, "no one else had tackled TV on
a system basis. . . . So David Sarnoff became a system entrepreneur—
the first person I know of in history to do so."

The cornerstone of his new systems management was the laboratory
in Camden. Research, he liked to say, was "the lifeblood of RCA." No
wonder his scientists felt they were doing "the most important job in
the world."

With an independent RCA now mustering its resources behind them,
the Zworykin team hit their stride. In early 1933 they finally built
a fully functioning all-electronic complete television system. The
latest-model Iconoscope was working to great satisfaction, picking up
"direct" pictures outdoors. It scanned the image with 240 lines twenty-
four times a second; the picture and sound were then relayed one mile
by radio to the transmitting station. From there the signals were retransmitted and picked up by the Kinescope. They were still using a
mechanical generator to create a synchronizing pulse, but otherwise
the system used no moving parts whatsoever.

The first half of 1933 raced on with a slew of patent applications flying out of Camden: Ogloblinsky's for "a means for maintaining the picture signal level," methods by Kell and Alda Bedford for projecting and
scanning from movie film, and a new synchronizing generator from
Campbell. Iams developed and patented his "Monoscope," the first
camera used to show call letters or other information discrete from
whatever else was being transmitted. The letters could either be

scratched on the screen, imparted with use of a mask, or created with different electrical characteristics from the background.

In February 1933, Zworykin spoke to the Optical Society of America about a new method of concentrating and focusing electron beams. Although the electrostatic method he had learned in Belin's Paris laboratory had been an improvement on his earlier magnetic focusing, he had continued to work on the latter, and on March 5, the *New York Times* reported his development of an "electro-magnetic lens." It used magnetic focusing with a thin wire coil to achieve "a point of intense brilliancy." And in his notebooks for February and March, Zworykin repeatedly wrote of experiments with "secondary emissions" (similar to Farnsworth's electron multiplier) as a means of improving the strength of the signal generated by the Iconoscope.

By June Sarnoff and Zworykin apparently felt that it was no longer advisable to keep the Iconoscope a secret. Better to garner the credit for creating the first commercially viable storage camera tube and expose their knowledge to competitors than to take the risk that one of those competitors might develop it first on their own. On Sunday, June 25, 1933, the *New York Times* shouted, "TELEVISION EXPERT TO REVEAL NEW ELECTRICAL EYE." Radio writer Orrin Dunlap Jr. reported that Zworykin would be speaking the following day in Chicago, presenting his new all-electronic television system to the annual summer meeting of the Institute of Radio Engineers.

And indeed the next day Zworykin presented a description (though no demonstration) of his new system. Sharing credit with Ogloblinsky, Essig, Iams, and Flory, Zworykin spoke of how ten years of research had finally resulted in the electrical equivalent of the human eye. He likened the Iconoscope to the retina and the Kinescope to the brain; the circuit was finally complete. Sensitivity was as good as photographic film, he said, and the Iconoscope could be used to scan an image with as many as five hundred lines. He admitted that the picture was imperfect, due to the fact that the scanning beam that was supposed to decharge the mosaic actually took things a bit too far and charged it negatively. He was far less modest, however, in an interview with Dunlap. Television "is ready [for the home] now," he said. "The electrical problems are solved. It now remains for the financial and merchandising experts to do their job. That is not my task."

Frank Gray and Herbert Ives at Bell Labs were cautious about their public acknowledgment of Zworykin's achievement, but there was an urgency to their internal memoranda. Zworykin's disclosure also set other labs in motion trying to develop a commercial electronic system, for with this announcement, everyone else was playing catch-up.

Though Farnsworth had had an all-electronic system working in the laboratory as early as July 1929, his Image Dissector didn't have the sensitivity to be commercially viable. And of course he also didn't have anything like the RCA publicity machine behind him. Now, in the summer of 1933, everyone knew that all-electronic television was not only possible but had been achieved. The only question was who would perfect it and manage it into a marketplace giant.

It was hard to bet against RCA.

3.   Though the pall of their child's death still hung over the Farnsworths, work in the new lab progressed well throughout 1933. Everson, from his new living quarters at the elegant Plaza Hotel in New York, was able to sell enough stock so that Farnsworth could increase his staff again. New hires included Tobe Rutherford's brother Romilly (Rom), who had worked for Farnsworth late in the Philco period; an expert glassblower, Albert Buttino, to help Gardner with the tubes; an engineer, Carl Smith; and an Italian immigrant, Joseph Spallone, who, it was said, could fashion anything out of anything.

Work progressed seamlessly after the move. On August 14, the San Francisco lab gave a demonstration to Admiral David F. Sellers, commander of the United States fleet, who watched a televised picture of McCargar engaged in one of the lab's favorite demo acts: blowing smoke rings. "What amazing possibilities lie before us," said Sellers when assured that a television system could be installed on an airplane. "We could scout the enemy with television equipment in a plane, direct the fire of our gunners and make great advances in aerial mapping."

Earle Ennis of the *San Francisco Chronicle* helped to publicize Farnsworth's feats, proclaiming him responsible for bringing "the magic box of science" to "Mr. and Mrs. Public" and announcing that commercial television was "promised for the latter part of 1933. . . . It is ready," wrote Ennis. "It works. It is here."

But despite the growth of his lab and the continual improvement of his picture, Farnsworth was growing despondent. Kenny's death had created a chasm between him and Pem, and the faint beginnings of a serious depression were stirring in him.

Despite his personal problems and Zworykin's galloping successes, Farnsworth still had some exciting moments. In early 1934 he found himself with the chance to make up for the disappointing demonstration he had given to Mary Pickford and Douglas Fairbanks in San Francisco four years before. Hearing that Pickford was appearing onstage in New York, he invited her to come to Philadelphia for another demonstration. She accepted, and this time it was a huge success; Farnsworth's picture was much larger and clearer, appearing on an Oscillite receiving tube with a screen twelve by thirteen inches that gave much better definition. He was also televising live subjects now, and Pickford agreed to sit under the hot klieg lights in front of the camera. "Whew!" she exclaimed after a few minutes. "This is hotter than color!"

He also managed to perfect his cold-cathode multipactor, or electron-multiplier, tube. He sent a sample out to the San Francisco lab, where a public announcement was made. Earle Ennis wrote in the *San Francisco Chronicle* on July 24:

> Development of an astonishing new radio-television tube that not only transmits television impulses, but may be used as an amplifier, director, rectifier and multiplier tube as well, and may make obsolete all known forms of radio tubes, was announced yesterday by the Television Laboratories, Inc. The new tube, according to the laboratories, is the long-sought "cold-cathode" tube which has been the goal of laboratories the world over. It is a multiplier of current to an astonishing degree.
>
>   . . . In the Farnsworth tube a single electron will build up or father

2,000,000,000,000,000,000,000,000,000,000,000,000,000,000, 000,000,000,000,000,000 electrons, all in the space of 1/1,000, 000th of a second.

A demonstration of the multipactor was held at the San Francisco plant of Heintz and Kaufman, with members of the Army Signal Corps, faculty from Stanford and the University of California at Berkeley, and other scientists present. Ralph Heintz placed the tube in the transmitter circuit of a wireless station and turned it on. There was no sign at all that the tube was operating until Heintz held an electric lightbulb taped to a yardstick within the tube's electric field; the bulb instantly glowed. They then used the tube to transmit a message of success to Farnsworth on the East Coast: "To Phil Farnsworth Greetings! This is the first message transmitted by your Electron Multiplier power tube."

Earlier in the summer, Farnsworth had presented a paper to the Franklin Institute in Philadelphia, after which one of their directors had come to him with a proposal. The institute had recently opened a new museum of cutting-edge technology, with features such as a giant robot programmed to greet visitors as they entered. Would Farnsworth be interested in giving public demonstrations of his new television system?

The offer came at just the right time. He had recently begun using cesium on silver oxide as a photosensitive coating for his Dissector tubes, and this had greatly increased their sensitivity. With his electron multiplier also finally working well, Farnsworth was now able to transmit live subjects effectively, both in and out of doors. And he had gotten his Oscillite tubes large enough now to produce a picture of twelve by thirteen inches, on 240 horizontal lines, just big enough to be seen by a large audience. He had also replaced the long magnetic coil around the entire receiving tube with a short coil only around the neck of the tube. This allowed him to apply some 4,200 volts directly to the anode, providing much greater brightness. His picture was now every bit as good as Zworykin's.

Farnsworth set to work putting the finishing touches on a mobile system with all his latest features, and Gardner began building spare

Oscillite tubes, since with the increase in size (they were now as large as a ten-gallon water jug) came an increased danger of implosion. The Franklin Institute announced a ten-day exhibition of television for August 1934.

There was only one detail that Farnsworth had overlooked: exactly what was he going to televise? That minor decision fell to Seymour "Skee" Turner, a young man who had showed up one day at the Chestnut Hill lab shortly after the break with Philco. He and his father, a San Francisco clothier, had invested heavily in the Farnsworth enterprise, and Skee had decided to come east and see what he could do to help the cause. Although Farnsworth had no money in the budget to hire him, he accepted lodgings in the bedroom on the Farnsworth's third floor and volunteered in the lab. Now, using the connections his wealth provided, he jumped into action, lining up acts for the demonstrations.

On August 24, 1934, visitors to the new museum at the Franklin Institute were greeted at the door by the eccentric-looking young scientist Phil Farnsworth, manning a black box on wheels "scarcely larger than a news photographer's camera." A few feet away they saw a four-foot-high cabinet displaying a small screen on which they could see themselves. And so began the first public demonstration of Farnsworth's all-electronic television.

After this initial exposure to the new medium, visitors paid an extra seventy-five cents to enter the two-hundred-seat auditorium where the main television exhibition was taking place. Every fifteen minutes, from 2:00 P.M. to 10:00 P.M. (10:00 A.M. to 10:00 P.M. on Saturdays), the room would empty and refill with four hundred eyes trained on the "greenish fluorescent screen about a foot square" on stage. In the next room, the acts Turner had rounded up performed before the camera and were transmitted via cable to the receiving unit. Everyone from the mayor and other local dignitaries to trained dogs, monkeys, and bears got their time in front of Farnsworth's camera. Turner, a tennis buff and member of the exclusive Philadelphia Cricket Club, brought in Davis Cup stars Frank Shields and Lester Stoefen, who "talked, swung tennis rackets and demonstrated their favorite grips." Chorus girls from the nearby theater district performed their routines, prompting a number of newsmen to leave the auditorium and catch the show live in the next room. A local cellist performed until the hot lights broke his strings.

When the weather was good, Farnsworth would take his camera to the front lawn or up on the roof and telecast outdoor scenes. Boys were recruited from the crowd to spar a few rounds in a makeshift ring or to play football. On the roof, he would point the camera to the traffic below or across the rooftops to the statue of William Penn on top of City Hall. These scenes all came through clearly to the audience inside.

One night the Farnsworth engineer manning the camera on the roof noticed a full moon rising above the city roofs and turned the camera up to it. A reporter wired news of the result to San Francisco, and a couple of days later the *Chronicle* reported:

> First recorded use of television in astronomy was announced yesterday in Philadelphia by Philo T. Farnsworth, young San Francisco scientist.
>
> And it was the man in the moon that posed for his first radio snapshot.
>
> Reproduction of the moon's likeness is just another sensational achievement by the young inventor.

Indeed, the Franklin Institute exhibition was a remarkable success for Farnsworth. "Some of the scientists who watched," reported the *New York Times,* "declared it the most sensitive apparatus yet developed." On the last evening of the exhibition, the entire floor show of a local nightclub crowded into the transmitting area to perform. Dr. Howard McClellan, secretary of the institute, watched the performance and sighed, "I never thought the staid old Franklin Institute would ever come to this. It will never be the same."

"But, Howard," said Dr. Barnes, the head curator, "we've taken in more money these past two weeks than in the last two years."

Television had forced its first compromise of dignity.

4. Meanwhile, in England, John Logie Baird was facing the decisive battle of his life. After a lifetime of struggle, punctuated with ephemeral successes and bitter failures, he was coming to his last great chance. He knew in his bones that if Baird Television failed, he would be broken. He had bounced back from falls in the past, but this time he had climbed too high.

Within a year after returning from America with his new wife, Baird found EMI ready to challenge him for the leadership role in British television. At the end of 1932 they suggested to the BBC that they had a cathode-ray receiver that could provide a picture much clearer than the one the Baird system offered, and they asked for a chance to demonstrate this. The demonstration was a complete success, with the BBC's chief engineer reporting to his superiors that the system was "by far the best wireless television I have ever seen." The BBC invited EMI to move their equipment into Broadcast House for further experimentation, with an eye to participating in the regular broadcast schedule.

Baird Television protested that the BBC invitation violated at least the spirit of the agreement between the BBC and Baird and that EMI wasn't really a British company at all. In a formal protest to BBC chairman Reith, Baird charged that EMI was "virtually controlled by the Radio Corporation of America, which surely controls quite enough of the world's communications without the home of British broadcasting taking it under its wing."

This was the same jingoistic argument that Baird had found so reprehensible when David Sarnoff had made it against the Baird interests in the United States. In this case it was only partially successful. The BBC decided to allow EMI to experiment from Broadcast House but not yet to make any publicly available broadcasts.

In the spring of 1933 the BBC asked for a head-to-head competition between the two companies, and EMI won easily as each demonstrated their capabilities: the cathode-tube receiver outdid Baird's mechanical sets at every turn. But still the BBC remained in Baird's corner; they had a full share of corporate inertia, and once having accepted Baird, they found it hard to desert him. EMI was now having the same problems that Baird had had earlier with the BBC.

On the other hand, the board of Baird Television saw clearly that the future of Nipkow disks and mechanical television was limited. Although Baird himself remained adamantly opposed to electronic systems, he was by this time no longer running a one-man show. Indeed, he had essentially retired to his laboratory, where he continued to tinker, and the company was coming to depend more and more on other engineers they had hired. So when the board decided to get started on cathode receivers, they turned to Captain A. G. D. West.

Captain West had been chief research engineer of the BBC when John Logie Baird put the advertisement in the *Times* back in 1923, and it had been West—together with E. H. Robinson—who had visited Baird's lab at Odhams's request. West had been suitably impressed—so much so, in fact, that by 1931 he had left the BBC and gone to work in television research for the Gramophone Company (later EMI). While there he had been sent to the United States to liaison with Zworykin at the RCA laboratory, so he was up to date on cathode receivers. Subsequently he left EMI, going to the Ealing motion-picture studios as their sound engineer, but he was eager to get back into television, and when Baird Television approached him, he accepted a position as technical director, bringing with him his full knowledge of RCA's and EMI's work on cathode receivers.

He was hired in May 1933; in July he informed the BBC that Baird Television was actively working on a cathode-tube system and hoped to have one ready for demonstration in the near future.

But Baird Television had been dragged squealing into the cathode-ray business only because the competition had already shown the inherent superiority of the system; Baird himself remained stubbornly attached to his old ideas. In an effort to get better resolution, he went to the flying-spot method, in which the Nipkow disk threw scanning beams of light onto the performer who was otherwise in total darkness. The resulting problems were formidable, particularly when the performer was involved in elaborate movements such as dance or acrobatics. Tony Bridgewater, one of the Baird engineers, recalled, "What with the darkness outside the beam and the flickering effect in people's faces, as soon as they were out of the scanning area, if they had to leap out in some act or gymnastic thing, they were liable to crash against the wall or fall on the floor."

No wonder that the Baird board of directors began to try to get rid of its founder. "One of the new directors," Baird lamented, "was an old employee whom . . . I had sacked. . . . Daniel in the Lion's Den was a poor show compared to Baird in the Baird board room. The first thing the boys did was to smash up the Marconi negotiations"—Baird had been pushing for a merger with Marconi; when these negotiations failed, Marconi merged with EMI—"and then they turned on me. Everything I did and had done was faulty." So, at the age of forty-five, he retired to his tinkering. "I had my own private lab, where I did research with my own staff independent of the general work of the company."

In 1934 Marconi-EMI was spending one hundred thousand pounds a year on research and development of the cathode-tube system. Baird Television again tried unsuccessfully to fight back, raising the old cry that Marconi-EMI was an American-owned subsidiary of RCA and that television—which, they claimed, was a British invention—was being stolen from the British people. EMI answered that "everything [in their system] down to the last screw was home manufactured." This, of course, begs the more important question of who had done the research, design, and development rather than just the manufacturing. EMI never would answer the question of whether they had based their designs on Zworykin's work—but of course, they had.

Baird Television changed its tack. Though Captain West had brought with him substantial knowledge of RCA's developments, the Baird company found that RCA held patents on that work that hamstrung Baird's ability to enter the field. The company therefore approached Farnsworth, asking him to bring his Image Dissector to England for a demonstration.

Several companies were now clamoring for attention, so the BBC and the Post Office set up a committee chaired by Lord Selsdon to look into the situation. After a lengthy investigation they recommended that the choice of British television should be between Baird and EMI. And so the final competition was set up: a two-year program of alternating EMI and Baird transmissions, at the conclusion of which the BBC would choose one system and would discard the other.

THIRTEEN

A Death Knell

Is it too late to protest before . . . this barbarous Graeco-Latin jumble ["television"] . . . passes irrevocably into the English language?

Sir John Risley, 1936

1. Farnsworth accepted immediately when he received Baird Television's invitation to demonstrate his system in England. Not only was his company in dire need of cash but here was a chance to gain international recognition. Having his system used for British television could hardly hurt his cause in the United States, where he was mired in ongoing patent litigation with RCA and, it must have seemed to him, likely to remain so for the rest of his life. Baird had no time to lose—they needed an effective demonstration for the BBC—so passage was booked on the next ship leaving for Europe: the SS *Bremen*. Farnsworth packed his clothes and all his equipment and set off with three assistants.

The five-day journey across the Atlantic was a much-needed vacation. For the first time in years Farnsworth was forced to relax with no option of going into the lab to fiddle with his television system. But as they neared Southampton, the stress began to build once again.

The *Bremen* carried no freight, so all the delicate television equipment had to be carried as personal luggage. And because of competition for the transoceanic trade, the German-owned *Bremen* wasn't permitted to dock in England; all passengers and luggage had to be transferred to a British boat at sea. British Gaumont, now the owners of Baird Television, sent a private launch to meet them. They boarded it, then watched as the *Bremen*'s loading crane lowered the carefully packed glass equipment down to the smaller boat. Just before the baggage reached deck, "a huge wave tossed the waiting deck up to meet the cargo, and they collided with a sickening crash."

The potential catastrophe was compounded when they reached shore; His Majesty's customs officials refused to allow the cargo to be admitted as personal luggage and promptly impounded it. Several hours later, after a British Gaumont representative had sorted out the trouble, the crates were transported to Baird Television's new laboratories at the Crystal Palace. One of London's great landmarks, the "palace" was a masterpiece of cast iron and glistening glass built originally in Hyde Park to house the Great Exhibition of 1851 and later torn down and erected again in the suburb of Penge. There, in the south tower, Farnsworth and his crew finally got to inspect their precious equipment. Baird engineers crowded around the boxes, eager to see the electronic tubes that were going to save their jobs, but they were quickly disappointed; the boxes opened to reveal a "jumble of chassis broken off their supports and lying in a heap at the bottom. They shrugged and went back to work, obviously not expecting much help from that direction."

But their gloom was premature. Left alone to unpack, the Farnsworth group found that miraculously all the tubes were unbroken and that the electrical components had also come through unscathed. The damage was superficial, mainly to the mechanical supports. Within a few days, the apparatus was set up and operating. Now the Baird engineers once again formed a crowd around the Farnsworth group, admiring the clear electronic picture.

As Farnsworth told it later to his wife, he went off immediately to find Baird himself, to show him the high-quality picture before something else went wrong:

> All the way back to the studio Mr. Baird was busily extolling the virtues of his mechanical system over Farnsworth's. As they came to the door, Mr. Baird, still in his argument, caught sight of the picture on

the monitor and became silent. He advanced slowly, as if hypnotized, until he was standing directly before it. He stood there for a time; then breaking the spell with a visible effort, he turned without a word and left. With great empathy, Phil watched him go, aware Mr. Baird had seen the death knell of his beloved spinning disc.

Farnsworth and his right-hand man, Skee Turner, met several times a week with a Baird group for hard-line negotiations regarding the patent licensing agreement. Sir Harry Greer, a member of Parliament and chairman of the Baird board of directors, began by pointing out Baird's superiority in manpower and facilities. "You may have the advantage at the moment," he told them, "but who knows? Next year it may be us." Baird Television was certain to make significant improvements in the Farnsworth system once it had full rein to work with it. With this in mind, Sir Harry felt that a simple cross-licensing agreement, in which neither side would have to pay patent royalties, was the appropriate contract.

Farnsworth and Turner didn't even consider accepting this offer. If they hadn't been in such need of immediate cash back home, they might have terminated the meetings right there. Instead, Turner spoke for both of them and informed Sir Harry that they would without question require royalties, as well as an immediate cash payment of fifty thousand dollars. Sir Harry replied gravely that when Mr. Ostrer, chairman of the board of British Gaumont, heard of such outrageous demands, he might cut off negotiations outright. Arguments flew back and forth in an apparent stalemate, until Turner asked if he might consult with Farnsworth alone for a moment.

Alone in an adjoining office, Turner and Farnsworth looked at each other helplessly. They couldn't sign an agreement without royalties, but they needed the cash much more than they were letting on. Then Turner saw a bottle of scotch whiskey and a glass on top of a cabinet. Although neither of them ever drank alcohol, "Skee poured a stiff drink and handed it to Phil, who gulped it down. Then he poured one for himself. Their eyes met, and they both knew what they were going to do."

Back at the conference table, they announced that they wouldn't budge from their position: an immediate cash payment and future royalties. Sir Harry repeated his doubts, and the meeting broke up for the day.

The next day, after a sleepless night, word came that Mr. Ostrer had capitulated; the fifty thousand dollars would be transferred immediately, and Baird Television would sign an agreement to pay royalties for using Farnsworth technology. Once again Farnsworth's determination to retain control of his own patents—aided by some fine single-malt scotch—had served him well. An inventor less confident in his creation might have taken a quick cash payment without future royalties. But for Philo Farnsworth, it would have been easier to sell his own child than to give up ownership of his electronic television system.

After two months on British soil, Farnsworth sailed home on the luxurious HMS *Majestic* with his child still in his arms and fifty thousand dollars in his pocket to help raise it to adulthood. He also had, though he didn't yet know it, the beginnings of a slowly developing reliance on the powers of hard liquor.

Back home, Farnsworth was planning on using the money from the new licensing agreements with Baird and Fernseh (who had been using Baird's mechanical system but now signed up with Farnsworth) to build a full-scale experimental broadcasting station, akin to the one he had built for Philco, in order to put their new system through the rigorous test of daily broadcasting. But McCargar would hear nothing of the kind. He and Everson were having enough trouble selling stock to finance the daily operations of the lab as it was; the newfound cash would be needed simply to keep things going. McCargar was increasingly irritated by the inventor's lack of touch with the real world, while Farnsworth was feeling more and more hampered by what he saw as McCargar's shortsightedness. Phil still had patent control over many of the basic ingredients of television, but he lacked the financial independence to take advantage of it. And meanwhile the competition was catching up with him—if they hadn't passed him already.

Then, in the summer of 1935, a momentous decision was handed down in the first of Farnsworth's great patent battles with Vladimir

Zworykin and RCA. Back on May 28, 1932, Farnsworth's attorneys had declared patent interference 64,027 against Zworykin. It involved Zworykin's 1923 patent application (still pending) for an electronic television system and Farnsworth's patent number 1,773,980 (filed January 7, 1927, issued August 16, 1930), which was based on Farnsworth's claim of being the first to build an operating electronic system.

In fact, the entire interference was based on one claim—that Farnsworth conceived "an apparatus for television which comprises means for forming an electrical image, and means for scanning. . . ." In their preliminary statement, the Farnsworth team alleged "conception, disclosure and drawings during the period January 1, 1922 to April 30, 1922, a written description on August 4, 1926, and a reduction to practice on January 7, 1927."

In the course of this legal battle, Don Lippincott traveled to Salt Lake City to find Justin Tolman, Farnsworth's high school teacher whom he had told about his television scheme. Tolman agreed to give a deposition, during which he recounted in exact detail his conversations of more than a decade before with the fifteen-year-old Farnsworth. He also "took from his pocket a well-worn sheet torn from a small pocket notebook whereon Phil had sketched his Image Dissector tube, saying, 'This was made for me by Philo early in 1922.'"

But this testimony, however dramatic, was eventually irrelevant; the U.S. Patent Office's examiner for the case ruled that Tolman's testimony had "no more weight than oral testimony," was "of no value in proving the date of the alleged originals," and was "clearly insufficient to enable a person skilled in the art to construct the Farnsworth device and practice the invention . . . and clearly insufficient to corroborate the testimony of Farnsworth that he disclosed a complete and operative embodiment of the invention."

That sounded bad, but the crucial question remained whether Zworykin had actually produced the system described in his 1923 application. A Mr. Mouromtseff, a Westinghouse engineer, testified that he was shown Zworykin's conception in 1919; other expert witnesses recalled being told of the device in 1921 and 1923, but none could corroborate that an actual working system had been built. On the other

side, Dr. Leonard Loeb of the University of California and others testified to the operation of the Farnsworth system. Both Farnsworth and
Zworykin submitted to intense cross-examination, and various attorneys for both sides were dispatched across the country collecting testimony. The battle cost Farnsworth's company over thirty thousand
dollars and RCA much more.

Final briefs were given on April 16, 1934, and a final hearing was
held eight days later. Fifteen months after that, on July 22, 1935, a
forty-seven-page decision was finally handed down, ruling that "Philo
Taylor Farnsworth, junior party, be awarded the priority of invention
on his system of television." The crucial reason given was that Zworykin's original device, even if it had worked, would not have satisfied
Farnsworth's definition of an "electrical" system:

> Zworykin has no right to make the count because it is not apparent
> that the device would operate to produce a scanned electrical image
> unless it has discrete globules capable of producing discrete space
> charges and the Zworykin application as filed does not disclose such
> a device.

This was to be Farnsworth's greatest victory. With it, David Sarnoff
was denied total control of television; it appeared that he would have to
share the prize.

Fresh from his legal victory, Farnsworth gave a demonstration to members of the Press and Radio Editors Association on July 30, 1935, at the
studio in Chestnut Hill. Two screens were shown, one receiving a signal by wire, the other by radio. The wire reception was on a fourteen-
inch screen that produced a clear black-and-white picture "of a very
high order of excellence, equal to the average home-movie in detail,
brilliance and contrast." The radio transmission was picked up on a
smaller, seven-inch screen that glowed with a greenish tinge. Both
showed pictures of 240 lines at twenty-four frames a second. The transmitter for both was located in the next room and sent pictures of
Mickey Mouse and a dancing chorus, both of which came from

On Christmas Eve 1883, a twenty-three-year-old Berlin engineer, Paul Nipkow, conceived of an *elektrisches Telescop*. It featured a spinning disk with a sequence of holes that spiraled inward, forever after known as the Nipkow disk. (*Bosch Technische Berichte* 1979)

In 1908 A. A. Campbell Swinton, a consulting engineer in London, was the first to propose that "the problem [of television] can probably be solved by the employment of two beams of kathode rays." He designed such a system but never built it. (Royal Television Society)

In 1906 a German engineer, Max Dieckmann, was the first person to attempt to create a picture with a cathode-ray tube. In 1925 he designed an all-electronic television system, but there is no evidence that he ever made it work. (*Bosch Technische Berichte* 1979)

Boris Rosing, a physicist at St. Petersburg's Institute of Technology, applied for the first cathode-receiver patent in 1907. In 1910 he made a far greater discovery: a young student named Vladimir Zworykin. (Hayka, Moscow, 1964)

In the 1890s Charles Francis Jenkins invented the world's first practical movie projector, only to see his idea stolen. "It's the old story," he wrote. "The inventor gets the experience and the capitalist gets the invention." (Virginia Roach)

Work on his motion-picture projector led Jenkins to develop an apparatus for "transmitting images to a distance by electricity." In 1922 he demonstrated his machine, which used a prismatic ring to scan photographs. (*Scientific American*)

Between 1923 and 1925 John Logie Baird, an eccentric, sickly Scotsman with no scientific training whatsoever, developed a working television system based on the Nipkow disk. His only previous success had been the "Baird Undersock." (Malcolm Baird)

In 1925 Selfridge's department store in London presented "The First Public Display of Television": John Logie Baird's Televisor. Viewers looked through a narrow tube to see "outlines of shapes transmitted only a few yards." (Malcolm Baird)

Captain Oliver George Hutchinson invested in his old colleague's television venture and became business manager. In 1927 the company went public, and "Hutchey" and Baird enjoyed lavish lunches daily. (Malcolm Baird)

Baird's favorite television model in 1925 and 1926 was "Stooky Bill," a ventriloquist's dummy. In October, 1925, Baird wrote, "the dummy's head formed itself on the screen with what appeared to me almost unbelievable clarity. I had got it!" (Malcolm Baird)

With the Nipkow disk, a bank of powerful light bulbs was needed to illuminate the subject to be scanned —in this case, Baird and his dummies in his laboratory. (Henley Publishing Company 1929)

Ernst Alexanderson, General Electric's top scientist, was already famous as "the man who made radio encircle the globe" when he turned his attention to television in 1923. "It behooves us to reason out," he said in late 1926, "whether the results we expect to get will be worthwhile even if our most sanguine hopes are fulfilled." (Hall of History Foundation)

Using a Nipkow-disk system, Alexanderson and GE presented the world's first televised drama, *The Queen's Messenger,* on September 12, 1928. One camera was trained on the head of each actor (who never moved), and a third showed the hands of "doubles" handling small props. (Hall of History Foundation)

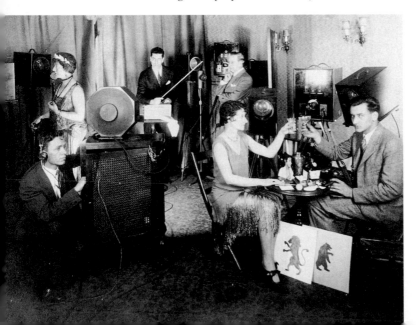

In 1928 Francis
Jenkins initiated the
first television boom
with his Radiomovies
broadcasts. Viewers
could purchase their
own Radiovisor
(above) or build their
own from instructions,
and tune in Monday,
Wednesday, and
Friday evenings for
"Pantomime Pictures
by Radio for Home
Entertainment" (right).
(Jenkins Laboratories)

Dénes von Mihály, a Hungarian physicist, published the first book exclusively about television in 1923. On May 11, 1928, living in Berlin and supported by the Reichspost, he gave a demonstration of his Nipkow-disk Telehor, misleadingly called "the first true demonstration of electrical television." (*Bosch Technische Berichte* 1979)

Philo Farnsworth, a farm boy with only a high school education, secured private financing for his television dream at the age of nineteen. Three years later, in 1928, he had built a cathode-ray system that could transmit from a motion-picture projector. It was the first working all-electronic television system. (Special Collections, Univ. of Utah Library)

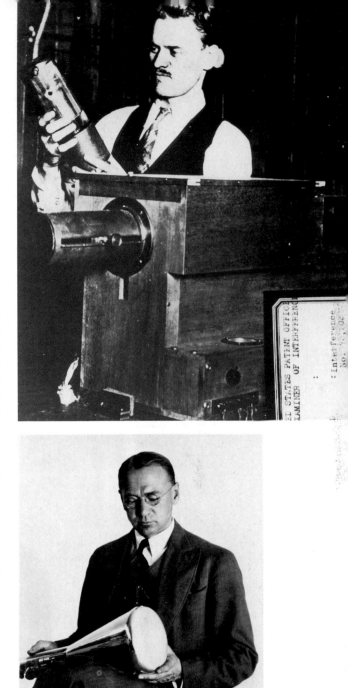

By 1928 the patent race was on between Farnsworth and Vladimir Zworykin. Farnsworth (top) posed for a patent photo with his Image Dissector camera tube around the time the *San Francisco Chronicle* proclaimed: "S. F. MAN'S INVENTION TO REVOLUTIONIZE TELEVISION." Zworykin (bottom) sat in 1929 with his Kinescope receiver tube, which was superior to Farnsworth's Oscillite. But Zworykin still didn't have a workable cathode-ray camera tube. (Farnsworth: Special Collections, Univ. of Utah Library; Zworykin: David Sarnoff Research Center)

A plastic model of Felix the Cat provided a willing test model for RCA's experimental transmissions in 1929 and 1930. Felix stood atop a phonograph turntable in front of a Nipkow-disk camera (above). The result was a 60-line picture on Zworykin's Kinescope receiver (left). (David Sarnoff Research Center)

By 1929 Farnsworth's all-electronic system was working well enough for him to form a public company with his investors. At twenty-two, he had made his dream a reality, and his share of his company's stock was worth well over $100,000. (Special Collections, Univ. of Utah Library)

The Flying Spot Scanner

Cathode radio television station on which Baron von Ardenne of Germany has been experimenting since 1928. The transmitter and receiver (inset) will be exhibited in a forthcoming Berlin Radio Exposition. The images are seen on the end of the tube in the square aperture of the receiver.

In 1931 German wunderkind Manfred von Ardenne's system grabbed the spotlight at the Berlin Radio Exhibition. It was hailed as "the world's first all-electronic system" despite the fact that Farnsworth had demonstrated his system three years before. (Manfred von Ardenne)

Baird gave experimental broadcasts in Berlin in 1929, was a founding member of the German Fernseh company, and in 1931 visited Manfred von Ardenne in his Lichterfeld laboratory. "Other broadcasting authorities are more interested in my television transmission than you are," he warned the BBC. (Manfred von Ardenne)

In late 1936 Farnsworth had a fully operating television studio in the Philadelphia suburb of Wyndmoor. Eleven-year-old "Smiles" Blum and "Baby Dolores," four, were favorite performers, along with the Nick Ross Orchestra. The audience was limited to the Farnsworth engineers and enthusiasts who built their own receivers (Special Collections, Univ. of Utah Library)

While various interests in the U.S. quarreled about broadcasting standards and whether commercial television was ready, the BBC strode forward. After EMI defeated Baird in the 1936 head-to-head competition, the BBC began the world's first commercial service, and receiver manufacturers such as Marconiphone raced to capture a new market.

On April 20, 1939, David Sarnoff stood before NBC television cameras at the World's Fair in Flushing, New York, and began the country's first regular television broadcasts. "Now," he said, "we add radio sight to sound." Farnsworth, embroiled in the bureaucratic mess of starting Farnsworth Television and Radio Corporation, was nowhere to be seen. (David Sarnoff Research Center)

After the war Zworykin no longer worked directly on television research, turning to other projects, but he remained RCA's television star. Over his objections, RCA would always proclaim him "the inventor of television." In sharp contrast to Farnsworth, he died a wealthy, well-honored man. (David Sarnoff Reasearch Center)

David Sarnoff masterminded RCA's "holy crusades" to develop a commercial television system in the 1930s and to create a compatible electronic color system in the 1950s. He was perhaps a more potent force than any one scientist or inventor in the drive to create television. (David Sarnoff Research Center)

motion-picture film. They also gave a transmission of a live orchestra. Despite the small screen, the *New York Times* described "a clarity and sharpness of definition that surprised many of the observers," although "the images could not be considered perfect because of an oscillation which sometimes distorted them."

In speaking to the group, Farnsworth declared his intention "to receive the picture on a small tube and then optically project it onto a screen of convenient size," once again letting his enthusiasm get the best of him, for he had no means of doing this at the time. He did admit that he was "not ready, however, to discuss this development" or estimate when he thought commercial television might happen, in view of the fact that "some former predictions haven't turned out too well." His reluctance once again fell by the wayside, however, when pressed on the latter issue—would it be three years, five years? "Sooner than that," he shot back. "It should come in less than a year. Receiving sets can be put on the market at any time. The obstacle is the erection of transmitting stations." To help traverse this hurdle, he said, he planned to build transmitting stations soon in Philadelphia and San Francisco, and later one in New York City. The radio industry needn't worry, he promised; he intended not to overthrow it but rather to improve it.

Farnsworth now felt urgent pressure to get commercial television going, since he was now in basic control of the important early patents of electronic television. His first patent, issued in 1930, would fall into the public domain in 1947, after which he would receive no credit or royalties; each year that passed by, he felt, was one year of royalties lost. Sarnoff and RCA, on the other hand, for the same reason stood only to gain by delaying the start of commercial television. And Sarnoff, with the financial power of RCA, had considerable lobbying influence with the nation's governing agencies. "Unable to make any headway in getting Washington to move on commercial television," wrote Pem, "Phil took every opportunity to announce to the press that television was indeed ready for the public."

Farnsworth also felt constant pressure from McCargar to keep costs down just when he wanted to open things up and move ahead with broadcasting. Everson, in New York, found himself forever between them, trying to keep peace even while he labored to sell stock to keep the operation going. It was around this time that Farnsworth began to turn to alcohol for relaxation from the pressures of his crusade. A glass of scotch may have gotten him through his negotiations with Baird, but in the future alcohol would only slow him down.

2.   By this time RCA was using the Iconoscope to scan images with 343 lines at a rate of thirty frames per second. They had previously been scanning twenty-four frames a second because this was compatible with the movie film they were transmitting, but with the new brightness levels achieved by the Kinescope, twenty-four frames (or forty-eight fields a second: remember, two fields were interlaced to form one complete picture frame) wasn't fast enough to eliminate the flicker phenomenon. They chose thirty frames (sixty fields) to correspond to the United States' uniform sixty-cycle power source, and this served to eliminate both the flicker and the problem of ripples flowing across the screen. In England (and the rest of Europe) the power source was fifty cycles, and so EMI was using twenty-five frames (fifty fields) per second. These differing standards have prevailed ever since, and that's why today a European television set will not work in the States, and vice versa.

In September 1934, Alda Bedford, who had worked on Alexanderson's GE television project in the late 1920s and had come over to RCA with the other GE and Westinghouse personnel in 1930, applied for the first American patent for a camera tube that combined Farnsworth's Image Dissector and Zworykin's Iconoscope. In the Image Iconoscope (Figure 14), the image would be focused onto a photoelectric plate that emitted electrons onto a secondary plate, as in Farnsworth's tube. Then, as in the Iconoscope, a high-velocity electron beam would scan the secondary mosaic, which operated on the storage principle. This new tube, combining the best of both systems, would eventually supplant the Iconoscope.

RCA's British partner EMI had already applied for an almost identi-

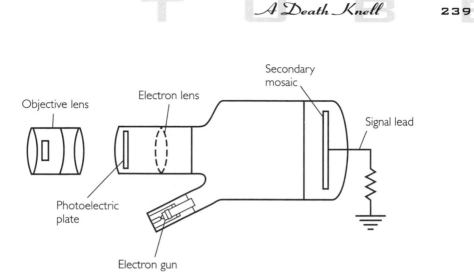

Figure 14. The Image Iconoscope

cal patent in May, designed by Hans Gerhard Lubszynski and Sidney Rodda. A patent interference ensued, and eventually Bedford was able to prove that he had conceived of the tube earlier than his English colleagues. RCA thus won the interference, and the Image Iconoscope (the name developed by EMI) became RCA's property (EMI would have to pay royalties for it and would call their eventual version the Super Emitron). As the television historian Albert Abramson put it, "When it came to patents and interferences, RCA recognized no one, including an ally such as EMI!"

In late 1934 Gregory Ogloblinsky, the most important scientist after Zworykin on the RCA television project, was killed in an automobile accident while vacationing in France. He had only been in the States a few years, but it was long enough to develop the Iconoscope into an impressive working electronic camera tube. Though he would never see the full fruits of his labors, he certainly could see in the months before his death that television was going to happen.

Some six months later, in May 1935, his Iconoscope took center stage. EMI had responded to the formal two-year competition with Baird by unveiling a 405-line "high-definition" system, using their version of the Iconoscope. Evidently shocked into action by this news from London, David Sarnoff made up his mind.

He had been waffling for some time. Despite his public assurances that television would never supplant radio, he had his private fears that a commercial television boom could cut into RCA's hugely profitable radio business. Consequently, he had made a decision to put television on a back burner for a few years while the Camden lab perfected their product and the radio industry forged a permanent niche in public demand.

In December of 1933 his old friend Major Edwin Armstrong, with four patents on his new FM radio system, had invited Sarnoff to come to his Columbia University labs for a demonstration. As described in the Prologue to Part One, Sarnoff was delighted with the high fidelity of this new type of radio transmission and invited Armstrong to use RCA facilities to further his research. In March of 1934, he had canceled all television transmissions from the Empire State Building and turned that facility over to Armstrong. On June 16, Armstrong made his first successful FM transmissions from the skyscraper, and he continued his tests throughout the rest of the year.

This move by Sarnoff gave a strong signal to radio's advertisers, merchandisers, and public that radio would dominate broadcasting for years to come. But now, barely one year later, the situation had changed. Actually, two factors had come together. Armstrong's tests had been very successful; indeed, they had been *too* successful. The advantages over normal AM radio were clear and overwhelming, but the system was too complex; when Sarnoff had asked Armstrong for a "little magic box" to eliminate static, he hadn't expected an entirely new system that could not be attached to the old. The last thing he wanted was to have to scrap all of RCA's immensely profitable radio sets and begin making new ones from scratch.

Second, the news from London of a 405-line television system, which promised much better resolution and less flicker than the RCA equipment, threatened to leave RCA and the United States in the back-water of television. Nightmares of RCA having to buy licensing rights and equipment from someone else cemented Sarnoff's decision.

Major Armstrong received the order to take his equipment out of the Empire State Building, and Sarnoff made a dramatic announcement at the annual RCA stockholders' meeting. At a projected cost of one million dollars, television was reemerging from the laboratory into the sunshine—back to the top of the Empire State Building. Sarnoff acted as though he had never canceled the earlier program of tests, and the *New York Times* bought it: "First Field Tests in Television, Costing $1,000,000, to Begin Here," ran the front-page headline. Sarnoff was "extending an invitation to the research experts to emerge from the seclusion of their scientific dens and use the great open spaces as a proving ground."

"Let me emphasize," said Sarnoff, still wary of upsetting the booming radio industry that had brought RCA enormous profits the previous year, "that while television promises to supplement the present service of broadcasting by adding sight to sound, it will not supplant or diminish the importance and usefulness of sound broadcasting." Carefully downplaying the advances made in Camden, he likened a television viewer's vantage point to watching a parade from the window of an office building or watching a World Series baseball game from a nearby rooftop.

He estimated that it would take the million dollars and twelve to fifteen months to install the new equipment and begin tests, according to a three-point plan: establish the most modern, high-tech transmitting station in the United States; manufacture a limited number of receiving sets to be placed at strategic positions for testing purposes; and "develop an experimental program service with the necessary studio technique to determine the most acceptable form of television programs." By transmitting from 1,200 feet above the ground, wrote Orrin Dunlap in the *New York Times,* RCA could "at least depend on the waves to blanket a twenty-five-mile area around New York. That encompasses a vast population, a great potential market for radio-vision receivers should 'the craze' spread."

This well-publicized announcement had two immediate consequences. First, Sarnoff made television research top priority, funneling
more money to Camden and letting his scientists know that he wanted
the most advanced system possible when the transmitter became ready
in a year's time. Second, he lost one of his best friends.

He offered to use Armstrong's FM for the sound component of television but told the Major clearly that he had no intention of revamping
his already-existing radio business. Armstrong would have no part of
that. He vacated the premises in anger and, selling off some of his RCA
stock, built his own four-hundred-foot FM transmitting tower in the
Palisades in New Jersey, across the Hudson river northwest of Manhattan.

Armstrong would never give up his fight for FM, a bitter struggle
that would eventually end in tragedy. By all accounts the most upright
and dignified of men, a figure of "scrupulous probity," Armstrong didn't
let his disagreement with Sarnoff tarnish his friendship or respect for
him—yet. At the stockholders' meeting in May, when Sarnoff made his
"one-million-dollars" announcement, Armstrong had already been
given his eviction notice; suspecting that Sarnoff was in need of support, however, he rose to his feet and addressed the assembly.

> I didn't come here to make a speech. I didn't come here to get into a
> row. I have been a stockholder since 1915, since the days of the old
> Marconi Company. I have seen the inside of radio from the beginning
> to the end. I want to say that the man who pulled this company
> through during the difficult times of the General Electric, Westing-
> house, RCA mix-up with the government was its president, Mr. Da-
> vid Sarnoff. I think you would have been wiped out if it hadn't been
> for him. I know what I am talking about. I tell you, I wouldn't have
> his job for $500,000 a year. I don't agree with everything, for I have a
> row on with him now. I am going to fight it through to the last ditch.
> I just wanted to tell you what you owe to Sarnoff.

The next day, Sarnoff, deeply moved, wrote a note to Armstrong:
"Doubtless I have made many mistakes in my life, but I am glad to say

they have not been in the quality of the friends I selected for reposing my faith."

Unfortunately, their friendship, however deep, could not survive the coming battle between FM and television. In 1948 Armstrong brought suit against RCA, claiming that the corporation "had conspired to discourage FM, had attempted to persuade the FCC to allocate to it an inadequate number of suitable frequencies, and had illegally obstructed an application of Armstrong's in the Patent Office." The suits dragged on for years; by 1953 Armstrong was devoting all of his time and considerable talents to the legal proceedings. His fortune was dwindling, and his nerves were frayed; he looked a decade older than his sixty-four years.

On the night of January 31, 1954, Armstrong wrote a sad but warm letter to his wife. His last words were "God keep you and may the Lord have mercy on my soul." Then he put on his hat and coat, pulled on a pair of gloves, and stepped out of a thirteen-story window. His body lay on the sidewalk until daylight, when a passerby found it.

The race to create television left Armstrong in its wake, bitter and miserable. But he was far from alone in that; by the time commercial television became a way of life, he would have copious and distinguished company.

3. On April 24, 1936, the Camden Fire Department, responding to a call, rushed to the scene of a supposed blaze. Reaching the site, they scaled their ladders to the top of a building and doused the rooftop, from which black smoke curled toward the sky. Pedestrians gathered on the sidewalk below, and traffic slowed to a crawl.

One mile away, another group watched the scene with far more excitement. They saw it in green-tinted black and white, on the five-by-seven-inch screen of a Kinescope television receiver. One year after Sarnoff's announcement of his new one-million-dollar television testing program, preparations were right on schedule. And now, two months before the new Empire State Building setup was to begin operating, RCA was staging a "preliminary" demonstration in Camden for the press. The fire was imaginary, the smoke artificial, but the all-electronic television transmission was quite real.

"Passers-by who gathered in the street were pictured unbeknown to them," wrote Dunlap in the *New York Times,* "as were automobiles rushing across the Philadelphia-Camden bridge in the background. Even the billboards and budding trees showed up clearly in the radio picture. The clamor of the community came clearly over the loud-speaker."

Not since May 22, 1932—four years earlier—had there been any demonstration of RCA's television activity; everything going on in the interim had been secreted in the remote, off-limits Camden laboratory. Now the results of those four years' research were startling. At that 1932 demonstration, when the Kinescope receiving tube had been shown for the first time, Zworykin's team had used a mechanical trans-mitter to send a picture with 120 lines at twenty-four frames per second. Now, not only were they using their Iconoscope, with no moving parts whatsoever, but their picture had 343 lines, transmitted thirty frames each second, and was sensitive enough to televise outdoor scenes with natural lighting.

Two months later, on June 29, thirteen and a half months after Sar-noff said it would take twelve to fifteen, RCA and NBC began their all-electronic experimental television broadcasts from the Empire State Building. With "no statement, no ballyhoo," as a company spokesman put it, they began broadcasting from the ten-kilowatt transmitting tower along a six-meter wave to between fifty and one hundred official receiving sets installed in homes and offices around the metropolitan area and to several mobile receiving units that monitored reception from various spots in the city.

The ballyhoo came a week later. On July 7, Sarnoff organized and presided at a gala event at Radio City, where he demonstrated the new system for all RCA licensees, "meaning virtually the entire industry." Both film and live shots of Bonwit Teller models parading before the au-dience and the camera were transmitted by cable and radio waves from Radio City to the Empire State Building; from there they were broadcast back to the Radio City auditorium. It was an elegant affair, with one RCA man for every five guests to ensure both fastidious attention and secrecy (no one was allowed to see inside the receivers). After the show, a fleet of a hundred taxis took everyone to a banquet at the Waldorf Astoria. "Each guest," Jesse McCargar wrote to George Everson in San Francisco, "had his own waiter, whose duty it was to see that the guest at least got enough to drink—and in most cases, more than enough. All during the demonstration and the talks at the dinner they kept emphasizing that July 7th was a great day in history that they would be able to tell their grandchildren about."

Sarnoff was either feeling sincerely magnanimous that night or else he was bent on projecting magnanimity: "There was room for all in this new industry of unfathomable potential," biographer Kenneth Bilby remembered him proclaiming; "television was too great in its promise for all mankind to be the exclusive preserve of any one company, and RCA was prepared to share the fruits of its pioneering with all others, including foreign licensees." Sarnoff even went out of his way to mention Farnsworth's name and to say that it was one "to be reckoned with."

His goodwill may well have been disingenuous. RCA had lost their important patent interference battle to Farnsworth just under a year before, with the U.S. Patent Office giving the young man (still only twenty-eight) "the priority of invention for his system of television." This was for the Image Dissector–type tube, not Zworykin's Iconoscope storage tube. But Bedford (and Lubszynski and Rodda) had already conceived of the Image Iconoscope, which combined the two types of tubes, and it was probably apparent to Sarnoff that this would be the way of the future. Although he may still have held out hopes that he could buy out Farnsworth, he must have begun to realize that his mighty corporation would eventually have to share patent control with the upstart independent.

4. In the fall of 1936, Farnsworth was called back to London: Baird Television, preparing for the BBC's two-year competition, was having trouble getting its system, using the Farnsworth camera, to produce a good enough picture. Farnsworth wasn't really feeling up to travel—financial pressures and the television race were getting to him—but he agreed to come if Baird would arrange a slow cruise ship and passage for his wife.

In London he spent long days at the Crystal Palace, tinkering with the Baird setup, while Pem enjoyed London and followed the scandal about King Edward and Wallis Simpson in the daily papers. At night, if Farnsworth wasn't collapsed in bed with a room-service meal, they went out for an elegant dinner or went dancing at the Hotel Savoy, where Pem wore her new wine-colored Spanish lace gown and Phil his top hat and tails. By the time the BBC demonstration was under way, Farnsworth was truly exhausted. His condition was not helped by the news from the States: "Cliff [Gardner] wrote that Jess McCargar had been causing problems again. He had sent Russ Pond, a former stockbroker, to take charge of the lab, and the situation was grave." Farnsworth wrote back asking Gardner to represent him in all management discussions, and he and Pem left for the French Riviera.

The next few weeks saw John Logie Baird's career come to a dramatic climax. The future of British television rested on the BBC and their decision as to which company's technology would be adopted as the official British system.

The future did not look good for Baird. The BBC was evidently swayed to allow Baird Television to remain in contention only because of Baird's stature as a pioneer and because he was using Farnsworth's Image Dissector. (Obviously, John Logie was not pleased: Farnsworth is a name that never once appears in Baird's autobiography. Of course, by now, no one in Baird Television was complaining about EMI's American connections; with their own reliance on Farnsworth, it would have been ridiculous to do so.) But for some reason, never established, Farnsworth's camera didn't produce the same quality in England as it did in the States, while EMI had their version of Zworykin's Iconoscope, which they called the Emitron, and a 405-line picture (compared to Baird's 240 lines). It has been reported, though we can find no verification, that the BBC's chief television engineer had earlier witnessed the EMI and Baird systems and had found EMI to be "infinitely superior. But to have granted the new system to EMI would have provoked a tremendous row in the press and throughout the country," since John Logie Baird had acquired the status of a folk hero. Thus the competition was set up, the result of which (according to this point of view) was a foregone conclusion.

The opening ceremony of the test period took place on November 2, 1936, at the Alexandra Palace, or the "Alley-Palley," as generations of English had called it. Twenty miles outside London, it had been built in 1873 as an exhibition hall; sixty-three years later it was widely known as the venue for the second rank of public entertainments: band concerts, dances, and trade shows. Its distance from central London was compensated for by its situation on top of a 306-foot hill; with the erection of a 300-foot "gaunt, lattice-steel mast" as a television antenna, the engineers obtained a broadcasting height of 600 feet above ground level, making for an impressive transmitting range.

Both companies transmitted the ceremony, with Baird going first and then EMI. The program began with speeches by the chairman of the BBC, the postmaster general, and the chairman of the board of Baird Television—by everyone, it seemed, connected with the development of television except John Logie Baird. Baird himself recalled the incident bitterly in his autobiography: "All the notabilities in any way connected with television appeared on the platform and were televised, all except Mr. Baird, who was not invited but sat in considerable anger and disgust in the body of the hall among the rank and file. Thus is pioneer work recognized. This little episode was but another addition to the host of slights and insults given to me by the BBC."

It was not only the opening ceremonies that displeased him; the test itself did not bode well. "Now we were faced at last with really serious competition," he wrote. "We had against us the whole resources of the vast RCA combine comprising not only the biggest companies in the USA but the great Telefunken Company in Germany and a host of others." As for the Baird organization itself, "we had the leadership of an elderly pedant with no grasp whatever of the situation, backed by an unimaginative and uninterested accountant. . . . As for myself, I at least had realized the situation but . . . was impotent. My codirectors . . . disregarded me."

Baird may have felt personally neglected, but television itself was on everyone's minds. As the tests progressed, the public was swept up in the excitement. People began to take seriously the question of what they—the people who watched the television programs—would be called. This was evidently sparked by publication of the Selsdon Committee's report that had suggested the competition, which referred awkwardly to the watchers as "lookers" or "lookers-in." Letters to the newspapers protested such silly language, suggesting more reasonable words. *Perceptor,* perhaps. Or *audiobserver* (since they both saw and listened to the programs). Similarly, and perhaps a bit simpler, was *lookener* (a hybrid of *looker* and *listener*). There were also *audoseer, invider, telegazer, teleseer, televist,* and *telspector.* Others offered *opticauris, visuel,* or *audivist.*

The word *television* itself was not yet settled. It seemed to make people angry. Aside from the editor of the *Manchester Guardian* ("Television? The word is half Greek and half Latin. No good will come of it"), there was Sir John Risley, a gentleman of the Athenaeum Club, who wondered in a letter to the *Times* whether it was not "too late to protest before . . . this barbarous Graeco-Latin jumble . . . passes irrevocably into the English language?" A few days later a Mr. Kenderdine wrote to the same paper that since the word means to see at a distance, the verb "to televise" must mean "to *see* the program" rather than to broadcast it; in other words, the television people had things quite backwards. It was a comment that would be made about television more and more frequently in times to come.

Alternative words were suggested to the *Daily Telegraph.* Why not call the system a *radioscope,* or a *lustreer, farscope, optiphone,* or *mirascope*? John Logie must have been pleased with the suggestion of *telebaird.* Apparently no one in 1936 came up with the simple words *telly* or *the tube.* As with those for people, the best nicknames for gadgets evolve naturally.

The opening-day broadcast lasted one hour. After the speeches came ten minutes of a Movietone newsreel, a variety show (Adele Dixon and Buck and Bubbles, comedians and dancers), and then the BBC Television Orchestra. This was all broadcast by Baird first and then repeated by EMI. The competition lasted for the rest of the year. According to modern history, there was never any doubt as to its outcome: "The first day was considered a victory for Marconi-EMI. The received pictures were sharp and clear. . . ." The newspaper reports indicated that EMI was sure to win the race, "so why continue?"

But this was not completely fair. True, the London *Times* reported on November 3 that "there was less flickering and more sharpness of detail in the second transmission of speakers than in the first," but then the paper went on to say that "in the transmission of the news events and the variety items there appeared to be little to choose between the two systems." Indeed, the *Times* argued that "the [Baird] system is suitable for televising subjects in the studio. The pictures shown by this method yesterday were excellent in every possible way." Furthermore, "the pictures, *especially those recorded either on ordinary film or on that made half a minute before the transmission,* were as clear in black and white as the usual film entertainment" (italics added). (It was the Baird system—not EMI's—that recorded the performers on quick-developing film and then televised from the film, instead of transmitting live.)

Baird fought hard, and for a while there was active discussion among "viewers" (the *Times*'s term, which was beginning to catch on) as to which system was better. But slowly, day by day, the Marconi-EMI system began to show its superiority. Not only was the Baird spinning-disk camera an idea that would never work well enough but the Farnsworth camera continued to give the Baird group troubles, and eventually they gave up on it entirely. Slowly, opinion began to grow that EMI was winning. And then, on November 30, a raging fire broke out in Baird's research laboratories in the Crystal Palace; by the time it was finally extinguished, there was nothing left.

When the test period was over, the victor was obvious. The BBC adopted the Marconi-EMI system, and suddenly there was nowhere for Baird to go. "After all these years, we were put out of the BBC," he lamented. Then, after going back to his old argument that the BBC should not have accepted what was basically an American system—forgetting once again his own company's desperate attempts to use the Farnsworth camera—Baird hit on the note that really hurt: "In an amazingly short time the Marconi publicity department had established in the public mind that Marconi invented television! All that reached [the public] consciousness was the continual trumpeting of the Marconi publicity—Marconi television, Marconi television. Poor Marconi was dead and buried and when alive he never knew one end of a television apparatus from the other. The first time he ever saw television was in my laboratory."

That was nearly the end for Baird. The company continued to sell receivers, and Baird himself pushed the effort toward pay television, with transmissions directed toward large movie theaters. But in September 1939, when the Nazis marched into Poland, more important matters were at hand. Television receivers became, in Baird's own words, "simply useless junk." Just a few months later, in time for that first wartime Christmas, John Logie sent his former board member and ally Sydney Moseley a terse cable: "Company unable to carry on through lack of funds. Note-holders have installed Receiver. A merry Christmas and a happy New Year!"

Now fifty-one, he tried to get involved with war work, in particular with radar, but the world had passed him by; the government offered him nothing. He tried to conduct research in his own home, but it was impossible under wartime conditions. Mainly he just tried to hold on until the war was over. He knew that television would boom then, and he had a host of plans for plunging right back into the heart of it again.

Sitting one day on the deserted beach of the resort town of Bude, he was staring out over the waters as he had done in 1923 at Hastings. He was lost in thought, sketching his ideas in a small notebook he always carried, when he was arrested by the police on suspicion of being a spy making notes for the coming German invasion.

In his anger, he sputtered incoherently. He told them who he was: "John Logie Baird!" They had never heard of him. That was the unkindest cut of all. They were about to take him away when his wife showed up and managed to convince them that he was, after all, only a "funny and curious" inventor, harmless, who had nothing at all to do with the war.

That was the sad truth. He spent the war years with his wife in "a rather shabby-genteel South London suburb, living in one of those quiet residential hotels which cater for decrepit old renters and aged ladies. It had the atmosphere of those boarding houses which I had known and shunned in my youth."

He lived to see the end of the war; he lived nearly long enough to see his earliest ideas justified as television took off, nearly long enough to start again. But in late 1945 he caught a cold, as he did nearly every winter. It developed into a major illness, as it nearly always did. His recovery was slow and unsure, as it nearly always was. There was only one difference: this time he died.

FOURTEEN

The Zeppelin over the Stadium

*Telefunken is the German arm of the great Radio
Corporation/Marconi group whose tentacles cover the
whole world and which endeavours either to engulf or
destroy all serious competitors who enter its field.*
John Logie Baird

1 .   After leaving England and Baird Television in the fall of 1936, Farnsworth and his wife crossed the Channel to France and tried to unwind. The last couple of years had been particularly stressful for him, with both successes and failures, and more and more he had been seeking refuge in alcohol.

Since leaving Philco, Farnsworth had been hampered by not having his own broadcasting station. There was nothing more important for his work: television could be based on theoretical work, but overwhelmingly its development had to be experimental, and he needed the means to test the changes he was making in his system.

Unfortunately, although broadcasting facilities were an absolute necessity from Farnsworth's point of view, the backers felt that there simply wasn't enough money available. The arguments between McCargar and Farnsworth were growing nasty, the frustrations and tensions between them were building to the breaking point, when Skee Turner announced at dinner one night (before the European trip, when he was still living with the Farnsworths) that he and his father had decided to fund the construction of a new broadcasting station. "Don't worry about the expense," he told Farnsworth. "It will pay for itself."

These were exactly the words Farnsworth had been longing to hear. Work on designing the building began the following morning. Two weeks later the foundation was laid, and a week after that the prefabricated building components were ready. A few months later, experimental broadcasting station W3XPF was on the air from Mermaid Lane in the Philadelphia suburb of Wyndmoor.

The programs were being coordinated by a thin six-foot-seven young man who had shown up two years earlier at the Farnsworth lab in Chestnut Hill looking for work. Lieutenant William Crawford Eddy, the progeny of a long line of high-ranking naval officers, had gone deaf as a child but had learned to read lips well enough to fool the navy—well enough, in fact, to be given the assignment of sound officer on his submarine. To do his job, he had to design an amplifier that turned sound signals from enemy subs into movements on a dial. He patented it as the Eddy Amplifier, and soon the entire navy was using it. Back in the States as a civilian, he became interested in television and decided that he should get into the nascent industry at ground level. Stuck in Philadelphia during a snowstorm, he looked Farnsworth up in the phone book, and by the end of the evening he was a Farnsworth employee.

Eddy had some experience staging shows in the navy, so now he was put in charge of studio operations at the Wyndmoor facility. He made one permanent hire, Nick Ross and his orchestra, with Nat Ragone on piano and Kay Allen, vocalist. Aside from them he depended on the willingness of local talent to perform for the exposure and the experience of the new medium. All ages were welcome: an eleven-year-old girl called "Smiles" Blum was always on call, willing to sing and dance as needed; she became known as "Little Miss Television." Eddy was also the discoverer of "Baby Dolores," a four-year-old who sang and danced on Farnsworth Television.

Like other broadcasting pioneers, the Farnsworth team soon learned the secrets of television makeup and clothing. Certain colors were picked up well, others weren't. Since the cesium photosensitive surface in the camera was ultrasensitive to red, for example, red clothing looked so bright it was almost white on the screen. This fact became apparent when a boxer wearing red shorts appeared to be naked when televised.

The Farnsworth "live" camera at this time had been condensed into a seventy-five-pound unit of only ten by twelve by fifteen inches. It included four lenses of varying focal length mounted on a rotatable disk and was capable of transmitting a 343-line picture with thirty frames per second. Farnsworth claimed that it required only forty foot-candles of light, an estimable improvement in sensitivity over Zworykin's Iconoscope, which needed a thousand foot-candles for a decent picture.

Nineteen thirty-six was a very productive year for Farnsworth. He managed to file for twenty-two patents, all of which were eventually granted. The long delay between filing and issuance would eventually be to his benefit, he knew, since the seventeen-year patent life would extend further into the era of commercial television, so he continued to prepare as many applications as possible. Nine of these patents were for the multipactor electron-multiplier tube alone. Also, as we've seen, Baird in England and Fernseh in Germany were using Farnsworth equipment for their broadcasts, to much acclaim (until Baird's failures late in the year). In the summer, Fernseh used his cameras to help broadcast the Olympic Games.

But money remained a problem. Bill Eddy recalled that he and the others didn't always get paid:

> To eat, we'd go to the Italian market in South Philadelphia and buy a gunnysack of week-old bread for one dollar. Bread, and rabbits that I raised on our farm, constituted my family's menu. We were either naïve or crazy. If morale dropped, Phil would get up on his platform and start spouting his ideas, and we were back in battery again.

The stress of trying to keep up with Zworykin's much better funded laboratory, combined with Farnsworth's own workaholic character, had nearly done him in by the time he was done helping Baird; Pem managed to convince him to take a couple of weeks off in France. His vacation, however, was interrupted in December by the numbing news of the Crystal Palace fire and the subsequent victory of Marconi-EMI. All his stressful work in London had been for naught. After New Year's the Farnsworths returned to England and waded through the mess left by the fire, stayed for a few days in London, and then flew to Germany, despite the warnings of Baird technical director Captain West.

Everywhere they had gone in France, people were on edge, wondering where Hitler would strike first and whether France would be among his targets. But Farnsworth had had several important visitors from Germany to his Philadelphia lab, including Dr. Paul Goerz, the director of Fernseh, and all of them had extended warm invitations to visit Germany. Also, Fernseh owed Farnsworth a good deal of money in royalties from their patent licensing agreement that had been tied up in government red tape, and Farnsworth hoped that by coming in person he would be able to collect it. Phil and Pem, like so many around the world in 1937, had little knowledge of the Nazis and even less political prescience. Enthusiastically, the Farnsworths took off for the land of Goethe and Beethoven.

2.   Their cocoon of naïveté began to unravel in Amsterdam, where they stopped for customs and lunch; their cash and traveler's checks were confiscated, and they were issued only enough reichsmarks to pay for minimal expenses. They were met at the Berlin airport by two uniformed men who introduced themselves as their "courtesy drivers" and took them to the Eden Hotel, an oasis for English and American tourists.

Captain West arrived the next day to facilitate their visit, since Baird had formerly been a partner in Fernseh. Dr. Goerz met them and helped allay their fears by arranging to have one of his own men drive them around. He also took responsibility for entertaining the Farnsworths, showing them all the sights in and around Berlin, including a succession of military parades featuring overpowering displays of artillery, goose-stepping soldiers, and Hitler himself.

On the surface, Germany was beginning to prosper. The trains were clean and running on time, armed conflicts in the streets were a plague of the past, and the countryside was full of happy marching children singing patriotic songs. Behind the facade, however, discerning observers could see ominous movements in the shadows.

One place Goerz wouldn't accompany Farnsworth, for example, was the office of the government official who had visited Philadelphia; apparently this man was very close to Hitler, and Goerz had been a member of the Elite German Cavalry, many of whom Hitler had had shot. Goerz had been spared because of his scientific worth, but he had no intention of popping up in a government office to remind the Führer of his magnanimity.

There were other uncomfortable glimpses of the new world order. A certain Herr Wild, the president of the Zeiss-Ikon Optical Company, one of Fernseh's parent companies, insisted that Farnsworth visit the Stuttgart plant. A vigorous man in his seventies, Wild was hanging onto his position despite his being a Jew. The Nazis had confiscated his cars, so he rode a bicycle to work every day, claiming cheerfully that it kept him in good shape for winter skiing. Alone with Farnsworth, however, he confided his fears for his son Rudolph, a law student. At his request, Farnsworth offered Rudolph a job in the States and got him safely out of Germany before the Holocaust reached a frenzy.

He was less successful in getting his money; Hitler had completely frozen the flow of reichsmarks out of Germany. Resigned to defeat in this matter, Farnsworth set about arranging for the passage home—he and Pem had seen enough of the Nazis.

To their shock, however, they found that their exit visas had been canceled. Repeated attempts to obtain new ones failed, and things were starting to look frightening when Dr. Goerz came to their aid. In a guarded telephone call, he told them to be ready before midnight. He picked them up at their hotel and took them to a train for Hamburg, where they were smuggled onto a transatlantic liner. "A feeling of great relief flooded over us," Pem wrote, "as the SS *Europa* weighed anchor and we headed for home."

3. Indeed, much had changed in Germany during four years of National Socialist rule, and the world of television research was far from immune. Siegmund Loewe, the principal owner of Fernseh as well as the leading manufacturer of radio home receivers, was Jewish, and he and the many other Jews in radio and television had felt the new wave of anti-Semitism for the first time at the annual Berlin Radio Exhibition in August 1933. They were the target of threats, both private and public; the postal official in charge of television, Friedrich Banneitz, was making it clear that no non-Aryans would be allowed to attain positions of importance in the new industry. And the widespread slogan, "Germans, don't buy from a Jew!" began to eat away at Loewe's radio business.

Still, as late as 1934, the hurricane of Nazi ascendancy had hardly caused a ripple in the deep well of American and British investment in German business, including television. The Hungarian Dénes von Mihály's lab was supported not only by the Reichspost but also by the well-known British aircraft industrialist Henry White Smith. Baird Television was still one of Fernseh's principal owners. And Telefunken had signed a patent-sharing agreement with RCA several years before.

By 1935, however, Hitler was insisting that no foreign power should own any part of a German company, and Baird Television withdrew from Fernseh A.G. The Bosch corporation, with the cooperation of partner Zeiss-Ikon, bought up all the Baird stock. The Loewe corporation, the principal owners of Fernseh, tried to protest, but as Luftwaffe Inspector General Erhard Milch later reported, "because the owners of the Loewe company were Jews, they had no success with their protest against Bosch." Over the next two years, Zeiss-Ikon's board would use the new anti-Semitic laws to force Loewe out of Fernseh altogether. In 1938 Siegmund Loewe lost his own once-mighty business, Loewe Radio, and fled to the United States.

Hitler's edicts also forced the dissolution of Mihály's television lab. In 1935, Henry White Smith withdrew his funding, and the lab fell apart, as Mihály no longer had money to pay his staff. He had been the great German hope of the late 1920s; now he was not only a foreigner in an increasingly xenophobic land but he was also barking up the wrong—mechanical—tree.

In 1935 Fritz Schröter, head of physics research for Telefunken, visited the RCA lab in Camden and came back with the exciting news that cathode-ray television was about to obliterate all mechanical systems, and also with a demonstration Iconoscope and the blueprints with which to construct their own models. Telefunken immediately took on the technological leadership and market power in Germany that RCA was about to enjoy in America.

At the beginning of the year, Lord Selsdon had visited Germany to inspect their television efforts and implied mistakenly that the BBC would be starting regular television broadcasting by the end of the year. (Actually, they were not intending to begin until the following year.) "At this, the head of State Radio, Eugene Hadamovsky, said that what the British were intending to do at the end of 1935 we could do well beforehand," said Gerhart Goebel, Germany's leading television historian and a Reichspost employee at the time. "And so on 22 March 1935, from one day to the next, the first television broadcasting service in the world was begun." (Once again, we have a "first" that ignores previous "firsts"; in this case, Jenkins's 1928 broadcasts were forgotten.)

The Reichspost's broadcasts were transmitted using Nipkow disks and consisted of both films and "live" shots with Telefunken's intermediate-film system (in which footage was filmed, immediately developed, and then scanned through the film projector by spinning disk). There were no private television sets in homes; instead, the telecasts were picked up on receivers in eleven public viewing rooms around Berlin.

No high-ranking Nazi officials attended the gala opening of the service, before an audience of fifty to one hundred (depending on whom you ask) invited guests—Reichspost officials, industry representatives, journalists, and some low-ranking Nazis standing in for their superiors. Kurt Wagenfuhr, a journalist present, said, "We suspected that this had been done because if everything went wrong, it could all simply be ignored. If things went well, a few good words about television could still be said in front of the camera." Hadamovsky, who had ordered the premature service, did his best to glorify the proceedings:

> Today, National Socialist broadcasting, in cooperation with the Reichspost and industry, starts regular television broadcasting, as the first broadcasting system on earth. One of the boldest dreams of mankind has become reality. . . . In this moment, on German soil, we are making cultural progress which will someday be considered the culmination of many individual technical developments of the last decades. While we are now breathlessly listening and watching here in the hall, a time of a new, incomprehensible wonder has begun.

Unfortunately, the initial service was less than wonderful, marred by the poor resolution and picture flicker that characterized mechanical television. And even the German press reported the event only in passing; in the *Frankfurter Zeitung*, for instance, it appeared on page twelve, under "World News."

In the end, the "first broadcasting system on earth" didn't amount to much. Before home receivers could be marketed, the whole system was destroyed by a fire at the Berlin Radio Exhibition in August. When German television came back on the air the next year, the British were right with them, and both countries were using Farnsworth and Zworykin electronic cameras.

But in March 1936, the Reichspost gained another "first": the opening of the world's first "television telephone." For twice the price of a regular telephone call, a Berliner could enter the *Fernsehsprechstelle* (television speaking station) at the corner of Kantstrasse and Hardenbergstrasse, just off the busy Kurfürstendamm, and sit in a dark, cramped booth. "Once one had sat down," remembered one customer, "a very harsh beam of light came towards one from out of an aperture, and it was most unpleasant. It dazzled one, and above this light aperture there was a Braun [cathode] tube which had the picture of the person at the other end."

The "other person" was sitting in a similar booth in Leipzig (or, later, in Munich), undergoing the same unpleasantness in order to be scanned by a flying-spot scanner. The *Fernsehsprecher* was one of the last hurrahs for the Nipkow disk, which was used as a transmitter even though the receiver was a cathode tube. When the war started, the service ended; only now, over fifty years later, is the idea of the "television telephone" (or "videoconferencing") resurfacing.

Early in 1936, while the Reichspost was setting up their mechanical "television telephone," an event began to take shape that would provide an opportunity for both Telefunken and Fernseh to showcase their new electronic product: the Eleventh Olympic Summer Games in Berlin. Horst Dressler-Andress was a former Communist and theater director who had become involved with the Nazi party in 1929, thinking that it could help him realize his dream of a German telecommunications network. In 1936, as a counselor in the Ministry of Propaganda, he targeted the Olympics as the event that would make Germany the world's television leader. His boss Joseph Goebbels had even grander designs: the televised Olympics would not only show the advanced state of German television but also the physical superiority of the magnificent Aryan athletes.

When the games opened on August 1 and black sprinter Jesse Owens and the rest of the U.S. athletes marched past Adolf Hitler and a hundred thousand Germans who stood with outstretched right arms in the Nazi salute, Telefunken and Fernseh were there. Fernseh, no longer affiliated with Baird or Loewe, still had their Farnsworth Image Dissector cameras, one transmitting live at the stadium and one in a mobile van that transmitted from intermediate film. Telefunken had three Iconoscope cameras, one at the swimming pool and two at the main stadium, with lenses of 250, 900, and 1600 millimeters—the "Olympia Cannon." Manning the "Cannon" was cameraman Walter Bruch—a former assistant to both von Ardenne and Mihály—who had been in charge of the team that built and fine-tuned it in the months preceding the games. As so often seemed to be the case, they barely made it. "A single time, on the last working Sunday," Bruch recalled, "did we point the camera out of the laboratory into the garden and deem it good enough. We quickly packed it all together, threw it in a truck, and went off to the stadium."

When Jesse Owens won the hundred-meter sprint, Bruch and the Cannon were positioned right at the finish line; Bruch boasted that he had a better vantage point than Hitler. The Führer, of course, probably wasn't too envious; after the black American flew by the great Aryan runners, Hitler quickly left the stadium. Things weren't so cozy down in the trenches, either, where Bruch found himself in a competition of his own with the German Radio commentator, "who kept referring to the brilliant colors of the scene," knowing of course that the Iconoscope was transmitting only in black and white. Bruch remembered:

> The commentator was always saying "Well here comes the Zeppelin over the stadium" or "Hitler is up there," but it was so high that I couldn't do anything with my camera because it wouldn't tilt so high—so what was left to me was to kick him in the back and sometimes even to curse [audibly into his microphone].

The action that Bruch could catch with his camera, though, was transmitted to an audience of about 150,000 over the fortnight, who watched in twenty-eight "television rooms" around the city, as well as in the Olympic Village. But Hitler needn't have regretted having to watch from the stands: the 180-line television picture, as reported by the London *Times*, shook uncontrollably, and "the eye strain being considerable . . . many didn't stay for the remainder of the afternoon events." Fernseh's Farnsworth system "delivered very sharp signals, free from interference components, but only in very bright weather."

Nevertheless, the Nazi government, ignoring Owens's great sprinting victories, celebrated both the show of German strength (they won eighty-nine medals, more than any other nation; the United States was a distant second with fifty-six) and the miraculous display of German scientific achievement in the form of the new television. They didn't bother to mention that their system had been designed by a Russian-American and a farm boy from Idaho.

FIFTEEN

Just Around
the Corner

And so by sunset tonight television will have come from around the corner in quest of its destiny: to find its role in the art of amusing Americans, and to fit in with the social life of the land.

New York Times, April 30, 1939

1. Mechanical television was now history; electronic television was here to stay. But that was not the end of the road. The race to invent TV was not like that for the atomic bomb, where the question was simply "Will it work?" and you had your answer when a section of desert instantly became a mountainous fireball. With television, tinkering and improvements would never end. The question was "How good can you make it in how short a time, staying ahead of the competition but delaying commercialization until the product promises a healthy profit?"

Around the world, television researchers were racing to answer this question. But none of them was able to harness the electron as Farnsworth and Zworykin had.

In Russia, where Boris Rosing had begun the world's first attempt at cathode-ray television, most of the work since 1912 had been based on mechanical systems. In the summer of 1934, Zworykin had accepted an invitation from the University of Moscow to return to his native land to give a series of lectures. Although the Stalin era was not the friendliest of times for former czarist military officers—and despite the U.S. State Department's warning that it could not extend protection to U.S. citizens returning to their country of birth—Zworykin could not pass up the chance to see his remaining family members once again. Sarnoff encouraged him to go; perhaps he could make connections that would lead to RCA doing business with the Soviets. In 1931 RCA had had a radio technical exchange agreement with the U.S.S.R., but this had quickly fallen apart. Sarnoff was now thinking ahead to the possibility of selling television equipment to Russia when it became a commercial commodity.

Zworykin stepped off the train from Berlin into a country far different from the one he had last seen in 1919. All remaining vestiges of his family's former life were gone. His sisters were working in Leningrad, and his mother had passed away during the civil war. "I inquired about Professor Rosing," he wrote later, "but most of the people I asked had never heard of him. Finally, I learned that he had been arrested . . . , was exiled to Archangel, and died soon after." In fact, Rosing had continued his work on television until 1931, when he had become one of the many thousands who fell victim to Stalin's purges. He was given a sentence of three years' deportation to Archangel; presumably his crime consisted of being an intellectual. Unwilling to give up his work, he convinced officials of the Forestry Institute there to give him space, but in 1933, just one year before Zworykin's visit, he suffered a fatal stroke.

Although Zworykin found that the state of the engineering laboratories in Moscow and Leningrad was poor, his lectures were well attended by enthusiastic students. The communications officials with whom he met were equally enthusiastic about buying television equipment from RCA as soon as it was available.

Actually, the Russians were building a lot of equipment of their own by that time, and their television research was energetic, although, since it was obscured by the great screen of Soviet propaganda, it is impossible to establish exact details. For instance, in 1926 "the transmission of moving images . . . was demonstrated" at the Fifth All-Union Convention of Physicists in Moscow, but since no non-Soviet scientists were allowed to attend, we have no confirmation of exactly what was "demonstrated," or even what the word itself meant in this context.

We know that a good deal of work was going on in the Soviet Union, however, from the simple existence of conventions such as the First All-Union Conference on Television, held in Leningrad on December 18, 1931. In that same year an announcement proclaimed that "on April 29 and May 2, in the television laboratory of the All-Union Electrical Engineering Institute, the first transmissions of images by means of radio will be carried out. Live images and photographs will be transmitted. Television amateurs will be able to view those working in the [laboratory] who made this achievement possible, and to see photographs of the leaders of the Revolution. . . . It is hoped that these trial transmissions will evolve into regular transmissions . . . and will increase the effectiveness of one of the most important sectors of the cultural front, one which also has great political significance."

On October 1, 1931, Moscow began a regular television broadcasting schedule, and transmissions were picked up by amateurs as far away as Odessa and Smolensk. But in a land where scientific decisions were made on the basis of politics, immediate results were more important than long-range progress. So in the country where Boris Rosing had begun the world's first attempt at cathode-ray television, research concentrated on the proven mechanical systems. And the world passed Mother Russia by.

In France, the Ministry of Posts, Telegraphs, and Telephones had inaugurated a cathode-ray television service of low definition in 1934, based on the work of Belin's group. The next year they upgraded it to a high-definition 240-line service, designed by M. Barthelemy. For the next few years their research continued, but they made no further significant progress.

In Japan, Kenjiro Takayanagi, an assistant professor at the Hamamatsu Technical College, had begun research into television in 1924. His story is an example of a man who had the right idea but who wasn't in the right place at the right time in history. From the beginning he saw that electronic television was the ideal. He claimed that in 1926 he was able to transmit simple characters, using a Nipkow disk for scanning and a cathode-ray tube for receiving; by 1927 he could transmit faces that were identifiable as faces but not as individuals. He found that he was limited by the gases in his tubes and spent the next few years concentrating on building a high-vacuum cathode-ray tube. By 1931 he was transmitting eighty-line pictures at twenty frames per second in Tokyo.

In 1934 he visited America and Europe and learned firsthand about Zworykin's work. From this point on, he concentrated on building an Iconoscope-type system, and within another year the Japanese research had flowered into a government-supported effort giving excellent results. The Japanese Broadcasting Corporation began to prepare for the next Olympic Games, to be held in Tokyo in 1940.

But by then the Manchurian Incident had metastasized into a full-blown invasion of China. Pearl Harbor followed and television research was no longer important in Japan. Takayanagi was simply in the wrong place at the wrong time.

In England in 1937, Marconi-EMI stood alone and unopposed. Together with the BBC they worked out their final details and began regular programming. Meanwhile, in prewar America, the competition between Zworykin and Farnsworth entered its final stages.

2.   Any improvement in Farnsworth's health from his relaxing stay on the French Riviera in the fall of 1936 was ancient history within twenty-four hours of his return to Philadelphia. First there had been the Crystal Palace fire, and then he arrived home to find his lab in disarray. While he and Pem had been in Europe, a leadership crisis had been erupting at home.

Jess McCargar had shown no respect for the men Farnsworth had left in charge: Arch Brolly, Cliff Gardner, and Frank Somers. So McCargar took it on himself to send Russell Pond to manage the lab in Farnsworth's absence; his son-in-law, George Sleeper, was also working in the lab at the time and seems to have tried to assume a leadership role as well. Together they completely undermined the authority of Brolly, Gardner, and Somers.

On November 5, McCargar wrote to Everson:

> If Archie and Frank had our real interests at heart I think they would welcome any help they could get, even if it were from my son-in-law. . . . Either it is a petty, short-sighted professional jealousy, or it is a frantic cooperation with our competitors.
>
> This situation calls for a strong hand and very prompt action. . . .
>
> Now for God's sake George, don't toss this off with the expression that I am having a pathological outburst.
>
> This situation is terribly serious!

Of course, his antics did suggest paranoia, partially brought on perhaps by the psychological wear and tear of years of financial investment in a risky venture, as suggested by his letter to Pond around the same time:

> I am satisfied in my own mind, as I have told you before, that Archie, Tobe and Frank, being very close, are afraid someone is going to show them up, because as you know, they have been working for years and years to get a picture and never have succeeded. They are pursuing a course that will wreck us unless we stop them.
>
> . . . With [possible phone tapping] in mind, and the continued failure to get a proper demonstration, is it possible that some of the people in whom we have placed every confidence are working against us? Now do not dismiss that idea with "oh, that isn't possible," because *it is possible.*

Just after New Year's, McCargar wrote Everson again:

> . . . and with Russ in Philadelphia to keep close track of things and display some business judgment, which all the rest seem to lack, I think we can go places. . . .
>
> P.S. I think it is of vital importance that Phil be not permitted to negative [sic], or upset, the good work that Russ has been doing. I hope you will keep this in mind constantly and keep Phil on the right track.

When Farnsworth returned from Europe, he exploded, immediately firing Pond and Sleeper and calling McCargar in San Francisco to tell him so. Four days later McCargar showed up in Philadelphia demanding that Farnsworth fire his entire lab. When Farnsworth refused, McCargar stormed into the lab, shouting, "You're all fired! Pick up your stuff and leave!"

Farnsworth furiously called Everson in New York to tell him what had happened and then called each of his employees to assure them they would be rehired. (Some, however, refused to work for McCargar any longer. Arch Brolly went to Philco, and Eddy found a job at RCA. Later, Eddy became famous for his pioneering programming in the 1940s on Chicago's experimental TV station, W9XBK.) Everson rushed down to Philadelphia and smoothed things over, but Farnsworth resolved to find a way to disassociate himself from McCargar.

To relieve his tension he took his family to Bermuda. When they returned a few weeks later, he arranged a meeting with Everson and Hugh Knowlton of Kuhn, Loeb, and Company, a prestigious New York banking house that had recently provided financial backing in return for Farnsworth stock. Farnsworth now presented a plan to form a new company, Farnsworth Television and Radio Corporation, which would encompass research, broadcasting, and set manufacturing.

At last he would be free of McCargar. Farnsworth favored firing him outright, but Everson, always the diplomat, insisted on offering him the position of chairman of the board of directors, which he was sure he would decline. And on April 25, 1937, Farnsworth wrote to his mother, "Jess is resigning from the company in favor of a highly paid technical executive. . . . I have been suggested as the new chairman of the board of directors."

As things turned out, it would be almost two years before the company could be born, but Farnsworth Television and Radio Corporation had at least been conceived.

3. Sarnoff's July 7, 1936, announcement at the Waldorf-Astoria had signified a change in RCA's tactics. Though Farnsworth still held important patents and it was clear that RCA's new camera tube owed a lot to Farnsworth's ideas, Sarnoff felt that now RCA had the technology to assume its heaven-appointed role as television leader. Characteristically, he took the offensive.

Zworykin had provided an all-electronic system that could televise indoors or out, in the studio or on the road via portable cameras; in other words, they now had a commercially viable television system. The General became an outspoken proponent of commencing commercial broadcasts, reversing his position of just a couple of years before. Now that RCA was in a position to clean up, why should the country delay? (The cartoon strip Li'l Abner would later feature a character named General Bullmoose, whose loudly proclaimed motto was "What's good for General Bullmoose is good for the country!")

The Communications Act of 1934 had created the Federal Communications Commission out of the seven-year-old Federal Radio Commission. The FCC, a seven-member panel appointed by the president and confirmed by the Senate, was given the mission of ensuring that in television, as well as radio, broadcasters acted "in the public interest, convenience, or necessity."

When it came to getting the new medium of television started on a commercial basis, however, the new commission had cold feet. They looked out on the television scene and saw, first of all, that RCA and Farnsworth were both operating with systems of 441 lines and thirty frames per second. But Philco was pushing for 605 lines and twenty-four frames, and DuMont insisted on 625 lines with fifteen frames. And Zenith and CBS were trying to stall, arguing that these discrepancies only proved that beginning a commercial service would be premature. Television receivers had to be perfectly synchronized with the transmitted signal, with regard to both lines per picture and frames per second, in order to get a picture at all. Failing to order a consistent and long-lasting standard would soon result in millions of obsolete sets, as well as outraged consumers.

Confused by the miasma of varying systems, the FCC hoped fervently that the radio industry would decide on a standard industry television system by themselves. Sort of like hoping the Yankees and

Giants would have a nice, clean World Series on their own, without umpires.

In late 1936, with Sarnoff's urging and the FCC's approval, the Radio Manufacturers Association turned their Television Committee to the task of recommending an industry standard for a commercial television system. Over a year later, in early 1938, they finally presented the FCC with their report: commercial television should be launched with 441 lines and thirty frames per second. Not surprisingly, the committee had chosen RCA's standards for the industry.

Things weren't going to be so easy for Sarnoff, however. Philco quickly disowned the report, claiming that RCA had an imbalance of influence on the committee. Zenith and CBS jumped right in, protesting that the FCC mustn't let Sarnoff push them into a premature commercial service. Disappointed by the dissent within the industry, the FCC backed away from a decision, declaring that technological research and testing must continue before a final standardization could occur.

Philco already had a history of resentment toward RCA. In the 1920s, following assurances from RCA that it would not be bringing out its new AC radio tube anytime in the near future, Philco had built up a huge inventory of its "B eliminators" for the coming season. When RCA came out with the AC tube anyway, it immediately made the "B eliminator" obsolete, and Philadelphia Storage Battery's (as it was then called) business collapsed.

In the early 1930s, when RCA had threatened to dominate television, Philco had fought back. First they hired Farnsworth; then, when that arrangement collapsed, they embarked on their own research and development program. One month after the gala RCA demonstration of July 7, 1936, Philco staged its own demonstration in Philadelphia, featuring a boxing match transmitted to a Philco cathode-ray receiver boasting a nine-by-eight-inch reflected screen. The transmitter was a regular Iconoscope, but clearly Philco intended to grab their share of the television market just as they had with radio—with their own distinctive line of home receivers.

Now, after the industry committee's report on standards, Philco filed suit in New York Supreme Court against RCA, claiming unfair trade practices; they charged that RCA had acquired confidential information on Philco's television patent materials in the most insidious of ways. RCA agents allegedly had targeted Philco's female employees, plying them with "expensive entertainment and intoxicating liquors at hotels, restaurants and nightclubs." Not only that, they supposedly "involve[d] them in compromising situations and did induce, incite and bribe" them in order to extract Philco's trade secrets. RCA scoffed at the charges as "sheer fabrication," and Philco was never able to prove its case.

Sarnoff by this time had become an executive of truly "baronial" stature. His salary climbed to one hundred thousand dollars (at the height of the depression), and he bought a six-story, thirty-room townhouse in Manhattan's east seventies, with servants' quarters, a private elevator, and a solarium. He was accompanied to his public appearances by an employee who carried his printed speech and handed it to him ostentatiously at the appointed time, after which it would be sent to newspapers around the country and to Washington for insertion into the *Congressional Record*. He stopped carrying cash, relying on his minions to pay for him and then apply for reimbursement.

As a fat cat, unrivaled government lobbyist, and industry power, he became an obvious target for RCA's rivals. Zenith took out a series of ads in trade magazines warning against a premature commencement of commercial television. A cartoon, which Sarnoff was convinced Zenith was behind, depicted Sarnoff as an oversized "televisionary" ape, trampling on a dying radio industry.

But Sarnoff, though financially comfortable to the point of decadence, had lost none of the fire that had brought him to this point. "Any effort to stop the progress of a new art in order to protect the existing art," he proclaimed, "is bound to be futile." Of course, this is exactly what he had done just three years or so before, when he canceled the Empire State Building tests and sent television back to the laboratory. But history didn't stand a chance under the onslaught of rhetoric.

> He poured invective on . . . all those in the industry who opposed
> him. They were "parasites," seeking to fatten themselves on radio to

the detriment of a newer service that could reinforce America's technological leadership in the world. It was always thus with the pioneer who led the way and took the risks, he averred publicly and privately. Not until the rewards were in sight would the "scavengers" crawl on the television bandwagon and join the feast.

This was just the sort of public battle in which Sarnoff thrived. He used his record of delaying television to his advantage, arguing that he had been patient when patience was necessary—but now television was ready, and it was time to act. On October 20, 1938, he addressed the annual meeting of the Radio Manufacturers Association and declared, "Television in the home is now technically feasible. The problems confronting this difficult and complicated art can only be solved from operating experience, actually serving the public in their homes." He had done everything he could to get the FCC to approve standards and allow commercial broadcasting to begin. But since they had dropped the ball, he was picking it up. He announced that RCA would commence regular broadcasting in the United States the following April, 1939, with the inaugural telecast coming from the opening ceremonies of the New York World's Fair.

4.   Early in 1937, Dr. O. E. Buckley, president of Bell Laboratories, Herbert Ives, and some other scientists from Bell Labs visited the Farnsworth team to see if they were interested in a cross-licensing agreement. Afterward Farnsworth personally delivered his entire patent portfolio to their New York offices for them to study. Months later the word finally came down that Bell was indeed interested in some sort of agreement, and on July 22, 1937, Farnsworth came back to New York and signed a contract. The agreement was nonexclusive, allowing each party to use the other's patents while maintaining the right to license other parties as well. From the very beginning, Farnsworth had held Bell Labs in the highest esteem; now, when they were finally recognizing him as an equal, he was so nervous that it was all he could do to add a wavering, barely legible "Philo T. Farnsworth" to the document.

Meanwhile, the Farnsworth studio in Wyndmoor, according to *Ra-*

dio News, was "one of the most complete and technically advanced television stations in the world"; Bill Eddy's acts, shuffled back and forth from Philadelphia on the commuter train, filled the studio, an impressive chamber forty feet long, twenty-four feet wide, and twenty-four feet high, "equipped in cinematic fashion with lights, props and full sized and miniature sets." The acts, well rehearsed and elaborate though they were, were still not officially intended for public consumption, but "any amateur within some thirty miles equipped with a receiver tuned to these channels"—a wavelength of 4.79 meters (62.75 megacycles), with a sound carrier of 66 megacycles—"and adjusted to the 441-line pictures with an interlace of two to one [could] get the program."

Farnsworth Television was also maintaining their Green Street lab in San Francisco, operated by "lone wolf" Bart Molinari. The son of a San Francisco baker, "Moli" had been an avid ham radio operator in high school, one of the first in the area to have his own transmission and receiving units. His obsession with radio kept him out of school so much that he never made it to college, but he did win the Hoover Cup awarded by the secretary of commerce for the best amateur shortwave transmitter. Soon after that he joined the Farnsworth lab.

In 1937, Everson and Molinari put on demonstrations of Farnsworth television in Hollywood in the hopes of coaxing some of the big money there to buy stock. Through Carter Wright, a local producer, Everson procured performers such as tap dancers, little-girl singers, and vaudeville acts for a five-week demonstration at a studio adjacent to the old Palomar Dancing Academy on Vermont Avenue. The dancing studio turned out to be "a fertile source of lovely young ladies who gladly seized the opportunity to be televised." They also provided a diverse range of skin and hair types, helping Molinari learn which would televise best. The men in the studio would place bets on which types would show up well on the television screen. Working with the Max Factor Company, they learned that the best lipstick was not pure blue, as they had used before, but "a little blue pigment mixed with the ordinary type of lipstick."

Television proved able to do for some of Hollywood's "beautiful people" what costly surgery does today. Since the color red televised as close to white, they found that if they applied red makeup liberally to wrinkles, the wrinkles disappeared from the television screen. Everson recalled televising a movie producer's wife, a former Follies beauty:

> She was well in her forties, and while the lines of her former beauty were still evident, her features were a bit heavy and there were distinct crow's-feet in her face. But with the skillful use of red lines on her cheeks and around the eyes, we succeeded in transmitting a television picture of her former loveliness.
>
> The producer, who was something of a wag, watching at the receiver, said, "My God, is that my wife? How much do these machines cost? I think I'll buy one if it can do that much for my wife's looks."

At any given time during this period, Farnsworth had between twenty-five and forty technicians and engineers working for him. An October 1936 *Collier's* profile of him, however, reminded readers: "He is now just thirty years old and his fair hair, blue eyes and slender build make him seem even younger, although when one talks with him the maturity of his outlook often gives the impression that he is older."

One of the visitors to the Hollywood demonstrations was a representative from Scientific Films, Inc., who did shorts for Paramount's *Eyes and Ears of the World*; soon afterward they came to Philadelphia to film Farnsworth working in the lab and giving a demonstration. Afterward, the camera moved into the reception area, which featured a Farnsworth receiver in a typical living room setting, where Pem and seven-year-old Philo were sitting. "Mother, can we see a television show?" asked the boy, to which she replied, "Yes, Philo, will you please turn it on?" He walked over to the set and turned a knob, and within seconds the picture came on bright and clear—as was the message: This was a system so simple even a child could operate it.

Despite the good show he put on for the cameras, though, Farnsworth was not well. In the spring of 1938, the Farnsworths drove up to Maine for a much-needed vacation and ended up buying a two-hundred-year-old farmhouse surrounded by sixty acres of mostly wooded land. They went back in August to take possession and stayed through the fall. "I can hardly tell you what acquiring this place in Maine means to us," Pem wrote to Everson in September.

> [In Philadelphia] Phil was all upset and nervous and hadn't eaten for two days—we had only been up [in Maine] a day when he started to eat. . . . After two days he developed a tremendous appetite and was sleeping with no trouble whatever. . . . So we are making tracks for Maine. . . . He is no good to the lab the way he is.

Farnsworth threw the same intensity and work ethic that had built the first electronic television into working on his new home, leaving patent interferences, financial pressures, and the constant threat of competition a thousand miles to the south. But he wasn't yet ready to forget television forever. The morning after a hearty Thanksgiving meal, the Farnsworths had a neighbor use his team of horses to pull their car through the winter's first snowfall to the paved road a mile away, and they headed back to Philadelphia.

5. Throughout 1938, Zworykin and his colleagues kept busy in the laboratory. The World's Fair telecast and subsequent service would be with the regular Iconoscope, but already the Camden team was finished with its successor. In June 1938, Harley Iams, George Morton, and Zworykin presented the Image Iconoscope in a paper at the annual Institute of Radio Engineers convention in New York. This was basically the same tube for which RCA's Alda Bedford had barely beaten EMI for the patent (applied for in 1934, interference decided in RCA's favor in 1937). RCA claimed that their Image Iconoscope was six to ten times more sensitive than the regular Iconoscope.

But even as they were presenting their paper in New York, Zworykin knew that the Image Iconoscope was at best a stepping-stone. Iams and Albert Rose were already hard at work in the lab perfecting a new tube, one that used a low-velocity electron beam to scan the image. In fact, Iams had already applied for the first patent on it.

At around the same time, Zworykin's original 1923 application for a patent on an all-electronic system was bouncing around in the final stages of its battle for acceptance. Pending for fifteen years, the application had been in litigation for twelve years, and the Patent Office had already ruled against it; now the case was in the District of Columbia Court of Appeals. Zworykin's lawyers were trying to prove that the photosensitive plate in the original application consisted of discrete potassium globules and that this was the first mention ever of such a construction. They finally succeeded in doing so, and on November 2, 1938, the court reversed the Patent Office's decision. With momentum in his favor, Zworykin proceeded to reapply for two previous patents: one was similar to the 1923 application, with two new claims involving an electrical condenser and a new circuit to utilize the discharge from the condenser; the other was from 1930 and added a couple of subtle new elements to the old Iconoscope design. When these new applications were finally granted to Zworykin in 1942, they would give him total control of the Iconoscope camera.

Of course, that wouldn't be enough to control television: the camera tubes of the future would combine his Iconoscope with key attributes of Farnsworth's Image Dissector, which Zworykin and RCA could never own. Still, these final Iconoscope patent victories must have been wonderfully gratifying to Zworykin as he approached his fiftieth birthday. Even before the patent decisions, he was beginning to find time for whimsy: an unusual sketch in his notebook from this time bears the caption, "Automatic Door Opener for RCA Lunch Room with Electron Multiplier."

There was also time for romance and adventure. In 1933, together with Loren Jones and two other friends, Vladimir had bought an open-cockpit biplane and learned to fly. In August of 1937, he asked Jones to fly him over Taunton Lake, about twenty miles southeast of Camden. He took a number of aerial photographs and said he was going to build a house on the lake. What he didn't tell Jones just yet was the lake's main attraction for him. Living there already were two fellow refugees of the Russian Revolution: a physician named Katherine and her husband Igor Polevitsky, the former mayor of Murmansk.

Katherine, slightly younger than Zworykin, was by all accounts a beautiful, intelligent, and charming woman. A trained ballet dancer as well as an educated woman, she was graceful in every way, physically and socially, a great contrast to Tatiana Vasilieff, Zworykin's first wife. Zworykin was smitten almost immediately on meeting her, and he vowed to marry her someday. His present marriage was not really much of an obstacle; he was already estranged from Tatiana, who lived with their daughters in nearby Haddonfield. Asked later why his marriage didn't last, Zworykin replied, "I couldn't think when she was around."

Igor Polevitsky, on the other hand, was a well-liked man—by Katherine as well as by all their friends—and Zworykin could not have had any hope that they would divorce. But Igor was considerably older than Vladimir and Katherine; time, Vladmir was sure, would bring them together.

He picked out a plot of land on the lakefront, close to the Polevitskys' house, but when he approached the ladies who owned it, they refused to sell. Never one to be deterred by illogical opposition, Zworykin went about building his house anyway, without the owners' knowledge or permission. Finally, in 1947, when his house was complete, he was able to convince the owners that the value of the rest of their property would rise, as his living there would turn it from unused land to prime lakefront real estate. They relented and sold, and he moved right in.

He moved into the Polevitskys' private life as well. During the next few years he was under surveillance by the FBI, suspected of being a Communist sympathizer. In fact, he was always unalterably opposed to the Soviet Union, insofar as his thoughts were political at all. But this was the McCarthy/Hoover era, when paranoia deemphasized the truth. His telephones were tapped, and he was followed by undercover agents, who found nothing to link him with any Russian spy ring but who did discover and formally report on many secret rendezvous with Mrs. Polevitsky, who was described succinctly as his "paramour."

Finally, in 1951, after Katherine's husband had died and Vladimir had gotten his divorce, they married.

By the end of 1938 David Sarnoff and RCA were busily preparing for their announced commencement of regular broadcasting in April 1939. The FCC had neither condemned nor sanctioned the plan, so

Sarnoff went full steam ahead. An impressive enough inauguration at the World's Fair, together with a subsequent regular entertainment program and the availability of home receivers for sale, would give the industry—and RCA in particular—a jump start. The FCC would have no choice but to authorize commercial service; the rest of the companies would then jump in and provide a thriving, competitive business, with RCA the undisputed leader.

On the afternoon of April 20, 1939, about a hundred invited guests sat before several Kinescope screens at Radio City to watch a television program. The first image they saw on the eight-by-nine-inch screens was that of veteran radio announcer Graham McNamee, who sat in front of a camera at Radio City and introduced the program. Suddenly the picture switched to an outdoor scene—Flushing, Queens, the site of the New York World's Fair. The voice of George Hicks narrated as the camera moved down the Avenue of Patriots, and the audience eight miles away saw the fair's landmark perisphere and trylon as well as hundreds of workmen lined up on the curb to watch the television apparatus make its promenade. Finally the camera reached the RCA building, where a bugle sounded and the Stars and Stripes could be seen climbing the mast. "Every detail was distinct," wrote the *New York Times* the next day, "even the fleecy texture of the clouds."

The occasion was the dedication of the RCA exhibit building at the fair and RCA/NBC's tune-up broadcast for their new regular service, to begin in earnest ten days later at the fair's opening ceremonies. Aside from the Radio City audience, several hundred more tuned in on home receivers throughout the metropolitan area, and about a hundred more watched on monitors at the RCA exhibit. After the flag-raising ceremony, Lenox Lohr, president of NBC, appeared before the RCA portable Iconoscope camera in the garden behind the building and briefly introduced RCA's president and the person most responsible for the telecast, David Sarnoff.

The viewers now saw a man, portly and nearly bald but with the bearing of a chief of state, appear on the screen. In the sunshine of a brisk but bright spring day, Sarnoff stood at a podium draped with the RCA banner, two NBC microphones framing his face. "Now," he intoned in his practiced bass voice, "we add radio sight to sound."

It is with a feeling of humbleness that I come to this moment of announcing the birth in this country of a new art so important in its implications that it is bound to affect all society. It is an art which shines like a torch of hope in a troubled world. It is a creative force which we must learn to utilize for the benefit of all mankind.

This miracle of engineering skill, which one day will bring the world to the home, also brings a new American industry to serve man's material welfare. In less than two decades, sound broadcasting provided new work for hundreds of thousands of men and women, added work in mines and forests and factories for thousands more, and aided the country and its citizens economically by causing the flow of hundreds of millions of dollars annually. Television bids fair to follow in its youthful parent's footsteps and to inherit its vigor and initiative. When it does it will become an important factor in American economic life.

The crowning moment of the new RCA service was supposed to have come ten days later with the telecast of President Roosevelt's opening ceremonies speech, but once again Sarnoff had grabbed the spotlight. It would not be FDR's visage but his own, beaming with confidence and seriousness just a few feet from the RCA camera, that would survive through the decades as the defining image of the beginning of regular television broadcasting in America.

Still, wrote Orrin Dunlap in the *Times,* the official opening day, April 30, 1939, would go down as "a historic date in the annals of science," much like November 2, 1920, generally considered the date when radio broadcasting began. "With all the exuberance of a boy with a new Kodak," Dunlap wrote, "the radio men pick up their electric cameras today and go to the World's Fair to televise the opening spectacle and to telecast President Roosevelt as a 'first' in this new category of broadcasting. . . . And so by sunset tonight television will have come from around the corner in quest of its destiny: to find its role in the art of amusing Americans, and to fit in with the social life of the land."

For the first time, a television camera took its place alongside the customary newsreel cameras to document a presidential speech. (In

England, television had been active on the political scene for some time. When Neville Chamberlain had returned from Munich in 1938 with "peace in our time," British viewers saw him waving for the cameras the slip of paper with Hitler's worthless signature on it.) Fewer than a thousand New Yorkers tuned in at the fairgrounds, at Radio City, and in a hundred or so private homes. The telecast began at 12:30 P.M. with a panoramic view of the fairgrounds and then covered the procession of dignitaries assembling to hear the president. As Mayor Fiorello La Guardia walked by, he stepped right up to the camera and ogled the lens, earning him the distinction voted by the engineers in the RCA van as "the most telegenic man in New York." The camera then followed the president's limousine as it entered the courtyard and showed him taking his place in the grandstand and later giving his dedicating remarks, calling the fair "a beacon of progress and hope"—much needed in a world soon to suffer the ravages of war.

Several observers from British television were on hand, more sophisticated than the Americans by several years' experience in television broadcasting, and were shocked at what they called "the nerve" of the Americans in having only one camera on the scene. The BBC, they assured reporters, would have had three or four shooting from different angles to provide fade-outs to various perspectives as well as insurance against technical failures. RCA certainly had more than one camera in existence, but someone in charge must have been confident. Asked about the possibility of a technical problem, one RCA engineer said, "That's not our luck, but should the optic go blind then we are licked."

It didn't, though, and the telecast was a great success. The following day, Monday morning, as promised, television receivers went on sale at several New York stores. Prices ranged from $199.50 for four-by-five-inch "telepicture attachment" for existing radio consoles to $1,000 for the largest set, with thirty-six tubes and a seven-by-ten-inch picture. Most of the dealers prepared dark "demonstration booths" in which customers could become acquainted with the new devices.

RCA also began their regular broadcasts, with the following schedule:

Wednesdays and Fridays, 8–9 P.M.: Live programming from the Radio City studio.

Wednesday, Thursday, and Friday afternoons: Live outdoor scenes from the NBC mobile van.

Mondays, Tuesdays, Thursdays, 11 A.M. to 4 P.M., and Wednesdays and Fridays 4–8 P.M.: broadcasting from film.

With an unwitting prescience, however, network officials were quick to "warn that the subject matter will be found repetitious" and also that the schedule might not be strictly followed.

Still, despite the primitive programming content and the fact that as the *New York Times* pointed out, "there has been no rush on the part of New Yorkers during the past week to have video sets installed," modern television broadcasting had begun. "From now on," wrote *Radio and Television Retailing,* "television will be in the open, where the public can see how it works, can see what it will and will not do, can appraise its capacity, its state of perfection, and its virtues. . . . Mr. and Mrs. Consumer are going to be the final judges of its actual worth."

In an effort to win over Mr. and Mrs. C., Sarnoff dictated a strong opening schedule of special live events. On May 17, NBC televised a Columbia-Princeton baseball game in what appears to be the first sports telecast in America. (Baird, remember, had televised the British Derby as far back as 1931, and of course the 1936 Olympics had been televised in Germany.) RCA followed the Ivy League match with the New York Giants and Brooklyn Dodgers from Ebbets Field and the Baer-Nova prizefight from Madison Square Garden. On June 11 they covered the parade in honor of King George VI and Queen Elizabeth, but sports were the most popular telecasts. Critiquing the telecast of the October 14 Fordham-Waynesburg football game, Dunlap wrote, "So sharp are the pictures and so discerning the telephoto lens as it peers into the line-up that the televiewer sits in his parlor wondering why he should leave the comforts of home." Though the number of sets sold was still in the hundreds, wives were already getting used to the sight of their husbands hunched over TV sets, shouting at the glowing tube.

As confidently as he had predicted radio sales of seventy-five million dollars for the first three years in his famous "Radio Music Box" memo of 1920, Sarnoff had projected sales of twenty to forty thousand television receivers in the year following the World's Fair introduction. Radio proved him a prophet, with an actual eighty-three million dollars in sales the first three years; television, however, threatened to throw egg on his face. Three months after introduction, only eight hundred sets sat in consumers' homes, while five thousand crowded the warehouses of dealers and distributors. Sarnoff slashed prices by a third—to no avail. Apparently his foes in the standards battle had convinced the public that buying now, while broadcasting was still an experiment, would be premature; if the RCA standards didn't hold, the sets would be obsolete. And at two hundred to one thousand dollars a set in 1939, that would be no minor personal financial setback. It would be like buying a new luxury automobile only to find that it couldn't ride on the new highways. If the FCC didn't finalize standards soon, Sarnoff faced the possibility of a mammoth failure and embarrassment.

While Sarnoff continued to pressure the FCC and fight his public battle for immediate authorization of commercial television, quiet progress went on in the laboratory. Zworykin, however, was no longer intimately involved. He settled into an administrative position as director of RCA's electronic research laboratory and no longer worked actively as a scientist. (He did, however, stay in the limelight. He insisted that he be listed as coauthor of every research paper that came out of RCA's television efforts, whether he had anything to do with the project or not. In fact, just like Baird, he would wander around the labs, poking his nose into everything that was going on, a noble and historic personage but a nuisance to the younger scientists who were actually doing the work. Sarnoff backed him in all of this, recognizing that Zworykin was his star, a man with name recognition to the reporters who followed television.)

On June 7, 1939, Iams and Rose made a presentation to the New York chapter of the Institute of Radio Engineers, disclosing details of their new low-velocity scanning tube. They called it the Orthiconoscope, or Orthicon, from the Greek *orthos*, meaning straight, because unlike the Iconoscope it produced a signal output linearly proportional to the input light. That is, while the Iconoscope's signal produced diminishing returns as the televised subject grew brighter, the Orthicon's picture would grow correspondingly brighter and brighter; it was deemed ten to twenty times more sensitive than its predecessor.

It also was the first RCA tube to use Farnsworth's 1933 idea of the low-velocity scanning beam. In this original Orthicon, light from the subject was focused directly onto a mosaic photoelectric plate. Just as in the Iconoscope, where the light was bright, that spot on the mosaic would emit an electron and acquire a positive charge; where the original subject was dark, no light would hit the mosaic, and that spot would remain uncharged. In the Orthicon, however, a low-velocity beam of electrons would then scan the mosaic. Since the potential of the mosaic and the electron-gun cathode were the same, the electrons slowed by the time they reached the mosaic to virtually zero velocity. Where the mosaic was uncharged, or "dark," the electrons would simply bounce off, but where it was "light" and charged positively, the barely moving electron would take the place of the electron that had been emitted and "discharge" that spot, or return it to its original potential. The discharging of each light spot on the mosaic created an impulse on the conducting signal plate on the back of the mosaic, and this impulse became the picture signal, which was carried to an amplifier and subsequently transmitted to the receiver.

Since the signal was produced directly by the replacing of electrons displaced by the light from the subject, the signal was directly proportional to the incoming light intensity, and the resulting graph of signal versus light input was a straight (*orthos*) line. Another way of putting it is that the conversion of photoemission into picture signal was virtually 100 percent.

Or at least that was the theory. In practice, this first low-velocity tube, which RCA promised would be ready for use by the beginning of 1940, was far from the perfect camera. It did not perform well under intensely lit conditions or under sudden bursts of light; the mosaic tended to "charge up" too much. And because of the linear relationship between input and output, it also didn't do well with dimly lit scenes.

So it lacked the Iconoscope's resolution and response to contrasts. But the Orthicon was still an important advance, and when RCA was finally able to combine its new characteristics with the best features of the Iconoscope and Image Dissector by the end of World War II, they would have the Image Orthicon, by far the best tube yet, a hundred times more sensitive than the original Orthicon.

The future looked bright, but there were still travails to be endured—and one, in particular, would stick like a stone in Sarnoff's craw.

SIXTEEN

Sarnoff's Folly

It is probable that television drama of high caliber and produced by first-rate artists will materially raise the level of dramatic taste of the American nation.

David Sarnoff

1. When Farnsworth, Everson, and Knowlton conceived of Farnsworth Television and Radio in 1937 with an eye to turning a profit by making and selling television sets, they hired E. A. "Nick" Nicholas away from RCA to head the manufacturing division of the future company. Soon he had found a radio manufacturing company, the Capehart Company of Fort Wayne, Indiana, that they could purchase, as well as an operating plant in Marion, fifty miles to the south; they would float three million dollars of stock to facilitate the deal and provide start-up capital. Nicholas set November 1938 as a goal to get all the paperwork squared away and to push the deal through the Securities and Exchange Commission.

But 1938 was a touchy year for the SEC. As Everson put it, "[we] were victims of a situation that had been created by flagrant abuses of buyers' confidence in public financing [of stocks]. The position taken by the Commission seemed to be that you were guilty until you proved your innocence. The attitude seemed to be one of daring us to prove that we were not all a pack of dishonest rogues."

Fresh in the commissioners' minds was the public spectacle and trial of Lee De Forest for having "fleeced" his investors with the Audion

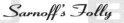

tube. (See Notes, page 386.) Despite the fact that De Forest had been found innocent of any wrongdoing and that his Audion had eventually proved to be the basis for the entire subsequent radio industry, what remained in people's minds was the scandal rather than the vindication. And that scandal was not the only one: the crash of 1929 was a recent event, and the whole country was still ensconced in its nightmarish aftermath.

So for the Farnsworth team, month after month went by, filled with "endless trips of accountants, lawyers, and executives to Washington." The registration statement and its supplement grew weightier than the New York telephone directory. As time passed, the Farnsworth group squirmed. Europe was quickly destabilizing, Hitler threatened to start war at any moment, and the stock market, on which the new venture depended, "was acting with a disconcerting uncertainty." If war started in Europe, the underwriters would certainly withdraw from the deal.

In September of 1938, Prime Minister Chamberlain had come home from Munich with "peace in our time," but by January of 1939, the British Foreign Office was convinced that far from having made his "last territorial demand," Hitler was planning an attack on the Western powers, and rumors and speculations of war were circulating within the American business community. If a general European war broke out, America might stay neutral, but American business would certainly be affected. Airplane and munitions corporation stock began to flourish, but businesses unrelated to war were becoming shaky investments. Under these conditions, television did not look like a good bet.

On March 15, Hitler dissolved Czechoslovakia; the Munich pact had collapsed. Anticipating the Nazis' next move, Chamberlain on March 30 sent an official assurance to Poland that "if . . . any action were taken which clearly threatened their independence . . . His Majesty's Government and the French Government would at once lend them all the support in their power."

On March 31, the last day on which the Farnsworth-Capehart deal could be legally consummated, the rumble in the press and on the ticker tapes was approaching a cacophony, and there still remained over a hundred documents to be ratified. Scores of bankers, government officials, lawyers, executives, and their assistants worked through the day until only one paper remained, the responsibility of one Allen G. Messick, who had decided to go out for a bite to eat. A search party finally located him, and the whole episode was commemorated in a poem by Don Lippincott, later published in *Savoir-Faire*:

A Television Picture

The clans are here from far and near,
And on the desks reposing
Are bales and blocks of common stocks;
There's going to be a closing.
Exchanging rafts of checks and drafts
And instruments of title
And all our fears and tears of years
Will meet with their requital.

So here are ranks of men from banks,
And many secretaries
And legal lights and parasites
And fiscal functionaries.
But what's this pall that grips them all
And stifles all this bunch:
They're waiting for an I.O.U.
And by the Gods they need it too
And Messick has the I.O.U.
And Messick's gone to lunch.

O praises be to Allen G;
Chambers of Commerce praise him!
No banker grim can trouble him
Nor tax collector faze him.
When tempers fail and strong men pale
He just lays out his hunch;
He knows the thing he has to do
And by the Gods he does it too!
He just writes out an I.O.U.
And calmly goes to lunch!

With a sigh of relief, Everson accepted a check for three million dollars. The next day he and Nicholas headed to Fort Wayne to launch the new Farnsworth Television and Radio Corporation manufacturing operation.

Until commercial television was a reality, the new corporation planned to finance itself by the sale of radios. The Capehart plant was still operating at the time of the sale, so the transition was smooth, and by the middle of August a complete line of Farnsworth radios and a national distributorship were ready. At their first distributors' conference, a million dollars' worth of radios were sold. At the same time, they were beginning to push the idea of commercial television. A July 1939 advertisement in *Radio Today* proclaimed, "Leading Distributors 'Go' Farnsworth," and "The history of television is the history of Farnsworth."

In the meantime, the television lab in Philadelphia was carefully packed and moved to Fort Wayne. The Farnsworths were spending the summer in Maine, hoping Phil would recuperate from the stress of all this hectic activity. A boost in morale came when biographer Durward Howes chose him as one of "America's Top Ten Young Men" for 1939, along with Lou Gehrig, E. O. Lawrence, William Paley, and Spencer Tracy.

Such a boost was needed after the disappointment of the World's Fair, where Farnsworth had intended to compete with RCA. He had promised reporters that "two trucks equipped with [Farnsworth] television cameras would be in use on the New York World's Fair grounds," but the company, in the midst of the SEC red tape, couldn't afford to prepare for the fair. So when RCA telecast President Roosevelt's speech, the Farnsworth Television and Radio Corporation was nowhere to be seen.

Still, Sarnoff was not to have the last laugh for 1939.

Farnsworth spent the entire summer in Maine, working on the farmhouse. Midway through the project, however, his "strength gave out," and his brother-in-law Cliff had to take over. Though only thirty-two years old, Phil had already been through enough power struggles, victories, and disappointments for an elderly retired executive, and he was feeling the effects.

In the fall, the Farnsworths left Maine and made the move from Philadelphia to Fort Wayne. Farnsworth radios were selling well, and for the first time ever the Farnsworth lab labored under no financial burden. But it was also no longer a small team that Farnsworth could lead himself, and he found it hard to get back into his creative work. Younger engineers constantly wanted his attention but more to impress him with *their* ideas than to seek his own; they made him feel respected but old and burned out.

Farnsworth had done all he could do to give birth to television. His scientific prophecy was fulfilled; the rest of the race was for the army of engineers and businesspeople who would flood onto the scene once commercial television was up and running. "There was only one matter of unfinished business," Pem wrote. "A license with RCA."

The mighty Radio Corporation of America had never before paid patent royalties to another company. In dominating the radio industry and promising to dominate the new television one, they had, like a Monopoly master buying up all the hotel chains on the board, simply purchased any and all patents that they felt they would need. It was a point of honor, as well as a company policy, never to be in a position of borrowing someone else's technology.

But in 1939 David Sarnoff began to realize that honor might have to be compromised where Farnsworth's television patents were concerned. In his two greatest patent victories, Farnsworth had retained ownership of the designs for his Image Dissector camera tube and the low-velocity scanning method to be used in RCA's Orthicon tube. He had also won a number of smaller interferences, giving him a solid chunk of the television-patent infrastructure—enough to make it impossible to succeed in the television market without him. If RCA couldn't buy rights to his patents for a flat fee, they would have to sign a patent-licensing agreement and pay him a specified amount for every camera they sold until his patents expired.

And he wouldn't sell.

In the summer of 1939 Sarnoff's vice president in charge of patents, Otto Schairer, and his assistants sat down with Nick Nicholas, Hugh Knowlton, and Farnsworth's new patent chief Edwin Martin to negotiate. Though these three men represented a new and smaller company, they had the experience and negotiating skill to stand up to the broadcasting giant (Nicholas had been the head of RCA's licensing division before coming to Farnsworth). As Everson put it, "at first, the two sides seemed so far apart that it looked utterly hopeless. Only the clear underlying fact that neither company could get along without the other kept the discussions alive."

From May through September, they hacked out negotiations. Finally, in late September, an agreement was reached. On October 2, 1939, after three hectic days of finalizing the contract, Schairer led the Farnsworth team and a group of RCA officials into the conference room at Radio City. First Nicholas signed, then it was Schairer's turn. As he bent over to put his name on RCA's first agreement ever to pay continuing patent royalties to another company, there were tears in his eyes.

2.   "Sarnoff's Folly," cried a *Radio Daily* headline in early 1940.

Well aware that Farnsworth's percentage was invisible to the public whose television sets carried the RCA logo, Sarnoff had shrugged off the humiliation of signing a patent royalty agreement and gone full steam ahead with NBC's broadcasts. Nothing he did, however, sparked sales. Philco, Zenith, and other competitors waged a media war against Sarnoff in an effort to keep consumers from buying receivers until standards were finalized. "I've had plenty of cats and dogs thrown at me," Sarnoff told a group of colleagues years later, "but never like that. Philco and Zenith were more interested in getting me than in creating a television industry."

In January of 1940 the FCC commenced public hearings. The commission's chairman, James Lawrence Fly, "an ardent New Dealer and antimonopolist of deep conviction," seemed determined from the start to prevent any one corporate giant from taking over the industry. It was quickly obvious to Sarnoff that the chasm between the two of them was too wide to bridge with polite talk, which he abandoned in favor of outright aggressiveness if not defiance.

After preliminary hearings, the FCC announced on February 28 that a limited commercial service would be authorized beginning on September 1. But they still hadn't finalized standards; research should continue, they said, until the best system was determined.

Sarnoff responded as though he had won a total victory. On March 20, full-page RCA ads ran in the New York papers announcing that the age of home television was here and that more extensive and exciting programming was on the way. Bloomingdale's and other department stores ran accompanying ads for RCA receivers at reduced prices.

Fly was outraged. Two days later the FCC suspended their authorization for September commercial service. The *New York Times* quoted the commission's response:

> The current marketing campaign of the Radio Corporation of America . . . is construed as a disregard of the commission's findings and recommendations. . . . Promotional activities directed to the sale of receivers not only intensifies the danger of these instruments being left on the hands of the public, but may react in the crystallizing of transmission standards at present levels.
>
> Moreover, the possibility of one manufacturer gaining an unfair advantage over competitors may cause them to abandon the further research and experimentation which is in the public interest.

The FCC announced further hearings to begin in April. In the meantime, debate raged in the media. *Newsweek* accused the FCC of imposing an "alien theory of merchandising" by protecting consumer interests beyond "acceptable bounds," and the *New York Times* called the FCC's action "absurd and unsound." Fly, responding on the radio, defended the commission's decision to resist "Big Business's bullying of the little fellows." Even President Roosevelt tried to step in, meeting with Fly and Sarnoff separately and suggesting in vain that the two men meet for lunch at his expense to work things out. "Our dispute is in the head, not the stomach," Sarnoff told the president.

Fly and Sarnoff had it out publicly during hearings of the U.S. Senate Committee on Interstate Commerce, called to determine if the FCC had acted correctly. Fly defended the suspension of service, admitting that the original authorization had been a misjudgment. "We begged the industry then not to fix the standards, not to let them become frozen," he said, but "within three weeks" came the RCA "blitzkrieg"—a potent image in 1940. Sarnoff countered that RCA was acting in the public's best interests:

> The purchaser of such a set knows exactly what he is paying for. He is paying for the unique privilege of seeing what is important or interesting today . . . which he cannot witness tomorrow or next year, however great the technical improvements.

The Senate hearings ended without any action being taken except to throw the mess back to the FCC, with the directive to find a solution soon. Public opinion applied added pressure to the commission; the people believed that television was ready, and they wanted it now.

The FCC's solution was to form yet another committee, the National Television System Committee (NTSC), comprised of engineering experts from the entire industry, appointed by the Radio Manufacturers Association. The NTSC would develop a final consensus of television standards; the FCC would vote on them, and then, if the standards were accepted, they would authorize a commercial service. When the FCC ascertained the time was right—not when David Sarnoff did.

In the meantime, the airwaves were hardly empty. By the end of 1939, RCA had a plethora of experimental broadcasting rivals across the country, some of which would wither and die in the competition while others would bloom. In the New York area, DuMont was broadcasting out of Passaic, New Jersey, with imminent plans for a New York City station, and both CBS and the Bamberger Broadcasting Service had stations under construction. General Electric was back on the air in Schenectady, broadcasting out of the Helderberg hills; General Television Corporation had a regular service going in Boston; and in Philadelphia, Philco continued their regular program of experimental broadcasts. In the Midwest, Zenith, Paramount Pictures, and CBS all had stations in Chicago. And in Los Angeles, radio pioneer Don Lee headed a list of at least seven regular broadcast stations. Using two portable Iconoscope cameras from RCA, the Don Lee station broadcast the 1940 Rose Bowl football game on New Year's Day, relaying the signal from Pasadena to W6XAO in Los Angeles nine miles away; from there it was broadcast to the metropolitan area.

Perhaps the high-water mark of this precommercial-broadcasting period came in June 1940 when NBC covered the Republican National Convention from Philadelphia. For thirty-three hours over five days, both an Iconoscope and an Orthicon mounted on the newsreel platform inside Convention Hall, along with special lighting equipment, transmitted the proceedings of the convention. The signal traveled by cable to AT&T's Philadelphia terminal, by phone line to New York, and by cable again to the Empire State Building; from there it was broadcast on W2XBS to the metropolitan area. Though this was not the first-ever telecast of a political event—remember GE's mechanical transmission of Governor Smith's acceptance speech twelve years before (chapter 6)—it was certainly the first of such magnitude, clarity, and popularity (a few thousand viewers). Philco also telecast the event to the Philadelphia area using their own cameras.

Orrin Dunlap remarked in the *New York Times* on how this landmark event would change politics forever:

> Sincerity of the tongue and facial expression gain in importance. . . . Naturalness is the keystone of success. . . . The sly, flamboyant or leather-lunged spellbinder has no place on the air. Sincerity, dignity, friendliness and clear speech . . . are the secrets of a winning telecast. More than ever, the politician must picture himself in the living room, chatting heart-to-heart with a neighbor. . . . How they comb their hair, how they smile and how they loop their necktie become new factors in politics.

Sarnoff concurred on the influence the new medium would have on politicians. Speaking of this telecast, he told the American Academy of Political and Social Science:

Political addresses are certain to be more effective when the candidate is both seen and heard. . . . Showmanship in presenting a political appeal by television will become more important than mere skill in talking or the possession of a good radio voice, while appearance and sincerity will prove decisive factors with an audience which observes the candidate in closeup views.

Over the summer of 1940, Farnsworth began to resign himself to the fact that television, when it did finally hit its stride after the war, would do so without him. He was an inventor, not an industrialist, and television was already becoming an industry. "Feeling he had to put television behind him," wrote Pem, "he entered into a frenzy of activity. He decided he would build his own lab [on the farm] and go on with what he did best, inventing." Improvements on the Maine house, however, continued to take up most of the summer and fall, as well as a portion of the Farnsworths' stock holdings. Farnsworth sold 2,000 shares of stock in August, 2,000 more in September, and 3,000 more the following February. In April 1941 he wrote to his mother asking her to sell 2,500 more shares for him so no one would know about it. "By the end of the summer," he wrote, "[we] will have an estate here worth a hundred thousand dollars and won't have a pennies [sic] encumbrance on it."

By September 1940, the Farnsworths had given up the idea of returning to Fort Wayne. Phil's drinking was getting worse, and he was also developing a dependency on chemical sedatives. His only hope, he and Pem felt, was to stay away from the stressful environment of the lab. "We have found a saner way of living than is possible in the city," he wrote his mother. Farnsworth Radio and Television was getting on fine without its founding father, and anyway, with war raging in Europe, television was going to take a backseat for a number of years. "Besides," said Pem, "we were now quite comfortable on our New England homestead, and so decided to settle in for the duration."

That same summer of 1940, while the NTSC was hashing out technical details and Spitfires were dogfighting Messerschmitts over England, Albert Rose and his RCA colleagues were steadily improving the Orthicon. They had decided that the answer lay in going back to a two-sided target. Zworykin and Ogloblinsky's critical decision in achieving a working Iconoscope in 1931 had been to abandon the two-sided tubes for one-sided ones. At that time, it had been too difficult to construct uniform, blemish-free, efficient two-sided targets, both for technical and economic reasons. But in 1940 Rose found the answer to this problem in something called "G-B."

"G-B" was the Corning Glass Company's classification for a special thin glass membrane that was otherwise similar to ordinary window glass. Rose found that by blowing a bubble of this glass onto a metal supporting ring and then heating it until the surface tension drew the glass flat, he could create a uniform sheet of glass less than 0.0002 inches thick. He then assembled a wire mesh signal screen next to this membrane. When the electron image was created on one side of the membrane, it created an analogous charged image on the other side, where it was then scanned with a low-velocity electron beam, as in the Orthicon. The result was a tube three to ten times more sensitive than the Orthicon and thirty to five hundred times more sensitive than the Iconoscope. Rose's patent, applied for in September 1940, was classified top secret during the war years and then never granted, but he had created the shape of things to come. The Orthicon was rendered obsolete in the same year that it was first used publicly.

From the last day of July 1940 to its last meeting on March 8, 1941, the NTSC deliberated on the standards to be used for American commercial television. David Sarnoff was noticeably reticent during this time. Apparently he had learned that he couldn't bully the government into accepting RCA's standards; he would have to rely on the good sense of the committee. Nine panels, concentrating on aspects from transmitter power to the famous lines-per-picture controversy, worked overtime to arrive at an industry consensus. Finally, by the end of February 1941, the panels submitted their findings to the general committee.

Engineer Donald G. Fink had been put in charge of recommending to the NTSC the number of lines and frames. He concluded from a survey of viewers' reactions that any number of lines within the range of

441 to 625 would be fine, given a constant video bandwidth (the committee had already chosen six megahertz). With that bandwidth, any increase in number of lines carried a concomitant decrease in horizontal resolution; the only difference would be the ratio of vertical to horizontal resolution, and "the typical viewer is not sensitive to the value of this ratio." As a compromise, therefore, he recommended a standard of 525 lines, with thirty frames per second to coincide with the U.S. AC power supply. Other panels made their recommendations of AM rather than FM for picture and synchronizing signals, FM for sound, and a ratio of four units horizontal to three units vertical, among others.

On March 8, 1941, the NTSC formally recommended these standards to the FCC in a report six hundred thousand words long—the result of four thousand man-hours of meetings, an equal amount of time in travel, and the witnessing of twenty-five full-scale demonstrations. On April 30, after brief hearings, the FCC approved the standards and authorized commercial broadcasting to begin on July 1, 1941.

Suddenly the long battle was over. Although the standards adopted were not RCA's, David Sarnoff had won again. RCA could easily convert its transmission standards, and commercial television—on which RCA figured to clean up—was finally about to begin.

Twenty-two television stations prepared for the July 1 starting date. When the day came, though, only RCA's station, NBC, was fully prepared. RCA closed down its Empire State Building transmitter to convert it to the new standards and opened ten service centers in the metropolitan area to convert consumers' receivers free of charge. On July 1, it opened commercial television in the United States with a USO fund-raising show, the news sponsored by Sun Oil, a television version of a radio show for Lever Brothers, and a quiz show presented by Procter and Gamble. (CBS had no sponsorship lined up yet, but they did telecast a dance lesson, a newscast, and an art exhibit, and DuMont continued their noncommercial broadcasting of film and live programming.) NBC also presented the first television commercial: a Bulova clock face, which remained on the screen as its second hand made one full revolution. The clock company paid four dollars for the minute of air time. (At the 1996 Super Bowl, one minute of air time on NBC would cost 2.4 million dollars.)

The other stations followed suit by the fall, but once again television failed to take off. This time it wasn't the fear of unstable standards but the fear of an unstable world. War was raging in Europe, and it was becoming clear that the United States could not remain neutral. This time Sarnoff didn't try to jump-start the sputtering television engine with advertisements or rhetoric. "By the summer of '41," he later recalled, "I was convinced we could not avoid war. . . . It was just too late in the game for television." With characteristic patriotism, he began organizing RCA's wartime role. The cathode-ray tubes developed for television would play a crucial part in radar and other military devices; the engineers who had learned their craft in the television research laboratories would take their place as the most important people in the United States arsenal. Sarnoff began spending more time in Washington meeting with various military officials, and in private meetings he assured President Roosevelt that RCA's global communications network could easily be put to work for the coming war effort.

After the attack on Pearl Harbor, Sarnoff immediately sent a telegram to Roosevelt: "All our facilities are ready and at your instant service. We await your commands." By April 1942 all radio and television production was banned; all raw materials and manufacturing capabilities were to be directed to the war effort.

It had been sixty-eight-years since the discovery of selenium's photoelectric properties, fifty-seven years since Nipkow designed his spinning disk, thirty years since Swinton had proposed electronic television, and two years of political haggling since the World's Fair. Television could certainly wait another five years for a war to run its course. When the smoke cleared, the new machine would be standing, irrepressible, ready to conquer the world.

"*Fulfillment
for Our
Long
Struggle*"

SEVENTEEN

The Color War

Everything looks worse in black and white.
Paul Simon

1 . Sixteen months before Pearl Harbor, while the new NTSC was trying to come up with national transmission standards and while RCA's engineers in Camden were furiously improving their Orthicon camera tube, a young accented voice momentarily disrupted the rush toward commercial television.

The voice belonged to television engineer Peter Goldmark, CBS's own television genius, who had emigrated to the United States from Hungary only seven years before. As CBS's delegate to the NTSC, he had sat for weeks squirming in his seat while he listened to debates over the various black-and-white television systems available at the time. Finally, he stood and addressed his older colleagues. You're beating a dead horse, he said. I've already perfected color television.

Even before the twentieth century, physicists knew that they could separate any image into its blue, red, and green components by using colored filters. What they didn't know was how to turn these three components into electric signals, transmit them, and turn them back into colored beams at the other end, mixing them again into the original color image.

In 1889, a Russian scientist by the name of Polumordvinov applied for a patent on a color television system that used spinning Nipkow disks and concentric cylinders with slits covered by red, green, and blue filters. He had none of the technology necessary to make such a scheme work, however; even a simple monochrome system was decades away. In 1902 a German, Otto von Bronk, patented a system using a mirror drum, selenium cell, and a grid of Geissler tubes with colored filters. Over the years, a ghostly army of inventors, with names like Adamian, Jaworsky, and even Frankenstein applied for patents on color systems that would never work.

Their basic concept, later called the "sequential" system of color transmission, was sound. They would first scan the picture with a red filter, then with a blue filter, then a green filter, and transmit each complete, tinted image one at a time. At the receiving end, the three components would be viewed in such rapid succession that the human eye would mix the colors and "see" the original multicolored picture. But none of these inventors had conceived of a receiving apparatus that could synchronize the three signals and mix and focus them accurately enough to produce a clear picture. And monochrome television itself was in such a primitive state that to be thinking about color was a bit quixotic.

Harold McCreary of the Associated Electric Laboratories of Chicago appears to have been the first to move beyond the sequential method, although his apparatus would never actually function. In 1924 he patented a "simultaneous" system that used cathode-ray tubes at both ends. To produce color, he separated the image into its three color components and used a separate camera tube to scan each component and transmit the three of them simultaneously. At the receiving end, three cathode tubes would reproduce the components. Each tube would be coated with a special chemical that when struck by the electron beam, would glow the proper primary color. Then the three colored images would be combined by a system of mirrors that would blend them into one realistic picture.

The next year, 1925, Vladimir Zworykin himself applied for a patent on a color system based on his still-pending 1923 application. He would turn that original design into a color instrument, he said, by inserting an "analyzing screen" between the two lenses that focused the image onto the photoelectric plate. The screen consisted of tiny square filters of red, green, and blue. Therefore the image that was formed on the photoelectric plate would consist of thousands of different signals for the three colors; by placing an identical screen on the receiving end, the image would be reproduced. The signals for red would send light only through red squares, for green only through green, and so on. Zworykin didn't determine how colors would actually be created on the screen. Still primarily absorbed with black-and-white transmission, he quickly went back to working on his earlier patent. He knew that someday the monster would surely run—if only he could teach it to walk.

By 1928, a host of inventors, including Herbert Ives of Bell Labs, had devised plans for color television, but no one had come close to making it work. Then, on July 3, 1928, word came out of London that color television had actually been demonstrated. John Logie Baird had taken his beloved spinning disk, cut three spirals into it, and covered each with a different colored filter. As the disk spun, it scanned the image with alternating lines of red, green, and blue. At the receiver a similar disk received the three tinted images one at a time, and flashed them on the screen. Screen colors were provided by special gas-filled cells: neon for red, helium for blue, and mercury for green. While one observer from the audience of reporters and scientists remarked that the reproduced color images of faces and flowers were "vivid," Baird, believing that color was little more than a distraction, went back to trying to convince the BBC of the worthiness of his monochrome device.

Then on June 27, 1929, Bell Labs gave the first American demonstration of color television and the first demonstration anywhere of a "simultaneous" system. They used spinning disks, like Baird, but employed a bank of photocells with colored filters to pick up the signals. At the receiver, three lights with filters reproduced the colored signals, and a system of mirrors mixed them on the screen. Although Bell Labs claimed their picture was "quite striking in appearance," and the *New York Times* concurred that "the colors reproduced perfectly," the screen was only the size of a postage stamp, to be viewed through a peephole in a dark room. It was doomed, too, as a mechanical system, using a disk with only fifty holes (thus constructing a fifty-line picture) that produced eighteen frames a second. As with black and white, good color television would require the cathode-ray tube.

Not much progress would be made on electronic color tubes before the war. In fact, color television was for the most part abandoned in the 1930s in the race toward commercial black-and-white TV. With the possibility of achieving commercial television so near, no one wanted to hear about a technology that was still years down the road.

And then, seemingly out of nowhere, Peter Goldmark appeared. He was only thirty-four years old in 1940 when he rose to address his colleagues on the NTSC:

> I calmly announced that we could transmit pictures in color, and I invited the assemblage to a demonstration in the CBS laboratory of a broadcast from the Chrysler Building.
>
> I couldn't have created a greater explosion if I had lit a stick of dynamite.

An RCA delegate immediately informed the committee that his company was well aware of CBS's experiments, that they had been monitoring them themselves, and that they were convinced that CBS color would never be of commercial quality. A debate ensued, with RCA, Farnsworth, and Philco forming a rare alliance against CBS color, while RCA's natural enemy Zenith backed CBS. It was finally agreed that all of them would have to see a demonstration for themselves.

And so on August 28 and September 4, 1940, selected members of the NTSC, as well as the FCC, met at the CBS labs on Madison Avenue to view color broadcasts from the Chrysler tower. On several screens only three inches wide, models could be seen parading in colorful dresses. Then bouquets of various flowers moved across the screen, their colors registering quite well. Everyone came away impressed, none more so than FCC chairman Lawrence Fly, who according to

Goldmark, "right then and there announced that he was a champion of color." In an official statement, Fly declared, "If we can start television off as a color proposition, instead of a black and white show, it will have a greater acceptance with the public."

2. Goldmark had had his first exposure to television while in graduate school in Vienna. He heard about Baird's do-it-yourself television kit and soon had his own Baird "televisor" complete with Nipkow disk and one-by-one-half-inch screen. Late at night, when the BBC allowed Baird to use its transmitter for his experimental broadcasts, Goldmark and his best friend received the signal from London: a tiny dancer flitting across the tiny screen.

Like so many other technologically minded young people in 1926, Goldmark became entranced with television. He set out immediately to enlarge the tiny Baird picture, and before long he had devised a system of mirrors to do so. He brought the entire contraption to the patent examiner along with his application and was awarded the first Austrian patent for television. After he finished his Ph.D. in physics, in 1931, he wrote a letter to Baird in hopes of getting a job in the new field. Baird replied with an invitation to meet him in London. The meeting was less than a success:

> [Baird] pulled my patent out of a briefcase. Writing and drawing sketches on the white tablecloth, he criticized my system through the remainder of lunch, down to the tarts. I don't know what disturbed me most, the disfiguring of somebody else's white tablecloth or the criticism of my invention. But I nodded to all of Baird's ideas and then, figuring there was nothing to lose, hopefully asked him for a job. He turned me down flat.

Goldmark did get a job in England, setting up a television research department for Pye Radio Ltd., but a year and a half later Pye felt the effects of the depression and got out of television. Goldmark returned to Vienna dejected but determined to continue working in the field.

To that end he set sail a few months later, in September 1933, for America.

In New York, he found an apartment in Brooklyn and before long got a job as a chief engineer for a radio manufacturing company, but he kept his eyes open for television opportunities and in the evenings worked on television designs at home. One of these designs was published in a British journal, and in late 1935 he received a call from an acquaintance at the Columbia Broadcasting Company. CBS was interested in getting into the television research game, and one of their engineers had noticed Goldmark's article. On New Year's Day, 1936, Goldmark began his career as a television engineer for CBS.

CBS had been created in 1927 when the United Independent Broadcasters (UIB), formed a few years earlier as a vehicle for promoting classical musicians, merged with the Columbia Phonograph Company (CPC) to form the Columbia Phonograph Broadcasting System. When the CPC withdrew soon after, the company decided to be known publicly as CBS. Despite huge investments by various individuals, the company was having trouble competing with David Sarnoff and NBC, so they turned to Sam Paley, millionaire founder of the Congress Cigar Company of Philadelphia. Paley's son, Bill, had shown his father the power of radio by advertising their cigars on a Philadelphia station; later his father had repaid him by putting him in charge of advertising their La Palina cigars on CBS. Now, although the elder Paley was reluctant to buy the broadcasting company, young Bill was champing at the bit. So, together, father and son bought out the majority of the company, and the next day, September 26, 1928, at the age of twenty-seven, Bill Paley "was elected president of a patchwork, money-losing little company called United Independent Broadcasters" ("CBS" was used only on the air).

Ten years later CBS was a well-respected broadcasting rival of RCA, and Bill Paley was a sort of younger alter ego of David Sarnoff. The two struck up a wary rivalry/friendship through frequent business meetings and lunches. Sharing Russian Jewish roots and an uncanny knack for taking winning business gambles, they engaged in an impassioned competition for broadcasting supremacy. "From the earliest days of radio," remembered Paley, "when he was the 'grand old man' and I was 'that bright young kid' we were friends, confidants, and fierce competitors all at the same time."

Paley, however, did not share Sarnoff's enthusiasm for technological research. He admitted that technology interested him little; it was broadcasting—entertainment—that he wished to conquer. So although CBS was a strong radio network by the mid 1930s, they had not joined in the race to produce television, aside from buying an RCA experimental system and carrying on some limited tests.

Then, in 1936, with a staff of three, Goldmark began his campaign to cajole and harass Bill Paley into supporting television research. At first they focused on black-and-white television, and Goldmark set out to improve means for transmitting motion-picture films on TV. Soon CBS gave him another engineer, making a total of five television researchers working on the tenth floor, who became known as CBS's "five-and-ten department." To assuage Paley's thirst for bettering Sarnoff, Goldmark oversaw the building of a one-million-dollar transmitting studio on top of the Chrysler Building, to compete with RCA's Empire State Building transmitter. As Goldmark said, "the urge to beat RCA and its ruler, David Sarnoff, was such an overriding force at CBS that it actually began to shape the direction of my own career." Nor had Goldmark forgotten that RCA was one of those companies that had declined to hire him in his early New York days.

How was he to beat them at television technology, though? Even CBS's great new studio was using RCA cameras, which were the state of the art. The answer came to him in March 1940 in Montreal, as Goldmark and his wife took a postponed honeymoon trip. While killing time waiting for their train back to New York, they decided to see the previous year's blockbuster movie, *Gone with the Wind*.

> For me it was a uniquely exhilarating experience, not because of the performers or the story, but because it was the first color movie I had seen, and the color was magnificent. I could hardly think of going

back to the phosphor images of regular black-and-white television. All through the long, four-hour movie I was obsessed with the thought of applying color to television.

During the intermission I slipped into a corner of the lobby, whisked out my notebook, and started to calculate what would be required for color in television. In the hotel and on the sleeper back to New York I continued to fill the pages with equations. It was perhaps fortunate that I had seen the movie at the *end* of my honeymoon trip.

As soon as he returned to the CBS lab, Goldmark got the OK to work on color, and for the next six months he and his staff were "consumed night and day" with making his notebook sketches into a practical television system. "We tore colors apart," he wrote, "put them together, studied their physiological effects on the eye, and otherwise turned ourselves into experts in the art and science of the subject now known as colorimetry, which once haunted Sir Isaac Newton."

Goldmark's plan was for a sequential color system with a spinning color-filter wheel, similar to Baird's except that it used a cathode-ray system instead of Nipkow disks. Behind the lens in the camera tube he put a spinning wheel with three sets of filters—red, blue, and green. By synchronizing the wheel perfectly with the scanning electron beam, he would be able to scan the image six times per field: red, blue, green, red, blue, green, with the last three images interlacing with the first three. A similar wheel in the receiving tube showed a red filter when the "red" signal came through, and so on, reproducing the original color image. So it was a hybrid, neither all mechanical nor all electronic, taking an electronic system and using mechanical wheels to "insert" a color signal.

By June 1940, Goldmark had his apparatus working well enough to demonstrate it to CBS management. With vice presidents and research directors (but notably not Paley) crowded into his laboratory, he presented a transmission from color slides, "including a lovely Spanish dancer—dressed in a strong red-and-white costume." It was a success, and Goldmark got the go-ahead to begin transmitting experimental broadcasts from the Chrysler Building, using color movies.

By August Goldmark was convinced he could take over the fledgling industry with his color system, and he made his bold announcement at the NTSC hearings. His demonstrations to the FCC and NTSC members followed, and for a moment it looked like he might be right.

But Goldmark underestimated the determination of the companies that had devoted themselves for so long to perfecting monochrome television. Most of all, he underestimated David Sarnoff. At a staff meeting just after Goldmark's demonstrations, Sarnoff declared that Goldmark's apparatus was mechanical, like the old Jenkins and Baird televisions that had fallen by the wayside years before. If the NTSC accepted CBS's color system, it "would set back the cause of our technology by a generation. . . . The RCA will never allow this counterfeit scheme to be foisted on the American people," he vowed.

Goldmark took offense at the characterization of his system as mechanical: "CBS's field-sequential system is electronic," he wrote later, "and not mechanical as later charged by RCA in an attempt to denigrate the system. The only mechanical part is really the device that inserts the color at the transmitter, and the only reason we used a revolving color filter at the receiver was that no color tubes capable of performing this function were available at the time." Of course, the electronic portion of the system was not Goldmark's at all but simply Farnsworth's Image Dissector tube. The only part that was his invention was the mechanical revolving filter.

But Sarnoff had unknowingly put RCA in a defensive position months earlier. The RCA labs in Camden had been working for some time on an all-electronic color system, and although it was far from perfected, Sarnoff had decided to demonstrate what they had to the FCC in February 1940. The colors were inaccurate and the image distorted, but that didn't seem to bother Sarnoff. "I didn't want to sell the commission on color," he said years later. "I wanted to show that its possibilities were still a long way off. The pictures were terrible, but the principles for electronic transmission were sound. My scientists could make mechanical color as well as anyone. It didn't require any basic discoveries. It was the quick and easy way, but it was wrong from the beginning, and I knew it." Still, RCA's primitive demonstration served only to underscore the high quality of Goldmark's system eight months later. Even

RCA's Vladimir Zworykin wrote that despite the unattractiveness of using a mechanical filter wheel, "it produces better results than any immediately available."

The debate went on for the next year. Had the FCC been inclined toward color, CBS certainly would have been the committee's choice; but they, like the rest of the industry, were reluctant to forgo the potential success of monochrome television before giving it a chance in the marketplace.

Meanwhile, Goldmark was still hard at work. At the September 1940 demonstration, he had been unable to transmit live subjects in color. He cleared this next hurdle quickly, in December, by switching from the Image Dissector tube to a modified RCA Orthicon, which had the sensitivity necessary to do the trick. The following June the FCC gave its permission to broadcast color on an experimental basis, and regular broadcasts began from the Chrysler Building.

Even RCA seemed unsure that CBS color would fade away; their own network, NBC, gave a demonstration on May 1, 1941, of a color system almost identical to Goldmark's. They were careful, though, to make it clear that although this was the simplest method at the present time for color transmission, the future belonged to all-electronic color—when it was finally perfected.

On July 1, 1941, commercial monochrome television began, and color was all but forgotten; the FCC ruled that CBS's color broadcasts had to be kept experimental. Sarnoff and his allies had succeeded in keeping the spotlight on black-and-white TV. Goldmark kept working on his system, broadcasting from the Chrysler Building, but his push for public support had slowed. And then on December 7, the war came to America, and color was placed on the back shelf alongside black and white.

3. In late 1944, David Sarnoff returned to New York from Europe, where he had taken part in the Allied invasion as Eisenhower's top communications expert. He had overseen the construction of a broadcasting station powerful enough to reach all the Allied forces in Europe, coordinated all communications channels between headquarters and the invasion forces, and masterminded the distribution of information to the various international media. After the Allies liberated Paris, Sarnoff followed them and took charge of restoring the French communications system. At the war's end and after many months of lobbying, he received the promotion he had lusted for: he was made official brigadier general, Army of the United States. Though it was an honorary and political appointment, from that moment on all but his closest friends would address him as General Sarnoff.

In December 1944 Sarnoff called together his top executives, including chief scientists Charles Jolliffe and Elmer Engstrom, to discuss his next battle strategy. "Gentlemen," he declared, "the RCA has one priority: television. Whatever resources are needed will be provided. This time we're going to get the job done. There's a vast market out there, and we're going to capture it before anyone else."

To oversee the various projects involved in making commercial television work, he formed an unofficial committee that included the chief of NBC, the chief of manufacturing, and various service representatives. Once a month they met in Washington. "Everything came out just like each person promised," said Ted Smith. "Because Sarnoff pounded on people, he made it impossible for them to say, We didn't do this."

So in late 1946, while most of the industry was still preparing their postwar campaigns, RCA's 630-TS television set, the "Model T" of television, began rolling off the production line. By the end of the year, the set, with its ten-inch screen, had sold 10,000 units at $385 each. The next year, 250,000 television sets were sold, four-fifths of them RCA. Broadcasting stations were popping up all over the country, and advertisers were paying a total of three million dollars to NBC for prime-time slots.

Goldmark had spent the war commuting between New York and Cambridge, Massachusetts, where he worked for the Office of Scientific Research Development (OSRD). The OSRD had been created as part of the war effort, and Goldmark joined Frederick Terman's lab at Harvard working on radar-jamming technology. He subsequently went to Europe to set up the OSRD's apparatus in England. He was also instrumental in supporting the D-day invasion by creating a diverting "ghost" invasion; a small fleet of wooden barges picked up German radar and retransmitted it so as to create the illusion of an entire Allied invasion fleet far from Normandy.

Back at CBS headquarters in New York after the war, Goldmark returned to color television, with an added dimension. In his work on radar countermeasures, he had become infatuated with ultrahigh frequency, or UHF. Using UHF, he thought he could give the public forty more channels, as compared to the six available on VHF (very high frequency) at the time. After a short time of tinkering with his color wheel and working on UHF, he found he was able to do it. It was easy enough to convince Paley; CBS's young millionaire president needed something big to stand up to Sarnoff's takeover of the new television industry. By the end of 1945, Goldmark was giving demonstrations of his latest apparatus at the CBS labs for special guests, including advertisers and prominent visitors from business and government. "I found myself in show business," he recalled, "giving performances at two and four o'clock. I must admit I loved it. We handed out questionnaires to collect people's reactions and found nothing but enthusiasm."

In early 1946, CBS decided it was time for a formal demonstration of Goldmark's color to the FCC. So on January 31, Charles Denny, new chairman of the FCC, and assorted other guests filed into the Tappan Zee Inn at Nyack, New York, overlooking the Tappan Zee, the widest part of the Hudson River, about twenty miles north of Manhattan. After many days of strained nerves and assiduous care, Goldmark's team had finished setting up several laboratory models of their color receiver, each sporting a twelve-inch screen. "After pleasantries had been exchanged," recalled Goldmark, "we all sat down and hunched forward in front of the TV sets."

I gave the necessary introduction to the assemblage, threw the switch, silently prayed a bit in Hungarian, and waited.

In an instant starlet Patty Painter, our nineteen-year-old heroine from Beckley, West Virginia, filled the tube. Her skin glowed a natural flesh pink, her long auburn blonde hair glistened, and the piquant smile and dancing blue eyes drew appreciative smiles from all of us.

Denny seemed as pleased with the picture as Goldmark, and they weren't the only ones. The *New York Times* called CBS color "superior to the Technicolor seen in the movies. . . . A few looks at [CBS] color television and black and white seems drab indeed." Harriet Van Horne of the *New York World-Telegram* wrote that the "brilliant young physicist named Dr. Peter Goldmark" had created "nothing short of a miracle. . . . [His color TV] is beautiful beyond description . . . and the vistas it will open should have a profound effect on every phase of the entertainment and advertising business, not to mention the arts, letters and sciences." And the *Wall Street Journal* had "little doubt that color television has reached the perfection of black and white."

All through 1946, while the FCC deliberated the commercialization of color, Sarnoff waged a public war against CBS, making "incompatible" the catchword of his campaign. Because Goldmark's color transmitter sent out three separate pulses, one for each primary color, ordinary receivers set up to receive one signal could not pick up the picture. If CBS color was authorized by the FCC, said Sarnoff, there were a quarter of a million sets out there that would show nothing but static. And the number was growing; the disaffected population would be in the millions by the time color got off the ground. While Goldmark had developed a converter to attach to black-and-white sets in order to receive his color signal—a device he called "relatively small, simple, and neat, one that I felt would add little cost to the set owner"— Sarnoff brushed off the contraption as "inefficient, ugly, and expensive."

RCA color, on the other hand, would be, when it was perfected, completely compatible with existing black-and-white sets (for reasons explained later). If the FCC could only wait the five years or so necessary to complete development, the public would be rewarded with five good years of black-and-white television, followed by color that would be much higher quality than CBS's and that could still be viewed on their old sets in black and white. They would not have wasted their money on their old sets, and they could switch to a new color set when their personal finances permitted.

CBS, knowing that each black-and-white set sold was another blow against their color system, put out a public relations campaign urging the public to wait for color before buying their television set and calling for the FCC to approve color quickly. As a show of their confidence, CBS declined to apply for licenses to operate VHF black-and-white stations in four major cities, retaining only their New York City license. Anticipating approval, they prepared to apply for UHF licenses all over the country. They put out the word, as Paley recalled, that "for anyone to invest in black and white would be a waste of effort and money."

Then, without warning, the tide seemed to turn against CBS. On January 30, 1947, the FCC declared that the CBS system was "premature" and required further testing before it could be approved. The FCC reaffirmed its monochrome standards, RCA happily flooded the market with receivers, and CBS "had to scramble to buy the four VHF licenses it had spurned," paying a new price that had risen by millions.

"We felt we had been dealt a foul blow," said Goldmark. They didn't feel any better six months later, when Denny accepted a post as vice president of NBC. Everyone at CBS "cynically noted" the coincidence and felt sure that David Sarnoff had once again seduced government and had his own way.

Sarnoff had certainly won a crucial victory. The FCC's decision would buy him an invaluable period of time for his lab to perfect their all-electronic color system; it also let him saturate the market with black-and-white sets, rendering CBS color more and more impractical every day.

But Goldmark could not accept that his dream was over. "I couldn't forget color TV," he said. "It was a burr in my soul." He found an outlet for his passion in 1948, when he was approached by a pharmaceutical firm regarding the possibilities of television as a tool for teaching surgery. Within a year, he and his lab had rigged their color system into a closed-circuit television adapted specially for medical use. On May 31, 1949, the first live operation in front of television cameras took place at the University of Pennsylvania, and in December Goldmark took his system to the American Medical Association's annual meeting in Atlantic City. Goldmark's team set up their equipment in the operating rooms of the Atlantic City Hospital and televised operations to fifteen thousand viewers in the convention hall. Reception was so good, said Goldmark, that "we began to measure the impact of our television shows by the number of faintings we could count."

The response from the press and the audiences was enormous, but Bill Paley, still reeling from the loss of pride and funds stemming from the FCC's decision, was fast losing confidence in Goldmark. When Goldmark returned from Atlantic City, he received word from management: "The chairman has decided he has no further use for the [television] lab. He'll give you just thirty days to shut down—and lay off the personnel." Goldmark responded with outrage and managed to get a ninety-day delay.

"The next few days and nights," wrote Goldmark, "I prowled the laboratory like a caged animal. When my staff spoke to me, I didn't hear what they were saying. My mind was dark with resentment. . . . At night, before I fell restlessly asleep, I tore through the paraphernalia of my brain, seeking to press it for ideas that I could build confidence in, enough confidence to sell others and to save the laboratory from extinction." Some of his staff left and found other jobs; one of his assistants resigned to enter the priesthood. "There seemed to be an air of depression around the laboratory."

Then Goldmark settled on a new course. If UHF was out, why not go back to VHF, simply molding his newest color system to the old transmission standards? After a month of "weight-losing, intensive concentration, and frenetic activity," he developed a new method of transmitting his color on the low frequencies, as well as a new process that he called "crispening," which sharpened the picture considerably. At the same time, word of their Atlantic City success was spreading—Congress even declared that CBS had made "an important contribution to mankind"—and people were wondering why Bill Paley was withholding his wonderful color system. The order to liquidate the lab was quickly forgotten.

The FCC's new chairman, Wayne Coy, was showing a definite friendliness toward CBS, and he invited its scientists to Washington to give more color demonstrations. CBS took out full-page ads announcing the color shows and, on January 12, 1950, presented the first public broadcast of their "new" color system. Influential voices such as Senator Edward Johnson, chairman of the Senate Commerce Committee, demanded that the FCC "clear the way for color" before too many useless black-and-white sets were sold.

4. RCA's development of an all-electronic color system had been progressing steadily since 1946 and had moved along particularly well since late 1949. Just as Goldmark was desperately staving off Paley's threats to dismiss his lab, the RCA team was stepping up its pace. Elmer Engstrom, the head of the Princeton laboratories, recruited Edward Herold, one of RCA's top research engineers, to coordinate the effort. Engstrom had taken over as director of the television project sometime in early 1934 as a liaison between Sarnoff and the Zworykin team, and he would one day succeed Sarnoff as president of RCA. Herold remembered how Engstrom, a devout fundamentalist Christian and future associate of Billy Graham, evangelized him with the Sarnoff gospel:

> I remember vividly that day in 1949—it was September 19—when Elmer Engstrom called me to his office. . . . Elmer asked me if I would coordinate a major company effort, a crash program so to speak, and show within three months that a color-picture tube was possible. He promised top priority to the project—all the manpower we could use, and "money no object," i.e., essentially unlimited funds. I don't know whether he thought I was too ignorant of the difficulty to object—after all, I wasn't a picture tube expert, and I wasn't even close to this work. In fact, however, I knew the job was just about impossible. Could unlimited effort reach an unattainable result? To be truthful, I didn't think so, but it sure was a challenge to try.

Meanwhile, Sarnoff was immersed in a constant public-relations battle. In 1949, as chairman of the board, he appointed a new RCA president who would be his aide-de-camp in this effort. Frank Folsom was a merchandising expert who had directed naval procurement in Washington during the war. "A tough, jowly, blunt-speaking extrovert with close-cropped graying hair," Folsom had been a favorite of Sarnoff's since he had come to RCA in 1947 to command the marketing campaign for the postwar television drive. He had quickly created the nationwide RCA Service Company to attend to problems any customer was having with an RCA set; the company was the first of its kind and a major factor in pushing RCA to the top of the sales charts.

Sarnoff had retained the services of one of the country's top public relations firms, Carl Byoir and Associates, to champion the cause of RCA electronic color, and now Folsom summoned the Byoir staff to his office. As one RCA manager remembered, "Folsom briefed the five Byoir men seated in front of his desk on the history and dimensions of the color conflict. It was, he assured them, the most fateful industrial conflict in American history. The future of electronics technology hung in the balance. If the forces of mechanical color triumphed, the march of science would be subverted by the horse and buggy. America's leadership of free world technology would be weakened. Stalin would love it. To one of the impressionable young Byoir staffers, a mental picture formed of dark and deserted scientific laboratories dotting the nation, grass growing in the streets."

Folsom told them that the public had formed an image of RCA as a wealthy, corpulent emperor of communications and of CBS as the underdog, riding on the invention of the brilliant scientist Goldmark. They had to stem CBS's momentum and buy time until electronic color could take over.

FCC hearings on color were under way once again, and throughout 1950 the color war raged in the papers, on radio, and before the commission. RCA's Engstrom pleaded with the commission to "specify compatibility as a requirement for any approved system." Frank Stanton, president of CBS, admitted that compatibility would be desirable but maintained that it was only a pipe dream. Goldmark testified that "the possibility of the RCA system ever becoming a practical broadcast service is extremely doubtful."

Both groups also participated in heavy lobbying and secret meetings with congressional leaders, hoping to sway them to their side. An air of espionage enveloped their activities. "To conceal our relations with Washington," said Goldmark, "we never took the Pennsylvania Railroad from New York because the press and RCA spies might wonder why. Instead, we took a circuitous route over the Baltimore and Ohio. When we arrived in the capital, we registered incognito in a small hotel and held meetings with various influential senators. I might add that these undercover precautions made little difference. The next day we read about our meetings in the papers." RCA representatives were just as busy, roaming the halls of Congress, chatting up anyone they felt had influence with the FCC.

In the media, the slurs flew back and forth. RCA derided the "slave sets" with their bulky converters that CBS was promising, the "Rube Goldberg contraptions" or "mechanical harnesses" to be attached to pure electronic television. Stanton fought back on CBS radio, saying, "These criticisms are not true. Present sets can be adapted at reasonable cost; compatibility can be built into all future sets at a lower cost." FCC Chairman Coy and Sarnoff accused each other publicly of outright lying.

On May 3, the hearings reached a climax, as Sarnoff delivered his testimony. He was in his element; after more than thirty years of working the courts, the Congress, and the industry like a champion salesman, the General now sat before the commission with the air of an emperor—but an emperor with the toughness and street knowledge of the working man. Unlike other executives, Sarnoff needed no one to explain technical details to him; he was as comfortable discussing electronics as sales projections.

"You are being urged," Sarnoff warned the commission, "to build a highway to accommodate the horse and buggy when already the self-propelled vehicle is in existence." CBS itself, he swore, "would shelve its mechanical system in favor of an all-electronic system" were it available, and available it would be, if only the public could wait a few more years. His scientists were working feverishly, he said, and new developments were coming out of the lab almost daily.

Even his scientists couldn't keep up with Sarnoff's pace. Kenneth Bilby remembered that "[Sarnoff's] day in that period often began with an office breakfast [meeting], then a morning-long strategy session . . . then the race for a train to Washington, then dinner [where he was] briefed on the political eddies, then past midnight studying his briefing books in preparation for the marathon testimony he would give the next day." The next morning, after more updates, it was "onto the witness stand for eight hours of grueling interrogation. . . . Then the race for a late train to New York. Clouds of cigar smoke would seep from a compartment of the *Congressional* as he postmortemed his testimony and devised follow-up strategy. As midnight approached, his limousine would deposit him at the Manhattan town house." More often than not, his greeting to his wife was "Well, I guess I'll go upstairs to the office and get some work done."

But his incomparable work ethic and impassioned testimony were in vain. Chairman Coy, by now clearly a supporter of CBS, called for immediate tests between the two color systems. Publicly, Sarnoff welcomed the competition; privately, he knew he stood no chance. It was too early for his electronic color to perform properly. He had failed to win the necessary delay of perhaps another year that would allow his scientists to catch up with Goldmark's spinning wheels.

The September competition was no competition at all. A *Variety* headline read "RCA Lays Colored Egg." Sarnoff would later recall with scorn, "The monkeys were green, the bananas were blue, and everybody had a good laugh." Goldmark's color picture, in contrast, looked brilliant.

On October 10, 1950, the FCC approved CBS's color television and the corresponding broadcasting standards and declared that the system could be commercially marketed at once.

Never one to take a beating lightly, Sarnoff struck back. After issuing a scathing official reaction, he ordered an escalation of manufacturing and marketing of black-and-white sets. "Every set we get out there makes it that much tougher on CBS," he said.

Paley had responded to his own earlier FCC setback by cutting back on television research, but Sarnoff now called for an even greater intensification of lab research, a holy crusade of science to bring the color tube to perfection and obliterate the spinning disk from the television landscape.

Much had changed since the days of developing the black-and-white Iconoscope. In 1942 the Camden labs, along with all other RCA research facilities, had moved to the RCA Research Center at Princeton, New Jersey. Zworykin was still a revered figure at RCA but was not working on color television; he had moved on to other projects, in particular the electron microscope. Sarnoff now had hundreds of scientists and engineers working under Ed Herold on color-related projects in various laboratories, churning out hundreds of patents designed to control the electronic color-TV market. The liaison between this staff and Sarnoff was still Elmer Engstrom, who had assumed the post during the Zworykin days in 1934.

Sarnoff ordered shifts expanded to sixteen hours, including weekends. All work unrelated to color was put aside, and no expense was to be spared. In fact, he offered rewards of thousands of dollars for key developments. And like a motivational football coach taping clippings to the locker-room wall, he circulated excerpts of Goldmark's FCC testimony. "I don't think field tests will improve the [RCA] system," Goldmark had said. Asked if RCA should "drop the system now," he had replied, "I certainly do." Below these quotes, Sarnoff added his own comment: "The above is the most unprofessional and ruthless statement I have ever seen made by anyone publicly about a competitor. I have every confidence that the scientists and engineers of the RCA will answer this baseless charge by the improvements which I have already seen since the first demonstration and which will be made during the coming months."

Months, not years.

In the meantime, Sarnoff filed suit in U.S. District Court in Chicago to "enjoin, set aside, annul and suspend" the FCC ruling, as it "contravened" the most respected technological knowledge within the industry and would lead to the dissolution of the still nascent billion-dollar black-and-white industry. The court at first granted a temporary injunction against CBS's color authorization, but then on December 22, 1950, it upheld the FCC's decision. So in March Sarnoff and RCA appealed to the U.S. Supreme Court.

On May 28, 1951, the final decision came down. With only one dissenter—Sarnoff's friend and personal correspondent Felix Frankfurter—the Supreme Court ruled that "the Federal Communications Commission was within its authority" in approving CBS color the previous fall and "could not be found to have acted 'capriciously,'" as charged by RCA. However, they conspicuously declined to comment on the technical validity of the two color systems, insisting that "it was not for the courts to overrule an administrative decision merely because the wisdom of the decision might be questioned."

This was a monumental victory for CBS. "We had taken on the great Sarnoff, the king of Radio City, and won," declared Goldmark. "David had beaten the Goliath of industry. We trumpeted our victory from the pages of every important newspaper in the country."

It must have been as meaningful a triumph for Paley as for Goldmark. For nearly a quarter century, he had nurtured his personal and corporate victories in Sarnoff's shadow. He had built CBS into a broadcasting power—but one that still paled next to "the king of Radio City." Lately he had built a string of successes by raiding radio talent from RCA/NBC and ABC and bringing such figures as Jack Benny, Bing Crosby, and Burns and Allen over to CBS, but when it came to technology, he could never touch his "friend and confidant," the "grand old man." "I always thought his strengths lay in the more technical and physical aspects of radio and television," wrote Paley, "while mine lay in understanding talent, programming, and what went on the air. I never could learn what made the insides of radio and television work." Goldmark noted that "Paley came away from the decision a transformed man. He had just trumped the General in the place it hurt—the prestige belt."

The victory was clear; less certain were its consequences. CBS was authorized to begin commercial color broadcasting—but who would see it? There were no CBS color sets out there, and CBS had no manufacturing capabilities at the time. They certainly didn't even dream of turning to the manufacturing king for help; "the Supreme Court can't order me to make color sets for CBS" was Sarnoff's comment. The rest of the manufacturing industry, primed to unload their monochrome sets on the market, was equally uncooperative.

And so the official premier of CBS color broadcasting on June 25, 1951, was largely invisible. It was "a gala, one-hour show" appropriately called *Premiere,* featuring Ed Sullivan and other CBS stars. FCC Chairman Coy also appeared before the camera, praising CBS in "this hour of triumph," and CBS supporter Senator Johnson telegraphed his congratulations "on this historic day in the progress of man." The only problem was that no one, aside from special studio parties, could pick up the celebration. There were twelve million television sets in existence, but only two dozen or so could receive CBS color. When the rest were tuned to CBS that night, they showed nothing but "snow."

This meant it was up to CBS to join the ranks of manufacturers. They purchased the Hytron Radio and Electronics Corporation and its subsidiary, Air King, one of the top fifteen TV set makers, and prepared to put out CBS spinning-wheel color receivers. But it would be years before they could turn out a line of TV sets in economical and profitable fashion. And in the meantime, they feared, RCA technology would be gaining on them.

In fact, it had already caught up. In the six months since Sarnoff had begun the legal proceedings, RCA's laboratory blitzkrieg had been marching forward without cease. Engstrom remembered it later as "the most intense, and exhilarating, experience" in his professional life. Twenty-four hours a day the various labs worked on, manned by specialists in camera tubes, receiving tubes, set design, fluorescent materials, electron guns, and radio transmission. Buoying them all with constant support, criticism, and domineering leadership was the General.

"It wasn't the normal boss-employee relationship," said Charles Jolliffe. "It was as if Sarnoff became one of the group. He was probing all the time."

"You have no idea what that did for our morale," said Merrill Trainer, a junior engineer. "For somebody of his importance to come down and suffer that torture just to see for himself really impressed us."

"Invention on demand," one engineer called it.

"He saw what was needed," said Engstrom, "and, applying wartime techniques, directed us at forced draft. Sarnoff taught us the word impossible had no place in our vocabulary."

By the time of CBS's "invisible" color premier, Sarnoff was ready to unveil the product of this indefatigable effort. At the end of his life he would say of it, "Never before have I witnessed compressed into a single device so much ingenuity, so much brain power, so much development, and such phenomenal results."

The apparatus to come out of Princeton was indeed ingenious. The major principles had existed for decades, but the intricate precision necessary to make it work had come only from the twenty-four-hour furnace of perspiration and inspiration fired by the General. The design that emerged was originally proposed by Alfred Goldsmith, who had directed RCA's old mechanical television lab at Van Cortlandt Park in the 1920s, and was perfected under the direction of Harold Law. "It's all done with mirrors," they say about certain acts of legerdemain, and indeed the RCA color camera started with mirrors.

Dichroic mirrors, to be precise. A blue dichroic mirror reflected only the blue component of the original image off to the side, where it was focused onto a regular monochrome camera tube. The rest of the light—the red and green components, that is—passed straight through and hit a red dichroic mirror. This reflected all red light off to the other side, where it was focused onto another monochrome camera tube. The remaining light, which by now was pure green, passed straight through and was focused onto a third monochrome camera tube.

So the color camera contained three black-and-white cameras. Each one scanned a picture comprised of a pure primary color and treated it like a black-and-white picture.

Wherever the original subject was pure blue, the "blue" tube transmitted a strong signal. Where it was pure red or green, the "blue" tube transmitted no signal. Where there was a mixed color, it transmitted a pulse corresponding to how much of that color was blue. So the color camera emitted three signals, corresponding to the red, green, and blue components of the image.

The RCA tricolor picture tube, or receiving tube, turned these black-and-white electronic signals back into color. The basic design was similar to a monochrome receiver: the received signal caused an electron gun to fire a beam of electrons, deflected and focused by magnetic or electrostatic plates, at a screen that glowed according to the intensity of the signal (and beam). In the color tube, however, there were three electron guns, each one connected to a signal corresponding to one of the primary colors. And on the screen was a matrix of hundreds of thousands of tiny triangles, each comprised of three discrete dots. Each dot was made of a different chemical, called a phosphor, which glowed a particular color when excited by an electron beam.

The electron beam corresponding to the blue component struck only the blue phosphors, which glowed blue according to the intensity of that beam. The "red" and "green" signals activated the "red" and "green" beams, which in turn hit only the red and green phosphors. A perforated "shadow mask" was placed right next to the screen and acted like a sieve, allowing through only those electrons that would hit the proper phosphor. Each tiny triangle would form a distinct color based on the relative brightness of its red, blue, and green phosphor.

So, for example, in the portions of the picture that were red, only the red phosphors were excited, and the green and blue phosphors were untouched by electrons. And so on. Where the picture was black, no electrons would be shot at any of the phosphors; and where it was white, the electron guns would hit the three phosphors with equal intensity.

The three color components were scanned simultaneously, not sequentially as in the Goldmark system. Every one-sixtieth of a second, the entire picture was scanned, separated into the three color components, and transmitted. And every one-sixtieth of a second, the receiver's three electron guns painted the entire picture simultaneously with red, green, and blue, left to right, line by line. The colored phosphor triangles were so tiny and so numerous that the human eye couldn't distinguish them; each triangle blended into one mixed color, and the matrix of triangles blended into one clear polychromatic picture.

The final ingenious aspect to RCA's color system was its compatibility. As discussed so far, the color signal, trifurcated as it was, would make no sense to an old black-and-white receiver poised to receive one signal only. So the RCA engineers specializing in radio transmission had to figure out how to make the signal comprehensible to black-and-white sets; this, after all, was Sarnoff's principal claim to superiority over CBS's system, his major argument for waiting for RCA color.

The answer lay in the physics of color optics. As it turns out, there are two different ways to specify any particular color on the spectrum. One is, as we've discussed, to give the relative brightness of the three primary colors. The other, however, is to give the total brightness, along with the relative hues of just two of the primary colors. This latter method is how RCA obtained black-and-white compatibility.

By complex electronic methods, the RCA researchers managed to convert the three color signals into two signals: the total brightness or luminance, called the "Y" signal, and a complex second signal containing the color information. The circuitry that manages this conversion at the transmitter exists in reverse at the receiver, where the Y and color signals are converted back into the simple red, green, and blue components.

The Y signal, or luminance, corresponds to a regular monochrome signal. After all, that's what black and white is: the total brightness of the scene, devoid of color information. They sent out the Y signal by the same standards as the old black-and-white signal, and any black-and-white receiver could pick it up. The color signal existed as an extra pulse, which the color sets with their sophisticated circuitry would pick up and mix with the Y signal. Black-and-white sets would simply ignore it.

Only a few months after Herold took over the color project, he recorded in his notebook, "A three-gun tube with H. B. Law's shadow-mask screen . . . was demonstrated by L. [Leslie] Flory [an important member of Zworykin's old TV team] . . . [a screen of] about 4" by 5" . . .

excellent registry in the center . . . good rendition of colors, and adequate brightness made this demonstration outstanding." Under Sarnoff's intense dictatorial program, it took just one more year to progress from this first success to a tube that would stand up to the scrutiny of a public demonstration.

So, at the end of June 1951, just a few days after CBS's "invisible" premier, Sarnoff and RCA proudly unveiled their new achievement in a demonstration at NBC's Washington studios. The following week they presented a larger demonstration at RCA Exhibition Hall in New York, a twenty-minute program for over two hundred invited guests from the industry and the media. It was a triumph. Nanette Fabray and Yma Sumac danced and sang show tunes, performing lovebirds fluttered their wings, and a troupe of swimmers and divers showed off at a nearby swimming pool—and the three electron guns in each of the receiving tubes painted the scenes over and over again, sixty times a second, in true living color.

Jack Gould of the *New York Times* reported that the demonstration "changes the whole outlook on the dispute over video in natural hues." The demonstration, he said, "put the FCC on a spot which is certain to become controversial and embarrassing. Technically, it ultimately may be proved that the FCC committed a classic 'boner.'"

Broadcasting Magazine declared that "no one could ask for better color," and the *Baltimore News Post* added that "all-electronic color is now an actuality." Allen DuMont, one of the industry leaders who had been suspicious of Sarnoff's color promises, jumped on the bandwagon, announcing that RCA color was "good enough to start commercial programs immediately." *Time* celebrated the occasion a few weeks later, remarking that though Sarnoff "lost a round to CBS last year . . . he did not stay down. . . . It looked as if radio's miracle man had not run out of miracles."

5.   Observers of RCA's demonstrations may have been forecasting the imminent commencement of commercial broadcasting in electronic color, but Sarnoff himself was less jubilant. Although his hour of triumph was apparently at hand, he insisted that the system was still two to five years away from commercial viability. Just as Sarnoff had resisted a premature launching of television in the 1930s that would have infringed on the radio market, so now he was reluctant to throw anything in the way of RCA's long-awaited monochrome gold mine.

And once again war was playing its part in the drama of unfolding technology: this time it was a small "police operation" in Korea. Productive capacity in general was slowed, and in particular the materials needed for production of color sets were deemed crucial to the war effort. CBS used the war as an excuse for delaying their production of spinning-wheel color sets, but in reality they were having trouble starting up a manufacturing business—just as Sarnoff had predicted. When in October 1951, Director of Defense Mobilization Charles Wilson ordered the suspension of color TV production for the duration of the war, both CBS and RCA happily complied.

For CBS, this took them off the hook, suspending the embarrassment of being unable to take advantage of their FCC victory. Sarnoff, however, couldn't have scripted it any better. As long as the war went on, RCA would continue to mass-produce their black-and-white sets, pulling in a fortune as the market leader and inundating the country with sets that couldn't receive CBS color. By the end of the war, there would be six million more strikes against CBS. At the same time, RCA engineers could continue to improve their color system, invisible to the constricting gaze of the public. Publicly, Sarnoff avowed that the ban was heaven-sent for CBS, saving them from ridicule for failing to capitalize on their victory. But he knew better than anyone that if the war was an act of God, then Someone up there was holding RCA stock.

When the war ended in 1952, CBS's color system was still the only one approved by the FCC, but there was little doubt that RCA color was the way of the future. Millions of black-and-white set owners were unlikely to shell out another hundred dollars for a CBS adapter. In fact, CBS was making little effort to push such adapters, and there were virtually no CBS color sets on the market. During the National Production Authority's hearings to consider revoking the color ban, Sarnoff accused CBS of favoring the ban because it relieved them of the burden of marketing an untenable product. CBS's Stanton retorted that Sarnoff was "abusing the processes" of the hearings to "carry on his bitter and desperate campaign to frustrate color." Meanwhile, the National Television Standards Committee was reestablished, consisting of two hundred engineers from ninety-one manufacturing companies; their goal was to create an "industry color system." Although the system they demonstrated to the press in August 1952 was virtually the RCA system, Sarnoff "was willing to play along since he recognized the political advantages of an industry system—a 'face-saving' device for the FCC, he privately called it."

On March 25, 1953, only two years after its huge FCC victory, CBS president Frank Stanton put up the white flag at a House committee hearing. With twenty-three million black-and-white sets in consumers' hands, he admitted, "it becomes economically foolish for us single-handedly at this time to resume a large scale broadcasting and manufacturing program." The *New York Times* headline the next day announced, "CBS Jettisons Monopoly on Color Video Production."

On December 17, 1953, the FCC officially reversed their 1951 decision and voted to accept for commercial broadcasting the RCA system that the NTSC had been demonstrating for over a year. It would officially be known around the world as the NTSC color system, but David Sarnoff didn't mind. RCA owned virtually all of the hundreds of patents controlling it.

In late December, Sarnoff ran full-page ads in the leading newspapers proclaiming RCA's "great victory." "We added sight to sound at the 1939 World's Fair," the ads read. "Now we add color to sight. . . . The opportunity to enrich the lives of people everywhere is a privilege of leadership." Industry rivals were incensed, and longtime RCA enemy Philco put out its own full-page ads declaring the new color standards were the result of an industry-wide effort, "not the work of any one company." This campaign was futile; Sarnoff made sure the public knew that the standards set by the NTSC were based on the system that had been invented and brought to commercial quality by RCA.

The FCC, meanwhile, was taking the pillorying prophesied by the *New York Times* two years before. They were portrayed in editorials as a group of nonscientific politicians who had set back the industry and punished the public with their ignorance. "The history of television," wrote the *Times,* "is a history of official procrastination, a history that brings out the danger in bureaucratic rule."

Still, progress had won out over bureaucracy; the ineluctable superiority of the electron, as Sarnoff would say, had finally won the day. And as soon as the massive RCA manufacturing machine could swing into action, the American public would be able to see the world on their little screens, in living color.

A year later, however, RCA color had lost all momentum; CBS may have surrendered, but the marketplace beachhead was far from won, and David Sarnoff was back on the warpath. He later called it "the toughest battle of my life."

In early 1954, RCA had followed through on promises of commercial production, and the first RCA color TV set rolled off the production lines. It was a model with a twelve-and-a-half-inch screen, and it cost a thousand dollars, as compared with the three-hundred-dollar, twenty-one-inch top-of-the-line black-and-white set. The idea, as with all new technological products since, was first to attract the wealthy buyers and then bring the price gradually down as sales increased. As he had for his Radio Music Box, Sarnoff announced bold sales predictions: 75,000 units in 1954; 350,000 in 1955; 1,780,000 in 1956; 3,000,000 in 1957; and 5,000,000 in 1958.

But at the end of the year, the warehouses were bulging with unsold sets; only 5,000 sets had been shipped out, not 75,000. Performing in a controlled demonstration was one thing, but mass-producing a set that could stand up in the hands of the average consumer was quite another. The RCA Service Company was receiving twice as many calls from the owners of color sets as from monochrome owners, and customers complained that they were unable to adjust their set for perfect color.

Sarnoff's enemies naturally jumped at this opening. Zenith announced they would produce no more color sets until the technology improved on RCA's "Rube Goldberg contraption." GE, Philco, and Westinghouse (which had actually beaten RCA to the punch by getting out the first commercial model) halted production as well. GE's revered chief, Ralph Cordiner, complained that "if you have a color set, you've almost got to have an engineer living in the house." CBS, which had already made the switch and was transmitting in NTSC (RCA) color, abruptly fell in line and canceled color broadcasts.

The general opinion, from Wall Street to various industry corporate offices (and even in the halls of RCA) was that Sarnoff had jumped the gun. *Time* called color TV "the most resounding industrial flop of 1956."

Sarnoff, having just celebrated his sixty-fifth birthday with a new, ten-year contract as CEO for two hundred thousand dollars a year, responded with a holy crusade. A marketing task force began the big push to get color into American homes. Advertising expenses tripled, and complimentary color sets were sent out to influential journalists, financiers, congressional leaders, and the White House. RCA organized neighborhood viewing parties for special NBC "colorcasts." And Sarnoff got his old pal and wartime boss, President Eisenhower, to appear on NBC dedicating the network's new Washington studios.

Sarnoff also began cutting the prices of his color sets, down to seven hundred dollars in 1955 and five hundred dollars the next year. But sales remained sluggish throughout the 1950s. By 1959, RCA had poured more than 130 million dollars into color development and marketing, still without recording a dollar of annual profit. As *Fortune* magazine later wrote, "for five years after it marketed its first set in 1954, RCA found itself the solitary tenant of the new world."

But by 1960 color was taking over American life in other ways, from pastel shark-finned automobiles, gaudy ties and clothes, and big color spreads in magazines to the now ubiquitous color movies. Sarnoff was more convinced than ever that color TV would inevitably follow.

That summer he made an important step in that direction, acquiring the popular Walt Disney television program from ABC, where it had been broadcast in black and white. NBC announced that they would begin showing the program that fall in color. From the moment it premiered, *Walt Disney's Wonderful World of Color* was a national hit. And the NBC peacock became famous, displaying its feathers in brilliant color.

Also by now, RCA had improved their color sets, with bigger screens, more stable color, and simpler controls. As the black-and-white market became saturated, the public slowly began to turn to the newest attraction. At the end of 1960, RCA announced that for the first time they had registered a profit from color sales. The next year RCA announced a one-million-dollar profit from color.

In 1961, longtime RCA foe Zenith finally gave in and placed an order for fifty thousand twenty-one-inch color tubes; four years later, twenty companies were manufacturing color sets using RCA tubes. Even CBS finally capitulated and quietly resumed color telecasts. Sarnoff declared 1965 "the year of fulfillment for our long struggle," and for good reason. Mainly due to color TV, RCA's net profit that year surpassed one hundred million dollars; Sarnoff ordered a fifty-million-dollar manufacturing plant expansion to meet the orders of the rest of the industry. Somewhere along the line, "V-C" day had passed; the color war was won.

As one might imagine, color television in the United States has undergone some development since the first NTSC-approved system. And officially at least, much of the rest of the world uses two different color systems. But basically the color television being broadcast all over the world operates on the same principles that came out of the David Sarnoff Research Center (as it was renamed in 1951).

In 1960, Japan adopted the NTSC color standards, but a few years later, Sony developed a new type of picture tube on which to receive them. Dubbed the Trinitron, it worked along the same principles of transforming the signal back into red, green, and blue components and then using these three signals to fire electrons at red, green, and blue phosphors on the screen. But the Trinitron screen, instead of having triangular clusters of the three phosphors, consisted of ultrathin phosphor stripes running the entire height of the screen, alternating red, green, and blue. A shadow-mask screen, similar to the original one but in this case having slits instead of holes, ensured that the electron beams hit only the color they were supposed to.

Spurred on by the Japanese achievement, which produced more stable colors, American engineers quickly modified their triad screens, and today American color tubes use screens with tiny rectangular strips of red, green, and blue, similar to the Trinitron scheme except that they are discrete rectangles instead of continuous stripes. If you put your face very close to your screen while it's turned on, you can easily see the separate phosphor rectangles.

In Europe, two different systems came into prominence in the 1960s. At the 1967 Berlin Radio Exhibition, Walter Bruch (who had worked in the television laboratories of Manfred von Ardenne and Dénes von Mihály before moving to Telefunken and manning the RCA-built Olympia Cannon at the 1936 Olympics) unveiled the Phase Altternation Line (PAL) system now in use in most of Europe. PAL is, however, basically the NTSC system with some modifications. In the NTSC system, the hue signal is phase modulated, as opposed to the Y brightness signal, which is amplitude modulated (AM), just like AM radio. This means that instead of changing the height, or amplitude, of the sine wave, you change its phase—you shift the entire wave to the left or right. Bruch found that if he reversed that phase shift every other line, any errors occurring in the transmission would be erased, and he would get a sharper picture.

France developed their own variant of the NTSC system, called SECAM (Système Électronique Couleur Avec Mémoire), and implemented it at around the same time as PAL. Its method of supposed improvement was—rather than transmitting the colors simultaneously—first to transmit a line of luminance and red, then a line of luminance and blue (remember, you only need the total luminance plus two of the three primary colors). It held the content of each line scan in storage (*mémoire*) until the next line came, when it would mix the two together. Why this should result in a better picture is an obscure and complex matter, but the French were convinced that their system was the best, and they managed to sell it to the Soviet Union as well.

So by 1970 color television around the world was set up pretty much as it is today, with North America and Japan using NTSC standards, France, its dependencies, and the former Soviet Union using SECAM, and the rest of Europe adopting Germany's PAL. But all these systems grew out of, and in essence are closely related to, the RCA tricolor camera and picture tube that emerged from the Princeton labs in 1951.

Peter Goldmark did enjoy some success at CBS, most prominently with the invention of the 33⅓ rpm long-playing record, which beat out RCA's 45 rpm record to be the music industry's staple for thirty years. But Bill Paley could never forgive his chief inventor for the color debacle, and he came to consider Goldmark "a thorn in [his] side"; "I couldn't wait until he reached sixty-five," he later remembered, "so I could retire him."

After his forced retirement, Goldmark formed his own company, Goldmark Communications Corporation, which quickly became a subsidiary of Warner Communications. Shortly afterward, he died in a car crash near his home in Westchester, New York. To the bitter end, Goldmark insisted that his sequential color system had been the best available at the time and that his aggressive pushes in 1940, 1946, and 1950 had served a vital purpose in history: to spur on color development and bring color to the American home years—even decades—earlier than might otherwise have happened.

He may indeed have served an important historical purpose as Sarnoff's foe in the color war. For certainly nothing spurred Sarnoff on like a direct challenge, particularly a challenge to "the electron." With black-and-white TV comfortably sweeping the country and profits increasingly pouring in, RCA may well have enjoyed the gradual saturation of the market and let the progress in the color labs proceed at a normal scientific rate. If not for Goldmark, that annoying, self-assured, persuasive thorn, Sarnoff never would have ordered round-the-clock research and ten-thousand-dollar bonuses for breakthroughs; he never would have rallied his troops into a six-month crusade in late 1950 to produce electronic color at all costs.

It was certainly the high point of an unequaled career in corporate battle. Looking back in 1981, Paley marveled at the performance of his old mentor, friend, and rival: "The way he refused to accept defeat . . . the way he kept coming back to Washington and rallying his people . . . the way he drove those scientists to perfect his system. No doubt about it, Sarnoff was magnificent in color."

EIGHTEEN

The Fading Days
of Lone Inventors

In its deceit, its outright lies, its spinelessness, its weak-mindedness, its pointless violence, in the disgusting personalities it holds up to our youth to emulate, in its endless and groveling deference to our fantasies, television undermines strength of character, saps vigor, and irreparably perverts notions of reality.

Frederick Exley, *A Fan's Notes*, 1968

1 . The metamorphosis of television from a dream into an industry made Philo Farnsworth a dinosaur at thirty-three. Over the winter and summer of 1940, as he lost control of his "baby" and his patents grew closer to expiration, he sank into an alcoholic depression. He had gone from clean Mormon abstinence to consuming several highballs a night. "It's come to the point," he told Pem, "of choosing whether I want to be a drunk or go crazy."

Doctors were no help. One prescribed chloral hydrate as a sedative, and it soon had him refusing to eat or move. Another suggested he take up smoking, thinking "a finger-habit may soothe [his] nerves." He took the advice, and the result was one more addiction added to his problems.

Nothing worked. "Phil had a nervous breakdown," according to his sister Laura. "There was a doctor who kept giving Phil uppers to try to help him out . . . [so] Phil had a drug problem as well as alcohol." Farnsworth Television and Radio became a major supplier of the war effort, but its eponym floundered. "Nothing I did seemed to help," said his wife. "He seemed bent on self-destruction."

He also fell completely out of touch with old friends. On October 29, 1943, Everson wrote him a bittersweet note:

> Farnsworth was admitted to trading on the NY, SF, and LA Stock Exchanges this morning. . . . Our baby is really of age now and can fend for itself.
>
> How are you getting on? Take time out and write to me.

After an operation for a strangulated hernia, he became dependent on the painkiller Pantipon. To combat it, he committed himself to the Baldpate Sanatorium near Topsfield, Massachusetts, where he underwent a drastic program including shock therapy. The war years, which ravaged Europe with firebombing and artillery, riddled the quiet inventor with depression and chemical dependency.

Peacetime brought no improvement. First his brother Carl died in a private-plane crash, and then the Maine estate burned down in an enormous forest fire, two days before a scheduled appointment to upgrade their insurance. Everything they owned was rubble, including Phil's laboratory, his library of over two hundred volumes, and Pem's heirlooms; the "estate . . . [without] a penny's encumbrance," into which he had poured so much of their fortune, was gone.

Farnsworth Television and Radio was unable to compete with RCA and other giants in the commercial television industry after the war. Farnsworth returned to Fort Wayne, but nothing could be done. After initially rejecting a takeover bid from ITT in hopes of saving the company, the board of directors in 1949 finally had to accept, and Farnsworth had no choice but to resign himself to the sale. He sent off a letter to his stockholders:

Dear Farnsworth Stockholder:

Most of you know that my entire working life has been devoted to the development of electronic television, the last 11 years with this company which bears my name. None of you can be more deeply concerned than I have been by the bitter facts which our company has had to face.

I write to you now as a Farnsworth stockholder holding over 10,000 shares, which I am voting in favor of the IT&T plan.

Farnsworth remained vice president in charge of research and advanced engineering, but the Farnsworth company disappeared from the commercial television scene. He worked on various other projects, but without the intensity of his youth. Jim McGarry, an ITT plant manager at the time, recalled Farnsworth's demeanor:

He spent most of his time in a personal think tank. He was a very quiet, introverted type person. If you walked into a room and said one of these 50 people is a shoe clerk, they'd probably pick out Phil Farnsworth.

In 1958, after three invitations, he finally agreed to appear on Garry Moore's *I've Got a Secret* TV show. Identified as "Dr. X," Farnsworth's secret, displayed to the audience and sought in vain by the panel, was "I invented electronic television in 1922—at the age of fourteen." His identity undiscovered, "time ran out, and Phil was declared the winner and handed his prize—an $80 check, a carton of Winstons, and Garry Moore's eternal gratitude: 'We'd all be out of work if it weren't for you.'"

But a game-show host's gratitude wasn't enough; by and large Farnsworth was a forgotten man, denied any credit for his television work. "For a while," said Pem, "he wouldn't even allow the word television to be used in our home. When the *Encyclopedia Americana* asked him to do the article on television he just threw the letter in the wastebasket." The *Encyclopaedia Britannica* didn't bother to ask; their entry on the invention of television fails to mention Farnsworth.

In the last two decades of his life, Farnsworth continued to suffer from depression, as well as a bleeding ulcer. Doctors removed two-thirds of his stomach in 1954. He also suffered from a misguided obsession.

Farnsworth was convinced that he had discovered the key to the greatest scientific goal of the post–H-bomb era: the harnessing of nuclear fusion for peaceful energy production. For over a decade he poured all of his energies and savings into pursuing his ideas, and he even garnered some brief publicity in the *New York Times* and other newspapers. He and his wife mortgaged their home, sold their stock holdings, and cashed in their life insurance policies, but it was all for nothing; this time there was no solid scientific ground beneath the obsession.

It was his final fight. "He told me he was all used up," said Pem. "He had nothing more to give. He prayed God to let him die."

In January 1971, Farnsworth came down with pneumonia. He refused to go to the hospital, so a doctor came to the house and gave him penicillin, but his fever still rose to 105 degrees. He recovered briefly, but "rather than willing himself to live," said Pem, "Phil was willing himself to die." Unable to eat, he withered away.

Philo Farnsworth had conceived of electronic television at fourteen and turned it into fame and wealth in his twenties. He died on March 11, 1971, at the age of sixty-four, impecunious and isolated from the scientific community.

After his death, his son Philo Jr. characterized his father's entire life as "a romance with the electron." And so it was, punctuated by the repeated cycles of hope, ecstasy, and disappointment that characterize any obsessive love affair.

2. During television's incubation period, the world of the lone inventor was changing. Fading away were the days when an independent visionary could retire to the basement and quietly work out the mechanism of a dimly imagined product: the telegraph, the airplane, radio . . . More and more, instead, the inventions of the twentieth century would be so complex and expensive that corporate or university sponsorship would be necessary. There would still be exceptions—Steve Jobs, who developed the Apple computer, and Bill Gates, of Microsoft, had not yet made their mark—but increasingly, those who defied the pressure to engage in sponsored corporate research would pay heavily for their intransigence. John Logie Baird died like Farnsworth, a broken, frustrated man. Charles Francis Jenkins was one of our most prolific inventors, ranking in the top ten in number of patents held, but television was a mountain he could not climb. "Within two years of his company's collapse, the little man from Akron who had fathered the first video boom in America died penniless and, according to associates, brokenhearted."

The two corporate engineers fared better. Ernst Alexanderson came to television late in his professional life, and when his ideas didn't pan out, he simply turned his back on it and busied himself with other work. He had no regrets; he never looked back. His company, GE, stepped out of the television development ring in the mid 1930s and let the others fight it out, concentrating instead on the manufacturing and broadcasting side.

Alexanderson continued his prosperous career in engineering, officially retiring in 1948 just before his seventieth birthday but staying active even after that. In the 1950s he worked as a consultant to GE and then RCA, filing a number of patents for motor-control systems, among other things. His final patent, for an adjustable-speed motor-control system, was filed in 1968 and issued in 1973. He died on May 14, 1975, at the age of ninety-seven, still lucid and with "extraordinary recall" but suffering from deafness, near blindness, and anemia. As far as television was concerned, he had been relegated to the sidelines from the 1930s onward, watching as television reached the commercial stage and developed into the fulcrum of American home life.

On November 24, 1960, the then eighty-two-year-old Alexanderson wrote a letter to John Crosby, a television commentator at the *New York Herald Tribune:*

Fourty [sic] years ago I had occasion to speculate on the impact on the world of radio and television. Now we know some of the answers and it has occurred to me that the four most popular programs could be described as follows using the classical verse measure of hexameter:

> *Fist fights and females and guns with horses and wagon as background*
>
> *Fist fights and females and guns with a river boat as a background*
>
> *Fist fights and females and guns with indians and horses as background*
>
> *Fist fights and females and guns with horses and cows as a background*

This is not a sarcasm, quite the contrary. The popularity of these programs proves that the world is yearning for an escape from modern art, modern music and the cold war, wishing to return to fundamental emotions.

I hope you will encourage such programs with themes from other ages such as The Vikings and variations as a substitute for fist fights. There is no substitute for females.

Vladimir Zworykin was the only one of the television pioneers who can be said to have fully succeeded. Backed by RCA, he lived to see his brainchild develop into a system of communication that has revolutionized our lives, *and* he received due credit. But of course, neither he nor Farnsworth can be called *the* inventor of electronic television. Swinton first published the concept but never built the machine. Farnsworth gets credit for the first all-electronic transmission, in 1927, but one black stripe hardly counts as the final product. Zworykin, who committed to the cathode ray even earlier than Farnsworth, led the RCA team to the first machine of commercial quality, but in the end they were forced to combine their system with Farnsworth's. And of course a great many lesser players made their contributions. The credit must be shared.

After Zworykin left television during World War II, he had a long, full career at RCA in other areas, including his pioneering work in the development of the electron microscope. He was awarded the Presidential Certificate of Merit, the Institute of Radio Engineers' Medal of

Honor, the National Medal of Science, the National Academy of Engineering's Founder's Medal, and Germany's Rhein Ring award; he was elected a member of the French Legion of Honor, and in 1977 he was inducted into the National Inventors' Hall of Fame. After retiring from RCA, he became director of medical electronics at the Rockefeller Institute, then finally retired for good to his homes in Princeton, Taunton Lake, and Miami Beach. In one corner of his living room in each city, he had a console television set. He almost never turned it on. "I hate what they've done to my child," he said. "I would never let my own children watch it."

NINETEEN

The Digital Future: Smart Television

> *Message came back from the Great Beyond:*
> *Fifty-seven channels and nothing on.*
>
> Bruce Springsteen

On a chilly January morning in 1928 the citizens of Berlin were greeted by a curious sight. Leafing through the *Berliner Illustrierte Zeitung* at their breakfast tables or while riding the *Strassenbahn,* they came upon a full-page drawing: a man was shown lying in bed, steering a mechanical apparatus on his lap while watching a mountain panorama on a projection screen. "Marvels that we might still experience: viewing the world from bed through television," read the caption. "The viewer operates, by remote control, an airplane that carries the filming apparatus."

The drawing was somewhat chimerical. After all, it had been only four months since Philo Farnsworth had transmitted the world's first electronic television image: a straight black line, sent from one end of his small San Francisco lab to the other. The Berlin artist had certainly never heard of Farnsworth; rather, he must have been inspired by the hopeful designs of his countryman Max Dieckmann or by Scotsman John Logie Baird, who had been enjoying much publicity lately for his "Televisor."

Such fantastical imaginings were forgotten while Farnsworth and Zworykin raced toward realizing electronic television and Baird floundered and died along with his beloved spinning disk. But the long-forgotten vision of that 1928 magazine artist, of viewers telling their televisions exactly what to broadcast, has resurfaced in the Information Age of the 1990s. The key word now is "interactive," and the technology that holds such promise is digital television.

A 1996 television receiver works on almost exactly the same principles as did those designed by Farnsworth and Zworykin in the 1930s. The advent of color TV in the 1950s didn't change the basic process: scan an image with a beam of electrons to create an electrical signal, and then re-create the image at the receiver by turning that signal back into an electron beam and bombarding a fluorescent screen.

But a new technology will soon transform television into a digital machine worthy of the times. Images will still have to be scanned before they can be transmitted, but the resulting analog signals will be converted into binary signals: the code of zeros and ones used by any computer or other digital device. Those signals will assign bits of binary code to each element in the picture, defining its color and brightness and re-creating the original image.

As straightforward as it may sound, that technology is rewriting the rules of broadcasting. The passing, in February 1996, of the Telecommunications Act of 1995—which replaces the Communications Act of 1934—has spurred a flurry of debates over digital broadcasting standards. No matter how the act shapes up, digital televisions will do more than show the same old programs. Within a few years you may be reading and sending E-mail (or video-mail) and accessing the Internet through your television, as well as choosing your favorite camera angle to watch the U.S. Open tennis tournament. Someday you may even steer that remote aircraft (or the virtual equivalent) through a breathtaking mountainscape.

This revolutionary change in television had its genesis, at least publicly, in a technology not nearly so innovative. The occasion was a demonstration in Washington in 1987 by NHK, Japan's public television network, of their new high-definition television (HDTV) system. Known by the acronym MUSE, it produced pictures of stunning quality by doubling the number of horizontal lines in the picture. It was still a conventional analog system, but it served to thrust "HDTV" into the public consciousness.

It also woke the American television industry out of doldrums that had been growing since the 1970s. The Japanese had already taken over the TV, VCR, and stereo businesses; now it appeared they would do the same with HDTV. The National Association of Broadcasters, stung by the demo, lobbied hard for an American HDTV system, and Al Gore even made it a campaign issue in 1988.

The FCC responded by creating the Advisory Committee on Advanced Television Service (ACATS), headed by former FCC chair Richard E. Wiley. ACATS declared an open competition to create an American HDTV system that it could recommend to the FCC, and twenty-three proposals promptly hit their desks. All were analog. The common wisdom was that digital television wouldn't be ready until the twenty-first century, and in any case no one in broadcasting had any interest in an incompatible new system that would require them to create a market from scratch.

Then, in June 1990, California provided another industry-shaking development. In 1927 it was Farnsworth's pioneering all-electronic transmission; now, General Instrument (GI) announced the world's first all-digital television system.

GI's San Diego subsidiary, VideoCipher, had built its business on scrambling systems for cable broadcasters like HBO to prevent consumers from capturing their programs for free with satellite dishes. After the MUSE demonstration, GI began looking into developing an HDTV system that would be compatible with existing satellite technology, so that their security system would still be relevant. The main obstacle to producing digital HDTV was the difficulty of compressing the necessary data into a six-megahertz television channel. But satellite TV used twelve-megahertz channels, and so, according to GI Vice President Robert Rast, "it was easier for the people in GI to conclude that you could go all digital."

Once the ACATS competition opened up, GI began to wonder whether they could make their digital system work in a six-megahertz terrestrial channel. Should they jump into the race or not? With the proposal deadline approaching, Woo Paik took a week off and went home.

Paik has been called the engineering world's "premier HDTV celebrity." Sixteen years before his breakthrough at GI he came to the United States from Korea to attend graduate school at the Massachusetts Institute of Technology. Immediately after receiving his Ph.D., Paik joined Linkabit, Inc. (which would later spawn VideoCipher), at the urging of Jerry Heller, another MIT Ph.D. In 1989 Heller put him in charge of a pet project: digital HDTV. Now, in the spring of 1990, Paik suddenly had to tell Heller whether or not he could deliver.

"We had the compression simulated," Paik said, "but the system requires transmission and other things, which I just had to develop right there in my mind. We hadn't even simulated the transmission. I had to extrapolate based on what was known and say we could make it work."

It went against the favored mode of attack of Paik, whom Rast called "a hands-on guy, more empirical than theoretical. He doesn't want to sit and analyze things forever, he wants to go and do it." But there was no time to build a prototype to "do it" with, so Paik did sit and analyze. A week later he had accomplished his mission—he told Heller the project was feasible—and GI submitted their proposal to ACATS at the last possible moment. Paik, Heller, and computer-simulation expert Ed Krause—together with the other twelve engineers in the HDTV lab—bumped up ACATS's digital TV timetable by a decade.

The fundamental problem that the Paik team was able to surmount was that of too much information. Digital high-definition television encompasses about 1,500 megabytes per second (1,080 lines times 1,920 picture elements—or pixels—per line times 30 pictures per second times 8 bits per pixel times three, for each color). The most that can be transmitted in six megahertz, however, is about twenty megabytes per second. So the signal, after it is digitized from an analog scanned signal, must be compressed into about 1 percent of its original space. The solution lies in what Rast calls "compression tricks."

Today's analog television system transmits a complete picture frame thirty times a second. But since most of the picture is unchanged from one frame to the next, a lot of redundant information is transmitted. GI's digital system took advantage of that by transmitting only changes in the picture, once it had presented a complete frame. When a newscaster is on the air, for example, almost nothing in the picture changes except his face. By not retransmitting the wall behind him and the desk, you can save millions of bytes per second. Another key is to take advantage of the fact that movement often involves an unchanging object being simply displaced. So you have only to define the motion vector and not repeat the description of the object.

There are other tricks as well, and of course every so often you have to refresh the entire picture. "But the fundamental rule," said Andrew Lippman, director of the MIT Media Lab's Television of Tomorrow research program, "is that you never, never send a frame if you can avoid it. Only transmit changes."

Lippman should know, because many labs other than GI's had been working on digital video for years, and MIT was one of the earliest. Another MIT physicist, William Schreiber, was instrumental in getting top technical and businesspeople from around the industry to sit down together in the mid 1980s and discuss the future of television. The businesspeople wanted an analog system compatible with present TV sets, but the scientists told them otherwise. "Bill Schreiber and I, and others, really explored that," said David Staelin, also of MIT. "We really gave analog an honest shot, because they put such high priority on it. In the end we had to come back and tell them that it simply wasn't going to work. It cost too much and the rewards were too small."

MIT then turned to digital research and quickly made great strides. "The digital technology in image processing was developing everywhere," said Staelin. Still, top industry management was resisting what the labs were telling them. It wasn't until GI made its announcement that the digital ball began to roll.

"MIT didn't have real money," said Staelin, "so for us to go digital was not nearly so meaningful as for GI to go digital—when they said they were going to come out with a digital standard, suddenly that made things click in the minds of the business types." Within a few months of GI's announcement, both Zenith and the David Sarnoff Research Center announced their own digital systems. Obviously, these labs weren't suddenly developing digital television within the space of a few months. "It wasn't really as slapped together as it appeared," said Staelin. "The technical people had been working on it in the back room for a long time; they just hid it. It was more a coming out of the closet than it was a crash effort."

"Other people had been working on this but were afraid to step up," said Rast. "There was a certain amount of risk with this. Most people just hadn't done enough work to satisfy themselves that it was feasible, didn't want to take the risk."

The next year, 1991, GI built its first prototype, DigiCipher I. "And the thing worked," said Rast. "It did. To the amazement of many people." The race was on: HDTV would provide a new proving ground, a second chance for American industry to thrive in the promised land of television.

The question remained, however, of who would reap the enormous financial rewards of providing the winning technology. It soon became clear that digital television was too big a territory for one pioneer to stake out; the answer would lie in collaboration. GI and MIT had recently pooled their HDTV efforts, and Zenith and AT&T had signed a similar agreement. Then in July 1992 the GI-MIT team signed a royalty-sharing agreement with Zenith-AT&T, and the digital television industry began to look like Europe in 1914, with treaties bonding entities that had long been fierce competitors.

"We had a situation," said Staelin, "where whoever won the race would own patent rights and could charge everyone else an arm and a leg to use them, and this created an atmosphere of uncertainty and fear among the contestants." This allowed ACATS chair Dick Wiley, who had the reputation of being a masterful deal maker, to bring the remaining players together in May 1993 and avoid war. The group—GI, MIT, Zenith, AT&T, the Sarnoff Research Center, Thomson Consumer Electronics, and Philips Consumer Electronics—chose a name borrowed from Winston Churchill himself: the Grand Alliance.

Free to combine the best features from a number of systems and unfettered by court actions between rival corporations, the alliance moved quickly. Within a year it had decided on the particular elements it would use—the exact compression methods, transport protocol, signal modulation, and audio system—and in November 1994 it held its first over-the-air field tests in Charlotte, North Carolina. The month after that, its members began a campaign of demonstrations in Washington and elsewhere designed to convince the FCC and all who might influence it that the age of digital television was here.

At a recent demonstration for the broadcast industry, it was hard to argue otherwise. A golfer hit out of a sand trap, and the individual grains fell off his club with perfect clarity. A snowy lake scene of a kingfisher diving for prey raised no pulses from a distance, but as one approached the screen the picture became eerily lifelike. At no matter how close a distance, no lines were visible, and the snowflakes remained distinct and sharp; one felt one was just seeing farther and farther into the panorama.

Experts outside the industry, though, provided a very different picture. "There are thirty-six ways of modulation being proposed, of which this is one," said Richard Solomon, associate director of MIT's Research Program on Communication Policy. "The alliance is just a bunch of entrepreneurs trying to peddle their own system." The alliance sees its system as the U.S. standard for many decades to come, and the broadcasting industry agrees, but Solomon and others see the entire concept of an approved, closed architecture as a mistake. "The bad news," wrote Nicholas Negroponte, founding director of MIT's Media Lab, "is that we are still mindlessly addressing the wrong problems, those of image quality—resolution, frame rate, and the shape of the screen. Worse, we are trying to decide once and for all on very specific numbers for each and to legislate these variables as constants. The great gift of the digital world is that you don't have to do this." Just as modems today already "handshake" with the other end of the line to determine the best common protocols with which they can communicate, so digital televisions should be flexible enough to adapt to various scanning rates and screen sizes. Today's PCs already have higher-resolution monitors than any TV; why not use an existing computer to receive digital television programs and then gradually upgrade? "So we get to HDTV, sure," said Solomon, "but we get to it by creeping up on it, the same way we got hi-fi."

"The Grand Alliance system has lots of limitations and problems," Bill Schreiber agreed. "It doesn't support inexpensive receivers. And many people are going to be surprised when they have to put up an expensive, heavy-duty antenna. You can forget about rabbit ears—they won't do the trick." Even the alliance admits that their first receivers would cost several thousand dollars, but they point out that the first television sets in the 1940s and the first color sets in the 1950s were just as expensive for their time.

The real question is whether the public wants HDTV at all. According to the MIT contingent, most consumers are relatively undemanding where television images are concerned. "Our studies showed that if people liked a program, then they would put up with terrible picture quality," Schreiber said, "as long as the sound was OK and the picture was reasonable."

"There is no overriding demand," agreed Solomon, "for people to spend thousands of dollars to upgrade their antennas and buy new cathode-ray monitors right now, just to see pictures that are slightly different."

According to Don West, editor of *Broadcasting and Cable* magazine, fewer than half of today's broadcasters are interested in transmitting high-definition programs. Why should they spend the ten billion dollars or so to convert their stations to digital, simply to show their viewers the same old programs? As Jonathan Blake, general counsel of MSTV, put it, "there will be no net gain in the eyeballs which they can sell to advertisers." Richard Solomon was even blunter: "I don't think there's any prospect for HDTV in our lifetime."

If HDTV is dead, though, digital TV remains the bright beacon of the future. For ever since television went digital, an entire range of new possibilities aside from high definition has emerged. The mantra now among many researchers, broadcasters, and government officials is "It's not about pretty pictures anymore."

From the very beginning, the scientists involved knew that the digital compression technology would not only allow them to show a high-definition picture over a regular six-megahertz channel but it would also give them the option of transmitting five or six programs of standard definition over that channel. It's no secret to broadcasters that they stand to make much more money by "multicasting" than by offering just one program with higher picture quality.

Digital television, however, will do much more than present six times as many soap operas at once. When the TV signal is digital, the home receiver is a computer in its own right. This means that broadcasters could offer not only entertainment programming but also computer services such as E-mail, two-way paging, and Internet access. And that's just the beginning. In the future, television itself will adapt to its new digital biology. There will be no reason for people to wait until 11:00 to see the news, for instance. As soon as a particular news report is prepared, it will be available to be plucked off a worldwide menu for instant viewing. Videocassettes and rentals will become obsolete, as cineasts find an entire library of films available to them instantly. Television will become more like a newspaper, as viewers pick out just the programs and reports that interest them and watch them whenever and wherever they want. They might be in their living room, in front of a flat active-matrix screen the size of the wall but only a few inches thick and clear as a window. Or they might be on the subway, watching a paper-quality laptop screen.

Negroponte predicts that someday "smart televisions" will scan through thousands of hours of available programming each day and pick out an hour or so of clips of particular interest to their owners. Instead of networks "broadcasting" everything to everyone, the individual viewers will "broadcatch" just what they want to see.

By that time, the Internet may well be a broadcasting venue of its own, with videos as well as text and photographs. Instead of "home pages," users will have their own virtual television stations on the Net.

"Any rational social commentator would have to say that television is going to become more like the Internet, and vice versa," said Lippman. Who will watch your personal sitcom is another question.

Technological visionaries, however, often disregard the sobering effect of the free market economy. Ernst Alexanderson was sending faxes and advocating a commercial service in 1930, but that technology was not available to the public until the mid 1980s. The German Post Office was running a video telephone service in 1936, but that innovation still hasn't found a market niche. When profits are questionable, or when big-business interest in old technology is threatened by a new technology, the public doesn't always get the full benefit of what the laboratories have discovered. Digital audiotape (DAT) is another example. The technology was there several years ago for the public to be able to create perfect digital copies of music compact discs. The music industry, however, was able to suppress this obvious threat to CD sales, and DAT effectively has been sabotaged by high prices and low visibility.

Technological visionaries also tend toward the quixotic regarding the effects their machines will have on the human race. Just as David Sarnoff in 1931 proclaimed that television would bring "a finer and broader understanding between all the peoples of the world," so Negroponte now predicts great harmonizing power for digital TV: "While the politicians struggle with the baggage of history, a new generation is emerging from the digital landscape free of many of the old prejudices. These kids are released from the limitation of geographic proximity as the sole basis of friendship, collaboration, play, and neighborhood. Digital technology can be a natural force drawing people into greater world harmony."

Sarnoff was wrong, and so will be Negroponte on this point. It is easy to be seduced by technology so that it appears to be a panacea for all the evils of the world, but the fact is that the kids who hang out on the Internet are no less racially prejudiced than working-class kids who hang out on the ball field. Radio and television contributed nothing to world harmony (witness Bosnia and Palestine), and neither will digital TV. Only human beings can do that. The limiting factor is not the technological capability to communicate but the human willingness to listen.

The digital pundits will undoubtedly be more accurate in their visions of what will physically become of television, although its exact shape is yet to be determined. In the short term, it will be up to the free market to determine whether broadcasters inaugurate digital television with high-definition pictures, multicasts of regular programs, a variety of computer services, or a combination of all. The last option is the most logical, as Negroponte points out: "At night, when few people are watching TV, you might use most of your license to spew bits into the ether for delivery of personalized newspapers to be printed in people's homes. Or on Saturday, you might decide that resolution counts (say, for a football game) and devote fifteen million of your twenty million bits to a high-definition transmission."

No matter which possibilities for digital television are realized and which fall by the wayside, television is about to metamorphose in dramatic ways. With or without the Grand Alliance system, television will probably go digital over the next fifteen years. In the new century, it will become as different from today's TV as the 1939 RCA World's Fair telecast was from radio.

If Philo Farnsworth had reached the age of ninety, he would have had to smile at the advent of digital television, for in a sense it is the ultimate realization of his hay-field dreams of 1921. The switch from analog to digital is analogous to the movement from mechanical television to electronic cathode-ray TV that he and Zworykin urged so passionately. Cathode-ray TV freed us from the crippling lassitude of the spinning disk, and digital TV frees us from the limitations of analog pictures. Just as electronic television made possible the transmission of moving pictures free from blur and flicker, the new television technology presents all the limitless possibilities—for manipulation and interaction—of the digital age.

Farnsworth's 1927 electronic transmission itself was an initial step toward digital TV. Today's digital TV camera first scans an image (with a chip instead of a cathode ray) to produce an analog signal, then digitizes that signal. But even a cathode-ray scanner is at the most basic level a digital device: the electrons flying out of the mosaic are quanta—individual "ones" as opposed to zeros. (When our machines can count this digital electron flow, we'll be able to skip the intermediate digitization step.) It's almost as if Philo knew, riding his hay mower back in Idaho, that all the countless scenes that would be sent through the air over the generations, from his assistant's smoke rings to men walking on the moon, were nothing more than information.

What thrilling lectures on solar physics will such pictures permit! . . .
What could be a more fitting theme for a weekly half-hour of television
than a quiet parade through some famous art gallery, pausing a moment before each masterpiece while the gifted commentator dwells
briefly upon its characteristics, explains its meaning, recounts the
story of its creation, its creator? What could be more richly entertaining, more uplifting, than such experience? . . . Can we imagine a more
potent means for teaching the public the art of careful driving safety
upon our highways than a weekly talk by some earnest police traffic officer, illustrated with diagrams and photographs?

Lee De Forest, 1950

Sir Thomas Beecham says he believes that television can do much to
improve the musical taste of the nation.

The London *Times*, September 1, 1936

In television the criterions of merit will inevitably be placed high. One
may dare a banality [in radio, but] the artist well knows this could not
be tolerated if he were beheld by his listeners. . . . Obviously the sponsor's advertising message must be much more politely, tactfully admin-
istered [than in radio], a much smaller pill, more sweetly coated.

Lee De Forest, 1950

I think it will be admitted by all, that to have exploited so good a scientific invention for the purpose and pursuit of entertainment alone
would have been a prostitution of its powers and an insult to the character and intelligence of the people.

Sir John Reith

We have perfected the biggest timewaster of all mankind.

Sir Isaac Schoenberg, EMI

Television? The word is half Greek and half Latin. No good will come of it.

C P Scott, editor, *Manchester Guardian,* 1928

Chronology

1872	Joseph May discovers that selenium's conductance of electricity is enhanced by light.
1878	Senleq proposes facsimile transmission using selenium scanner and telegraphy.
1880	First articles in *Nature, English Mechanic,* and *Scientific American* about early models of television.
1884	Paul Nipkow patents television scanning disk.
1900	First use of term *television* by Perskyi at International Electricity Congress, part of 1900 Paris Exhibition.
1906	Max Dieckmann builds rudimentary fax machine using cathode-ray tube.
1907	Boris Rosing at Saint Petersburg Technical Institute designs mechanical scanner with cathode-ray-tube receiver.
1908	Allan A. Campbell Swinton proposes cathode-ray tube for both scanning and receiving.
1911	Rosing patent for synchronization. With college student Vladimir Zworykin as assistant, he achieves first distant transmission of images. Receives gold medal of Russian Technical Society. Swinton describes cathode-ray system in detail. An article in *Scientific American* discusses future uses of television; entertainment is not among them.

1919	RCA formed as a subsidiary of GE by combining patent holdings of American Marconi, GE, and the navy. Twenty-eight-year-old David Sarnoff is named commercial manager.
1921	Philo T. Farnsworth, age fourteen, has hay-field vision of electronic TV scanning.
1922	C. Francis Jenkins transmits still pictures by wireless with mechanical system.
	Farnsworth explains electronic TV system to his high school teacher Justin Tolman.
1923	Working for Westinghouse in Pittsburgh, Zworykin files patent application for all-electronic television system; still unable to build and demonstrate it.
	John Logie Baird begins TV work. Achieves "world's first" TV picture.
	Jenkins applies for his first TV patent.
	Hungarian Dénes von Mihály, working in Berlin, files patent for "Phototelegraphic Apparatus." His book, *Das elektrische Fernsehen und das Telehor,* the first book exclusively about television, appears.
	Ernst Alexanderson begins his TV work at GE.
1924	Kenjiro Takayanagi begins work in Japan.
1925	Jenkins transmits picture of "readily recognizable moving objects" (a windmill) in Washington.
	Zworykin demonstrates a system to Westinghouse; told to "work on something more useful."
	Baird demonstrates his system at Selfridge's in London.
	Dieckmann's apparatus on display at the German Transport and Traffic Exhibition in Munich (not shown to work).
1926	Baird gets first license ever to transmit television.
	Farnsworth meets George Everson in Salt Lake City. Financed with Everson's $6,000, they form partnership. Farns-

worth marries Elma Gardner and moves to Los Angeles to begin research. Receives backing of Crocker syndicate and moves lab to Green Street, San Francisco.

Alexanderson speech in Saint Louis; press already crowning him "inventor of television."

1927

January: Alexanderson demonstrates mechanical TV to Institute of Radio Engineers.

April 7: AT&T gives demonstration of its mechanical system, televising Secretary of Commerce Herbert Hoover's speech from Washington to New York via phone cables; also wireless demonstration from New Jersey to New York City. Hailed as "the transmission of sight, for the first time in the world's history."

September 7: Farnsworth transmits a straight line via electronic system. "THE DAMNED THING WORKS!"

1928

January 13: Alexanderson and Sarnoff present GE mechanical system to the press: "the radio art has bridged the gap between the laboratory and the home." GE system hailed as the world's first television. May 11: GE begins regular TV broadcasting. August 22: They televise Governor Al Smith's acceptance speech. September 12: They televise a play, *The Queen's Messenger.*

May 11: Mihály demonstrates mechanical system in Berlin. Calls it "the first true demonstration of electrical television."

July 2: Jenkins begins broadcasting, and the First Television Boom is on. December: Jenkins Television Corporation created with $10 million in common stock.

Baird transmits from London to New York.

Takayanagi demonstrates cathode-ray system in Japan.

September 2: Farnsworth demonstrates his system to the press in San Francisco. The first demonstration ever of all-cathode-ray television. *Chronicle's* headline: "S.F. Man's Invention to Revolutionize Television."

1929

January: Zworykin meets with Sarnoff at RCA headquarters in New York. Predicts two years and $100,00 to produce electronic television. Sarnoff agrees to fund his work.

June: Fernseh A. G. formed in Berlin, combining Baird, Loewe, Bosch, and Zeiss-Ikon.

Summer: Farnsworth team replaces motor generator with vacuum-tube generator. Now has first truly all-electronic system, with no moving parts whatsoever.

November: Zworykin announces development of the Kinescope, his cathode-ray receiver.

1930

January 3: David Sarnoff becomes RCA president at the age of thirty-eight.

April: Zworykin visits Farnsworth's San Francisco lab, praises the Image Dissector camera tube: "I wish that I might have invented it."

In new Camden laboratories, Zworykin tries to develop a camera tube as good as Farnsworth's Image Dissector, to go along with Kinescope.

May 22: Alexanderson's demonstration at Proctor Theater, Schenectady. Mechanical system televises orchestra, other acts. Alexanderson's last hurrah.

Baird telecasting three nights a week on BBC; his large-screen system shown in London, Berlin, Paris, and Stockholm.

In England, HMV Gramophone and Columbia Gramophone join to form EMI, partly owned by RCA Victor. Baird International, Ltd. is formed.

1931

April: Sarnoff visits Farnsworth's lab, makes $100,000 offer, which is rejected. States "there's nothing here we'll need."

May: Zworykin turns toward using one-sided camera tubes. Summer: Sanford Essig bakes photoelectric mosaic too long, accidentally creating beautiful mosaic of insulated globules—the "final link." October: Zworykin names his new

tube the Iconoscope. November 9: First successful Iconoscope tested. Zworykin finally has his all-electronic system, at least in theory.

June: Farnsworth signs contract with Philco, moves lab to Philadelphia.

August: Berlin Radio Exhibition features Manfred von Ardenne's cathode-ray system. Called "the world premiere of electronic television."

1932   First Television Boom dissolves, and so does Jenkins Television Corporation. Its assets sold to De Forest Company and then to RCA.

Sarnoff demonstrates RCA system in New York, then drapes curtain of secrecy over lab. Last RCA demo for four years.

Baird televises British Derby in movie theater.

Viewing public in London estimated at ten thousand, based on Baird Televisor sales.

1933   April: Farnsworth applies for patent on first low-velocity storage camera tube.

June 26: Zworykin announces his Iconoscope (with no demonstration). In lab, finally has his all-electronic system performing.

BBC conducts test comparing Baird and EMI, won by EMI. Baird company begins cathode-ray research.

Under pressure from RCA, Philco drops Farnsworth. Farnsworth sets up his own lab in Philadelphia.

1934   March: Sarnoff cancels television broadcasts from Empire State Building and turns that space over to Major Edwin Armstrong for tests on his FM radio system.

August: Farnsworth demonstrations at the Franklin Institute's new museum in Philadelphia.

Baird using cathode receivers, but still needs electronic camera. Invites Farnsworth to visit and demonstrate his Dissector. September: Farnsworth goes to England, demonstrates his system, and secures patent-licensing deal.

Francis Jenkins dies.

1935   Patent interference 64,027 between Zworykin and Farnsworth, declared in 1932, finally ruled in favor of Farnsworth. This decision will prevent RCA from gaining total patent control of television.

June: Pressured by EMI's success in London and fearing FM's potential takeover of radio market, Sarnoff evicts Armstrong from the Empire State Building and announces million-dollar research and testing plan for television.

In Germany, Hitler's antiforeign, anti-Semitic edicts force Baird and Loewe out of Fernseh. Mihály's lab is dissolved when foreign investment pulls out. Telefunken, however, is able to sign licensing deal with RCA and use their Iconoscope. March: The Reichspost begins what they call "the first television broadcasting service in the world." Quality is poor, receivers are few.

1936   April: First RCA demonstration in four years. Using all-electronic system, they are transmitting pictures of 343 lines at thirty frames per second.

Farnsworth transmitting entertainment programs from Wyndmoor, Pennsylvania, station, also at 343 lines and thirty frames per second.

Summer: Berlin Olympics televised by Telefunken and Fernseh, using RCA and Farnsworth equipment, respectively.

Fall: Farnsworths travel to England to help Baird in his competition with EMI. They then go to France and Germany.

November 2: BBC begins two-year Baird-EMI competition, broadcasting from Alexandra Palace (called "world's first, public, regular, high-definition TV station").

November 30: Fire destroys Baird labs at Crystal Palace.

1937   February: BBC declares EMI victor in competition.

The coronation of King George VI and the Wimbledon tennis tournament are televised in England. Nine thousand sets are sold in London.

France orders world's most powerful transmitter to be constructed in Eiffel Tower. In the U.S., eighteen experimental stations are operating.

1938   Farnsworths buy farm in Maine in the hope that spending time there will ease Phil's growing depression and alcoholism.

June: RCA announces Image Iconoscope, a camera six to ten times more sensitive than Iconoscope.

Radio Manufacturers Association recommends to the FCC that commercial television be launched with standards of 441 lines and thirty frames per second (RCA's standards). Philco, Zenith argue vehemently against it. October: Sarnoff announces that RCA will inaugurate regular broadcasting at the World's Fair next April.

1939   March 31: Farnsworth Television and Radio is incorporated; operations begin in Fort Wayne, Indiana.

April 20: In broadcast from the World's Fair in Flushing, Queens, Sarnoff announces, "Now we add sight to sound." Ten days later, at opening ceremonies, FDR is the first president to be televised. Television sets go on sale the next day, and RCA (NBC) begins its regular broadcasts.

June 7: RCA announces its Orthicon low-velocity camera tube, ten to twenty times more sensitive than the Image Iconoscope.

Twenty thousand sets operating in England.

October 2: Farnsworth signs patent-licensing agreement with RCA. First time RCA has ever agreed to pay royalties to another company.

1940   Sarnoff, FCC wage media war over whether commercial television should begin. FCC announces September 1 starting date, then cancels when RCA jumps the gun with advertising. Forms the NTSC to decide on industry standards. In the meantime, there are twenty-three experimental broadcast stations in the U.S.

June: RCA and Philco televise the Republican convention from Philadelphia.

August: Peter Goldmark announces to the NTSC that CBS has marketable color technology.

1941   March: The NTSC recommends standards of 525 lines and thirty frames per second. FCC authorizes commercial broadcasting beginning July 1.

July 1: NBC begins commercially sponsored broadcasts; CBS, DuMont, and others follow in the fall.

December 7: Pearl Harbor.

1942   Commercial production of TV equipment banned for duration of war. NBC's commercial TV schedule canceled.

1946   CBS's color demonstration to the FCC at Nyack, New York. Publicly lauded as having "reached the perfection of black and white."

Baird dies.

RCA model 630-TS, the "Model T" of television, rolls off the assembly line. Sells 10,000 units by end of year, at $385 each.

1947   FCC declares CBS color "premature." RCA is flooding market with black-and-white sets.

1949   RCA steps up development of all-electronic color system.

Farnsworth Radio and Television sold to ITT. Philo Farnsworth, at forty-three, suffering from alcoholism and drug dependency, is out of television.

1950   Goldmark and CBS present new improved VHF color system, still using mechanical color wheel. Throughout year, CBS and RCA wage media war. Sarnoff calls CBS system a "horse-and-buggy" system, a "mechanical harness" to be put on black-and-white sets.

September: "RCA lays colored egg" in competition. October: FCC approves CBS color for commercial broadcasting. However, CBS has no means of mass production and the market is flooded with black and white. Sarnoff orders "holy crusade" in the RCA laboratories to perfect electronic color.

1951   June 25: CBS televises one-hour gala color premier, featuring Ed Sullivan and others. But only two dozen sets in the country can pick it up.

End of June: RCA demonstrates its new electronic color system. "Changes the whole outlook," says the *New York Times*.

October: Color TV production suspended for duration of Korean conflict.

1953   March 25: CBS concedes victory to RCA in the color war.

December 17: FCC officially reverses its own decision, authorizes NTSC color (basically the RCA system, standardized by the NTSC) for commercial broadcasting.

1954   Early in year, first RCA color set put on the market, with twelve-and-a-half-inch screen, for $1,000. By end of year, only 5,000 sets sold.

Following years of fruitless lawsuits against Sarnoff and RCA, Edwin Armstrong commits suicide.

1956   *Time* calls color TV "the most resounding industrial flop of 1956."

1960   NBC acquires Walt Disney TV program from ABC, premiers *Walt Disney's Wonderful World of Color.*

After more than $130 million spent in development and marketing, RCA records first profit from color TV. The next year, that profit jumps to a million dollars. In 1965, profits surpass a hundred million.

1971	Philo Farnsworth dies at sixty-four, impoverished and heart-broken.
1985	Zworykin dies, wealthy and well honored.
1987	Japanese television network gives demonstration in Washington of MUSE, their analog high-definition TV system (by this time, only one American company still manufactures TV sets). FCC creates Advisory Committee on Advanced Television Service, to find an American high-definition system.
1990	General Instrument's VideoCipher division announces an all-digital high-definition system, a decade before anyone thought digital TV would be possible.
1991	GI builds first working digital prototype, DigiCipher I. Other companies follow suit.
1996	February: Congress passes the Telecommunications Act of 1995, replacing the Communications Act of 1934 and paving the way for the new era of digital television.

Notes

All letters relating to Philo Farnsworth, as well as his journals, are located in the Farnsworth file of the Archives division of the University of Utah library in Salt Lake City. Ernst Alexanderson's letters and journals are at the Schaffer Library, Union College, Schenectady, New York; other GE and Alexanderson material is at the Hall of History at GE in Schenectady. Vladimir Zworykin's journals are at the David Sarnoff Research Center in Princeton, New Jersey. All other references are to the Bibliography.

Part One, Prologue: A Note from the General

5   *The General* . . . Sarnoff's rank was granted at the end of the Second World War in recognition of his administrative work and his prominence in civilian life. It was an honorary title; he never held a general's command, but forever afterward he liked to be addressed as "the General."

6–7   *In ordinary AM* . . . Lewis.

One: The Dream

10   *"My dear Latimer Clark . . ." Journal of the Society of Telegraph Engineers* 2 (1873): 31.

11   *"Selenium's sensibility to light is extraordinary . . ."* The phenomenon was given the name *photoconductivity*; later, when the electron was discovered toward the end of the century, it was understood as a transfer of energy from the impinging light to the atomic electrons. This loosened them from the bond of the nucleus and thus made them more mobile, and since electric current is simply a flow of electrons, it made the selenium more conductive to electricity.

11   *very quickly the basis for both schemes was shot down when* . . . Sale, R. E., "Action of Light on the Electrical Resistance of Se," Royal Society of London *Proceedings* 21 (1873): 283.

11   *"complete means of seeing by telegraphy . . ."* Nature (Sept. 23, 1880): 499.

13   *"sealed description of a method of seeing by telegraph". . .* Scientific American (June 5, 1880).

13   *"While we are still quite in ignorance . . ."* Nature (Sept. 23, 1880): 499.

13–14   *Dr. Hicks of Bethlehem, Pennsylvania . . .* English Mechanic (April 30, 1880).

16   *LeBlanc was not able to do this . . .* Abramson (1987), 11.

16   *Two years later William Lucas published his ideas . . .* W. Lucas, "The Telectroscope," English Mechanic (April 1882).

17   *"It was television over the telephone wires . . ."* Dunlap, 129.

19   *"a national technological myth was created . . ."* Elsner et al., 207; Halloran, 159.

Two: Puir Johnnie

21   *"Never since the days when King Robert Bruce . . ."* Tiltman, 16.

21   *"tranquility and freedom from adventure . . ."* Mowat, 145.

23   *"when his name was mentioned . . ."* McArthur and Waddell, 48.

23   *"frequent ill-health . . ."* This and subsequent quotes and anecdotes from J. L. Baird (except where noted).

29   *The word itself had just come into use . . .* Abramson (1987), 23.

30   *He went down to the Hastings public library . . .* Margaret Baird.

30   *"The only ominous cloud on the horizon . . ."* Journal of Scientific Instruments 4 (1927): 138.

31   *"he had little money . . ."* R. W. Burns, "The First Demonstration of Television," Electronics & Power (Oct. 9, 1975).

32   *According to Norman Loxdale . . .* Wheen, 13.

32   *Victor Mills was known in town as a wireless buff . . .* Wheen, 14.

33–34   *"It was mostly his back we saw . . ."* Margaret Baird, 46.

Three: The Three Lessons of Invention

38   *"within one year we shall be watching . . ."* Nature (June 4, 1908): 105.

38   *and by the age of six . . .* Tony Bridgewater, in Television (Sept. 1981).

38   *"problem can probably be solved by the employment of two

	beams of kathode rays . . ." Campbell Swinton, in *Nature* (June 18, 1908).
38–39	*"The Possibilities of Television"* . . . A. G. Jensen, in JSMPTE (Nov. 1954).
39	*Francis . . . was born of Quaker parents . . .* This and other biographical information in this section comes from Jenkins (1929).
40	*As a child on the farm* . . . Jenkins, unpublished autobiography.
41	*"It's the old story over again . . ."* Jenkins letter, quoted by Hollenback.
41	*the machine didn't go quite fast enough* . . . Jenkins (unpublished).
42	*In 1894 he had proposed a method* . . . Jenkins (1929).
43	*"developing radio movies to be . . ."* Jenkins (unpublished).
44	*"Invention is to me a very satisfying occupation . . ."* Scientific American (Nov. 1922).
45	*In June of 1925 he demonstrated a moving picture of a windmill* . . . Udelson, 27.
45	*"Congratulations were in order . . ."* Jenkins (unpublished).
45	*"I have just left the laboratory of Mr. C. Francis Jenkins . . ."* H. Gernsback, in *Radio News* (Dec. 1923).
45	*"Folks in California and Maine . . ."* Jenkins (1929).
45	*"in a more or less perfect form . . ."* Radio News, cited in Hollenback.
46	*an enthusiastic observer* . . . S. R. Winters, in *Radio News* (April 1925).

Four: They All Laughed . . .

47	*Memo from BBC producer to House superintendent* . . . Cited in Swift.
47–48	*In an attempt to obtain some financial backing* . . . This and following anecdotes come from J. L. Baird.
49	*"SELFRIDGE'S PRESENT . . ."* Various London newspaper advertisements (1925).
51	*"I cannot make you see the Statue of Liberty . . ."* London *Times* (Dec. 9, 1922).
54	*"a wonderful character, a churl . . ."* Susan Douglas, interview on PBS's *Empire of the Air*.
57	*"One could not help feeling sorry for his restless nature . . ."* Swift.

57	"I attended a demonstration of Mr. Baird's apparatus . . ." Quoted in Burns, op. cit.
59	"apparatus designed by Mr. J. L. Baird . . ." London Times (Jan. 28, 1926).
59	"the international race . . ." New York Times (Jan. 28, 1926).
61	With Baird's new success appeared an old friend . . . Tiltman, 43.

Five: Slumbering Giants

65	Two screens were shown. . . . Udelson, 31.
65	After the tour, the demonstration began. . . . Bell Laboratories Record 4 (May 1927): 302.
66	On January 11, 1927 . . . Udelson, 33.
67	"Our work in developing methods for transmitting pictures . . ." Alexanderson memo to Adams (March 10, 1923).
67–68	But television was not the object of obsession . . . This and the following biographical material concerning Alexanderson from Brittain.
68–69	"You'd be talking to him . . ." and "I once met him . . ." Kisseloff, 19–20.
69	"At the luncheon and dinner given this week . . ." Alexanderson memo to Adams (Jan. 5, 1923).
69	"This feat is conceivable." Alexanderson memo to Adams (March 10, 1923).
70	"Personally, I believe that short waves hold possibilities . . ." Alexanderson memo to Pratt (July 24, 1924).
70	"sixteen independent photo channels, each covering . . ." Alexanderson memo to Davis (Aug. 12, 1924).
70	"I have seen this device in operation . . ." Alexanderson memos to Allen (Dec. 10, 12, 17, 1924).
71	"I have no reason to change my opinion . . ." Alexanderson memo to Davis (Dec. 19, 1924).
71	"the test demonstrated the operativeness of all the principles . . ." Alexanderson memo to Lunt (Jan. 17, 1925).
71–72	"in one-tenth of a second . . ." Alexanderson memo to Lunt (April 21, 1926).
72	"Our work on picture transmission and television . . ." Alexanderson memo to Lunt (June 2, 1926).
72–73	He began his talk . . . Alexanderson, speech in Saint Louis (Dec. 15, 1926), in GE Review (Feb. 1927).

Six: The Path to Glory

76	*The picture that Baird was transmitting* . . . This and following quotations are from J. L. Baird.
79	*"the Baird apparatus not only does not deserve a public trial . . ."* Wheen, 21.
79	*In mid July of 1928 Campbell Swinton* . . . Letter to the Editor, London *Times* (July 19, 1928).
79–80	*"Baird and Hutchinson are rogues . . ."* Norman, 54.
80	*The BBC agreed with Campbell Swinton.* . . . Wheen, 22.
80	*They decided that Baird should set up a television transmitter* . . . J. L. Baird.
81–82	*Dénes von Mihály . . . "there can no longer be any doubt . . ."* Goebel, 281–82.
82	*To the engineering experts in attendance, Karolus's systems . . .* Hempel, 154; Riedel, 14–15; Goebel, 282–83.
82–83	*On June 11, he entered into a formal partnership* . . . Rudert, 236–37.
83	*"The march of progress is necessarily slow . . ."* *Tulsa World* (Jan. 2, 1927); *New York Herald* (May 22, 1927).
84	*"almost every conceivable type of scanner was suggested . . ."* Burns, op. cit.
86	*"The two beams work alternately," Alexanderson reported* . . . Alexanderson to Huff (May 7, 1927) and to Lunt (May 21, 1927); as reported by Abramson (1987), 103, 290.
86	*"One of the important simplifications . . ."* Alexanderson memo to Lunt (Oct. 28, 1927).
87	*he declared his next step* . . . Alexanderson memo to Allen (Nov. 2, 1927).
87–88	*On January 13, 1928 . . . "A diminutive moving picture . . ."* *New York Times* (Jan. 14, 1928); GE press release (Jan. 13, 1928).
89	*And Francis Jenkins was in it for keeps* . . . Udelson, 31.
89	*"a 36-inch diameter disk is required . . ."* Jenkins, 61.
89	*"The whole family," he joyfully pronounced* . . . Jenkins, cited in Hollenback, 147.
89	*That same year the Federal Radio Commission* . . . Udelson, 50.
90	*"much love at the breakfast table . . ."* Udelson, 51.
90	*"Needed will be a $^3/_4$ inch board . . ."* Jenkins, 21.
90	*"That evening the first scheduled broadcast . . ."* Jenkins (unpublished).

90	Despite the limitations of his programming . . . New York Times (May 13, 1928), in Hollenback, 165.
90–91	"For the past week I have been able to receive . . ." Radio News (Nov. 1928), in Hollenback, 173.
91	"What thrilling lectures on solar physics . . ." De Forest, 353.
91	In December 1928, the establishment of the Jenkins Television Corporation . . . Udelson, 54; New York Times (Dec. 5, 1928).
92	"Synchronism is obtained by moving the motor board . . ." This and following quotes from Jenkins, 29–35.
92	"in a more or less perfect form . . ." W. B. Arvin, Radio News (Sept. 1925).
93	"This test appears convincing . . ." Alexanderson memo to Dunham (March 17, 1928).
94–95	A press release announced that television programs . . . GE press release (May 1928).
95–96	"made clear at the outset . . ." This and subsequent quotations are from GE Historical File, Alexanderson statement (Sept. 4, 1928).
97	"The pictures . . . were sometimes blurred and confused . . ." New York Times (Sept. 12, 1928); GE press release (Sept. 11, 1928).
97	"the picture of the little Dutch girl comes in good . . ." Udelson, 51.
98	"We offer the radio amateur kit parts for the construction . . ." Jenkins, cited in Udelson, 52.
99	"that caught the fancy of the audience . . ." New York Times (Oct. 23, 1931).
99–100	There were other television systems . . . Udelson, 52.

Part Two, Prologue: The Wireless Operator

105–7	Formation of RCA. Bilby, 45–52.
107–10	Sarnoff early history. Bilby, 11–30.
110–12	The Titanic incident and aftermath for Sarnoff. Lyons, 59; Sarnoff, 22–23; Bilby, 30–55; Dreher, 28–29; Lewis, 107; Barnouw, 18.

Seven: Two Russian Immigrants and One Farm Boy

| 119–21 | Zworykin was born . . . This and the following biographical information about Zworykin (except where noted) are from Olessi, 1–25. |

121–24	*Zworykin might have stayed in Saint Petersburg after graduation* . . . Olessi, 30–33; Abramson (1995), 1–53.
125–26	*As the beam scanned across and down the scene* . . . Abramson (1987), 63–64; Abramson (1995), 1–54; Eddy, 36 ff.
126–27	*a fourteen-year-old-boy* . . . Elma Farnsworth, 34–37.
127	*Philo was named* . . . Collier's (Oct. 3, 1936); Elma Farnsworth, 32–34; Everson, 18.
127–28	*On entering Rigby High School* . . . Everson, 20 ff.
129–34	*After his freshman year at Rigby High* . . . This and following anecdotes are from Elma Farnsworth.
131–34	*"looked much older than his nineteen years . . ."* This and other quotes are from Everson, 40 ff.

Eight: The Damned Thing Works!

135–36	*In 1924 he received his naturalization papers* . . . This and the following anecdotes from Olessi, Udelson, and Abramson (1987).
136–37	*"Mr. Davis asked me a few questions . . ."* Olessi, 84.
137–38	*In June of 1926* . . . Elma Farnsworth, 48–50; Everson, 46–48.
138–39	*Now the three partners combed the city* . . . Everson, 48–49.
139	*Pem Farnsworth remembered her husband* . . . Elma Farnsworth, 50.
139	*"Strange packages were being brought in . . ."* This and following quotes from Elma Farnsworth, 51 ff.
140–43	*Farnsworth got up to explain his work* . . . *"Well, that is a damn fool idea . . ."* Collier's (Oct. 3, 1936); Everson, 53–63.
143–44	*Fagan had a technical expert inspect the plan* . . . Everson, 65; Elma Farnsworth, 59–60.
144–46	*A few weeks later, on September 22, 1926* . . . Elma Farnsworth, 63 ff.
146–47	*The next day, after deeming the vacuum pure enough* . . . Elma Farnsworth, 76–79; Everson, 77–79; Farnsworth lab notes (Sept. 5, 1926, and March 2, 1927).
147	*Dieckmann had been working on television systems* . . . Abramson (1987), 95–97, 74–75.
148	*"Cliff's skills increased . . ."* Elma Farnsworth, 83.
148	*"I had everything set up to show a line picture . . ."* Farnsworth letter to Everson (Feb. 13, 1927).
149–50	*"Because there were no shield-grid tubes on the market . . ."* This and other quotes from Elma Farnsworth, 86 ff.

150   *"The Image Dissector tube was excited by the ten-cycle ..."* Farnsworth lab notes (Aug. 30, 1927).

151   *" 'Put in the slide, Cliff ...' "* Elma Farnsworth, 90–91.

152   *"The Received line picture was evident this time ..."* Farnsworth lab notes (Sept. 7, 1927).

152   *"became very jubilant ..."* Elma Farnsworth, 90–91.

Nine: Two Years and One Hundred Thousand Dollars

154   *"There has been a lot in the papers lately ..."* Farnsworth letter to Everson (Feb. 18, 1928).

154   *"Line pictures can be transmitted with the amplifier system ..."* Farnsworth lab notes (Jan. 24, 1928).

155   *The team was also working to synchronize ...* Farnsworth lab notes (April 10 to May 6, 1928).

156   *After countless futile strategies ...* Farnsworth lab notes (April 10 to May 6 and May 7–12, 1928).

156–57   *"In one room the dissector tube ..."* through *"A square luminescent field ..."* Everson, 89.

156   *"We showed them the ability of our tube ..."* Farnsworth lab notes (March 1, 1928).

157–58   *The men shook hands ...* Everson, 90–91; Elma Farnsworth, 96–97.

158–59   *Next came a demonstration for ... he could achieve these goals in one more month.* Elma Farnsworth, 98–99.

159–160   *on May 22 ... never even considered this offer.* Abramson, "Pioneers of Television: Philo Taylor Farnsworth," *SMPTA* (*Society of Motion Picture and Television Engineers*) *Journal* (Nov. 1992).

160–67   *In June, Carl Christensen ...* This and following anecdotes from Elma Farnsworth, 98 ff.

160–67   *The black box ...* This and following anecdotes from Everson, 95 ff., 129–31.

163–64   *Cliff Gardner had by this time become an expert ...* Elma Farnsworth, 106–7.

164   *On August 24, 1928, Farnsworth gave a demonstration ...* Abramson (1987), 125.

164–65   *Reporters described the picture ...* San Francisco Chronicle (Sept. 3, 1928).

167   *Farnsworth devised a substitute made of cesium oxide ...* Abramson (1987), 110.

168	*The first was Gregory Ogloblinsky* . . . Loren Jones interview (March 30, 1994); Abramson (1987), 295.
169	*The final problem was that the electron beam* . . . Abramson (1987), 123.
169–70	*A private note written in 1929* . . . Abramson (1995), citing a Bell Labs memo.
170	*"I had learned by this time . . ."* Olessi, 84.
170	*According to Loren Jones* . . . Jones interview.
170–71	"Radio Music Box" memo. Sarnoff, 31–33.
171–73	*Sarnoff's proposal seemed . . . truly the king of radio* . . . Bilby, 52–62, 70–88.
173	*"I believe that television, which is the technical name . . ."* Sarnoff, 88.
174	*In a speech before the Chicago Association of Commerce* . . . Sarnoff, 90.
174–75	*On that January day in 1929* . . . Bilby, 121.
175	*"Zworykin had the spark in his eye . . ."* Jones interview.
175	*"My first impression of Sarnoff . . ."* Olessi, 89.
175	*"proved to be one of the most decisive . . ."* Bilby 121–22.

Ten: Tube Wars

177–78	*He also worried . . . "If we had only . . ."* J. L. Baird, 98.
178	*By March of 1930 . . . appeared bright and clear.* J. L. Baird, 101.
178	*In 1929 His Master's Voice* . . . Abramson (1987), 131.
178–79	*The new company's work* . . . Schoenberg and colleagues, interview by Peter Ranger, in *Television* (Dec. 1986): 316 ff.
179	*Schoenberg badgered his group* . . . London *Times* (Jan. 7, 1931).
179	*At the Physical and Optical Society's . . . Baird's argument was thrown out.* Abramson (1987), 161.
179	*Four months later . . . carried out by Zworykin.* Abramson (1987), 164.
180	*This American venture . . . "which gave a remarkably bright . . ."* J. L. Baird, 104.
180	*By 1932 . . . "but was too overcome . . ."* J. L. Baird, 117.
181	*"If an inventor . . . and they have the paper."* J. L. Baird, 128.
181	*The engineering was now being done . . . Scottish mistress and her husband.* J. L. Baird, 123.
181–82	*"a beautiful young woman with raven black hair . . ."* This and following quotations from McArthur and Waddell, 164–67.

182   *"The only way to get anything done in America . . ."* J. L. Baird, 126.

183   *At Van Cortlandt Park . . . Alfred Goldsmith and Ted Smith.* Abramson (1987), 134.

183   *Smith soon had a patent application . . . the still nascent NBC.* Abramson (1987), 134, 137.

183   *Meanwhile, in Pittsburgh . . . "the result proved . . ."* Abramson (1987), 132, 138–39, 295.

184   *RCA's Chairman Owen Young . . . continued their work undisturbed.* Bilby, 102–3.

184   *On November 16 . . . before accelerating it.* Abramson (1987), 141–43.

184–85   *Two days later . . . Zworykin's living room.* Abramson (1987), 143–45.

185   *At the last moment . . .* Olessi, 89–90.

185–86   *The British periodical . . . "of very little promise." Television* 2 (Jan. 1930): 528, and Ives memo to Charlesworth (Dec. 16, 1929), both cited in Abramson (1987), 299.

186   *"Zworykin's tube was the most important . . ."* Abramson (1987), 145.

186   *A new corporation . . . all research activities.* Abramson (1987), 137.

186   *Under the new plan . . . direction of Vladimir Zworykin.* Abramson (1987), 147.

186–87   *Then, on January 3 . . . mightiest corporations.* Bilby, 103.

187   *"incorporate the electron multiplier . . . seven-inch picture."* Elma Farnsworth, 118–19.

187   *on August 1 . . . "This marks an important step."* Farnsworth lab notes (Aug. 17, 1929).

189   *"it is necessary to supply . . ."* Farnsworth lab notes (Dec. 1, 1926).

189   *"charging a very large capacity . . ."* Farnsworth lab notes (Oct. 1, 1928).

190   *patent litigation that followed . . . victory for Farnsworth.* Elma Farnsworth, 106.

190   *The vacuum-tube . . . no moving parts whatsoever.* Abramson (1987), 131.

190   *The lab at 202 Green Street . . . "their best picture yet."* Elma Farnsworth, 119, 125–26.

191–92   *"Dr. Zworykin spent three days" . . . to begin work at the new*

Camden laboratory. Elma Farnsworth, 128–30; Everson, 125–27; Abramson (1987), 149–51; Abramson, "Pioneers of Television: Philo Taylor Farnsworth," 9–12; Hofer interview with Elma Farnsworth (June 20, 1975).

192 *Farnsworth received a letter . . . "description of such apparatus."* Mann letter to Farnsworth (April 17, 1930).

193 *On May 1 . . . "a modified Farnsworth type."* Abramson (1987), 148–51.

193 *"M. Farnsworth . . . such a focussing is entirely possible."* Zworykin notebook (May 15, 1930).

194 *"I believe that a public showing . . ."* Alexanderson letter to Sarnoff (April 2, 1930).

194 *In the nineteen months . . . to push for a commercial service.* Brittain, 194–95.

194 *Alexanderson had also by now considered . . . "receiver of the future."* Alexanderson memo to Young (Oct. 12, 1928).

194–95 *On April 30 . . . entertainment possibilities.* Alexanderson letter to Tullar (May 1, 1930); Brittain, 214; Alexanderson speech, "Television and Its Uses in Peace and War."

195–96 *on May 22 . . . impression on the audiences.* GE press release (May 22, 1930).

196 *That night Alexanderson spoke . . . guided through the fog by television.* GE Historical File, "Development and Future of Television," speech transcript (May 22, 1930).

196 *"I have read Mr. Zworykin's report . . ."* Alexanderson memo to Dunham (June 4, 1930).

197 *The week of July 15, 1930 . . . to work in Zworykin's lab at RCA.* Abramson (1987), 155–56, 158.

197–98 *While Karolus . . . over their shoulder.* GE Engineering Report for 1930; *New York Times* (Feb. 13, 1931), 15:3.

198 *On October 3 . . . "with spectacles visible."* Alexanderson letter to Sarnoff (Oct. 3, 1930).

198 *"I regret I cannot . . ."* Sarnoff to Alexanderson (Nov. 10, 1930).

198 *"Dear Mr. Sarnoff . . ."* Alexanderson to Sarnoff (Nov. 13, 1930).

199 *In early 1931 . . . fundamental electrical research.* Brittain, 218.

199 *His research on ultrashort wave . . .* GE Historical File, "Television on a Light Beam"; Alexanderson memo to Dunham (Dec. 3, 1931).

Eleven: Coast to Coast

200–1   *Born in 1907 . . . "still more impressive success."* Von Ardenne,
            15–18, 50–64, 74–76, 94–102; von Ardenne interview, Dres-
            den (May 19, 1994); Bruch, 34.

202   *Ten days later . . . "in the world."* Bruch, 35.

202   *In the periodical . . . "on the transmitting side."* Abramson
            (1987), 164.

202–3   *In August 1931 . . . a true electronic television camera.* Von Ar-
            denne, 107; von Ardenne interview; Bruch, 35–36; Abram-
            son (1987), 170.

203   *RCA began construction . . . Farnsworth would be able to do it.*
            Abramson (1987), 163, 166–67.

203–4   *The two-sided tubes . . . shape of things to come.* Abramson
            (1987), 167.

204   *The Camden team's toughest problem . . . as large as four by four
            inches.* Olessi, 87–88.

205   *"Zworykin's tube was a great improvement . . ."* Ted Smith in-
            terview, Philadelphia (March 30, 1994).

205–6   *On October 23 . . . worthy of patenting.* Zworykin notebook
            (Oct. 23, 1931).

206   *Four days later . . . operable tube of this kind at the time.* Ab-
            ramson (1987), 173–75.

206–7   *On May 30, 1930 . . . "That's how Sarnoff made us feel."* Bilby,
            105–6, 122, 228.

207   *"Zworykin is the greatest salesman . . ."* Bilby, 123.

208   *Since Zworykin's visit . . . the Farnsworth enterprise.* Elma
            Farnsworth, 133.

208   *The Farnsworth team now felt ready . . . experimentation on
            these air transmissions.* Everson, 120–21; Abramson, "Pio-
            neers of Television: Philo Taylor Farnsworth," 12.

208–9   *In December 1930 . . . train from California.* Elma Farns-
            worth, 134.

209   *On December 3 . . . reputation would suffer for it.* Everson,
            120–25.

209–10   *For months Farnsworth had been working . . . flaw in his rea-
            soning.* Everson, 120–25.

210   *"We have succeeded in narrowing . . ."* Farnsworth letter to
            McCargar (Oct. 25, 1930).

210   *"I am quite anxious . . ."* Farnsworth letter to McCargar (Nov.
            22, 1930).

210   *In a Bell Labs memo . . . obscurity in the annals of television.*

Bell Labs memo (Dec. 19, 1930); Abramson (1987), 160–61; Everson, 120–25.

210–11   *"housed in a box . . ." New York Times,* Sec. 10 (Dec. 14, 1930), 14:6.

211   *David Sarnoff and RCA . . . to Philadelphia to discuss a sale.* Udelson, 119–20.

211–12   *"A fast-talking promoter by the name of Cox" . . . delay the meeting with Philco.* Elma Farnsworth, 135–38.

212   *"Sarnoff seemed impressed . . ."* Everson, 199.

212   *he made an offer . . . "There's nothing here we'll need."* Abramson (1987), 168, 304; Elma Farnsworth, 131; Everson, 199.

212–13   *By the beginning of June 1931 . . . to be set up within a year.* Everson, 133; Elma Farnsworth, 138; Abramson (1987), 167–68.

213   *The Farnsworths traveled back to San Francisco . . . Pullman car . . .* Elma Farnsworth, 138.

Twelve: Mavericks from the West

214–15   *You could charter a Pullman . . . their fans arrived.* Elma Farnsworth, 140.

215   *"I have been working on . . ."* and other quotations, not included, which show that he was still working on this problem. Farnsworth lab notes (Sept. 18, Nov. 23, Dec. 7, 1931).

215   *"I. To simplify . . ."* Farnsworth lab notes (April 10, 1932).

215–16   *On July 14 . . . a screen two square feet in size.* Abramson (1987), 169.

216   *Farnsworth traveled to Washington . . . call letters W3XE.* Elma Farnsworth, 145.

216   *For some time he had been picking up . . . renewal of RCA licensing agreements.* Elma Farnsworth, 145.

216–17   *Relations between Farnsworth and Philco . . . Farnsworth and Philco parted ways.* Elma Farnsworth, 143–45; Everson, 135; Abramson (1987), 195.

217   *In April 1933 . . . storage camera tubes of the future.* Abramson (1987), 196–98.

217   *McCargar now wanted . . . a staff of two.* Elma Farnsworth, 146; Everson, 135–36.

218   *"the business sun . . ." New York Times* (May 22, 1932).

218   *"Our Company still does not consider . . ."* Abramson (1987), 189, 193.

218   *The audience strained . . . no more RCA television demonstra-*

tions for four years. New York Times (May 22, 1932); Abramson (1987), 180 (for more technical description, see *Proceedings of the IRE,* Dec. 1933).

219–20   *Indeed, Sarnoff was the central figure . . . David Sarnoff would never again share power at RCA.* Bilby, 105–10; Dreher, 136–40; Smith interview (March 30, 1994).

220   *"Finally, I had the authority . . ."* Bilby, 124.

220   *"Sarnoff was a genius . . ."* Smith interview.

220–21   *"It would not be enough . . ."* Bilby, 124.

221   *"In the whole world . . ."* Smith speech at RCA Lunch Club (Dec. 14, 1992).

221   *Research, he liked to say . . . "the most important job in the world."* Bilby, 125.

221–22   *In early 1933 . . . signal generated by the Iconoscope.* Abramson (1987), 193–94; Zworykin notebooks.

222–23   *On Sunday, June 25, 1933 . . . "That is not my task." New York Times* (June 25, 27, July 2, 1933); Abramson (1987), 198–200 (see also *Proceedings of the IRE,* June 1933 and Jan. 1934).

223   *Frank Gray and Herbert Ives . . . internal memoranda.* Abramson (1987), 199–200; Bell Labs Case 33089 memos.

223   *Though the pall . . . anything out of anything.* Elma Farnsworth, 147–49.

223   *"What amazing possibilities . . ." San Francisco Chronicle* (Aug. 15, 1933).

224   *"the magic box" . . . "It is here." San Francisco Chronicle* (Aug. 20, 1933).

224   *Kenny's death . . . were stirring in him.* Elma Farnsworth, 149.

224   *Hearing that Pickford . . . "This is hotter than color!"* Elma Farnsworth, 159.

225   *A demonstration of the multipactor . . . "your Electron Multiplier power tube."* Elma Farnsworth, 176; Everson, 137–40.

225   *He had recently begun using cesium . . . His picture was now every bit as good as Zworykin's.* Abramson, "Pioneers of Television: Philo Taylor Farnsworth," 17.

225–27   *Farnsworth set to work . . . "more money these past two weeks than in the last two years."* Elma Farnsworth, 160–64; Everson, 142–45; Abramson (1987), 209; *San Francisco Chronicle* (Aug. 25, 1934); *New York Times* (Aug. 25, 1934).

228   *"by far the best wireless television I have ever seen."* Wheen, 23.

| 228 | *The BBC invited EMI* . . . Abramson (1987), 191. |

228   *The BBC invited EMI* . . . Abramson (1987), 191.

228   *"virtually controlled . . ."* Wheen, 23.

229   *Captain West had been . . . his full knowledge of RCA's and EMI's work on cathode receivers.* Abramson (1987), 172–95.

229   *"What with the darkness . . ."* Wheen, 24.

230   *"One of the new directors . . ."* J. L. Baird, 129.

230   *"everything [in their system] down to the last screw was home manufactured."* Seldson Committee report, cited in Abramson (1987), 208.

Thirteen: A Death Knell

231–34   Farnsworth's visit to England. Elma Farnsworth, 165–69.

234   *Back home, Farnsworth . . . hadn't passed him already.* Elma Farnsworth, 170.

234–36   *Then, in the summer of 1935 . . . "Zworykin application as filed does not disclose such a device."* Patent Interference no. 64,027, Philo T. Farnsworth v. Vladimir K. Zworykin, Final Hearing (Washington, D.C.: United States Patent Office, April 24, 1934); Hofer, 75–81; Abramson (1987), 179–80; Everson, 152–53; Elma Farnsworth, 154–57.

236–37   *Fresh from his legal victory . . . but rather to improve it.* Abramson (1987), 220–21; New York Times (July 31, 1935).

237   *"Unable to make any headway . . ."* Elma Farnsworth, 178–79.

237–38   *Farnsworth also felt constant pressure from McCargar . . . relaxation from the pressures of his crusade.* Elma Farnsworth, 179.

238–39   *In September 1934, Alda Bedford . . . "including an ally such as EMI!"* Abramson (1987), 206–11, 211.

239   *In late 1934 Gregory Ogloblinsky . . . could see in the months before his death that television was going to happen.* Abramson (1987), 219; Jones interview.

241   *Sarnoff made a dramatic announcement . . . "a great potential market for radio-vision receivers should 'the craze' spread."* New York Times (May 8, 12, 1935); Sarnoff, 97–99.

242–43   *He offered to use Armstrong's FM for the sound . . . His body lay on the sidewalk until daylight, when a passerby found it.* Dreher, 203–8; Lyons, 212–14; Bilby, 198–200.

243–44   *On April 24, 1936, the Camden Fire Department . . . was sensitive enough to televise outdoor scenes with natural lighting.* New York Times (April 25, 1936).

244   *Two months later, on June 29 . . . several mobile receiving units that monitored reception from various spots in the city.* New York Times (June 29, 1936).

244–45   *On July 7 . . . "RCA was prepared to share the fruits of its pioneering with all others, including foreign licensees."* McCargar letters to Everson (Aug. 5, 13, 1936); Bilby, 126.

245–46   *In the fall of 1936 . . . he and Pem left for the French Riviera.* Elma Farnsworth, 181–85.

247   *Twenty miles outside London . . .* Swift, 72.

247–48   *"All the notabilities . . ."* This and following quotes come from J. L. Baird, 134–38.

248   *Letters to the newspapers . . . "to televise" must mean "to see the program" rather than to broadcast it . . .* London Times (Feb. 2, 9, 1935).

248   *Alternative words were suggested . . . the suggestion of* telebaird. Burns, 353.

248–49   *The opening-day broadcast . . . "so why continue?"* Abramson, Journal of the Antique Wireless Association 29 (Feb. 1989), 24–26.

249   *True, the London* Times *reported . . . "were as clear in black and white as the usual film entertainment."* London Times (Nov. 3, 1936).

249   *Farnsworth camera continued to give the Baird group troubles, and eventually they gave up on it entirely.* Abramson (1987), 234.

249–50   *"After all these years, we were put out of the BBC . . ."* J. L. Baird, 139.

250   *"Company unable to carry on through lack of funds . . ."* Moseley, 229.

250   *Now fifty-one, he tried to get involved with war work . . .* There has been some effort (McArthur and Waddell, 1986) to describe his war years as being involved with secret work, in particular with radar. But when one of us (DEF) searched all available records in preparation for a book on the British development of that weapon (*A Race on the Edge of Time* [New York: McGraw-Hill, 1988]), no mention of his name was ever found. In Baird's own words, "I sent my name in to the authorities and expected to be approached with some form of government work, but no such offer materialized."

250–51   *Sitting one day on the deserted beach . . . nothing at all to do with the war.* Moseley, 234.

251   *"a rather shabby-genteel South London suburb . . ."* Moseley, 242.

Fourteen: The Zeppelin over the Stadium

252   *"Telefunken is the German arm . . ."* J. L. Baird, 121.

252–53   *Skee Turner announced at dinner one night . . . the Philadelphia suburb of Wyndmoor.* Elma Farnsworth, 170–72.

253   *The programs were being coordinated by . . . by the end of the evening he was a Farnsworth employee.* Kisseloff, 14, 37, 80.

253–54   *He made one permanent hire . . . appeared to be naked when televised.* Elma Farnsworth, 170–72.

254   *The Farnsworth "live" camera . . . a thousand foot-candles for a decent picture.* Abramson (1987), 231, 245.

254   *Nineteen thirty-six was a very productive year . . . the Olympic Games.* Elma Farnsworth, 176–79; Abramson (1987), 233.

254   *"To eat, we'd go to the Italian market . . ."* Kisseloff, 37.

255–56   The Farnsworths' trip to Germany. Elma Farnsworth, 188–91.

257   *he and the many other Jews in radio . . . began to eat away at Loewe's radio business.* Hempel, 142.

257   *Mihály's lab was supported not only . . . a patent-sharing agreement with RCA several years before.* Riedel, 19; Abramson (1987), 149.

257   *The Bosch corporation . . . fled to the United States.* Hempel, 143.

257   *Hitler's edicts also forced . . . to pay his staff.* Riedel, 20.

258   *In 1935 Fritz Schröter . . . construct their own models.* Riedel, 22.

258   *At the beginning of the year . . . "first television broadcasting system in the world was begun."* Wheen, 29.

258   *The Reichspost's broadcasts . . . eleven public viewing rooms around Berlin.* Abramson (1987), 217; Wheen, 31.

258–59   *No high-ranking Nazi officials . . . "incomprehensible wonder has begun."* Elsner et al., 206; Wheen, 29.

259   *Unfortunately, the initial service . . . using Farnsworth and Zworykin electronic cameras.* Abramson (1987), 217–18; Wheen, 31; Elsner et al., 206–7.

259–60   *But in March 1936, the Reichspost gained . . . to be scanned by a flying-spot scanner.* Postmuseum Berlin brochure; Wheen, 244.

260   *Horst Dressler-Andress was a former . . . magnificent Aryan athletes.* Hempel, 127–33, 154.

260–61	*When the games opened . . . "only in very bright weather."* Riedel, 22–23; Elsner et al., 193, 208; Wheen, 31–32; Abramson (1987), 232.

Fifteen: Just Around the Corner

262–63	*In the summer of 1934 . . . "was exiled to Archangel, and died soon after."* Olessi, 90–99; Jones, "Experiences in Russia," self-published monograph.
263	*In fact, Rosing had continued . . . a fatal stroke.* Abramson (1995), 124.
263	*Although Zworykin found . . . as soon as it was available.* Olessi, 93–99.
263–64	*Actually, the Russians . . . research concentrated on the proven mechanical systems.* P. K. Gorokhov, "History of Modern Television," *Radio Engineering (Radiotekhnika)* 16 (1961): 71–80.
264	*In France, the Ministry . . . no further significant progress. Radio News* (Aug. 1935); Abramson (1995), 147, 175.
264–65	*In Japan, Kenjiro . . . television research was no longer important in Japan.* Abramson (1995).
265–66	*Jess McCargar had shown no respect . . . authority of Brolly, Gardner, and Somers.* Elma Farnsworth, 193–94.
266	*"If Archie and Frank had our real interests at heart . . ."* McCargar letter to Everson (Nov. 5, 1936).
266	*"I am satisfied in my own mind . . ."* McCargar letter to Pond, undated.
266	*"and with Russ in Philadelphia . . ."* McCargar letter to Everson (Jan. 4, 1937).
267	*When Farnsworth returned from Europe . . . Farnsworth Television and Radio Corporation had at least been conceived.* Elma Farnsworth, 192–99; Everson, 182–86.
267	*Arch Brolly went to Philco . . . Chicago's experimental TV station, W9XBK.* Kisseloff, 40, 80–81.
268–70	*The General became an outspoken proponent . . . Philco was never able to prove its case.* Udelson, 119–21, 124–25; Bilby, 128–31.
268	*DuMont insisted on 625 lines . . .* Allen B. DuMont had been chief engineer for the De Forest Radio Company and founded his own laboratory in 1931. Enamored of the cathode-ray tube, he made many technical advances in its design and production, and this led him into electronic television. By the

late 1930s, he was both manufacturing sets and operating a fledgling network.

270   *Sarnoff by this time . . . apply for reimbursement.* Bilby, 129–30.

270–71   *Zenith took out a series of ads . . . coming from the opening ceremonies of the New York World's Fair.* Udelson, 124–26; Bilby, 130–32.

271   *Early in 1937, Dr. O. E. Buckley . . . a wavering, barely legible "Philo T. Farnsworth" to the document.* Everson, 155–59; Abramson, "Pioneers," 21.

271–72   *Meanwhile, the Farnsworth studio . . . "with an interlace of two to one [could] get the program."* New York Times (Jan. 10, 1937); Radio News (May 1937).

272–73   *"lone wolf" Bart Molinari . . . "She was well in her forties . . ."* Everson, 228–33; Elma Farnsworth, 204–5.

273   *Farnsworth had between twenty-five and forty technicians . . .* Everson, 163–65.

273   *"He is now just thirty years old . . ."* Collier's (Oct. 3, 1936).

273   *One of the visitors to the Hollywood . . . a system so simple even a child could operate it.* Elma Farnsworth, 205.

273–74   *In the spring of 1938, the Farnsworths drove . . . and they headed back to Philadelphia.* Elma Farnsworth, 200–3.

274   *"[In Philadelphia] Phil was all upset . . ."* Elma Farnsworth letter to Everson (Sept. 26, 1938).

274   *In June 1938, Harley Iams . . . had already applied for the first patent on it.* Abramson (1987), 245–46.

275   *Zworykin's lawyers were trying to prove . . . total control of the Iconoscope camera.* Abramson (1987), 248–49.

275   *"Automatic Door Opener for RCA Lunch Room with Electron Multiplier."* Zworykin notebook (March 15, 1938).

275–76   *In 1933, together with Loren Jones . . . and he moved right in.* Jones interview.

276   *He moved into the Polevitsky's private life . . . who was described succinctly as his "paramour."* Abramson (1995), 182.

277–78   *On the afternoon of April 20, 1939 . . . "it will become an important factor in American economic life."* New York Times (April 21, 1939); Bilby, 133.

278–80   *Still, wrote Orrin Dunlap . . . "Mr. and Mrs. Consumer are going to be the final judges of its actual worth."* New York Times (April 30, May 1, 1939); Bilby, 133.

280–81   *On May 17, NBC televised . . . slashed prices by a third—to no avail.* Abramson (1987), 252; Udelson, 138–39; *New York Times* (Oct. 15, 1939) 9:12; *Business Week* (Aug. 12, 1939): 24.

281   *He settled into an administrative position . . . to the reporters who followed television.* Abramson (1995), 154.

281–83   *On June 7, 1939, Iams and Rose . . . a hundred times more sensitive than the original Orthicon.* Udelson, 114–17; Abramson (1987), 252, 264.

Sixteen: Sarnoff's Folly

284   *When Farnsworth, Everson, and Knowlton . . . "a pack of dishonest rogues."* Everson, 235–38.

284–85   *the public spectacle and trial of Lee De Forest . . .* In 1912, when De Forest tried to market his Audion, he had been prosecuted as a fraud for trying to sell stock in such a preposterous device. His American De Forest Wireless Telegraph Company had been set up in conjunction with a crooked stock manipulator named Abraham White, who sold stock for more than the company's assets were worth. When the scheme finally burst, they were arrested. At the trial, the prosecutor showed that nearly two million dollars had been raised from stock sales, but that less than half a million ever reached the company; the rest had gone into De Forest's and his partners' pockets, and from there directly to real estate agents, automobile dealers, nightclubs, and mistresses. The prosecutor lifted the Audion high above his head and charged that De Forest had promised the gullible suckers that he would send music and voices across the ocean with "this worthless piece of glass." The jury found his codefendants guilty but De Forest innocent. They later said that he seemed "actually to believe" that his device would work; he should be committed to an asylum, they thought, but not to jail. In the end, of course, the Audion was the device that finally made radio—and television—a reality.

285   *month after month went by . . . "was acting with a disconcerting uncertainty."* Everson, 235–38.

285   *by January of 1939, the British Foreign Office . . .* Halifax to Lindsay, in the *British Foreign Policy Journal,* quoted by Taylor, 194.

285   *"if . . . any action were taken . . ."* Taylor, 205.

285–87	*On March 31, the last day . . . the new Farnsworth Television and Radio Corporation manufacturing operation.* Elma Farnsworth, 206–7; Everson, 235–38.
287	*Until commercial television was a reality . . . a million dollars' worth of radios were sold.* Everson, 239.
287	*"Leading Distributors 'Go' Farnsworth," and "The history of television is the history of Farnsworth."* Farnsworth file, University of Utah Library.
287	*In the meantime, the television lab in Philadelphia . . . E. O. Lawrence, William Paley, and Spencer Tracy.* Elma Farnsworth, 209.
287	*"two trucks equipped with" . . . was nowhere to be seen.* Elma Farnsworth, 209; Abramson (1987), 251–52; *New York Times* (Nov. 15, 1938).
287–88	*Farnsworth spent the entire summer . . . "A license with RCA."* Elma Farnsworth, 213.
289	*In the summer of 1939 Sarnoff's vice president . . . there were tears in his eyes.* Elma Farnsworth, 213–14; Everson, 242–47; Abramson (1987), 254.
289	*"Sarnoff's Folly," cried a* Radio Daily *headline . . . "than in creating a television industry."* Bilby, 135.
289	*"an ardent New Dealer and antimonopolist of deep conviction"* Bilby, 135.
290	*After preliminary hearings, the FCC . . . until the best system was determined.* Udelson, 148.
290	*On March 20, full-page RCA ads . . . RCA receivers at reduced prices.* New York Times *(March 20, 1940).*
290	*"The current marketing campaign . . ." New York Times* (March 24, 1940).
290	*The FCC announced further hearings . . . "Our dispute is in the head, not the stomach."* Udelson, 149; *Newsweek* (May 13, 1940): 64; *Business Week* (April 20, 1940): 22, 24; Bilby, 136.
291	*"We begged the industry then . . ."; "The purchaser of such a set . . ."* Udelson, 149–50, from U.S. Senate Committee on Interstate Commerce, Development of Television, 76th Cong., 3rd sess. (April 10–11, 1940): 59–61.
291	*The Senate hearings ended . . . and they wanted it now.* Bilby, 137.
291	*The FCC's solution . . . authorize a commercial service.* Bilby, 137; Abramson (1987), 262.

291–92	*In the New York area, DuMont . . . from there it was broadcast to the metropolitan area.* Udelson, 133–37; Abramson (1987), 257.
292	*For thirty-three hours over five days . . . to the Philadelphia area using their own cameras.* Udelson, 139–40; Abramson (1987), 261.
292	*"Sincerity of the tongue . . ."* New York Times, Sec. 9 (June 30, 1940): 10.
293	*"Political addresses are certain to be . . ."* Sarnoff, 104–5.
293	*"Feeling he had to put television behind him" . . . "Besides, we were now quite comfortable . . ."* Elma Farnsworth, 221–23.
293	*Farnsworth sold 2,000 shares of stock . . . "By the end of the summer" . . . "We have found a saner way . . ."* Farnsworth file in University of Utah Library; Farnsworth letter to his mother, April 24, 1941.
293–94	*Albert Rose and his RCA colleagues were steadily improving . . . obsolete in the same year it was first used publicly.* Abramson (1987), 264–66.
294–95	*From the last day of July 1940 . . . commercial broadcasting to begin on July 1, 1941.* Udelson, 152–56; Bilby, 137; Abramson (1987), 268.
295–96	*Twenty-two television stations prepared . . . all raw materials and manufacturing capabilities were to be directed to the war effort.* Udelson, 156–58; Abramson (1987), 270–72; Bilby, 187–88.

Seventeen: The Color War

299	*The voice belonged to . . . I've already perfected color television.* This and all Goldmark quotes, biographical information, and information from his point of view are from Goldmark, *Maverick Inventor.*
299–300	*In 1889, a Russian scientist . . . patents on color systems that would never work.* Abramson (1987), 22–24, 27.
300	*Harold McCreary of the Associated Electric Laboratories . . . blend them into one realistic picture.* Abramson (1987), 67.
300–1	*The next year, 1925, Vladimir Zworykin . . . for green only through green, and so on.* Abramson (1987), 78.
301	*By 1928, a host of inventors . . . images of faces and flowers were "vivid" . . .* Abramson (1987), 118, 121.
301–2	*Then on June 27, 1929, Bell Labs . . . that produced eighteen*

frames a second. Abramson (1987), 135–37; *New York Times* (June 28, 1929).

302–3   *"I calmly announced"* . . . *"it will have a greater acceptance with the public."* Goldmark, 60–62; Bilby, 178; Abramson (1987), 262–64.

304   *CBS had been created in 1927* . . . *"United Independent Broadcasters" ("CBS" was used only on the air).* Paley, 32–37.

304–5   *The two struck up a wary* . . . *"friends, confidants, and fierce competitors all at the same time."* Paley, 200; Bilby, 175–76.

307   *At a staff meeting just after Goldmark's demonstrations* . . . *"scheme to be foisted on the American people,"* he vowed. Bilby, 179.

307   *But Sarnoff had unknowingly put RCA* . . . *"wrong from the beginning, and I knew it."* Bilby, 179.

308   *He cleared this next hurdle quickly* . . . *but his push for public support had slowed.* Goldmark, 63–64; Bilby, 179.

308–9   *In late 1944, David Sarnoff returned to New York* . . . *would address him as General Sarnoff.* Bilby, 143–51.

309   *In December 1944 Sarnoff called together his top executives* . . . *"we're going to capture it before anyone else."* Bilby, 172.

309   *To oversee the various projects* . . . *"he made it impossible for them to say, We didn't do this."* Ted Smith interview.

309   *So in late 1946* . . . *three million dollars to NBC for prime-time slots.* Bilby, 173.

311   *"superior to the Technicolor seen in the movies . . .";* *"brilliant young physicist named Dr. Peter Goldmark . . .";* *"little doubt that color television has reached the perfection of black and white."* Bilby, 186–87.

311   *"inefficient, ugly, and expensive."* Bilby, 181.

312   *CBS, knowing that each black-and-white set sold* . . . *"would be a waste of effort and money."* Paley, 184.

314   *"I remember vividly that day in 1949 . . ."* Dreher, 210–11.

314–15   *In 1949* . . . *he appointed a new RCA president* . . . *buy time until electronic color could take over.* Bilby, 174, 187–88.

315   *FCC hearings on color* . . . *"ever becoming a practical broadcast service is extremely doubtful."* Lyons, 293.

316   *RCA representatives were just as busy* . . . *accused each other publicly of outright lying.* Bilby, 189–90.

316   *On May 3, the hearings reached a climax* . . . *new developments were coming out of the lab almost daily.* Lyons, 293–94.

317   *"[Sarnoff's] day in that period often began . . ."* Bilby, 204–5.

317   *Publicly, Sarnoff welcomed the competition . . . the system could be commercially marketed at once.* Bilby, 184; Lyons, 292–95.

317–18   *After issuing a scathing official reaction . . . obliterate the spinning disk from the television landscape.* Bilby, 184–85; Lyons, 295.

318   *Sarnoff now had hundreds of scientists and engineers . . . "which will be made during the coming months."* Bilby, 185–86.

318–19   *In the meantime, Sarnoff filed suit . . . "merely because the wisdom of the decision might be questioned."* New York Times (May 29, 1951); Bilby, 186, 190.

319   *"I always thought his strengths lay . . ."* Paley, 200–1.

320   *"the Supreme Court can't order me" . . . and prepared to put out CBS spinning-wheel color receivers.* Bilby, 191–93; Paley, 208.

320–21   *Engstrom remembered it later . . . "the word impossible had no place in our vocabulary."* Bilby, 191–92.

321   *"Never before have I witnessed compressed into a single device . . ."* Bilby, 223.

321   *The apparatus to come out of Princeton . . . perfected under the direction of Harold Law.* Dreher, 211; Abramson (1987), 112.

323–24   *"A three-gun tube with H. B. Law's shadow-mask screen . . ."* Dreher, 211.

324   *So, at the end of June 1951 . . . "radio's miracle man had not run out of miracles."* "The General," Time (July 23, 1951): 74; Lyons, 298–99; Bilby, 192.

324–25   *Although his hour of triumph was . . . both CBS and RCA happily complied.* Lyons, 298–99; Bilby, 193–94; Paley, 208.

325–27   *When the war ended in 1952 . . . "a history that brings out the danger in bureaucratic rule."* Bilby, 194–95, 207; Paley, 221.

327–29   *A year later, however, RCA color . . . manufacturing plant expansion to meet the orders of the rest of the industry.* Bilby, 208–18.

329–30   Description of Trinitron. *Encyclopaedia Britannica.*

330   Description of French and German systems. *Encyclopaedia Britannica.*

331   *"a thorn in [his] side . . ."* Paley, 227.

332   *"The way he refused to accept defeat . . ."* Paley, 227.

Eighteen: The Fading Days of Lone Inventors

333   *consuming several highballs a night . . . one more addiction added to his problems.* Elma Farnsworth, 217.

333–34	*"Phil had a nervous breakdown . . ."* Thomas Ropp, "The Real Father of Television," *Arizona Republic Magazine* (May 6, 1984).
334	*"Farnsworth was admitted to trading . . ."* Everson letter to Farnsworth (Oct. 29, 1943).
334	*After an operation . . . where he underwent a drastic program including shock therapy.* Elma Farnsworth, 231–32.
334	*First his brother Carl died . . . so much of their fortune, was gone.* Elma Farnsworth, 238–44.
334–35	*Farnsworth Television and Radio was unable . . . "I am voting in favor of the IT&T plan . . ."* Elma Farnsworth, 252–59.
335	*"He spent most of his time in a personal think tank . . ."* Ropp, *Arizona Republic Magazine.*
335	*In 1958 . . . "'We'd all be out of work if it weren't for you.'"* Elma Farnsworth, 263–64.
335	*"For a while . . . he wouldn't even allow the word television . . ."* Kisseloff, 41.
336	*In the last two decades of his life . . .* Elma Farnsworth, 34, 279–331.
337	*"Within two years of his company's collapse . . ."* Bilby, 123.
337	*Alexanderson continued his . . . suffering from deafness, near blindness, and anemia.* Brittain, 283, 286, 294, 305.
337–38	*"Fourty* [sic] *years ago I had occasion to speculate . . ."* Alexanderson to Crosby (Nov. 24, 1960).
338–39	*After Zworykin left television . . . "I would never let my own children watch it."* Abramson (1995), 204; Denis Robinson interview, Arlington, Mass. (Sept. 14, 1992).

Nineteen: The Digital Future: Smart Television

340	*On a chilly January morning . . . Berliner Illustrierte Zeitung* (Jan. 8, 1928).
342	*. . . demonstration in Washington in 1987 by NHK . . . All were analog. New York Times,* Sec. 3 (Jan. 22, 1995), 1:2.
342–43	*GI's San Diego subsidiary, VideoCipher . . . Woo Paik took a week off and went home.* Robert Rast interview, Washington (Nov. 9, 1995).
343	*"premier HDTV celebrity." Design News* (July 11, 1994): 58.
343	*"We had the compression simulated . . ."* Woo Paik interview (Nov. 21, 1995).
343	*"a hands-on guy . . ."* Rast interview.

344   *GI's digital system took advantage . . . refresh the entire picture.*
      Rast interview.

344   *"But the fundamental rule . . ."* This and all other Lippman
      quotes are from Lippman interview (Nov. 20, 1995).

344   *Another MIT physicist, William Schreiber . . . "Bill Schreiber
      and I . . ."* This and all other Staelin quotes are from Staelin in-
      terview (Nov. 20, 1995).

346   *"There are thirty-six ways of modulation being proposed . . ."*
      This and other Solomon quotes are from Solomon interview
      (Nov. 20, 1995).

346   *"The bad news . . ."* This and other Negroponte quotes are
      from *Being Digital.*

347   *"The Grand Alliance system has lots of limitations . . ."* This and
      other Schreiber quotes are from Schreiber interview (Nov.
      16, 1995).

347   *According to Don West . . . "which they can sell to advertisers."*
      Association for Maximum Service Television annual meeting
      (Nov. 1995).

350–51 *But even a cathode-ray scanner is at the most basic level . . .*
      Woo Paik interview.

Bibliography

Abramson, Albert. *Electronic Motion Pictures*. Berkeley: University of California Press, 1955.

———. *The History of Television, 1880 to 1941*. Jefferson, N.C.: McFarland, 1987.

———. *Zworykin: Pioneer of Television*. Champaign: University of Illinois Press, 1995.

Aitken, Hugh G. *Syntony and Spark: The Origins of Radio*. New York: Wiley/Interscience, 1976.

Appleyard, Rollo. *Pioneers of Electrical Communications*. London: Macmillan, 1930. Reprinted by Books for Libraries.

Ardenne, Manfred von. *Die Erinnerungen*. Munich: Herbig, 1990.

Baird, John Logie. *Sermons, Soap and Television*. London: Royal Television Society, 1988.

Baird, Margaret. *Television Baird*. Cape Town: Haum, 1973.

Barnouw, Erik. *Tube of Plenty*. New York: Oxford University Press, 1975.

Baughman, James L. *Television's Guardians: The FCC and the Politics of Programming, 1958–1967*. Knoxville: University of Tennessee Press, 1985.

Bilby, Kenneth. *The General*. New York: Harper and Row, 1986.

Birmingham, Stephen. *The Rest of Us*. London: MacDonald, 1985.

Blum, Daniel. *A Pictorial History of Television*. Philadelphia: Chilton, 1959.

Bogart, Leo. *The Age of Television*. New York: Ungar, 1956, 1958, 1972. (1972 edition is a facsimile reprint of the 1956 edition, with extensive added notes.)

Braun, Ernest, and Stuart MacDonald. *Revolution in Miniature: The History and Impact of Semiconductor Electronics*. 2nd ed. Cambridge: Cambridge University Press, 1982.

Briggs, Asa A. *The Golden Age of Wireless: The History of Broadcasting in the United Kingdom (1926–1939)*. London: Oxford University Press, 1965.

———. *The War of Words: The History of Broadcasting in the United Kingdom (1939–1945)*. London: Oxford University Press, 1970.

———. *Sound and Vision: The History of Broadcasting in the United Kingdom (1945–1955)*. London: Oxford University Press, 1979.

———. *The BBC: The First Fifty Years*. London: Oxford University Press, 1986.

————. *History of Broadcasting in the United Kingdom.* London: Oxford University Press, 1961.

Brittain, James E. *Alexanderson.* Baltimore: Johns Hopkins University Press, 1992.

Brown, Les. *Les Brown's Encyclopedia of Television.* 2nd ed. New York: Zoetrope, 1982.

Bruch, Walter. *Kleine Geschichte des deutschen Fernsehens.* Berlin: Haude & Spenersche Verlagsbuchhandlung, 1967.

Bucher, Elmer. *History of Radio and Television Development in the U.S.A.* Princeton, N.J.: David Sarnoff Library, 1952.

Buchsbaum, Walter H. *Fundamentals of Television.* New York: John F. Rider Publisher, 1964.

Buehler, E. C. *American vs. British System of Radio Control.* New York: H. W. Wilson "Reference Shelf" Series, 8:10, 1933.

Burns, R. W. *British Television: The Formative Years.* London: Peter Peregrinus, 1986.

Davis, Henry B. *Electrical and Electronic Technologies: A Chronology of Events and Inventors.* Metuchen, N.J.: Scarecrow, 1981–1985.

De Forest, Lee. *Father of Radio: The Autobiography of Lee De Forest.* Chicago: Wilcox and Follett, 1950.

Dreher, Carl. *Sarnoff: An American Success.* New York: Quadrangle, 1977.

Dummer, G. W. A. *Electronic Inventions, 1745–1976.* Oxford, England: Pergamon Press, 1977.

Dunlap, Orrin, Jr. *Radio's One Hundred Men of Science.* New York: Harper & Row, 1944.

Eddy, William. *Television: The Eyes of Tomorrow.* New York: Prentice Hall, n.d.

Elsner, Monika, Thomas Müllner, and Peter M. Spangenberg. "The Early History of German Television: The Slow Development of a Fast Medium," *Historical Journal of Film, Radio, and Television* 10, no. 2 (1990).

Everson, George. *The Story of Television: The Life of Philo Farnsworth.* New York: Norton, 1949. Reprinted by Arno Press, 1974.

Farnsworth, Elma. *Distant Vision: Romance and Discovery on an Invisible Frontier.* Salt Lake City: PemberlyKent, 1990.

Federal Trade Commission. *Petition of Radio Corporation of America and National Broadcasting Company, Inc., for Approval of Color Standards for the RCA Color Television System.* Washington, D.C.: Federal Trade Commission, 1953.

Felix, Edgar. *Television: Its Methods and Uses.* New York: McGraw-Hill, 1931.

Flatow, Ira. *They All Laughed.* New York: HarperCollins, 1992.

Glut, Donald F., and Jim Harmon. *The Great Television Heroes.* New York: Doubleday, 1975.

Goebel, Gerhart. "Das Fernsehen in Deutschland bis zum Jahre 1945." *Archiv für das Post- und Fernmeldewesen* 5 (Aug. 1953).

Goldmark, Peter C. *Maverick Inventor: My Turbulent Years at CBS*. New York: Saturday Review Press, 1973.

Graham, Margaret B. W. *RCA and the VideoDisc: The Business of Research*. New York: Cambridge, 1986.

Gross, Ben. *I Looked and I Listened: Informal Recollections of Radio and TV*. 2nd ed. New Rochelle, N.Y.: Arlington House, 1970.

Gross, Lynne Schafer. *The New Television Technologies*. 2nd ed. Dubuque, Iowa: Wm. C. Brown, 1986.

Hempel, Manfred. "German Television Pioneers and the Conflict between Public Programming and Wonder Weapons," *Historical Journal of Film, Radio, and Television* 10, no. 2 (1990).

Hofer, Stephen F. *Philo Farnsworth: The Quiet Contributor to Television*. Ph.D. dissertation, Bowling Green University, 1977.

Hollenback, David Arthur. *Contributions of Charles Francis Jenkins to the Early Development of Television in the United States*. Ph.D. dissertation, University of Michigan, 1983.

Hubbell, Richard W. *Four Thousand Years of Television: The Story of Seeing at a Distance*. New York: Putnam, 1942.

Jenkins, Charles Francis. *Radiomovies, Radiovision, Television*. Washington, D.C.: Jenkins Labs, 1929.

———. *Boyhood of an Inventor*. Unpublished autobiography.

Jespersen, James, and Jane Fitz-Randolph. *Mercury's Web*. New York: Atheneum, 1981.

Keller, Wilhelm. *Hundert Jahre Fernsehen*. Berlin: VDE-Verlag, 1983.

Kempner, Stanley. *Television Encyclopedia*. New York: Fairchild, 1948.

Kennedy, Philip D. *Understanding Television*. Indianapolis: Howard W. Sams, 1976.

Kilbon, Kenyon. "History of the RCA Laboratories." Vols. 1 and 2. Princeton, N.J.: David Sarnoff Library, 1965.

Kisseloff, Jeff. *The Box: An Oral History of Television 1920–1961*. New York: Viking, 1995.

Le Duc, Don R. *Cable Television and the FCC: A Crisis in Media Control*. Philadelphia: Temple University Press, 1973.

Lessing, Lawrence. *Man of High Fidelity*. Philadelphia: Lippincott, 1956.

Leinwoll, Stanley. *From Spark to Satellite*. New York: Scribner, 1979.

Lewis, Tom. *Empire of the Air*. New York: HarperCollins, 1991.

Lichty, Lawrence W., and Malachi C. Topping, eds. *American Broadcasting: A Source Book on the History of Radio and Television*. New York: Hastings House, 1975.

Long, Mark. *World of Satellite TV*. Winter Beach, Fla.: Long Enterprises, 1988.

Lyons, Eugene. *David Sarnoff*. New York: Harper, 1966.

McArthur, Tom, and Peter Waddell. *The Secret Life of John Logie Baird.* London: Hutchinson, 1986.

Marschall, Rick. *History of Television.* New York: Gallery Books, 1986.

Math, Irwin. *Morse, Marconi, and You.* New York: Scribner, 1979.

Moseley, Sydney A. *John Baird: The Romance and Tragedy of the Pioneer of Television.* London: Odhams, 1952.

Mowat, Charles Loch. *Britain Between the Wars.* Boston: Beacon Press, 1955.

Negroponte, Nicholas. *Being Digital.* New York: Knopf, 1995.

Norman, Bruce. *Here's Looking at You.* London: BBC/Royal Television Society, 1984.

Olessi, Frederick. *Iconoscope: An Autobiography of Vladimir Zworykin, Drawn from His Writings.* Unpublished, 1971.

Paley, William. *As It Happened: A Memoir.* New York: Doubleday, 1979.

Reid, T. R. *The Chip.* New York: Simon & Schuster, 1984.

Riedel, Heide. *Walter Bruch: Ein deutscher Fernseh-Pionier.* Mainz: Fernseh- und Kinotechnischen Gesellschaft e.V., 1988.

Rowland, John. "The Television Man: Story of John Baird." New York: Roy, 1966.

Rudert, Frithjof. "50 Jahre 'Fernseh', 1929–1979." *Bosch Technische Berichte* 6 (1979): 236–67.

Sarnoff, David. *Looking Ahead: The Papers of David Sarnoff.* New York: McGraw-Hill, 1968.

Schwartz, Bernard. *The Professor and the Commissions.* New York: Knopf, 1959.

Sendall, Bernard. *Independent Television in Britain: Origin and Foundation, 1946–62.* London: Macmillan, 1982.

———. *Independent Television in Britain: Expansion and Change, 1858–68.* London: Macmillan, 1983.

Settel, Irving. *A Pictorial History of Television.* New York: Ungar, 1983.

Settel, Irving, and William Laas. *A Pictorial History of Television.* New York: Grosset & Dunlap, 1969.

Sheldon, H. Horton, and Edgar Norman Grisewood. *Television: Present Methods of Picture Transmission.* New York: Van Nostrand, 1929.

Shiers, George, ed. *Technical Development of Television.* New York: Arno Press, 1977.

———, with May Shiers. *Bibliography of the History of Electronics.* Metuchen, N.J.: Scarecrow, 1972.

Skornia, Harry J., and Jack William Kitson. *Problems and Controversies in Television and Radio.* Palo Alto, Calif.: Pacific Books, 1968.

Sobel, Robert. *RCA.* New York: Stein & Day, 1986.

Sterling, Christopher H. *Stay Tuned.* Belmont, Calif.: Wadsworth, 1978.

Swift, John. *Adventure in Vision: The First Twenty-Five Years of Television.* London: John Lehmann, 1950.

Taylor, A. J. P. *The Origins of the Second World War.* New York: Fawcett, 1968.

Thomas, Dana L. *The Media Moguls.* New York: Putnam, 1981.

Thomas, Lowell. *Magic Dials: The Story of Radio and Television.* New York: Lee Furman, 1939.

Tiltman, Ronald F. *Baird of Television.* London: Seeley Service, 1933.

Tyne, Gerald. *Saga of the Vacuum Tube.* Indianapolis: Howard W. Sams, 1977.

Udelson, Joseph. *The Great Television Race: A History of the American Television Industry 1925–41.* University, Ala.: University of Alabama Press, 1982.

Waldrop, Frank C., and Joseph Borkin. *Television: A Struggle for Power.* New York: Morrow, 1938.

Wheen, Frances. *Television: A History.* London: Century, 1985.

Wicks, Keith. *Television.* Vero Beach, Fla.: Janos Marffy and Jim Dugdale, The Rourke Corporation, 1984.

Winship, Michael. *Television.* New York: Random House, 1988.

Wyver, John. *The Moving Image.* Oxford, New York, London: Basil Blackwell, BFI Publishing, 1989.

Index

Abramson, Albert, 186, 239
ACATS (Advisory Committee on Advanced Television Service), 342–43, 345
Adams, Ira, 67, 69
advertising:
  in early commercial broadcasts, 295
  on experimental stations, 97–98, 100
  fees paid for, 295–96, 309
  and FRC, 100
  and home entertainment, 171
aerials (antennas):
  for digital television, 347
  and radio waves, 4, 53–55
Air King, 320
airmail service, 208
airplane:
  invention of, 105
  television on, 119, 223
Albu, Margaret, 181–82
Alexanderson, Ernst F. W., 66–74
  alternator invented by, 68, 69, 74
  apparatus of, 71, 195–96, 197
  birth and background of, 67–68
  and color television, 199
  and competition, 153, 177, 196–97, 203
  death of, 337

demonstrations by, 71, 195–96
and facsimile, 194, 349
and Farnsworth, 159, 192, 196
genius and abstraction of, 68–69
and home television, 87, 88
and Karolus's light valve, 82
late career of, 337–38
low profile of, 83, 95
and mechanical system, 73–74, 84–90, 93–97, 132, 186, 193–99
and mirror drum, 86
and patents, 199, 337
research budget of, 197
and Sarnoff, 71, 198
and screen size, 93
and shortwave radio, 69–70
alkali earth elements, photoconductivity of, 55
Allen, Gracie, 319
Allen, Kay, 253
alternator, Alexanderson and, 68, 69, 74
aluminum oxide:
  insulator, 184
  surface layer, 125
AM (amplitude modulation):
  vs. FM, 6–7, 240
  and Y signal, 330
American Marconi Company, 105–6